BUTLER'S
LIVES OF THE SAINTS

NEW

FULL EDITION

JULY

BUTLER'S
LIVES OF THE SAINTS

NEW FULL EDITION

Patron
H. E. CARDINAL BASIL HUME, O.S.B.+
Archbishop of Westminster

BUTLER'S
LIVES OF THE
SAINTS

NEW
FULL EDITION

JULY

Revised by
PETER DOYLE

BURNS & OATES

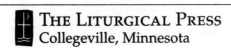

THE LITURGICAL PRESS
Collegeville, Minnesota

First published 2000 in Great Britain by
BURNS & OATES
Wellwood, North Farm Road,
Tunbridge Wells, Kent TN2 3DR

First published 2000 in North America by
THE LITURGICAL PRESS
St John's Abbey, Collegeville,
Minnesota 56321

Butler's *Lives of the Fathers, Martyrs and other principal Saints* ... first published
1756-9. First revised edition, *Butler's Lives of the Saints*, ed. Herbert Thurston,
S.J., 1926-38, copyright © Burns, Oates & Washbourne Limited. Second revised
edition, ed. Herbert Thurston, S.J., and Donald Attwater, 1954-8, copyright ©
Burns & Oates Limited.

ISBN 0 86012 256 5   Burns & Oates
ISBN 0-8146-2383-2   The Liturgical Press

The emblems appearing at the foot of some pages are taken from W. Ellwood Post,
Saints, Signs and Symbols: A Concise Dictionary. © Copyright 1962, 1974 by
Morehouse Publishing, with the permission of the publishers.

Library of Congress Catalog Card Number: 95-81671

Typeset by Search Press Limited
Printed in the United States of America

CONTENTS

Contents

PREFACE

Alban Butler wrote in the original preface to his *Lives of the Fathers, Martyrs and Other Principal Saints*: "Who is not awakened from his spiritual lethargy, and confounded at his own cowardice, when he considers the fervour and courage of the saints? All our pretences and foolish objections are silenced when we see the most perfect maxims of the gospel demonstrated to be easy by example." Such example, he went on, is "of all others, the shortest, the most easy, and the best adapted" way of leading people to virtue; "though we cannot imitate all the actions of the saints, we can learn from them to practise humility, patience, and other virtues in a manner suiting our circumstances and state of life." Recent research has shown beyond doubt that devotion to the saints in the past cut across social barriers: the élite as well as the ordinary among the population, clerical and lay, prayed to, depended on, and were proud of their saints. The varieties of saintliness to be found in the Church's calendar for July means that there is "something for everyone" looking for examples to follow or patrons to appeal to.

Above all, perhaps, July is a month rich in saints and blessed who have enriched the Church with new families of religious. Two obviously take pride of place, St Benedict (11th) and St Ignatius Loyola (31st), who present quite different problems for the writer: we know little about the former's life, while we have almost too much knowledge about the latter—so much that the task of compression becomes almost impossible. The impact of their distinctive traditions, however, continues to be outstanding and universal and is the surest witness to their personal sanctity. Several other founders whose feast-days are celebrated this month have re-interpreted the vision of a life lived in total dedication to the gospel message of loving God and our neighbour, a vision as old as Christianity itself, and have left a rich legacy of Orders and Congregations, many of them with a direct involvement in caring for the sick, educational work, and the foreign missions: St John Gualbert (*c.* 995-1073; 12th), founder of the Vallambrosan branch of the Benedictines; St Bridget of Sweden (1303-73; 23d), visionary foundress of the Bridgettines; St Antony Zaccaria (1502-39; 5th), founder of the Barnabites; St Camillus de Lellis (1150-1614; 14th), founder of the Ministers of the Sick; St Bartolomea Capitanio (1807-33; 26th), co-foundress of the Sisters of Charity of SS Bartolomea Capitanio and Vincenza Gerosa (also known as the Sisters of the Infant Mary or the Capitanio Sisters); St Mary Magdalen Postel (1756-1846; 16th), foundress of the Sisters of St Mary Magdalen Postel (originally the Sisters of the Christian Schools of

Mercy); Bd Anne Marie Javouhey (1779-1851; 15th), foundress of the Sisters of St Joseph of Cluny; Bd Clelia Barbieri (1847-70; 13th), co-foundress of the Minims of Our Lady of Sorrows (now merged with the Servants of Mary); Bd Mary Teresa Ledóchowska (1863-1922; 6th), foundress of the missionary Sodality of St Peter Claver; Bd Peter Poveda (1874-1936; 28th), founder of the Teresian Association, and Bd Pauline of the Suffering Heart of Jesus (1865-1942; 9th), foundress of the Little Sisters of the Immaculate Conception. Such a list is almost sufficient witness in itself to the varieties of sanctity to be found across the generations.

Among the new saints and blessed to be found in July, special mention may be made of Bd Peter ToRot (17th), a catechist killed by the Japanese in wartime New Guinea; Bd Titus Brandsma (26th), a Dutch Carmelite friar killed in Dachau for his opposition to the Nazis and his defence of the freedom of the Catholic press; Bd Alphonsa Muttathupadathu (28th, formerly 8 Feb.), the first Indian *beata* of the Syro-Malabar rite; St Leopold Mandic (30th), a Capuchin friar inspired by the ideal of reunion between the Orthodox and Catholic Churches, and the large numbers of martyrs from the Spanish Civil War (22d). The heroism of those who stood firm during earlier periods of persecution is also celebrated this month in the feast of St Oliver Plunkett (1st), the last of those to be executed for their faith in England, and the large number of feast-days of English and Welsh martyrs.

The month also has its learned theologians and masters of the spiritual life in three Doctors of the Church, St Peter Chrysologus (30th), St Bonaventure (15th), and St Laurence of Brindisi (21st). It has its outstanding missionaries, one of whom at least deserves to be better known and could easily serve as a contemporary model—St Justin de Jacobis (31st). Finally, there are the saints better known for the popular cults that have grown up around their names than for what we know about them historically: St Mary Magdalen (22nd), St Veronica (12th), and St Christopher (24th)—historical research may question their identity, and even their existence in some cases, but popular devotion will be slow to give them up.

Changes have taken place in the Calendar of saints as a result of the revisions of 1969 and the ongoing work of revising the Roman Martyrology. It may be helpful to readers to have a list of some of the more important of these changes as they affect this volume. Saints whose feast-days have been moved from July include St Irenaeus of Lyons (to 8 Feb.), SS Cyril and Methodius (to 14 Feb.), SS John Fisher and Thomas More (to 22 June), St Vincent de Paul (to 27 Sept.), and St Jerome Emiliani (to 8 Feb.); the Visitation of the Blessed Virgin Mary has moved to 31 May. Others have been brought in from other months: St Bridget of Sweden will be found on 23 July, instead of 8 October, and St Disibod on 8 July instead of 8 September. The following saints have changed days within the month: Oliver Plunkett (from 11th to 1st), Elizabeth of Portugal (from 8th to 4th), Swithin (from 15th to 2d), and Camillus de Lellis (from

18th to 14th). Some former feast-days that had entries in *B.T.A.* have been omitted altogether: these include Our Lady of Mount Carmel (formerly 16 July), the Seven Sleepers of Ephesus (27th), St Neot (31st), SS Nazarin and Celsus (28th), and both St Christina the Martyr and St Christina the Astonishing (both formerly on 24th). Since the relevant month of the new Roman Martyrology was not available when this volume was being prepared there will, no doubt, be further changes in the Universal Calendar for July; a few of these have been noted in the present volume and the rest will be included in future editions.

Changes have also been taking place for some years now in the way the Lives of the saints are being studied. This may reflect an increasing secularism and a tendency to study the saints as products of a particular social context and their Lives as providing us with valuable insights into the social milieu of the early hagiographers rather than detailed information about the saints themselves. The present-day hagiographer must take note of these changes in approach and may often use them to advantage without, of course, losing sight of the essentially spiritual message of those being written about. The fact that many medieval canonizations, for example, were politically motivated, or the interesting new approaches to early Lives of the Irish saints serve to enhance our understanding of the complexity and richness of the ways saints have been perceived at different times. Selectivity and even special pleading on the part of hagiographers is nothing new: St Oda (4th), archbishop of Canterbury, commissioned a new life of St Wilfrid (12 Oct.) to justify his theft of the saint's relics to enhance the cathedral at Canterbury and made sure that it carefully avoided mentioning how Wilfrid had quarrelled seriously with former archbishops. Bd James of Voragine (13th) had his own agenda in the selections he made for his great *Golden Legend*, the influential medieval bestseller, while Alban Butler was careful about what he included of the miracle stories to be found in earlier sets of Lives, arguing that a "detail of all miracles, though authentically attested, is not the design of this work." Just as the holy founders re-interpreted the gospel commands to suit their own times, the hagiographer takes from the rich treasure of sanctity what seems best suited to the taste of the day; as Herbert Thurston, the first serious reviser of Butler's work, put it: "no good purpose would be served by attempting completeness . . . completeness of any sort is a simple impossibility." I can only hope that the present compilation does not disappoint by its omissions of some saints altogether or of some of the more popular legends.

Everyone interested in the lives of the saints is indebted to the vast project of the *Acta Sanctorum* launched by the Bollandists in the seventeenth century and to their current bi-annual publication, the *Analecta Bollandiana*. There is also the indispensable Italian *Bibliotheca Sanctorum*, published between 1960 and 1970, with a supplementary volume published in 1987. This multi-volume work is based on authoritative scholarship and has the added attraction of being well illustrated. Another extremely useful multi-volume Italian work is the *Dizionario degli Istituti di Perfezione*, providing information and analysis of founders, ancient and modern, and their Congregations or Orders. The present pope has beatified and canonized a large number of people; it is, perhaps susprisingly, sometimes difficult to find out very much about them beyond their basic biographical details, and in these cases I have consulted the official Vatican publications *Notitiae* and *A.A.S.* In English there are David Hugh Farmer's *Oxford Dictionary of the Saints* and J. N. D. Kelly's *Oxford Dictionary of the Popes*, which are both invaluable, as is the *Oxford Dictionary of the Christian Church* for background information on people, movements, and events in the Church's history. For the sections on art and iconography I have relied mainly on the *Bibliotheca Sanctorum* and on Peter and Linda Murray's *Oxford Companion to Christian Art and Architecture*.

I would like to acknowledge the invaluable assistance received from a number of people and institutions: Jean Olwen Maynard for substantial help with the entries on the Martyrs of the Spanish Civil War (22d), St Justin de Jacobis (31st), and the Salcete Martyrs (25th). The Teresian Association provided valuable information on their founder Bd Peter Poveda and Bd Victoria Díez (28th), as did Sr Monica Sheehan of the Sisters of St Joseph of Cluny on their foundress Bd Anne Marie Javouhey (15th). I am also indebted to Antony Joseph Ugesh for information on the Indian cult of St Thomas the Apostle (3rd). Paul Burns has been his ever-helpful and understanding self; in addition to providing general assistance he wrote the long entry on the Martyrs of the Spanish Civil War and provided much information on the Vietnam martyrs whose feast-days are celebrated this month (see 12th, 20th, 28th). The entry on St Disibod was written by Sarah Fawcett Thomas. I offer my apologies to any one who has helped but whom I have omitted here.

Without the support and interest of my wife, Barbara, and our son, Matthew, this hagiographer's task would have been even more daunting than it has been.

---

1 July 1999, Feast of St Oliver Plunkett, Bishop and Martyr

Peter Doyle

Abbreviations and Short Forms

A.A.S.	*Acta Apostolicae Sedis. Commentarium officiale.* Rome, 1908-.
AA.SS.	*Acta Sanctorum,* 64 vols. Antwerp, also Rome and Paris, 1643-.
A.C.M.	H. Musurillo, S.J. *Acts of the Christian Martyrs.* Oxford, 1972.
A.C.O.	E. Schwartz (ed.). *Acta Conciliorum Oecumenicorum.* Strasbourg, 1914-.
Anal.Boll.	*Analecta Bollandiana.* 1882-.
Anal.Eccles.	*Analecta Ecclesiastica.* 1893-.
Anal.Franc.	*Analecta Franciscana.* 1885-.
Anstruther	G. Anstruther, O.P. *The Seminary Priests,* 4 vols. Ware, Ushaw, and Great Wakering, 1968-77.
Archiv. Fratrum Praed.	*Archivum Fratrum Praedicatorum.* 1931-.
A.S.C.	*The Anglo-Saxon Chronicle,* in *E.H.D.,* 1 and 2.
Baring-Gould and Fisher	S. Baring-Gould and J. Fisher. *The Lives of the British Saints,* 4 vols. London, 1907-13.
Bede, *H.E.*	The Venerable Bede. *Historia Ecclesiastica* (ed. L. Sherley-Price and D. H. Farmer). 1955; revised ed., 1990.
B.H.L.	Society of Bollandists. *Bibliotheca Hagiographica Latina,* 2 vols. Brussels, 1898-1901.
Bibl.SS.	*Bibliotheca Sanctorum,* 12 vols. Rome, 1960-70; Suppl. 1, *Prima Appendice.* Rome, 1987.
B.T.A.	H. Thurston and D. Attwater (eds.). *Butler's Lives of the Saints,* 4 vols. London & New York, 1953-4; the previous edition of this work.
Catholic Encyclopaedia	C. Herbermann (ed.). *The Catholic Encyclopaedia,* 17 vols. New York, 1907-14.
Catholicisme	G. Jacquemet et al. (eds.). *Catholicisme: hier, aujourd'hui, demain.* Paris, 1948-.
C.C.	*Corpus Christianorum.* Turnhout, 1954-.
C.C.S.G.	*Corpus Christianorum, Series Graeca.* Turnhout, 1977-.
C.M.H.	H. Delehaye et al. (eds.). *Commentarius Perpetuus in Martyrologium Hieronymianum,* in *AA.SS.,* 65. 1931.
Coptic Encyc.	A. S. Atiya et al. (eds.). The *Coptic Encyclopedia,* 8 vols. New York and Toronto, 1991.
C.R.S.	Publications of the Catholic Record Society. London, 1905-.

C.S.C.O.	*Corpus Scriptorum Christianorum Orientalium*. Paris and Louvain, 1903-.
C.S.E.L.	*Corpus Scriptorum Ecclesiasticorum Latinorum*. Vienna, 1866-.
D.A.C.L.	H. Cabrol and H. Leclerq (eds.). *Dictionnaire d'archéologie chrétienne et de liturgie*, 15 vols. Paris, 1907-53.
D.C.B.	W. Smith and H. Wace (eds.). *Dictionary of Christian Biography*, 4 vols. London, 1877-87.
D.H.G.E.	A. Baudrillart et al. (eds.). *Dictionnaire d'histoire et de géographie ecclésiatiques*. Paris, 1912-.
Dict.Sp.	M. Viller, S.J., et al. (eds.). *Dictionnaire de spiritualité*. Paris, 1937-.
Diz. dei Papi	B. Mondin. *Dizionario enciclopedico dei Papi: storia e insegnamenti*. Rome, 1995.
Diz. Ist. Perf.	G. Pellicia and G. Rocca (eds.). *Dizionario degli Istituti di Perfezione*, 10 vols. Rome, 1974-.
D.N.B.	L. Stephen and S. Lee (eds.). *Dictionary of National Biography*, 63 vols. London, 1885-1900.
D.N.H.	F. Holböck (ed.). *Die neuen Heiligen der katholischen Kirche*. Stein am Rhein, 1994.
D.T.C.	A. Vacant, E. Mangenot, and E. Amman (eds.). *Dictionnaire de Théologie Catholique*, 15 vols. Paris, 1903-50.
E.E.C.	*Encyclopaedia of the Early Church*, 2 vols. 1992.
E.H.D.	D. C. Douglas et al. (eds.). *English Historical Documents*. London, 1953-.
E.H.R.	*English Historical Review*. London, 1886-.
Encic.Catt.	*Enciclopedia Cattolica*, 12 vols. The Vatican, 1948-54.
Foley	H. Foley (ed.). *Records of the English Province of the Society of Jesus*, 8 vols. London, 1877-83.
Gillow	Joseph Gillow. *A Literary and Biographical History, or Bibliographical Dictionary of the English Catholics. From The Breach with Rome, in 1534, to the Present Time*, 5 vols. London, 1885-1902; rp. London, 1999.
G.P.	William of Malmesbury, *Gesta Pontificum*, ed. N. E. Hamilton. London, 1870.
Grove	*The New Grove Dictionary of Music and Musicians*, 20 vols. London, 1980.
I.E.R.	*The Irish Ecclesiastical Record*. Dublin, 1869-1968.

The Irish Saints	D. D. C. Pochin Mould. *The Irish Saints*. Dublin and London, 1964.
Jedin-Holland	A three-vol. abridgement (New York, 1993) of H. Jedin and J. Dolan (eds.). *History of the Church*, Eng. trans., 10 vols. London & New York, 1965-81.
J.E.H.	*Journal of Eccelsiastical History*, 1950-.
K.S.S.	A. P. Forbes (ed.). *Kalendar of Scottish Saints*. Edinburgh,1872 .
L.E.M.	E. H. Burton and J. H. Pollen (eds.). *Lives of the English Martyrs*, 2d series. London, 1915.
Léon	Léon de Clary, O.F.M. *Auréole Séraphique*. Eng. trans., *Lives of the Saints and Blessed of the Orders of St Francis*, 4 vols. Taunton, 1887.
L.P.	L. Duchesne (ed.), *Liber Pontificalis*, 2 vols. Paris, 1886-92.
M.G.H.	G. Pertz et al.(eds.), *Monumenta Germaniae Historiae*, 64 vols., Hanover, 1839-1921. The *Scriptores* series is split into sub-series: *Auctores antiquissimi; Scriptores rerum merovingicarum; Poetae Latini; Epistolae; Scriptores.*
M.M.P.	R. Challoner. *Memoirs of Missionary Priests*. London 1741-2; new ed. by J. H. Pollen, 1924.
Murray	P. and L. Murray. *The Oxford Companion to Christian Art and Architecture*. Oxford, 1996.
N.C.E.	*The New Catholic Encyclopedia*, 14 vols. New York, 1967.
N.D.S.	D. Attwater. *A New Dictionary of Saints*, rev. ed. by John Cumming. Tunbridge Wells and Collegeville, Minn., 1993.
N.L.A.	C. Horstman (ed.). *Nova Legenda Angliae*, 2 vols. London, 1901.
Notitiae	*Congregatio de Cultu Divino et Disciplina Sacramentorum. Notitiae.* Rome, 1965-.
N.S.B. 1	T. Lelièvre. *100 nouveaux saints et bienheureux de 1963 à 1984*. Paris, 1983.
N.S.B. 2	T. Lelièvre. *Nouveaux saints et bienheureux de 1984 à 1988*. Paris, 1989.
O.D.C.C.	F. L. Cross and E. A. Livingstone (eds.). *The Oxford Dictionary of the Christian Church*. Oxford, New York, and Toronto, 1957; 2d. ed., 1974; 3d. ed., 1997.
O.D.P.	J. N. D. Kelly. *The Oxford Dictionary of Popes*. Oxford, 1986.

O.D.S.	D. H. Farmer. *The Oxford Dictionary of Saints*. Oxford and New York, 3d ed., 1993; 4th ed., 1997.
Office of Readings	*The Divine Office. The Liturgy of the Hours according to the Roman Rite*, 3 vols. London, Sydney, and Dublin, 1974.
Pastor	L. Pastor. *The History of the Popes from the Close of the Middle Ages*. London, 1891-1953.
P.B.	F. Guérin (ed.), Vie des Saints des Petits Bollandistes, 17 vols. Paris, 1880.
P.G.	J. P. Migne (ed.). *Patrologiae Cursus Completus. Series Graeca*, 162 vols. Paris, 1857-66.
P.L.	J. P. Migne (ed.). *Patrologiae Cursus Completus. Series Latina*, 221 vols. Paris, 1844-64.
Procter	J. Procter (ed.). *Short Lives of the Dominican Saints*. London, 1900.
Propylaeum	*Propylaeum ad Acta Sanctorum Decembris*. Brussels, 1940.
R.H.	*Recusant History*, the journal of the C.R.S., 1951-.
R.H.E.	*Revue d'histoire ecclésiastique*, Louvain, 1900-.
S.C.	Sources chrétiennes. Paris, 1940-.
S.C.H.	*Studies in Church History*. London, Leiden, Oxford, 1964-.
Stanton	R. Stanton. *A Menology of England and Wales*. 1892.
Vies des Saints	J. Baudot et P. Chaussin (eds.). *Vies des Saints et des Bienheureux*, 13 vols. Paris, 1935-59.
V.S.H.	C. Plummer (ed.). *Vitae Sanctorum Hiberniae*, 2 vols. 1910; 2d. ed., 1968.

1

ST OLIVER PLUNKETT, *Bishop and Martyr* (1625-81)

Oliver Plunkett was born on 1 November 1625 at Loughcrew in County Meath, Ireland. Through his mother, Thomasina Dillon, he was related to the earls of Fingall and of Roscommon, while his father, John Plunkett, came from a well-to-do landed family. Very little is known about Oliver's early years except that he was educated privately by a Cistercian cousin, Dr Patrick Plunkett, brother of the earl of Fingall and later abbot of St Mary's, Dublin, and bishop, first of Ardagh and then of Meath. This cousin and other members of Oliver's family took a prominent part in the Confederation of Kilkenny, which led the great Irish rebellion of 1641; Oliver himself was not directly involved, although it was through moving in Confederate circles that he met Fr Pier Francesco Scarampi, an Oratorian priest sent by the pope as envoy to the Confederacy. When Scarampi returned to Rome in 1647 Oliver went with him to study there for the priesthood. From a letter written after Scarampi's death from the plague (caught while ministering to those in quarantine) it is clear that Oliver had a high regard for the Italian priest who continued to help him spiritually and financially during his early years in Rome.

After studying at the Irish College Oliver was ordained in 1654; he asked to be excused from his student oath to return to Ireland immediately after ordination and instead became chaplain to a house of Oratorian priests. He took up the study of law and in 1657 was appointed to lecture in theology and apologetics at the Propaganda College in Rome; he also worked for a time for the Sacred Congregation of the Index, reviewing a number of books. He kept his post at Propaganda until his appointment as archbishop of Armagh and Primate of All Ireland in 1669. It appears that his appointment was the result of personal intervention by the pope, Clement IX, though there is a letter from Oliver to the cardinals of Propaganda in which he said that he "desired to return to his country for the service of souls" and asked to be made archbishop of Armagh. He was consecrated at Ghent and arrived in his diocese in March 1670.

His arrival coincided with a period of relative calm for the Church in Ireland, though the new archbishop still felt it wise at first to go about as a layperson with the alias Captain Brown, wearing a sword and carrying pistols. He admired the faith of his people: "What pleases me most is to find in this people such devotion, such piety and such constancy in the faith for which they have suffered to the limit of human endurance," but a great deal needed to be done to make good the effects of the severe persecution that had followed the failed rebellion. There was a shortage of priests, and many who had been ordained had not been properly trained; many thousands of people had not been confirmed, there was a long-running conflict between secular and religious clergy and between different orders of friars, and the authority of some of the bishops was uncertain. The appointment of a friendlier and more tolerant viceroy in May 1670 allowed Oliver to move freely about the country, and "he hoisted full sail into the favourable wind," as he put it. In 1670 alone he held a number of diocesan synods, organized a meeting of the bishops in Dublin, confirmed about ten thousand people, held a provincial synod, made visitations of six dioceses, and opened schools to be run by the Jesuits in Drogheda. This set the pattern of his work for the next two years; he was tireless in his pastoral activity and also found time to publish a book, *Jus Primatiale*, as part of his controversy with the archbishop of Dublin over who should be regarded as primate of the country.

In 1673 the English Parliament forced Charles II to adopt a stricter policy against Catholics, and edicts were issued in Ireland banning the bishops and all religious from the country. By Christmas the bishops were back in hiding and the Drogheda schools had been closed. This state of affairs lasted for about seven months, but even when the immediate danger passed there was no return to the earlier freedom of movement. In a letter to Rome Oliver likened the uncertainties and dangers of the times to the situation of the Church under the Roman emperors; he hoped they would be "made glorious and rich by the sufferings and martyrdoms of the northern peoples" and was sure the Irish bishops would not turn out to be "hirelings": unless dragged away by force they would not abandon "either lambs or sheep." From mid-1675 onward he seems to have been able to live in semi-hiding in the houses of relatives, and he continued his efforts to bring order to the Church in Ireland. In 1678 he held a provincial synod and set out on another diocesan visitation; this had to be cut short when the false revelations of the Popish Plot brought on a fresh outbreak of persecution. In 1679 a price of £10 was put on the head of all the Irish bishops, and Oliver was back in hiding. Despite the danger, he visited Dublin to see his old teacher, Bishop Plunkett, who was dying; he was arrested and imprisoned in Dublin Castle in December.

In July 1680 he was tried at Dundalk on a ridiculous charge of trying to bring seventy thousand French soldiers into Ireland; not surprisingly, the main prosecution witnesses failed to appear and he was returned to prison in Dublin, where he was reconciled with his old adversary over the primacy, Archbishop Talbot, who was also in prison. The authorities in England realized that it would be almost impossible to mount a successful case against the archbishop in Ireland, where he was respected by Catholics and Protestants; they still needed a conviction to add some credibility to the supposed plot. In October 1680 they had him moved to London to stand trial for treason, even though at that time the English courts did not have jurisdiction over people accused of crimes committed in Ireland, and in any case, the length of time between the supposed offence and the indictment was longer than that allowed by statute. On 3 May 1681 he was formally charged with "endeavouring and compassing the king's death, and to levy war in Ireland, and to alter the true religion there, and to introduce a foreign power." (Curtis). He was given five weeks to bring his witnesses from Ireland, but it proved impossible to do so in the time available, and the trial went ahead in June.

The witnesses for the prosecution were a sorry lot—ex-friars, suspended and apostate priests, and convicted criminals. They showed to the court's satisfaction that a plot to bring in the French had existed in Ireland, and it was assumed that the archbishop, the leader of the Irish Catholics, must have been involved in it, although no evidence of this could be adduced; much was made of the fact that he had collected money in Ireland and sent some of it to Rome—this was taken to be the money to pay for the French invasion. He was found guilty of treason, condemned to death, and hanged, drawn, and quartered at Tyburn on 1 July (N.S., 11 July). His body was taken to the English Benedictine abbey of Lambspring in Germany in 1684 by Fr Maurus Corker, O.S.B., who had been in prison with Oliver under sentence of death for his part in the plot but was released in 1683. In 1883 the remains were moved to Downside Abbey in Somerset. Fr Corker took the martyr's head to Rome and gave it to Cardinal Howard; eventually it was given to the archbishop of Armagh, who gave it to the Dominican convent in Drogheda; it is now in the Oliver Plunkett Memorial Church in Drogheda. Oliver was beatified in 1920 and canonized in 1975.

There are 230 of the saint's letters that survive, almost all of them written by him personally. Most of them date from between 1669 and 1681, the years of his episcopate, and most are of an official nature. Even so, they give an invaluable picture of the ideals and the work of the archbishop and of "his human qualities, accomplishments and weaknesses" (Hanly) in the very difficult Irish situation of the time. The final letters, written while he was in prison awaiting trial and after his condemnation, are very moving. Overall, the letters show a man of learning, devotion to pastoral duty, and the courage to do always what his conscience told him was right—"Let the world perish, but let justice be done!" was one of his favourite sayings. At times he used harsh language to condemn his opponents and was clearly impatient with those he felt were putting obstacles in the way of his reforms; he demanded the highest standards of his priests and was uncompromising with those who gave scandal in any way (*ibid.*). While under sentence of death he wrote to Fr Corker: "Happy are we who have a second baptism, nay a third; water we received, the sacrament of penance we got, and now we have . . . the baptism of blood." He thought the sufferings that he would undergo at Tyburn only a "flea biting" compared with what Christ suffered for us; it was Christ's "fears and passions" that enabled him to be free from fear. Since he was "the first of my countrymen in this age who suffered here, I desire to lead the way, and since I exhorted others by word in Ireland, it is fitting that I should strengthen them now by example. . . . I ought therefore cheerfully desire it [*i.e.*, Tyburn], heartily covet it, and joyfully embrace it, it being a sure way, a smooth path by which I may in a very short time pass from sorrow to joy."

There is an excellent critical edition and translation of St Oliver's letters: Mgr John Hanly (ed.), *The Letters of Saint Oliver Plunkett 1625-1681* (1979), from which the quotations above are taken; incidentally, the letters show clearly that he always spelled his name Plunkett. Emmanuel Curtis, O.C.S.O., *Blessed Oliver Plunkett* (1963), is a reliable account and reprints some of the prison letters; it also contains a very good bibliography and list of sources for the saint's life. See also *M.M.P.*, pp. 574-82; A. Curtayne, *The Trial of Oliver Plunkett* (1953); T. Ó Fiaich and D. Forristal, *Oliver Plunkett, his life and letters* (1975).

There is a portrait of St Oliver in the National Gallery of Ireland, perhaps painted by Garret Morphey and dating from *c.* 1690; this shows a man with a long, aristocratic face, with a moustache and small beard, in episcopal dress and holding a crucifix. A commonly reproduced engraving by Van der Vaart was based on this portrait. There is a large mosaic of the saint by Boris Anrep in Westminster Cathedral, which also has a relic of him.

SS Julius and Aaron, *Martyrs* (*c.* 304)

St Bede (25 May) tells us that Aaron and Julius suffered martyrdom at the same time as St Alban (21 June), which would mean that they died during the reign of Diocletian in the early years of the fourth cenury. Their place of death may have been Caerleon-on-Usk in Monmouthshire. Bede adds that they endured "many horrible physical tortures," after which "their souls entered the joys of the heavenly city." His source seems to have been St Gildas (*c.* 500-70; 29 Jan.), whose learned work *De excidio Brittaniae* is often not historically trustworthy. There is some doubt whether Diocletian's anti-Christian decrees were ever promulgated in Britain, and Gildas himself admits that placing the martyrs in that period was no more than an inference. On the other hand, an ancient cult of the two saints certainly existed, and this has been used as evidence of a Christian presence in the south-east of Wales in Roman times. In the twelfth century the *Book of Llandaff* claimed that there was a martyrs' chapel in their honour near Caerleon—the Welsh word *merthir* usually indicated a chapel built over a grave site, and there is some sixth-century evidence of the existence of such a building. There is a strong tradition that two chapels dedicated to the martyrs existed to the east and west of Caerleon, about two miles apart; a farmhouse named Saint Julian's, once a manor house belonging to Lord Herbert of Cherbury, probably occupies the site of St Julius' chapel, while St Aaron's may have been near the Roman camp of Penrhos. There were a small number of other church dedications in their honour in the area as well as one at Silchester. Aaron gave his name to one of the Welsh holy wells.

Bede, *H.E.*, 1, 7; *O.D.S.*, p. 274; *Bibl.SS.*, 6, 1235-7. See also Baring-Gould and Fisher, 1, pp. 101-3; E. G. Bowen, *The Settlements of the Celtic Saints in Wales* (2d ed., 1956); P. Grosjean in *Anal.Boll.* 72 (1954), p. 458.

St Shenute, *Abbot* (*c*. 466)

Shenute (Shenoudi) was born about the middle of the fourth century at Shenalolet in Egypt and became a monk at Dair-al-Abiad (later known as Dayr-Anba-Shinudah, or the White Monastery), which had been founded by his uncle near Atrib in the Thebaid. About the year 385 he succeeded his uncle as abbot. His long reign was important for the development of Egyptian monasticism, and he is linked with St Antony (17 Jan.) and St Pachomius (9 May) as one of its outstanding figures. He ruled over a very large community, reputed to have numbered at its height about four thousand monks and nuns, and was noted for the severity of his discipline, introducing flogging and imprisonment for minor faults and generally moving away from Pachomius' more humane rule. He was quick-tempered by nature and had a rather violent disposition, but the monastery flourished under his direction and attracted large numbers of recruits. He set out to impose a greater regularity in the observance of the monastic life and instituted something like the three monastic vows of poverty, chastity, and obedience: the monks and nuns covenanted to observe continence, not to steal or lie, and not to do any evil in secret upon pain of incurring God's anger and forfeiting their salvation. He believed that obedience was the most important virtue for a religious and became depressed when his authority was not accepted without question: it is clear that he considered himself inspired by God in his dealings with those under his care.

Those who had proved themselves in the monastic life were allowed to become hermits, but he opposed the extreme bodily penances that had become something of a hallmark of Egyptian monasticism and condemned the false mysticism that he thought often accompanied them. He forbade his monks and nuns to engage in secular study and, indeed, discouraged study of any kind; he was not learned himself, though he wrote sermons and many letters of spiritual direction in a very forthright style. He knew Greek, but his own writings were in Coptic. They are concerned almost entirely with the running of the monastery; while they show a good knowledge of the scriptures, he does not seem to have understood the complex nature of the important theological controversies of the day, and there is some evidence that he adopted Monophysitism (the belief that Christ had only one, divine, nature) toward the end of his life. He was an organizer rather than a theologian.

Some accounts say he played an important part in the Council of Ephesus alongside St Cyril of Alexandria (27 June) in 431; this is uncertain, though his presence at the council may be accepted as fact and it may have been as a result of his support for Cyril that he was made archimandrite, a sort of abbot general over all the monastic foundations in Egypt. His influence spread beyond the monastery, and visitors sought his advice on many subjects, not all of them religious; he seems to have undertaken pastoral and social work throughout a wide area and won praise for the way he supported the poor and attacked rich employers. His most violent language, however, was reserved for pagans and their religious practices; he personally led attacks against their temples and destroyed idols and other religious objects.

The exact date of his death is not known, but it took place about the year 466, when he was reputedly 118 years old. His monastery was still in existence in the nineteenth century; only its ruins remain today.

A key source for his life are his own writings: these were popular among Egyptian monks for several centuries after his death, and fragments are still being collected and edited. There is also a Life written by his pupil Bêsa; this and other Lives abound in extravagant miracle stories but also contain useful information. Shenute's writings and Bêsa's Life are in *C.S.C.O.*, 2 (1906); 4 (1908); 129 (1951); 75-6 (1982). See also P. Ladeuze in *R.H.E.* 7 (1906), pp. 76-83; G. Lefebvre in *D.A.C.L.*, under Deir el Abiad, 4, 1 (1920), 459-502; *Coptic Encyc.*, 7, pp. 2131-3, with up-to-date bibliography; D. N. Bell, *Bêsa: The Life of Shenoute* (1983).

St Theodoric, *Abbot* (533)

Theodoric (or Thierry) was born at Aumenancourt-le-Grand near Reims in northern France. His relatives forced him to marry, but he persuaded his wife that they should give up their marital rights so that he could become a priest; other sources, however, say that he failed to persuade her and so just abandoned her. Eventually he founded a monastery at Mont d'Or, near Reims, and became famous for the number of converts he attracted by his zeal. One of these was his father, a man of evil reputation who had made a living from armed robbery but ended his life as a monk under Theodoric's direction. One of the miracles attributed to him was the cure of King Theodoric I (*c.* 455-526) of a serious eye disease, while Flodard relates how he restored the king's daughter to life and was rewarded by large royal donations to his monastery. Most accounts give the date of death as 1 July 533. The Roman Martyrology said that he was a disciple of St Remigius (13 Jan.), but there are no early sources to support this. His relics were translated in 976 to the abbey, which had been restored in 933; when the house was suppressed in 1776 they were transferred to the parish church.

AA.SS., July, 1, pp. 56-85, gives a tenth-century account by Flodard and two short Latin Lives; none of these is historically reliable. See *Bibl.SS.*, 12, 230-1.

St Carilefus, *Abbot* (*c.* 540)

Carilefus (or Calais) was born in the Auvergne region of France and brought up in the monastery of Ménat, near Riom. Here he became a friend of St Avitus (17 June), and the two of them decided to dedicate themselves to the religious life. They moved to the abbey of Micy, near Orleans, where they were ordained. Carilefus, however, wanted to lead a more solitary life and so went off with two companions to Maine, where they attempted to follow a régime based on the rigours of the ancient Egyptian Fathers. According to tradition, Carilefus' fame spread, and so many people sought his guidance that in the end he founded a monastery for them at Anisole on the river Anille, in the diocese of Le Mans. It now appears, however, that he was neither the founder nor the abbot of this monastery but lived as a hermit near or on its site. A royal charter of 693 mentions a monastery founded in honour of Carilefus, "a holy confessor." The date of his death is uncertain but was probably about the year 540. A document of 712 or 715 refers to him as "most blessed," while another slightly later one refers to him as "saint." During the Norman invasions his relics were moved to Blois for safekeeping and in 1663 were moved again to Saint-Calais, a small town that had grown up around the monastery. He is honoured as the founder of monasticism in that part of France.

St Gregory of Tours gives details of Carilefus in his *Historia Francorum*, 5, ch. 14. Three Lives have come down to us; one is of no value, the other two date from the ninth century; the more reliable of these was edited by B. Krusch in *M.G.H., Scriptores rerum merov.*, 3, pp. 386-94. See also *Anal.Boll.* 24 (1905), pp. 29-31, 44-101, 484-6; *Bibl.SS.*, 3, 786-7.

St Gall I of Clermont, *Bishop* (*c.* 486-551)

Gall was born about the year 486 in Clermont in the Auvergne region of France. His parents came from the leading families of the area, and his father wanted to betroth him to the daughter of a senatorial family. About the year 507, however, Gall was miraculously cured at the tomb of St Julian of Brioude (28 Aug.) and decided on the religious life. He left home to join a monastery at Cournon but was admitted only after gaining the consent of his father. The local bishop, Quinziano of Clermont (515-25), thought highly of him and appointed him to be his representative at the court of King Theodoric; here his fine singing voice gained him the post of official cantor in the royal chapel. He was also responsible for the destruction of some pagan temples and escaped the anger of the people only with some difficulty. When Quinziano died in 525 the king appointed Gall as his successor, and he became widely known for his charity and pastoral zeal. Accounts of his life stress his meekness and patience in the face of injuries and insults. He organized a council at Clermont in 535 that was attended by fourteen bishops, and he attended those held at Orleans in 541 and 549. During the last years of his life he devoted a great deal of time to training his nephew, the future St Gregory of Tours (17 Nov.). He died on 14 May 551 and was buried in the church of Saint Laurence; his epitaph was composed by the poet Venantius Fortunatus (*c.* 530-610; 14 Dec.). A strong local cult developed, and miracles were reported at his tomb, which seems to have been well known until the tenth century. His feast-day was fixed as 1 July in the fifteenth century.

What is known of St Gall comes mainly from the *De vita patrum* of Gregory of Tours and his *Historia Francorum*; see *AA.SS.*, July, 1, pp. 103-9. See also *Bibl.SS.*, 6, 5-12.

St Eparchius (504-81)

Eparchius was the name given by St Gregory of Tours (17 Nov.) to a French monk better known as Cybard or Ybar. He was born in Trémolet in the Périgord in 504. He was intelligent and received a good education. When he was fifteen years old he was appointed chancellor by his grandfather, but very little is known in detail about these early years. At the age of thirty he entered a monastery, either that at Seyssac near Saint-Aquilin or that at Saint-Cybard near Mouleydier in the Dordogne. His holiness was outstanding, and so many people sought his advice and begged him to work miracles in their favour that he worried about becoming proud and self-satisfied; he left the monastery to live in solitude near Angoulême, with the approval of Aptone, the local bishop. At some point he was ordained priest, perhaps at the instigation of the bishop. He soon attracted disciples and agreed to direct them as long as they abstained from all manual labour and relied only on the alms of the local people; when they complained of having to go without food he would quote St Jerome's (30 Sept.) saying, "Faith never feared hunger." There are some doubts about the nature of his secluded life: Gregory of Tours calls him abbot and implies he lived some sort of monastic life with a number of disciples, but there is a strong tradition that he lived alone in a specially built grotto on the northern walls of the city. He cared for the sick and prisoners, using the alms he was given for food to look after them and to buy the freedom of prisoners and slaves. This last seems to have been his main work, and there exists in the Angoulême cartulary a document of 558 giving 175 slaves their freedom as a result of his intercession. These works of charity explain why he is usually shown either emptying a sack of money for his disciples to distribute or holding a set of chains.

He died in 581—some authorities give 558—and a considerable cult soon developed; he was especially remembered as a miracle-worker. A monastery founded during the reign of Pepin I (817-38) was dedicated to St Cybard; it was sacked by English soldiers in the fourteenth century and again by Protestants in 1558, when the saint's relics were burned. The supposed site of the grotto on the city walls has been known since the ninth century; it was restored and enlarged in 1673 and again in 1851.

The fullest source for the life of Eparchius comes from St Gregory's *Historia Francorum*, 6:8, and *In gloria Confessorum*, 101. A Latin Life, for a long time thought to be contemporary, probably dates from the ninth century. See J. de la Martinière, *S. Cybard, étude critique d'hagiographie* (1908); *Bibl.SS.*, 3, 1249-52. *Catholicisme*, 3, 392-4, discusses the sources and the authenticity of the famous freeing of slaves.

St Symeon Salus (Sixth Century)

Nothing is known of Symeon's early life except that he was a Syrian and that his mother lived in Edessa. While on a pilgrimage to the Holy Places he met another Syrian, John, and they travelled together back from Jerusalem. Both men were well educated, especially in Greek. On the way they passed through Jericho and saw the monasteries that stood by the river Jordan; both were attracted to a life of solitude and decided to become monks. The hallmark of Symeon's approach to the spiritual life was humility; he believed that not only should we accept willingly the humiliations sent us by God in everyday life, we should also on occasion actively seek to be humiliated and not be guided by human considerations in these matters. He left the desert to live at Emesa (present-day Homs) in Syria, where he was given the Greek nickname *salos* (mad) because he deliberately copied the ways of those who were mentally disturbed in order to be thought a fool. Alban Butler commented that although we are not obliged to imitate Symeon's eccentricity in all respects unless we have a special call from God to do so, yet his example should make us ashamed when we consider how badly we receive anything that hurts our pride. The former edition of this work says that God rewarded Symeon's humility by granting him extraordinary graces and the power to work miracles; it also adds that it seems likely that at times his mind was unhinged. A modern commentator suggests instead that Symeon's absurd behaviour and the physical discomfort and abuse that accompanied it had a clear purpose in his spirituality: to hide his identity as a holy person and to "transcend his body" by this unusual, although not unique, form of asceticism (Krueger).

The Syriac version of the Greek Life makes out that Symeon was a Monophysite (believing that Christ had only one, divine, nature), presumably to make him a member of the Syriac Church, which was itself Monophysite. It also changes the account of Symeon's burial: the Greek version tells us that when John had the simple tomb opened in order to have the body moved to a more fitting one the body was not there, "for the Lord, to glorify him, had translated it." This would explain why there was no body to venerate, but the Syrians apparently wanted to claim to have the body, and so their version states that some holy people had taken the body and put it in the monastery on the outskirts of Emesa, where St John the Baptist's head was already venerated.

Symeon used to be venerated with his companion, St John, on 21 July in many of the ancient calendars. In the sixteenth century Baronius for some reason separated the two and moved Symeon to 1 July.

The historian Evagrius (*c.* 536-600) gives a fairly full account of Symeon in his *Historia Ecclesiastica*, 4, 34, and there is a long Greek Life by Leontius, bishop of Neapolis in Cyprus, from the following century; see *AA.SS.*, July, 1, pp. 129-69. See also *Bibl.SS.*, 11, 1115-6, and 6, 863-4, under John; A. Festugière and P. Van Deun, *Vie de Syméon le Fou* (1974); Derek Krueger, *Symeon the Holy Fool: Leontius' Life and the late antique city* (1996), which includes an Eng. trans. of the Life. *Vies des Saints*, 7, pp. 18-9, deals with St Symeon and the phenomenon of "fools for Christ's sake."

BB George Beesley and Montford Scott, *Martyrs* (1591)

George Beesley was born in Goosnargh, Lancashire, in 1562. He studied for the priesthood at the English College in Reims, where he was ordained in 1587. When he returned to England in the following year he used the *alias* Passelaw and worked for a time in Laton, near Lancaster. We know that he was in London in about April 1590, for he officiated at the marriage of Richard Webster, a schoolmaster who was in prison in the Marshalsea. Late in the same year he was committed to the Tower and tortured; in 1591 he was moved to Newgate and on 1 July was hanged, drawn, and quartered in Fleet Street. Challoner says that he was the brother of Richard Beesley, a priest who also worked in Lancashire, but this is not certain.

Montford (or Monford) Scott was born in Hawstead, Suffolk. He studied at Cambridge before going to Douai in 1574. For some reason he returned to England as a subdeacon in 1576 along with Fr Dominic Vaughan; both were captured, but Montford was back in Douai the following year and was ordained in Brussels in June 1577. He was sent to work in England later that same month but was soon arrested again, this time in Cambridge. The bishop of London ordered the vice chancellor of the university to send the captive to London, together with "such books, letters, writings, and other trash" taken with him. We do not know what happened to him as a result—he may have been exiled—but he was back working as a priest in East Anglia in the early 1580s. He had a reputation for fasting, taking only bread and water on weekdays and "but little more on Sundays and holydays," and also for spending many hours in prayer. Topcliffe, the famous pursuivant, is said to have boasted particularly about his capture of so widely venerated a priest. Sometime in December 1590 he was arrested in the house of William Kilbeck in his native Hawstead and sent to London and imprisoned. He was hanged, drawn, and quartered in Fleet Street with George Beesley on 1 July 1591.

Both martyrs were beatified in 1987.

George Beesley's date of birth is known from an inscription he made while in the Tower, which is still visible. See *M.M.P.*, pp. 166-8; Anstruther, 1, pp. 28, 303-4. See also the general entries on the English and Welsh Martyrs under 4 May and 25 October.

Bd Thomas Maxfield, *Martyr* (c. 1585-1616)

Thomas Maxfield was born at Maer Hall, Enville, in Staffordshire about the year 1585. His father, William, was a staunch Catholic and at the time of Thomas' birth was under sentence of death for harbouring a priest, Robert Sutton, who was executed in Stafford in 1588. He was in prison until 1606, when he was able to purchase his release, and he died peacefully four years later. Thomas himself was born in prison because his mother Ursula was also under arrest for the same crime. When he was about eighteen years old Thomas went to Douai, but he was sent home in 1610, partly for health reasons and partly because he was considered unsuitable for the priesthood; when he returned in 1612 he was in trouble for "sedition," but he was ordained in 1614 and the following year was sent to work on the English mission. He used a number of aliases: Cleaton, Field, and Fylde; Challoner says the family's name was sometimes given as Macclesfield.

After only three months he was arrested in London by John Wragg, a well-known pursuivant, and lodged in the Gatehouse prison. He was questioned in the usual way about his priesthood and the work he had been doing in the country; he admitted being a priest and said he would obey the king in all civil matters but refused to take the Oath of Allegiance. He was left in prison for eight months and then tried to escape by being let down from a high window on a rope. Unfortunately he landed in the arms of a passer-by and was returned to the prison, where he was beaten severely and kept tied up in a filthy underground cell. A few days later he was moved to Newgate gaol to be tried. He was condemned to be hanged, drawn, and quartered because he was a priest and had refused a second time to take the Oath of Allegiance, though he acknowledged King James as "his true and lawful sovereign."

The Spanish ambassador, the duke of Gondomar, intervened on Thomas' behalf and asked for the sentence to be reduced; when this was not granted, the duke sent one of his chaplains to the prison to comfort and assist him in preparing for death. The execution took place at Tyburn on 1 July 1616 and was watched by a very large crowd; it was reported that the authorities had tried to keep it as quiet as possible and were particularly annoyed to find that the gallows had been decorated with flowers as though for a celebration. In his speech to the crowd Thomas claimed to have returned to England on the same mission and with the same authority as St Augustine of Canterbury (27 May): to instruct the English people in the true faith of Jesus Christ. The crowd insisted that he be allowed to hang until he was dead before the drawing and quartering took place. The Spanish ambassador recovered the body; part of the remains are at Gondomar and part at Downside Abbey. He was beatified in 1929.

Six of Thomas' letters were published in C.R.S., 3 (1906), pp. 48-57. Dr Kellison, president of Douai, published a Life of the martyr in 1616, and a reliable eyewitness account of his death was published the following year; see *ibid.*, pp. 30-48. See also *M.M.P.*, pp. 344-53; Anstruther, 2, pp. 214-6; Gillow, 4, pp. 362-7, under Macclesfield, and pp. 367-9, for Thomas' father. See also the general entries on the English and Welsh Martyrs under 4 May and 25 October.

Bd Ignatius Falzon (1813-65)

Ignazio Falzon was born in 1813 in Valetta, the capital of Malta. His father, Francesco, was a lawyer, and he and his wife, Mary Teresa Detono, were fervent Catholics. As a boy Ignazio showed signs of unusual holiness, and while he was studying law at the local university he spent his evenings teaching catechism to young people at the local church, urging them to receive the sacraments and join confraternities. He also began preaching to the soldiers in the English garrison, an apostolate he was to make his own. Later on he received the tonsure and minor orders but refused to go on to the priesthood, feeling himself too unworthy despite the encouragement of the local bishop that he should be ordained. He had a very strong devotion to Our Lady and recited the whole rosary every day. He died from cancer at the age of fifty-two on 1 July 1865. His cause was introduced in 1904, and his cult, which was very popular in Malta, was officially approved the following year.

Bibl.SS., 5, 449.

2

St Monegundis (570)

Monegundis was a native of the town of Chartres in France. When her two daughters died young she decided to become a religious because, as the previous edition of this work put it, she feared "lest in her grief she should become so centred in herself as to be unmindful of God." With her husband's consent she built a cell in the town and lived there in solitude, subsisting on as little food as possible and with no furniture except a floor mat on which to sleep. To avoid the fame caused by her miraculous powers of healing she moved to Tours and lived in a cell near the shrine of St Martin (11 Nov.), following the same strict rule of life. She was joined by a large number of women who were keen to dedicate themselves to God, and the cell became the nucleus of the convent of Saint-Pierre-le-Puellier. She died in 570, and her tomb became a place of pilgrimage, especially for the sick; many cures were attributed to her intercession. The shrine was destroyed by the Huguenots in 1562, but most of her relics were saved; they were solemnly re-enshrined in 1697. Her name features in some versions of the Hieronymian martyrology and in some Benedictine calendars, although she had no obvious Benedictine connections.

St Gregory of Tours is the main source of information; see his *De vitis patrum.* See also *Catholicisme*, 9 (1982), 565; *Bibl.SS.*, 9, 544-5.

St Swithin, *Bishop* (862)

Swithin, or Swithun, was born in Wessex about the end of the eighth century. Very little is known about his early life except that he was educated at the Old Minster in Winchester and became chaplain to King Egbert of Wessex (802-39). He is recorded as one of the witnesses to a royal charter granted to the abbey of Croyland in 833, and he was responsible for the education of Egbert's successor, Aethelwulf, who chose him to be bishop of Winchester in 852. Winchester was the capital of Wessex and as such was an important see; this importance increased as Wessex gradually became the leading English kingdom. The king appears to have leaned heavily on the bishop for advice. Swithin became famous for his works of charity and his building of churches; as the chronicler William of Malmesbury put it, "He was a treasury of all the virtues, and those in which he took most delight were humility and charity to the poor; in the discharge of his episcopal functions he omitted nothing belonging to a true pastor." He died on 2 July 862 and was buried, as he had requested, in the ordinary cemetery outside the west door of the Old Minster, "where his grave might be trodden on by passers-by and the rain fall upon it." His cult was very popular; there were fifty-eight medieval churches dedicated to him in England.

His feast-day was traditionally celebrated on 15 July, the date of the translation of his relics a century after his death. The rebuilding of the cathedral by St Aethelwold (1 Aug.) in 971 led to the inclusion of the saint's tomb within the building as a separate chapel; three years later another shrine was erected in the cathedral, perhaps containing the saint's head. The cult of Swithin may be considered to have begun in earnest with the building of these shrines. When St Alphege (19 Apr.) moved from Winchester to Canterbury in 1005 he seems to have taken the head of the saint with him. Many cures were reported to have taken place on this occasion, and Aelfric reports that the walls of the chapel were hung from end to end with the crutches of those who had been healed. When a new cathedral was built in the eleventh century Swithin's shrine was moved there on 15 July 1093; this remained a place of pilgrimage until the Reformation, when it was destroyed. The shrine was rebuilt in 1962.

The origin of the strong tradition that if it rains on St Swithin's day (15 July) it will rain for forty days afterwards is not clear. There was, apparently, a heavy rainfall on the occasion of the first translation in 971, and this was taken to be a manifestation of the saint's power. It should be noted that similar traditions attach to other saints, for example St Médard (8 June) in France, St Cewydd in Wales, and SS Processus and Martinian, who were also venerated on 2 July.

Lives of St Swithin were written by Aelfric, Wulfstan, and Lantfred; another, of uncertain date, used to be attributed to Goscelin. The scanty sources are gathered together in *AA.SS.*, July, 1, 321-37, and are also printed in Latin in *Anal. Boll.* 4 (1885), pp. 367-410; 7 (1888), pp. 373-80; 58 (1940), pp. 187-96. See also F. Bussby, *Saint Swithin* (1971); M. Lapidge and M. Winterbottom, *Wulfstan of Winchester: Life of St Ethelwold* (1991); *O.D.S.*, p. 446; *O.D.C.C.*, p. 1565; M. Lapidge, *The Cult of St Swithun* (forthcoming).

St Otto of Bamberg, *Bishop* (*c.* 1062-1139)

Otto was a member of the Mistelbach family of Swabia. When their parents died he and his brother moved to Poland and opened a school to earn some money. He was ordained and entered the imperial service sometime before 1090, eventually being appointed chancellor by the emperor Henry IV. He was appointed bishop of Bamberg in 1102 and in 1105 was chosen by the Diet to go to Rome in an attempt to make peace between pope and emperor. While he was in Rome he was solemnly consecrated bishop by Pope Paschal II (1099-1118). Some accounts say Otto had refused to accept consecration from any of Henry's bishops because of the emperor's quarrel with the pope over investiture and his support for the antipope, but this does not seem to have been the case. When Henry died his son at first promised to end the quarrel but then reverted to his father's policies. Otto kept in communion with Rome and tried to ensure that the rights of the Church in his diocese were not threatened. Because of his obvious holiness and sincerity Otto was highly regarded by both the imperial and the papal parties; he was an exemplary bishop, reforming clerical abuses, establishing and reforming the religious Orders, and living a life of personal austerity. He was responsible for fifteen major monastic foundations and six lesser ones, earning the title "Father of monasticism." His reforming activities extended beyond the confines of his own diocese, and he held a number of synods.

When Boleslaus III of Poland conquered part of Pomerania he invited Otto to undertake the evangelization of the area. In 1124 the bishop took a number of priests and laypeople and worked there for about a year, baptizing large numbers (some reports say up to twenty thousand) and organizing the priests to carry on the missionary work when he returned to his own diocese. He was back in Pomerania in 1128 in an attempt to re-convert the towns of Stettin and Julin, which had reverted to paganism, and also to evangelize the more remote areas. He died in Bamberg on 30 June 1139 and was canonized in 1189. He is regarded as the apostle of Pomerania, and his remains are venerated in the church of Saint Michael in Bamberg.

The sources for the life of Otto are plentiful. The important *Relatio de piis operibus Ottonis* is in *M.G.H., Scriptores*, 15, pp. 1156-66, and there are other early Lives—see *AA.SS.*, July, 1, pp. 349-465. See also *Anal.Boll.* 42 (1924), pp. 452-3; *Bibl.SS.*, 9, 1316-8.

The earliest depictions of Otto—some eleventh-century miniatures and the fourteenth-century tomb sculptures—show him in episcopal robes and holding a book. Later pictures add other elements: he is shown holding the model of a church to mark his reputation as a founder, and sometimes with a dog to mark the fact that he is invoked in Germany as a protector against rabies. He is sometimes shown holding arrows, which it is said he used to collect to make into nails for the building of the cathedral.

Bd Peter of Luxembourg, *Bishop and Cardinal* (1369-87)

Peter was born in 1369, the sixth son of Guy of Luxembourg, count of Ligny, and his wife, Mahaut of Châtillon; both his parents had died by the time he was four years old. He was educated by an aunt at Saint-Pol and as a boy was known for his piety and intelligence. At the age of ten he was sent to Paris to begin his formal studies and came under the influence of the famous Peter d'Ailly. Despite his age he was made a canon of Notre Dame in 1378, archdeacon of Dreux and Brussels in 1381, and canon of Cambrai in 1382. In the winter of 1380 he spent some months at Calais as a hostage for his elder brother who was a prisoner of the English. His family connections and wealth made him famous, and Pope Clement VII, the French antipope at the beginning of the Great Schism, appointed him bishop of Metz in 1384; two months later he made him a cardinal. Peter had to rely on the armed help of his brother to enter Metz, as it was occupied by the supporters of Pope Urban VI and already had another bishop. Once he was in charge of the city Peter had a Dominican priest consecrated bishop to act as his assistant in the visitation of the diocese, which he insisted on carrying out in person. He corrected clerical abuses and showed every sign of being a zealous pastor. Before long, however, he was forced out of the city by his political opponents. He resigned his see in 1385 and retired to Ligny and then to Paris, until Clement VII called him to Avignon in the autumn of 1386.

Peter attempted to live a life of penance and almsgiving in the papal court; his austerities were so extreme that Clement had to order him to mitigate them for the sake of his health. When his money ran out he sold his episcopal ring to have something to give to the poor. He planned a diplomatic mission to the kings of England and France in an attempt to bring peace, but in the early months of 1387 his health deteriorated and he moved across the river to Villeneuve, where the air was said to be better and he could relax in the Carthusian monastery. He died on 2 July and was buried, according to his wishes, in the cemetery of the poor in Avignon. His tomb soon became a place of pilgrimage, where miracles were reported, and in 1432 he was declared to be patron of the city. He was beatified in 1527. His remains are venerated in the church of Saint Didier in Avignon.

The principal source of information about Bd Peter is the documentation put together for the beatification process and containing the testimony of a number of contemporary witnesses; see *AA.SS.*, July, 1, pp. 486-628. See also *Bibl.SS.*, 10, 705-9.

A fifteenth-century picture of Bd Peter in Romainmôtier, Switzerland, shows him in ecstasy and contains the words that apparently he often quoted: "Contempt of the world, contempt of yourself: rejoice in your own contempt, but despise no other person." He was often depicted dressed as a cardinal, with the Luxembourg heraldic shield but with bare feet—presumably to show his humility; later pictures add a halo. The Worcester (U.S.A.) Art Gallery has a fourteenth- or fifteenth-century painting of him in the act of recommending a benefactor to Our Lady.

St Bernardino Realino (1530-1616)

Bernardino Luigi Realino was born in 1530 in Carpi, near Modena in northern Italy. His parents were Francesco Realino and Elisabetta Bellentani; the Bellantani were the more distinguished of the two families. Bernardino in later life wrote gratefully of his father, "who made it convenient for me to study and did not wish to send me to court." He studied with great success at the academy of Modena and then went to the university of Bologna to study arts and medicine; he finished his medical studies in 1551 and thought about practising as a doctor. Instead he began to study civil and canon law, apparently at the request of a lady he had fallen in love with and who thought that he would make a good lawyer. Bernardino, however, saw these legal studies as giving him a foundation for a career in government or public administration. In 1556 he was awarded a doctorate *utriusque juris*. His father was then in the service of Cardinal Madruzzo, the prince-bishop of the city of Trent and governor of Milan, and it looked as though Bernardino was set for a successful public career. He held a number of important posts in various towns and finally became auditor and general superintendent in the kingdom of Naples of the marquis of Pescara. It is clear from his letters that he was also developing spiritually during these years. He wrote to his brother: "I have no desire for the honours of this world but solely for the glory of God and the salvation of my soul," while he wrote to his sick father: "God is always seeking the good of his creatures, though this frail and miserable flesh, inclined as it is to pleasure, does not wish to acknowledge this."

It was in Naples that he first came into contact with the Jesuits, and after a great deal of prayer he decided to join them, finally persuaded by an apparition of some kind of Our Lady and the Child Jesus. He wrote to his father to say that he had been called to serve the Lord, from whose hands he hoped "to win in a short time joy, honour and reward without measure," and to enter a "flock of the most dear souls God has on earth, that is the Society of Jesus." He became a novice in 1564 and was ordained priest in 1567; he was very soon appointed novice-master, an indication of the respect that he had already won among his superiors. When the novitiate was moved from Naples he remained in the city working among the poor and the Muslim slaves, preaching (though not very successfully, it seems), hearing confessions, acting as diocesan censor of books, and directing an aristocratic lay confraternity. In 1574 he moved to Lecce in Apulia to set up a new Jesuit house and college, and he spent the rest of his life there, being at different times rector, vice rector, and ordinary teacher.

Outside the college he became known for his gentleness and patience. He was consulted by people from every walk of life on secular and religious matters, earning the nickname "father of the city" because of his concern for anyone who was in trouble or suffering from illness. Several miracles were attributed to his intercession. He continued his apostolate to prisoners and the slaves, converting a large number of the latter to Christianity and, as in Naples, found himself to be more effective in counselling individuals than in public preaching. He set up a sodality for priests to help reform the secular and religious clergy of the city. He died in 1616 and was beatified in 1895 and canonized in 1947. St Robert Bellarmine (17 Nov.) said of him: "I have never heard a single complaint about Fr Realino, though I have been his provincial; even those who were ill-disposed to the Society, who seized every opportunity to speak unfavourably of it . . . always made exception for Realino. . . . Everyone knows that he is a saint." Shortly after his death the city council chose Bernardino as Lecce's official patron.

Certain physical phenomena relating to some phials of his blood were associated with his cult. These involved liquefaction and were described in detail in the previous edition of this work, where they are shown to have been well documented and to have lasted until the middle of the nineteenth century. A biographer in 1895, however, failed to find any relic of the blood preserved in a liquid state. The editor concluded: "It has seemed worthwhile to give these

17

details, which may not have anything whatever to do with the holiness of St Bernardino Realino, because they are a well-authenticated example of such prodigies, which raise an interest and excitement out of all proportion to their importance or significance."

A collection of his spiritual letters was published in 1854: G. Boero (ed.), *Lettere spirituali inediti*; Bernardino's book, *In Nuptias Pelei et Tethydis Catullianas Commentarius*, exists only in the 1551 edition and is very difficult to find; he destroyed as much of his early classical writings as he could find on becoming a Jesuit, and most of what survived was lost when the Society was suppressed in 1773. The best Life is G. Germier, *San Bernardino Realino* (1943). A sound English biography is Francis Sweeney, S.J., *Bernardine Realino, Renaissance Man* (1951). See also *Bibl.SS.*, 2, 1322-6. For the blood phenomena, see *B.T.A.*, 3, pp. 13-14, and a series of critical articles on the subject in general by H. Thurston in *The Month* 149 (Jan.-Mar. 1927), pp. 44-55, 123-35, 236-47.

ST THOMAS—patron of builders
Spear with silver head and tawny handle,
for his martyrdom; carpenter's square with silver blade
and gold handle, on red field

3

ST THOMAS, *Apostle* (First Century)

All that is known for certain about Thomas comes from the New Testament. He is mentioned as one of the twelve apostles in all four Gospels and is nick-named Didymus, "the twin," in John's Gospel (11:16; 20:24). It is John's Gospel that recounts three episodes in which Thomas features prominently and one where he appears among a group: first, he suggested to the other disciples that they too should go to Jerusalem with Jesus and die with him (11:16). Then, during Jesus' last great discourse with his disciples after the Last Supper, Thomas interrupted to say that they did not know where Jesus was going and therefore could not know the way, to which Jesus replied, "I am the Way, the Truth and the Life." (14:4-6).

Third, and most famously, "doubting Thomas" refused to believe that Jesus had risen from the dead until he had seen him with his own eyes and put his finger into his wounds; this brought Jesus' response, "Doubt no longer but believe," to which Thomas replied, "My Lord and my God" (20:24-9). This last was the only occasion when a disciple declared a belief in Christ's full divinity (Peter had acknowledged him as the "son of the living God" in Matthew 16:13-20), and it gave Our Lord the opportunity to stress the importance of faith. Finally, Thomas is mentioned as being one of the disciples on the shore of the Sea of Galilee after the resurrection who witnessed the miraculous catch of fish (John 21: 1-14). Thomas' importance in the mind of the early Church can be seen from his appearances at key points in the Gospel narrative, and from his spoken words that lead on to pivotal statements by Our Lord. It has even been suggested by a recent scholar that it was Thomas and not John who was the "beloved disciple."

There are a number of traditions about where Thomas preached the gospel after Pentecost. One of these, supported by the historian Eusebius, says he preached to the Parthians, to the south-east of the Caspian Sea in what is now Iran; Parthians had been among those who had heard the apostles preaching at Pentecost. The strongest tradition, however, links Thomas with southern India and says that he founded a Christian Church there after preaching first in Syria and Persia. The Syriac Christians of Malabar still call themselves "Christians of St Thomas" and claim that he was martyred and his body buried at Mylapore, near Madras, in the year 72. There is a tradition that his body was translated to Edessa in Syria in 394 and eventually to Ortona in Italy, but the Indian Christians believe that he is still buried in what they call San Tome. An ancient stone cross dating from between the sixth and the eighth centuries is preserved in the church that was built over the supposed place of his martyrdom. The tradition was mentioned by a large number of early writers, Eastern and Western, including St Ephraem (9 June), St Gregory Nazianzen (2 Jan.), St Ambrose (7 Dec.), St John Chrysostom (13 Sept.), and St Jerome (30 Sept.), who wrote, "Christ dwells everywhere, with Thomas in India and with Peter in Rome." St Gregory of Tours (17 Nov.) knew of the story of Thomas' martyrdom, having heard it from "Theodore who visited those parts." The tradition became so well established that King Alfred of Wessex sent alms "to India to St Thomas," as well as to Rome (*O.D.S.*). Later, Marco Polo, reporting on his visit in 1293, wrote that both Christians and Saracens visited Thomas' tomb on pilgrimage, and when the Portuguese landed in India for the first time in 1498 they found a number of well-established Christian communities. The tradition is still strong, and the Indian government issued postage stamps in Thomas' honour in 1964 and again in 1972 to mark the nineteenth centenary of the apostle's death.

Four apocryphal writings were attributed to Thomas. The *Acts of Thomas* had its origins in Gnosticism and seems to have been written before the middle of the third century, perhaps in Edessa; it is mainly a long account of Thomas' work in India and of the transfer of his relics to Mesopotamia. The *Apocalypse of Thomas* was written at the end of the fourth century; it deals with the end of the world and the last things, and it was popular in Anglo-Saxon England. The *Gospel of Thomas* was originally written in Greek about the year 150 and is known almost entirely through a Coptic version discovered in the 1940s. It contains sayings and parables of Jesus and may have a few genuine sayings not to be found in the canonical Gospels. Finally, the *Infancy Gospel of Thomas* exists in a variety of versions in different languages and claims to tell of the miracles worked by Jesus as a child: "These are often without theological point or justification, so that the Lord appears callous and irresponsible" (*O.D.C.C.*).

The cult of St Thomas has been strong in the West, and his name became one of the most popular Christian names. About fifty ancient church dedications exist in England. Until recently his feast was celebrated in the West on 21 December, the traditional date of his death, with a celebration of the translation of his body on 3 July. The Syriac Church and the Malabar Christians, however, claim that he died on 3 July, and this has been adopted in the recent revision of the Roman Calendar. The Greek Church celebrates his feast on 6 October. He is the patron saint of builders (see below) and of the blind.

O.D.S., pp. 458-9; *O.D.C.C.*, p. 1370; *N.C.E.*, 14, p. 101.

In art the scene of Thomas' doubting and Christ's appearance is that most usually portrayed—the earliest is a tenth-century ivory in Berlin, and there is a twelfth-century mosaic in Monreale, Sicily, showing Christ guiding Thomas' hand toward his side. The most famous of these representations is a Verrocchio bronze in San Michele, Florence (1483). There are also several copies of a painting of the subject by Caravaggio (*c.* 1598), including one in the Uffizi, Florence. Among the finest are the painting by Guercino in the

National Gallery, London (1621), and by Rubens in Antwerp. In groups of the twelve apostles he sometimes holds a spear to indicate his martyrdom, sometimes a builder's T-square. The latter originated in the story in the *Acts of Thomas*, repeated in *The Golden Legend*, that in India he built a palace for a local king. A twelfth-century English bronze bowl in the British Museum gives his life in seven scenes, which include one of the marriage of the king's daughter (*O.D.S.*). *The Golden Legend* relates how Thomas received a girdle from Our Lady after her assumption, which he had doubted just as he had doubted the resurrection; this became a favourite subject with artists—see, for example, Benozzo Gozzoli's *Assumption, with St Thomas receiving the girdle* (1450; Vatican Museum), and Matteo di Giovanni's *Assumption . . . girdle* (1474; National Gallery, London). See Murray, pp. 522-3.

St Anatolius of Laodicea, *Bishop* (*c.* 283)

Nothing is known of the personal life of Anatolius. He was renowned as a philosopher and mathematician and ran an Aristotelian school in Alexandria. When a rebellion broke out in Bruchion, a suburb of the city, the Roman army laid siege to it, probably in the year 263, and caused considerable suffering by cutting off the food supplies. As a result, famine and disease threatened to kill many innocent people, but, according to tradition, Anatolius persuaded the Roman general to let them leave the city; the rebel leaders at first refused to allow anyone to go, but again Anatolius used his prestige to save the non-combatants.

Some time later Anatolius was in Palestine, where he became assistant bishop in the city of Caesarea. On the occasion of the Second Council of Antioch in 268 he went to Laodicea in Syria, where his friend Eusebius was bishop. On the latter's death Anatolius was chosen to succeed him. There is no information about his activities as bishop. He died about the year 283.

St Jerome speaks highly of Anatolius in his *De viris illustribus*, but the main source of information about him is the historian Eusebius. He quotes at some length from a book about Easter that was attributed to Anatolius, but a later Latin version of this, *Liber Anatoli de ratione paschali*, was written by Irish monks on Iona in the sixth century. Parts of ten treatises that he wrote on arithmetic have survived and were published in *P.G.*, 10, 232-6. See *Bibl.SS.*, 1, 1084-5.

St Heliodorus of Attino, *Bishop* (*c.* 405)

Information about Heliodorus comes mainly from the writings of St Jerome (30 Sept.). He had probably been a soldier and belonged to a group of clergy who formed themselves around Valerian, the bishop of Aquileia. He met St Jerome when he stayed in Aquileia from 370 to 373 and accompanied him to Palestine, where they lived the monastic life together for a time. Heliodorus refused to follow Jerome in a more austere way of life and returned to Italy, where we find him bishop of Attino: he was probably the city's first bishop. He was consecrated some time before the year 381, when he took part in a meeting of bishops in Aquileia. Jerome regarded Heliodorus' return to Italy as a desertion of the monastic life and wrote at length to rebuke him, pointing out in his letter all the advantages of the life of desert solitude. As usual, Jerome did not mince his words: Heliodorus had chosen the inheritance of the world and so could not be a "co heir with Christ"; why would he not fight when he was prepared for battle? They remained friends, however, and later on Jerome wrote to him and St Chromatius (2 Dec.), bishop of Aquileia and friend of Heliodorus, asking for money and books to help him with his translation of the Bible; he dedicated some of his translations to the two bishops. When Heliodorus' nephew, Nepotian, gave up the life of a soldier to become a priest, Jerome wrote that he could have no better model as a pastor than his uncle. The date of Heliodorus' death is unknown, but it seems to have occurred before the year 410.

St Jerome's letters are in *P.L.*, 22; see especially 14, 52, 60. There is a late Life full of fables in *AA.SS.*, July, 1, pp. 645-51. See also *Bibl.SS.*, 4, 1076-7.

St Anatolius of Constantinople, *Patriarch* (458)

Anatolius was a native of Alexandria. He seems first to have come to notice at the Council of Ephesus in 431, when he was an outspoken opponent of the Nestorians, who believed that there were two distinct persons in Christ. Before this he may have been sent by St Cyril of Alexandria (27 June) to be his representative at the imperial court in Constantinople, and this may help to explain how he came to be appointed patriarch of Constantinople in succession to St Flavian (18 Feb.), who had died as a result of the injuries he had received at the "robber council" of Ephesus in 449. Anatolius was consecrated by Dioscorus of Alexandria, a Monophysite bishop, and this, along with the manner of his appointment, led some to have doubts about his orthodoxy. The pope, St Leo the Great (10 Nov.), sent legates to try to discover whether these doubts were justified or not, and so Anatolius organized a synod to prove his orthodoxy. It formally accepted the letter that had been sent by Leo to Flavian; this letter, the so-called "Tome of Leo," set out clearly the orthodox teaching on the Incarnation, with special reference to the two natures in Christ. After the synod Anatolius had it copied and sent to his metropolitan bishops for their acceptance. He hoped that this would help to win the approval of the pope and recognition of himself as Flavian's legitimate successor; Leo still had reservations, however, because Anatolius had accepted consecration from a heretic—in the end he agreed to recognize him "rather in mercy than in justice."

Anatolius played a prominent role in the Council of Chalcedon in 451, which defined the Faith in line with Leo's teaching and also deposed Dioscorus. Against the wishes of the papal legates the council went on to declare that Constantinople was second in importance as a see only to Rome and that its bishop should have a corresponding precedence as patriarch. Leo objected to this decree on the grounds that both Alexandria and Antioch could claim seniority over Constantinople and in answer to Anatolius, who had written personally to put his case, replied: "A Catholic, especially if he be a priest of the Lord, should not be corrupted by ambition any more than involved in error." The patriarch died on 3 July 458.

The previous edition of this work said it was unfortunate that we know nothing of Anatolius' private life, "for his public career is rather equivocal for one who is acclaimed as a saint." It added that Baronius, when drawing up the Roman Martyrology in the sixteenth century, condemned him "for the way he received his see, for ambition, for conniving at heresy, and on other grounds." While the Bollandists acquitted him of these charges, others have continued to view him rather severely, not so much for any doubt about the orthodoxy of his beliefs but for being by temperament and in practice an opportunist (Jugie). His cult has always been strong in the Eastern Church.

There is an anonymous Life in Greek, which is of little historical value; see *AA.SS.*, July, 1, pp. 571-85. Leo's letters are in *P.L.*, 54, 912-27; 991-1010; for Anatolius to Leo, see 975-84. See also M. Jugie in *D.H.G.E.*, 2 (1914), 1497-1500; *B.T.A.*, 2, pp. 12-3.

St Leo II, *Pope* (683)

Leo was a Sicilian by birth. He had been trained in the papal choir-school and was admired for his competence in Greek and Latin. The date of his election to the papacy was probably January 681, but he had to wait for the emperor's official approval before he could be consecrated. The sixth general council was in session at the time in Constantinople, and the emperor, Constantine IV (668-85), refused to approve Leo's election until he was sure that the new pope would ratify the findings of the council. Among the most important of these was a condemnation of the Monothelite heresy and its followers, who believed that Christ had only one, divine, will and so was not truly human. An earlier pope, Honorius I (625-38), had failed to condemn the heresy and, in some people's eyes, had even accepted it himself. The emperor was determined that the council should condemn Honorius by name and that this condemnation should also be approved by Leo. It took many months to persuade the papal legates to the council to agree to this, and they did not return to Rome until July 682, taking with them Constantine's approval of Leo's consecration. For the sake of peace between the papacy and the emperor, Leo agreed to ratify the council's decisions, including its condemnation of Honorius. In return, Constantine allowed the pope to have a permanent representative at the imperial court and reduced the taxes on some of the papal territories. He also declared that the archbishops of Ravenna, the imperial city in the north of Italy, should in future be consecrated by the pope and come under papal control.

While Leo spoke of Honorius' "profane betrayal" of the true faith in one of his letters to the emperor, elsewhere he spoke merely of his predecessor's negligence in not taking steps to prevent the spread of heresy. He also refrained from inflicting punishments on those whom the council had removed from office: his interest was peace between the various factions, and he believed that clemency would win over more than severity.

The *Liber Pontificalis* speaks of Leo's care for the poor and his almsgiving. It also describes how he took the relics of several martyrs from the catacombs to place them in a special chapel restored for the purpose in Rome. He also restored the church of San Giorgio in Velabro for use by the Greek community. He died on 3 July 683. His feast was celebrated on 21 June until 1921; in 1960 it was removed from the universal Calendar.

Leo's letters are in *P.L.*, 96, 387-420. See especially *O.D.P.*, pp. 78-9 and references. See also *O.D.C.C.*, p. 787, on Honorius and p. 1106 on Monothelitism.

St Raymund of Toulouse (*c.* 1050-1118)

Raymund Gayrard was born in Toulouse about the middle of the eleventh century. He became a chorister at the local church of Saint-Sernin and later married. When his wife died shortly afterwards he decided not to re-marry but to devote himself to God's service. He remained a layman and spent his money and time in the care of the poor and other needy people in the city, causing comment, apparently, because he included some Jews in his works of mercy. He founded and endowed an almshouse for thirteen poor people, in memory of Our Lord and the twelve apostles. He also built two stone bridges. Eventually he was ordained and became a canon in the collegiate church of Saint-Sernin, devoting all his energies to completing the building of the church and increasing its collection of relics, which made it a famous shrine for the rest of the Middle Ages. At some stage he was elected provost of the college of canons. He died on 3 July 1118, probably before the church had been finished, and was buried in the almshouse that he had founded. His tomb became the centre of a local cult, and a large number of miraculous cures were attributed to his intercession. The cult was approved in 1652. The Canons Regular of the Lateran keep his feast on 8 July.

AA.SS., July, 1, pp. 589-603, gives the biographical detail taken from an Office in his honour but compiled over a century after his death; this was probably based on an earlier, relatively reliable Life. See also *Bibl.SS.*, 11, 25-6.

4

ST ELIZABETH OF PORTUGAL (1271-1336)

Elizabeth was born in Zaragoza in Spain, the daughter of King Peter III of Aragon. She was given the name Elizabeth at Baptism in memory of her great-aunt, St Elizabeth of Hungary (17 Nov.), who had died forty years earlier, but in her own country was always known under the Spanish form of the name, Isabella. The young princess was brought up in a pious atmosphere and showed signs of being more interested in religious matters than in those relating to the court. When she was twelve years old she was married to Diniz, the king of Portugal, who "allowed her an entire liberty in her devotion, and esteemed her piety without feeling called to imitate it" (*B.T.A.*). Their first child, Constance, was born in 1290 and their son, Alfonso, in 1291. Her husband led a profligate life and fathered a number of illegitimate children; Elizabeth also cared for these and saw to their education. Diniz was, however, an able ruler, and his reign was later described as a golden age; he himself was nicknamed "the Justinian of Portugal" because of the wisdom of his laws.

Alfonso took up arms against his father, mainly because of the favours shown by the king to his illegitimate son. Elizabeth earned a reputation as a peace-maker for her efforts to end these quarrels, as well as those involving Ferdinand IV of Aragon (who had married her daughter, Constance) and various other princes. For a time Diniz banished her from the court, thinking she was giving too much support to his son, and during this period of exile Elizabeth lived her life according to a strict rule, with set hours devoted to prayer and almsgiving. She intensified her works of mercy and became known for her charity to the sick and the poor and her care of pilgrims; she provided marriage dowries for poor girls and established hospitals for penitent prostitutes. She was eventually reconciled with her husband, who rewarded her for making peace between him and his son, who had rebelled a second time in 1323 and laid siege to Lisbon.

The king died after a long illness in 1325, during which Elizabeth nursed him herself; she then decided to devote the rest of her life to good works and gave as much of her wealth as she could to the poor. Dressed as a Franciscan tertiary, she made a pilgrimage to Compostela and afterwards decided to join the Poor Clares in a convent that she had founded at Coïmbra. She did not immediately make any vows, however, but lived simply in a house attached to the convent. She died on 4 July 1336 at Estremoz in Portugal, where she had gone, despite being very ill, on another mission to reconcile her son, now King Alfonso IV, and the king of Castile. She made her religious vows on her death-bed and was buried in the chapel of the Poor Clares in Coïmbra. Miracles were attributed to her intercession, although the well-known story of a page saved miraculously from death in a lime-kiln can be traced back to Goan folklore and was attributed to Elizabeth only in the sixteenth century. Documents were gathered together in 1576 to begin her cause, and her body was exhumed in 1612 and found to be incorrupt. She was canonized in 1625 and is the patron saint of Coïmbra and one of the patron saints of Portugal.

An almost contemporary Life is in *AA.SS.*, July, 2, pp. 169-213. See also V. McNabb, *St Elizabeth of Portugal* (1937), which uses extracts from her few remaining letters; *Bibl.SS.*, 4, 1096-9; *O.D.S.*, p. 156.

Elizabeth is often depicted with her great-aunt, St Elizabeth of Hungary, sometimes with her head covered as a religious and wearing the cord of a Franciscan tertiary, sometimes wearing a crown. Both saints are sometimes depicted with crowns of roses because of the legend told of both of them that when they were about to give money to the poor and were stopped by their husbands, who objected to their generosity, the money they were carrying miraculously turned to roses. Other pictures show Elizabeth with two crowns, one on her head to show her royalty and one in her hand to show her sanctity. The two saints are also shown caring for the sick, especially those with repugnant skin diseases; it is not clear which of the two is depicted in Murillo's *Works of Mercy* in the Prado in Madrid. A drawing by Goya in the royal palace in Madrid shows Elizabeth of Portugal caring for the sick.

St Bertha of Blangy, *Abbess* (*c.* 725)

Bertha was born near Thérouanne in the Pas de Calais region of France and was the founder of the monastery of Blangy near Hisdin in Artois. According to a late Life she was the daughter of Count Rigobert, married a nobleman, and had five daughters. When her husband died she decided to become a religious and so entered the convent that she had founded at Blangy; her two eldest daughters, Gertrude and Deotilla, entered with her. She became abbess and after establishing regular observance of the Rule among the community left Deotilla in charge while she retired to a cell to devote herself to prayer. She died about the year 725. Her relics were transferred to Erstein, near Strasbourg, in 895 to keep them safe from the Norman invaders; in 1032 they were taken back to Blangy, which by then had been restored as a Benedictine monastery.

AA.SS., July, 2, pp. 47-60, prints a late and unreliable Life written about two centuries after Bertha's death and after the destruction of Blangy and all its records by the Normans; see also *Bibl.SS.*, 3, 90; *D.H.G.E.*, 8, 944-5; *Catholicisme*, 1, 1499.

St Andrew of Crete, *Bishop* (*c.* 660-740)

Andrew was born in Damascus about the middle of the seventh century. At the age of fifteen he went to Jerusalem and became a monk of Saint Sabas and the Holy Sepulchre. In 685 Theodore, the patriarch of Jerusalem, sent him to Constantinople to confirm Jerusalem's acceptance of the decrees of the Sixth

Council of Constantinople against Monothelitism (the belief that Christ had only one, divine, will). While he was in the imperial city he was ordained deacon and given charge of an orphanage and a hospice for the elderly. Sometime after this, probably about the year 700, he was appointed archbishop of Gortyna, the metropolitan diocese of Crete. In 711 there was another attempt to establish Monothelitism as the official belief of the empire, when Philippicus Bardanes seized the imperial throne and called a synod to repeal the decrees of the previous council. Andrew attended the synod and for a short time accepted its heretical decrees, until Bardanes had been driven out and the patriarch of Constantinople had sent a letter of apology and retractation to the pope on behalf of those who had attended the synod.

Andrew's fame was as a preacher and hymn writer. Twenty-one of his fifty remaining sermons have been published, and while it is not true, as used to be claimed, that he was responsible for introducing the type of hymn known as a *kanon* into the Byzantine liturgy, he wrote a large number of them, some of which are still in use. One he wrote is known as the "Great *Kanon*" and consists of 250 strophes, to be sung in Lent "with much hard work and weariness of the lungs," as one critic said, but on the whole they are "remarkable for the originality of their metric and musical form" as well as their length (Grove). His sermons are important in the development of devotion to Our Lady. He died on the island of Lesbos about the year 740. He should not be confused with another St Andrew of Crete, "the Calybite" (20 Oct.), who was martyred in 766.

Andrew's works are in *P.G.*, 97, 790-1444; an English trans. of "The Great Canon" was edited by D. J. Chitty in 1957. See also *O.D.S.*, p. 21; *O.D.C.C.*, p. 60; Grove, 1, p. 412.

St Oda of Canterbury, *Bishop* (958)

Oda (sometimes mistakenly Odo) was born in East Anglia of Danish parents. Scandinavians in England became Christians in large numbers after the conversion of the Danish leader Guthrun following Alfred's Treaty of Wedmore, and Oda became a Christian early in his life and went on to be ordained priest. He served as a counsellor to King Athelstan (924-39) and became bishop of Ramsbury in Wiltshire in the year 927. He was a regular attender at royal councils and led a diplomatic mission to restore Louis d'Outremer, Athelstan's nephew, as king of the Franks. According to legend he was present at the battle of Brunanburgh in 937 when King Athelstan won a great victory, establishing the authority of the kings of Wessex over northern England, and played an important role in the battle by restoring miraculously the king's sword; it is, however, unlikely that Oda was there at all.

In 942 he was appointed archbishop of Canterbury by King Edmund I; at first, it is said, he refused to accept the appointment on the grounds that he was not a monk, but at the king's insistence he received the monastic habit at Fleury-sur-Loire and was consecrated archbishop. The episode is not clear, and it is more likely that Oda had received the monastic habit earlier, perhaps when he was in France on the diplomatic mission already mentioned. The episode may have been invented to stress his sympathy and active support for reformed monasticism, which are not in doubt. As archbishop he encouraged the important monastic reforms of St Dunstan and helped his own nephew, St Oswald of Worcester (28 Feb.), to become a monk at Fleury.

He was popularly known as "Oda the Good" because of his work in restoring churches and raising the standards of his clergy. Sometime between 942 and 946 he drew up a list of ten constitutions dealing with matters of faith and morals, based partly on earlier English decrees and partly on a collection of Irish canons and other sources. They deal with a range of issues, including the immunity of the Church from taxation, the duties of priests and clerics, the proper observance of Sundays and feast-days, the duty of every bishop to visit and preach in each parish of his diocese at least once a year, fasting, and the duties of the king. He wrote to his suffragan bishops exhorting them to be diligent in caring for their flocks in both material and spiritual matters. He also set about re-organizing the Church in his native East Anglia, badly disrupted by the Danish armies in which his own father may have served, and restored the see at Elmham. At Canterbury he restored the cathedral and rebuilt its walls, raising them by twenty feet in the process. A new altar was installed to house the relics of St Wilfrid (12 Oct.), stolen from Ripon in 948 when the minster had been destroyed by Eadred. The possession of such important relics added to Canterbury's standing, and Oda exploited this by having a monk, Frithegod, write a new verse Life of the great northern bishop. Oda wrote a preface to this explaining the "translation" of the relics on the grounds that religion was decaying in the north and that it was the will of God that Oda should "receive" the relics that had been carried away by "certain men"; it was a rather disingenuous defence of himself against a possible accusation of having stolen the relics. Frithegod's Life obscures the fact that Wilfrid had quarrelled seriously with the archbishops of Canterbury.

Oda was also a keen defender of the rights of the Church against lay interference and of the see of Canterbury against all comers, but he maintained good relations with the king and was one of Edmund's valued counsellors. He ceased to attend royal councils in the last year of his life, and some have seen in this a cooling off of relations between the archbishop and the new young king, Eadwig, whose personal life was open to criticism; on the other hand, it could have been the result of age or illness. He died in 958 and was buried in the cathedral, close to the high altar; his remains were later moved to the Trinity Chapel. His name features in several ancient calendars; a number of legendary miracles were attributed to him, including one by which he persuaded some of the Canterbury clergy of the truth of the Real Presence in the Eucharist by showing them a host dripping with blood. His pastoral zeal and personal holiness provided a model for later reformers; it is said that St Dunstan of Canterbury (19 May) never passed his tomb without kneeling in prayer before it. The most recent history of Canterbury describes him as "the most distinguished of Canterbury's churchmen in this period" (Collinson *et al.*).

Eadmer wrote a *Vita S. Odonis*; see *P.L.*, 133, 933-44; this is wrongly ascribed to Osbern in *AA.SS.*, July, 2, pp. 67-73. There is information about him in the Life of his nephew, St Oswald. The Latin text of the *Constitutiones Odonis* and Oda's letter to his suffagans may be found in D. Whitelock, *et al.* (eds.), *Councils and Synods and other documents relating to the Church of England* (1981), 1, pp. 65-74. See also N. Brooks, *The Early History of the Church of Canterbury* (1984, repr. 1996), pp. 222-37; *O.D.S.*, p. 361; P. Collinson, *et al.* (eds.), *A History of Canterbury Cathedral* (1995).

St Ulrich of Augsburg, *Bishop* (890-973)

Ulrich was born into the family of the counts of Dillingen in Augsburg in southern Germany in 890 and was educated at the famous Swiss monastery of Saint-Gall. He became friendly with St Wiborada (2 May), a recluse who lived near the monastery and who apparently foretold that her young friend would become a bishop. After completing his studies Ulrich returned to Augsburg, where his uncle, St Adalbero (locally venerated on 6 Oct.), was bishop; he lived for a time in his uncle's household and at some stage was ordained priest. Adalbero died in 909, and in 923 Ulrich became bishop of Augsburg himself through the influence of his maternal grandfather, the duke of Swabia.

The Magyars invaded the area in 926, killing Wiborada, plundering Augsburg, and burning its cathedral. Ulrich set about restoring order and rebuilding his people's confidence and prosperity; he was an able administrator and a devoted pastor and carried out a visitation of his diocese every year. He founded the monastery of Saint Stephen in 968 and restored that of Saint Afra, as well as restoring a number of parish churches. This active pastoral life was all the more remarkable given his involvement in politics as one of the emperor's closest counsellors. Otto finally defeated the Magyars in 955 and attributed the victory in great part to Ulrich, who had defended Augsburg successfully, building a protective wall around the city and organizing its military defences. Throughout his years as bishop Ulrich was a strong supporter of Otto and his imperial policies. His busy public life was based on an inner life of prayer and austerity and an almost monastic régime in the episcopal household. As evidence of his dedication to the precepts of the gospel it is said that he visited the hospital in Augsburg daily to wash the feet of twelve poor people and distribute alms.

Toward the end of his life he wished to retire to a monastery, and so in 972 he resigned from his see and appointed his nephew Adalbero in his place. He was criticized for this act of nepotism and was called before a synod at Ingelheim to explain it, but Adalbero died before he could take up his post. Ulrich died in

973, and a local cult began straightaway. Miracles were reported at his tomb, and at the request of his successor as bishop of Augsburg he was canonized by Pope John XV in 993 at a synod held in the Lateran, the first recorded papal canonization. Motives behind the rapid canonization were mixed, and the pope was acting at least in part to please the emperor in Germany, but there is no doubt about Ulrich's sanctity and exemplary reign as bishop. Ulrich is one of the two principal patron saints of Augsburg and is also the patron saint of a number of other German towns. His tomb in the basilica of SS Ulrich and Afra in Augsburg is still a place of pilgrimage.

There are abundant sources for the life of Ulrich. The most important is the contemporary Life by Gerhard, provost of Augsburg, printed in *M.G.H., Scriptores*, 4, 377-425. Another early Life by Berno, the abbot of Reichenau, is in *P.L.*, 113, 1183-1204. See also H. Kohl, *Bischof Ulrich: ein Lebensbild . . .* (1963); *Bibl.SS.*, 12, 796-8.

In art Ulrich is normally depicted conventionally as a bishop, often alongside St Afra, but also with St Barbara. Some pictures show him holding a fish as a reminder of the legend that once he was offered meat to eat on a Friday; when he did so he was accused of having broken the Church's law, but was able to show his critics that fishbones were all that was left on his plate.

Bd John Cornelius and Companions, *Martyrs of Dorchester* (1594)

John Cornelius was born in Bodmin in Cornwall in 1554 or 1557. His parents were Irish, and the family name may have been Cornellys; when he was working in Cornwall as a priest John used a large number of aliases—mostly Irish but also the Cornish Mohun—and it has been suggested that his mother's maiden name was O'Mahon or O'Mahoney. The family was poor, and it was thanks to a local benefactor, Sir John Arundell of Lanherne, that John was educated and able to go to Exeter College, Oxford, where he became a fellow in 1575. Three years later, however, he was expelled because he was a Catholic. He decided to go abroad to study for the priesthood, first in Reims and then in Rome, where he was ordained, probably in 1582. He had already gained a reputation as a gifted preacher and had been chosen to preach before the pope in the Sistine Chapel at Christmas 1581. John Gerard, in his *Narrative of the Gunpowder Plot*, says that John Cornelius was "so famous in preaching that all Catholics followed him as children do their nurses when they long for milk."

He left for England in September 1583 and worked mainly as chaplain to the Arundell family. Because of his Catholicism, Sir John had been required to live in London where he could be watched by the government, and Fr John spent some years there with the family. On Sir John's death in 1590 he went with Lady Arundell to Chideock Castle in Dorset, where he worked for a few years before being arrested in April 1594, owing to the treachery of one of the servants. Two other servants were arrested with him, John Carey and Patrick Salmon, both of whom were Dubliners; another layperson, Thomas Bosgrave, a nephew of Sir John, was also arrested, apparently for offering a hat to the priest as he was being taken away.

John was interrogated locally by, among others, Sir Walter Raleigh and then taken to London and tortured to make him reveal the names of those who had assisted him in Cornwall. When he refused to divulge any names he was sent back to Dorchester for trial. According to a letter to Fr Henry Garnett, S.J., written while a prisoner in the Marshalsea in London, John asked to be allowed to make his profession as a Jesuit; he had tried to enter the Society much earlier, in Rome, and spoke of his grief that he was not "one of you in number and merit." This time his request was granted, and he took his vows in prison in the presence of two laymen and a religious commissioned by Garnett. On 2 July he was found guilty of being a seminary priest ordained abroad but living in England and was condemned to be hanged, drawn, and quartered; the three laymen were found guilty of helping him and were also condemned to death by hanging. All refused the offer of freedom in return for giving up their Catholicism, and the executions took place in Dorchester on 4 July 1594. John signed a final letter from prison, "Yours, John, one about to die for a moment that he may live for ever." Raleigh attended the execution and prevented John from addressing the crowd as he had planned.

The four were beatified in 1929. Another priest, Bd Hugh Green, was executed in Dorchester on 19 August 1642; the group of five are known collectively as the Dorchester Martyrs.

There is a full Life of John Cornelius in Foley, 3, pp. 435-74, and see Leo Hicks, S.J., "John Cornelius: An Irish Martyr, 1554-1594," *Studies*, Dec. 1929, pp. 537-55. See also *M.M.P.*, pp. 198-202; C.R.S., 5, pp. 269-70; Anstruther, 1, pp. 88-9—but he makes no mention of the companions. See also the general entries on the English and Welsh Martyrs under 4 May and 25 October.

Bd William Andleby and Companions, *Martyrs* (1597)

William Andleby, or Anlaby, was the second son of John Anlaby of Etton, near Beverley in Yorkshire, and was born about the year 1552. He was brought up as a Protestant but seems to have led a fairly irreligious life. He graduated from St John's College, Cambridge, in 1572. When he was twenty-five years old he visited Flanders on his way to join the Dutch Protestants in their fight against the Spaniards. Out of curiosity he visited the English College in Douai and had a number of discussions with its founder, William Allen; eventually these led to his conversion to Catholicism and a decision to study for the priesthood. He was ordained at Cateau-Cambrésis in 1577 and sent to England early in 1578. He worked mainly in Yorkshire but at different times was in Durham, Huntingdonshire, and Lincolnshire. At considerable risk to themselves, he and Bd Thomas Atkinson (11 Mar.) ministered to Catholic prisoners in Hull gaol. Challoner says of him: "Wonderful was the austerity of his life in frequent watchings, fastings, and continual prayer. He never spoke but where the honour of God and his neighbour's good required it . . . even upon his journeys he was always in prayer, mental or vocal, with his soul so absorbed in God he

31

often took no notice of those he met." The details of his eventual arrest seem to be unknown; he was tried and condemned at York in 1597, on the charge of ministering as a priest, and hanged, drawn, and quartered there on 4 July.

Thomas Warcop and Edward Fulthrop, both laymen, were executed with him, the first for having sheltered the priest and the second for having converted or been reconciled to Catholicism through his ministry. Another layman, Henry Abbot from Holden in Yorkshire, was also hanged, drawn, and quartered on the same day at York, having been condemned for trying to persuade a Protestant minister to become a Catholic. He had been tricked into this by the minister, who then reported him to the authorities. He does not seem to have been associated directly with William Andleby.

William and the three laymen were beatified in 1929. The former edition of this work included with them three other laymen executed at York, BB George Errington, William Knight, and William Gibson, but they were executed in 1596 and were not connected with William Andleby; they are venerated on 29 November.

M.M.P., pp. 231-2; Anstruther, 1, p. 9—but he does not mention Edward Fulthrop or Henry Abbot. See also the general entries for the English and Welsh Martyrs under 4 May and 25 October.

Bd Peter George Frassati (1901-25)

Pier Giorgio Frassati was born in Turin in 1901. His father, Alfredo, was a senator of the kingdom of Italy, founder and director of the famous newspaper *La Stampa*, and Italian ambassador in Berlin; his mother was Adelaide Ametis. He was educated by the Jesuits and then attended the polytechnic in Turin to study industrial and mechanical engineering, specializing in mining. In 1919 he joined a circle of the Italian Catholic University Federation (F.U.C.I.), a student movement founded at the end of the nineteenth century as an important branch of Catholic Action, with one of it aims the formation of a strongly Catholic lay élite; it became the focus for anti-fascist views and publicity. He also became a member of the anti-fascist *Partito Popolare Italiano* and tended toward the left wing of the movement, favouring an alliance with the socialists and helping to found *Il pensiero popolare*, a left-wing journal, in 1923. He was arrested in 1921 during the Congress of Catholic Youth in Rome and in 1924 was the victim of fascist violence. He travelled abroad, especially to Germany after his father became ambassador there, made contacts with the international movement known as *Pax Romana*, and attended its first annual congress in Ravenna in 1921. He became involved in the political struggles for control of the student movement in the university of Turin and was again to be found collaborating with the socialists in the anti-fascist cause. When Matteotti was murdered in 1924 he joined the Anti-fascist University Alliance.

At the same time Peter George was an active member of a number of religious societies and associations; he joined the Confraternity of the Rosary in 1919 and the university students' "nightly adoration of the Blessed Sacrament" sodality in the following year. He became a Dominican tertiary in 1922, taking the name Jerome, apparently in memory of the Florentine Dominican reformer Savanarola, who had been burned in the fifteenth century. He was also a member of the St Vincent de Paul Society, and it may have been through visiting the sick that he caught a virulent form of poliomyelitis and died suddenly in July 1925. His funeral was remarkable for the large number of poor people who attended it. He was buried at Pollone, near Vercelli, where his family had originated.

His deep spirituality and ardent political convictions were not immediately apparent beneath an easygoing, extrovert, and warm personality; he was a keen mountaineer and sportsman and played a full part in student life. He was intransigent, however, when it came to defending his beliefs, whether it was a question of the importance of democracy or of the truth of Catholic doctrine. His political activity was motivated by his religion: he wanted to reform the state on truly Christian principles, chief among which was his belief in each individual's importance as a person loved by God and redeemed by Christ. Although his life was so short, it was an exemplary model of a lay life lived to the full and inspired by a personal spirituality that necessarily included an active concern for the well being of others.

One of his teachers, Prof. Cojazzi, wrote a lively biography of him shortly after his death, and this helped to make him very widely known—it sold over 100,000 copies and was translated into fifteen languages, including Chinese and Japanese. A large number of university student groups were inspired by his example and used his name in their title. His cause was introduced in the diocese of Turin in the mid-1930s and he was beatified in 1990, when the pope spoke of faith and charity as the forces that motivated his life: these made him play a busy, energetic role in his family, at school and university, and in society at large and transformed him into a joyful and enthusiastic apostle of Christ and a passionate follower of Our Lord's message and love. According to the pope, Peter George typified St Peter's admonition: "Simply reverence the Lord Christ in your hearts, and always have your answer ready for people who ask you the reason for the hope that is in you" (1 Pet. 3:15).

A.A.S. 82 (1990), pp. 460-2, for the miraculous healing of a paraplegic, and pp. 1515-9, for the beatification. A. Cojazzi, *P. G. F., Testimonianze* (1928), and L. Frassati (Peter George's sister), *Lettere di P. G. Frassati* (1950; 2d ed., 1976), are indispensable sources, as are L. Frassati's Life in several parts under the general title *Mio fratello Pier Giorgio* (1953-82). See also *D.H.G.E.*, 18 (1977), 1054-5; F. Molinari in *Dizionario storico del Movimento Cattolico in Italia*, 2 (1982), pp. 209-12; P. Soldi, *Verso l'Assoluto* (1982); *Bibl.SS.*, Suppl. 1, 513-5, with photograph.

5

ST ANTONY ZACCARIA, *Founder* (1502-39)

Antonio Maria Zaccaria was born in Cremona in northern Italy in 1502. He studied medicine at the university of Padua and practised as a doctor for a short time back in his native town. In the words of the previous edition of this work, "here he soon learned that his vocation was to heal souls as well as bodies," and under the spiritual direction of the Dominicans he developed a special apostolate of teaching religion to the poor. They encouraged him to become a priest, and he was ordained in 1528. He became spiritual director to Louisa Torelli, countess of Guastalla, and in 1530 moved with her to Milan. Under Antony's guidance she founded a Congregation of women known as the Angelicals, dedicated to works of mercy and especially to the protection of women who were in danger of falling into prostitution; the phrase "of St Paul Converted" was added to their title later. He himself founded and directed a number of lay groups that became involved in reforming the way of life of lay society in the city.

He became a member of the Confraternity of Eternal Wisdom and so met two Milanese nobles who were also members: Bartolomeo Ferrari and Jacobo-Antonio Morigia. Together they decided to establish a Congregation of priests who would "regenerate and revive the love of divine worship and a properly Christian way of life by frequent preaching and faithful ministering of the sacraments." With Louisa Torelli's help they opened their first house, and the five members of the new Congregation preached in local churches and the streets, stressing Our Lord's redeeming passion and death and urging people to repentance and a more fervent way of life based on the Eucharist. They ministered to the victims of the plague and won widespread acclaim for their pastoral work; Ferrari's brother was a papal secretary, and he brought their work to the notice of Pope Clement VII, who approved the Order in 1533. In 1535 Pope Paul III confirmed that approval, and the Order adopted the name Clerks Regular of St Paul; in 1552 they added "of St Paul Beheaded" to the title. They faced violent opposition from the local clergy because of the reforms they tried to introduce and were reported to Rome for heresy in 1534 and again in 1537; on both occasions their work and teachings were fully vindicated by the Roman tribunal.

Antony was elected as the first provost general but resigned in favour of Morigia and moved to Vicenza to set up a second house. He is credited with having introduced to the city the Milanese custom of exposing the Blessed

Sacrament for three days' public veneration. Some have claimed that he founded this devotion while in Milan, but it had existed already as a private devotion in the Confraternity of the Eternal Wisdom. What he did start was the custom of ringing the church bells on Friday afternoons to remind people of the death of Our Lord. He organized conferences for the clergy and set up associations of "married couples devoted to St Paul." He continued his open-air preaching and looking after the sick. His sermons were based solidly on doctrine, without any rhetorical ornamentation, and he preferred not to have music during public services. His spirituality was based on devotion to the Blesed Sacrament and to the crucifix—it is clear from his letters that this dominated his thinking. His teaching was very strongly Pauline in inspiration, and he shared with other early-sixteenth-century reformers a desire to avoid later medieval theological complexities in favour of a return to the texts of the New Testament and especially to St Paul. Apparently he was a very gentle person, but he demanded a total commitment to Christ from those he advised, whatever this cost in human terms. He wrote, "Let us run like fools not only to God, but also to our neighbour, who is the intermediary to whom we give what we cannot give to God." The members of the Order lived an austere life of strict poverty.

In the last year of his life he began negotiations for the church of St Barnabas in Milan to become the headquarters of the Congregation, and this was why its members became better known popularly as Barnabites. While giving a mission at Guastalla he fell dangerously ill and was taken to his mother's house in Cremona, where he died on 5 July 1539, aged only thirty-seven. He was canonized in 1897. In 1893 his relics were moved from the chuch of St Paul in Milan to the crypt of the Barnabite church, where they are still venerated.

After strong initial opposition the Barnabites flourished but have never become a large body: "They still labour in modest obscurity among the outcasts of great towns; they educate, for wherever is a Barnabite community there is a centre of learning; and following their founder they preach the gospel with special reference to the epistles of St Paul" (*B.T.A.*). They had houses in North and South America, Italy, France, and Belgium, with a small missionary branch in Africa. Their foundation in the 1530s was part of a strong reform movement in the Italian Catholic Church that owed nothing to Protestant attacks on it: a number of reformers realized that there was need for a new type of religious Order to reform both clergy and people, and the Barnabites may be viewed alongside the Theatines, Somaschi, and Oratorians (and St Angela Merici's Ursuline nuns—see entry for 27 Jan.) as sharing in that religious vitality. In Milan itself they paved the way for the reforms of St Charles Borromeo (4 Nov.).

St Antony did not publish anything himself, but some of his letters and sermons and his draft Constitution for the Order are extant. See G. Cagni, *Le Lettere di S.A.M.Z.* (1952); G. Cagni and F. Ghilardotti, *I Sermoni di S.A.M.Z.* (1952 and 1959), and *Le Costitutzioni* (1954). See also G. Chastel, *Saint Antoine-Marie Zaccaria, Barnabite* (1930); *Bibl.SS.*, 2,

216-20; *Dict.Sp.*, 1, 720-3. On the Barnabites see *N.C.E.*, 2, p. 103, and long article in *Diz. Ist. Perf.*, 2 (1975), 945-74.

There is no authentic portrait of the saint. He is always shown wearing a black beard and holding a chalice, a host, and a cross, sometimes with a lily; early pictures show him with the other two founders. A seventeenth century painting by Santagostino in Milan shows St Paul with a chalice and host appearing to the three men dressed as priests. In 1909 a statue of St Antony was erected in St Peter's, Rome, among the founders of religious Orders.

St Athanasius of Jerusalem, *Martyr* (451)

Athanasius was a deacon in the church of the Resurrection in Jerusalem in the first half of the fifth century. During the Council of Chalcedon (451) a monk named Theodosius took advantage of the absence of the bishop, Juvenal, at the council to rouse the people of Jerusalem against it. He declared himself to be the leader of the Eutychians, a group that had formed itself around Eutyches of Constantinople, who denied the true humanity of Christ and had been condemned and exiled by the council. In general the monks of Palestine rejected Chalcedon's solution to the disputes about Christ's two natures and wanted a new bishop elected. Athanasius publicly rebuked Theodosius for the scandal that he was causing in dividing the Church and firmly upheld the council's findings. Theodosius regarded Athanasius as an embarrassment and an obstacle to his leadership and so had him murdered, or even murdered him himself.

Athanasius was not listed in the Eastern synaxaries and did not feature in the Greek liturgy. His name was added to the Roman Martyrology by Baronius in the sixteenth century under today's date as a champion of orthodoxy and a martyr in its cause.

What is known about Athanasius comes mainly from Theophanes' *Chronographia* and Nicephorus Callistus' *Church History*. See *D.H.G.E.*, 4, 1312; *Bibl.SS.*, 2, 551. On the general background to the troubles in Palestine see W. H. C. Frend, *The Rise of the Monophysite Movement* (1972).

St Athanasius the Athonite, *Abbot* (*c.* 920-1003)

Abraham was born in Trebizond about the year 920. He studied at Constantinople and became a teacher there. He made friends with both St Michael Maleinos and the future emperor, Nicephorus Phocas. Abraham became a monk in St Michael's monastery at Kymina in Bithynia, taking the name Athanasius in religion. The monastery was a *laura*, where the monks lived in separate cells grouped around a church under the control of an abbot, and Athanasius stayed there until about the year 958. To avoid election as Michael's successor he fled to the famous Mount Athos, or Holy Mountain. This was inhabited at the time by small groups of hermits without any proper organization. For a time he hid his identity, taking the name Dorotheos and pretending to be uneducated. He was found out, however, by agents of Nicephorus Phocas, who wanted him to help organize and give his blessing to an expedition against the Saracens. Very unwillingly Athanasius did so; the expedition was successful, and when Athanasius asked to be allowed to return to Mount Athos he was given as a reward a large sum of money to build a monastery. In 961 he began the building of what was to be the first monastery on Mount Athos and dedicated it to the All-Holy Mother of God; it is now known as the monastery of St Athanasius, or simply, "The Monastery."

At first the monastery and Athanasius' position were resisted by the hermits already living there, and attempts were even made on his life, but through the support of two emperors, Nicephorus Phocas and John Tzimisces, it flourished, and eventually Athanasius was recognized as abbot general of all the communities on Mount Athos—there were fifty-eight of these by the time of his death. In adopting the *laura* system he was reversing the policy of St Basil (2 Jan.) and St Theodore the Studite (11 Nov.) and returning to the early Egyptian monastic tradition, although the Rules he wrote relied heavily on those of Theodore. He insisted on unity among the monks, on study, and on an austere diet composed mainly of uncooked vegetables and oil. His influence was of great importance in the development of Byzantine monasticism. He died about the year 1003 as the result of an accident when the cupola of a church that he was inspecting collapsed suddenly.

Two works by Athanasius, his *Typicon* and his *Testament*, were printed in P. Meyer, *Die Haupturkunden für die Geschichte der Athosklöster* (1895). A detailed Greek Life written by a monk who was closely associated with Athansius' successor and another long biography based on it were ed. by J. Noret in *C.C.S.G.*, 9 (1982). See also J. Leroy, O.S.B., "Les deux vies de saint Athanase l'Athionite," *Anal.Boll.* 82 (1964), pp. 409-29; *Bibl.SS.*, 2, 547-9. On Mount Athos see *O.D.C.C.*, p. 122; *N.C.E.*, 1, pp. 1008-10.

Bd William of Hirsau, *Abbot* (1091)

William was a monk in the abbey of Saint Emmeram in Regensburg who, about the year 1069, was elected abbot of the abbey of Hirsau in the Black Forest. After a period of decay the abbey had been re-settled by a group of monks from Einsiedeln; the occasion of William's election was the deposition of the previous abbot, Frederick, who had been trying to reform the older monks and restore the abbey to its former eminence as a place of learning. William regarded the deposition as both unjust and uncanonical and refused to adopt the title of abbot until after Frederick's death, but he immediately set about continuing the work of reform and was so successful that he is sometimes regarded as Hirsau's founder. He visited Rome in 1075 to have the abbey's privileges confirmed by the pope. It was an important visit because it also confirmed William in his support for Pope St Gregory VII's (25 May) reforming ideals.

William took the great monastery of Cluny as his model, and the most detailed account of Cluniac monastic life comes from the customary composed at

Cluny for William's use, with permission to make what changes he thought suitable for the different conditions at Hirsau. The abbey did not become part of the Cluniac association, or "union", but formed its own loose federation of associated houses, which became in its own right an important centre of monastic reform. Hirsau was chosen by St Gregory to be a hub of reforming activities in Germany, partly because of its own standing as a refomed house and partly because of William's support for the pope in the investiture conflicts with the emperor. It may be that the abbey became too involved in these disputes, and some have argued that it was this that caused Hirsau's failure to develop after William's death. While he was alive, however, William's personal reputation for holiness and his ability as an administrator attracted a number of good recruits to Hirsau, and he was able to re-open the school for which the abbey had previously been famous. He drew up the Constitutions of Hirsau, and these became the Rule for the monasteries that he founded to deal with the large number of those who wanted to become monks under his direction. Other monasteries followed suit, and eventually there were about 120 houses using them, though they did not form a union or federation in any formal sense. William's Constitutions differed from those of Cluny in one important respect: he did not seek exemption from episcopal supervision and visitation of his houses and, indeed, seems to have been happy with it.

William was responsible for spreading a development that was to be important in the future of monasticism. His fame attracted numerous laymen of the lesser nobility to take the monastic habit, often in middle age, as *conversi,* or "lay monks." It is not the case that the development arose from William's concern for "the spiritual and material well-being of the serfs" on the monastic and other manorial lands and that he "aggregated its servants to the monastic community" (*B.T.A.*). They were not "lay brothers" as later understood, but "lay monks," too uneducated in some cases to go on to receive Holy Orders but taking full monastic vows and bound by the obligation to recite the divine office while dedicating themselves to a life of practical service to the monastery. They are evidence of a demand for an extension of the monastic way of life as lived in the reformed houses under the direction of inspirational abbots such as William, who combined a rigid personal asceticism with kindness and affability to others.

William had a reputation as a learned man, being particularly skilled in music and astronomy and accomplished in poetry and mathematics; he even invented a clock for monastic use. He rewrote some of the music for the hymns of the office and was probably one of those who were trying to bring plainchant in line with contemporary musical theories; he left a treatise *De musica et tonis* ("On music and its tones") in the form of a dialogue between himself and one of his early teachers at Emmeram, where the treatise had probably been written. In the preface William described the work as an introduction to the subject, mixing old and new ideas, but it is a complex work, certainly not for beginners. Some modern critics say it was influential in the development of medieval musical theory, but others say it was of purely local interest. He also left a treatise on astronomy.

A biography by a contemporary prior of Hirsau has a great deal of unhistorical material in it; the more reliable parts are in *M.G.H., Scriptores*, 12, pp. 200-25. See *P.L.*, 150, 927-1146 for the Constitutions, and 1639-41 for the preface to the astronomical treatise. See also *Bibl.SS.*, 7, 474-5; Grove, 20, p. 419; *Dict.Sp.*, 6 (1967), 1210-12.

BB George Nichols, Richard Yaxley, Thomas Belson, and Humphrey Pritchard, *Martyrs* (1589)

These four martyrs suffered together at Oxford on 5 July 1589. George Nichols and Richard Yaxley were priests, Thomas Belson and Humphrey Pritchard (or ap Richard) laymen. They were beatified in 1987.

George Nichols was born in Oxford and educated at Brasenose College. In 1581 he went to Reims to study for the priesthood, was ordained there in 1583, and the following year was sent to England. He apparently worked in the Oxford area and was responsible for reconciling a number of people to the Church. In 1589 he was betrayed to the authorities by a false convert and arrested in the Catherine Wheel inn in the city. Richard Yaxley was a native of Boston in Lincolnshire and had gone to study in Reims in 1583. Ordained in 1585, he had returned to England the following year, and he is known to have been working in Cornwall in 1588, using the alias Tankard. He was in Oxford staying at the same inn as George Nichols at the time of the latter's arrest.

Thomas Belson, a native of Brill, near Aylesbury, had also studied at Reims in the early 1580s but had not been ordained. At the time of George Nichols' arrest he was staying in the same inn in Oxford, apparently in order to see Fr Nichols, his confessor. He was taken with the others. The fourth member of the group, Humphrey Pritchard, from Wales, was pot-boy at the inn and had worked there for about twelve years, giving what help he could to Catholics who were on the run or in hiding. There is some evidence that the innkeeper, a widow, was also arrested, but she was not brought to trial. The inn was clearly a meeting place for Catholics, and presumably the false convert knew this and was able to strike at just the right time to catch the whole group.

After being interrogated in Oxford they were taken to London, where the priests were put in the Bridewell and tortured. After a month they were sent back to Oxford, tried, and condemned to death, the priests for having exercised their priesthood in England and the two laymen for having helped and sheltered them. While he was in prison awaiting execution George Nichols reconciled a condemned highwayman to the Church; his name was Harcot, and he was executed on the same day as the martyrs, reciting the psalm *Miserere* on the way to the scaffold. Attempts were made to persuade Humphrey Pritchard to give up his beliefs on the grounds that he did not know enough to understand what being a Catholic meant; he refused to argue, however, saying, "What I cannot say in words I will seal with my blood."

An Italian account of the executions was printed in Rome in 1590. See *M.M.P.*, pp. 153-9; Anstruther, 1, pp. 250-2, 389-90. See also the general entries on the English and Welsh Martyrs under 4 May and 25 October.

6

ST MARIA GORETTI, *Martyr* (1890-1902)

Maria Teresa Goretti was born in October 1890, the third child of Luigi and Assunta Goretti, who were poor farmers in Corinaldo, near Ancona, in Italy. Reports of her as a child comment on her unusual piety and helpfulness but also on her cheerfulness and general good humour. The family's farm was not large enough to sustain the four children (one son had died in infancy), and so in 1898 they moved to Ferriere di Conca, in the Pontine Marshes, where they became tenant farmers. Her father died in 1900, and so her mother had to spend more time working in the fields to support the family, which seemed to be getting even poorer; it fell to Marietta, as she was known, to look after the house and younger children and to teach them their prayers. Her mother told her that she would have to put off receiving her First Communion because she had had no education, but Marietta went of her own accord to the local town for special lessons and in May 1902 was able to receive Communion; she then became a weekly communicant.

The Serenelli family had moved from Corinaldo at the same time as the Gorettis and worked as their partners; the two families shared accommodation above an old barn. Alessandro Serenelli was almost twenty years old; he had worked for a time in the nearby docks and had received a little education. He was a good worker and reasonably devout, attending Mass regularly and joining in the saying of the family rosary. Maria seems to have accepted him as an elder brother, but during June he twice made sexual advances to her, threatening to kill her if she told anyone. On 5 July she was on the verandah outside the house looking after her baby sister while the rest of the family were in the fields. Alessandro returned to the house and forced Maria inside; when she refused to submit, he stabbed her several times and fled. She was taken to hospital with severe internal injuries and operated on, but she died the next day. She had been conscious for much of the time after the attack and was able to receive the Last Sacraments and to say that she forgave Alessandro "for the love of Jesus" and hoped that God would forgive him also. Alessandro was found guilty and sentenced to thirty years in prison—he was too young for the death penalty.

In 1910 Alessandro expressed remorse for what he had done, moved by a dream in which Maria had appeared and offered him some lilies. In 1929, when her body was moved by the Passionists to their sanctuary of Our Lady of Grace, the process for her beatification began, and Alessandro, now out of prison, gave testimony at it, stressing that during his attack Maria's appeals had been for the safety of his soul and that she had urged him not to commit such a grave sin. Maria was beatified in 1947; a number of miracles followed, and she was canonized in 1950 in the presence of her mother and other members of her immediate family.

Some recent feminist writers have seen the canonization in problematic terms. According to the Church, they argue, Alessandro's sin was his attempt to engage in illicit sexual behaviour; if Maria had consented, no matter how unwillingly, she would also have been guilty of grave sin. What is lacking here, according to the feminist approach, is any sign of condemnation by the Church of Alessandro's violence against Maria as a sin in itself, still less of the patriarchal system dominant in Italy that encouraged young men to expect young women to give in to them, and in which a raped woman could be forced to marry her assailant. "A true canonization of Maria Goretti by the faithful could arise from a refusal to accept her as anything other than a martyr to violence nurtured by a church which was willing to sacrifice the powerless in the name of its own patriarchal interests" (Stenzel).

Maria's cult was extremely popular, especially in Italy, and her canonization took place before what was claimed to be the biggest crowd ever assembled in Rome for such an occasion. She became the patron of the Children of Mary and of teenage girls.

M. C. Buerhle, *Saint Maria Goretti, Saint and martyr* (1952) is a popular, very sentimental account; J. Carr, C.S.s.R., *Bl Maria Goretti, Martyr for Purity* (1948); F. Ciomei and S. Sconocchia, M.R.P., *Santa Maria Goretti, Nelle Palude Pontine* (1978); Ann Ball, *Modern Saints, Their Lives and Faces* (1983), pp. 163-71. For a modern feminist study see Eileen J. Stenzel, "Maria Goretti: Rape and the Politics of Sainthood," in E. S. Fiorenza and M. S. Copeland (eds.), *Violence Against Women* (Concilium, 1994/1), pp. 91-8. See also M. Turi, "'Il brutto peccato.' Adolescenze e controlle sessuale nel modello agiografico di Maria Goretti," in B. Papi (ed.), *Bambini Santi* (1991), pp. 119-46.

A sentimentalized portrait, painted in 1938, was approved by Maria's mother and the postulator of her cause as the "official" portrait; it shows her with a halo of light and holding white lilies.

St Sisoes (*c.* 430)

Sisoes was an Egyptian who became a monk at the famous desert monastery of Scetis under Abba Or. After the death of St Antony (17 Jan.) in 356, Sisoes left Scetis because it had become too popular and went to live on St Antony's mountain with a disciple named Abraham. The place was deserted, which may indicate that he arrived there sometime after the Saracen raids of 357; he lived there for a very long time, probably over seventy years. At some stage, perhaps when he was too old for the rigours of life in the desert, he lived for a time at Clysma, a town near the Red Sea. He died about the year 430.

About fifty items in the *Apophthegmata Patrum* (Sayings of the Fathers) mention Sisoes (or Tithoes, a variant of the name), and they seem mostly to refer to the Sisoes venerated today, but there is at least one other monk of the same name who lived at that time and is mentioned in the *Apophthegmata*. These sayings are the main source of information about Sisoes and show him as a humble lover of solitude, with a boundless trust in God's mercy, and often lost in contemplation; his disciple often had to say to him, "Abba, get up and eat," and Sisoes would reply, "Have we not eaten, my child?" When the disciple said they had not yet done so, Sisoes would say, "If we have not eaten, bring the food, and we will eat." On humility and submission to the divine will he is reported to have said: "Let yourself be despised, cast your own will behind your back, and you will be free from care and at peace." Numerous miracles, including raising a dead child to life, are attributed to him, and it is reported that when he was dying God said, "Bring me the chosen vessel of the desert."

For the *Apophthegmata Patrum* see Thomas Merton (trans.), *The Wisdom of the Desert* (1960; n.e., 1998); also Benedicta Ward, S.L.G. (trans.), *The Sayings of the Desert Fathers* (1975), pp. 178-86; on desert monasticism see her introduction to Norman Russell (trans.), *The Lives of the Desert Fathers* (1980), pp. 3-46. See also *Coptic Encyc.*, 7, p. 2141.

St Palladius, *Bishop* (432)

Nothing is known about the origin and early life of Palladius. He may have studied at Auxerre under St Germanus (3 Aug.) and was clearly a person of some standing, perhaps a deacon in Rome. According to St Prosper of Aquitaine (25 June), he went to Rome to persuade Pope Celestine I (422-32) to send St Germanus to combat the Pelagian heresy in Britain and consolidate Christianity there. That was in 429, and it seems likely that Palladius accompanied Germanus to Britain and returned to Rome to report on the mission. In 431 he was himself consecrated bishop by the pope and sent to Ireland as the first bishop of the Irish. He landed at Arklow and worked mainly in County Wicklow, where the sites of three of his churches have been identified, but he was not successful in his missionary work and left soon afterwards. This lack of success may well have been exaggerated by biographers of St Patrick (17 Mar.) to highlight their hero's achievements in a difficult situation; it is more likely that Palladius' mission to Ireland had been intended to be of limited duration, just as Germanus' mission to Britain had been. Some Scottish sources say that he left Ireland for Scotland and worked there for twenty-three years before dying at Fordun, near Aberdeen, where his relics were venerated in the Middle Ages. This cannot be true, as there is no doubt that he died in 432, probably on his way back to Rome. Pope Celestine had died earlier that year, and it may be that Palladius wanted to be back in Rome for the election of his successor; he may even have been a possible candidate himself.

Attempts have been made to identify Palladius with St Patrick, who had studied at Auxerre and knew St Germanus, but, again, this seems far-fetched, and it is better to think of Patrick as his successor as "bishop to the Irish," who landed in Ireland shortly after Palladius had left, about the year 432.

The only reliable historical source for our knowledge of Palladius is Prosper of Aquitaine; there is plenty of largely legendary material in various Lives of St Patrick. See *O.D.C.C.*, p. 1211, which has a useful bibliography. See also P. Grosjean in *Anal. Boll.* 63 (1945), pp. 73-86, 112-7, on the historical problems, and R. P. C. Hanson, *Saint Patrick: His Origins and Career* (1968). D. N. Dumville (ed.), *Saint Patrick, 493-1993* (1993), contains a number of articles dealing with the complex issues of dating and Palladius' relationship to Patrick.

St Sexburga, *Abbess (c. 699)*

Sexburga was the daughter of Anna, king of the East Angles; her sisters were SS Etheldreda (23 June), Ethelburga (7 July), and Withburga (8 July), and she was half-sister of St Sethrida (7 July). She married King Erconbert of Kent and had two sons and two daughters by him—the daughters were St Ercongota (7 July) and St Ermengild (or Ermenilda; 13 Feb.). She founded a convent at Minster-in-Sheppey and after her husband's death in 664 retired there and became its abbess. After a time she decided to lead a life of greater seclusion and moved to the abbey of Ely, leaving her daughter Ermenilda as abbess at Minster-in Sheppey. In 679 she became abbess at Ely in succession to her sister Etheldreda, the abbey's founder, and was responsible for enshrining her sister's body in the abbatial church. According to the story in Bede, she could not find a suitable piece of stone for the coffin in the swampy area around Ely and so sent men to search for one; they returned with an ancient Roman tomb of white marble that they had found at Grantchester. Unfortunately, nothing is known for certain of her reign as abbess; the Latin Life says that she was Etheldreda's sister not so much by blood "as by imitation of her good works."

Sexburga died on 6 July, probably in the year 699. In 1106 her remains, along with those of SS Etheldreda, Withburga, and Ermengild, were moved to new shrines in the abbey church, where they remained objects of veneration until the Reformation. She features in sculptured scenes of the life of Etheldreda in Ely Cathedral. Minster-in-Sheppey was destroyed by the Danes and rebuilt in 1130 in honour of Our Lady and St Sexburga.

Bede, *H.E.*, bks. 3, ch. 8, and 4, ch. 19. Sexburga is mentioned in some Anglo-Saxon fragments; a Latin Life is of no historical value apart from its quotations from Bede. See E. O. Blake (ed.), *Liber Eliensis* (1962).

St Godeleva (*c. 1050-70*)

Godeleva (or Godelieve) was born of noble parents about the year 1050 near Boulogne in northern France. At the age of eighteen she married a Flemish lord, Bertulf of Ghistelles; it seems that the marriage was not consummated and that he soon deserted her, leaving her in the charge of his mother, who treated her with remarkable cruelty. Godeleva returned to her parents, who appealed to the local bishop to persuade Bertulf to mend his ways and live with his wife. For a time he did so, but he then decided to get rid of her altogether by having her murdered by two of his servants; they strangled her and hid her body in a well. The date of her death is variously given as 6 or 30 July. Bertulf married again but was said to have been so full of remorse for his crime that he ended his days in a monastery. Traditionally Godeleva has been considered a martyr, but as the previous edition of this work put it, it is hard to see why, since "she did not endure death for any article of the faith or for the preservation of any Christian virtue or for any other act of virtue relating to God—unless indeed her supernatural patience finally provoked her husband to his wicked violence."

The site of her death, outside the castle of Ghistelles, became a place of local pilgrimage, and several miracles were reported to have taken place there, including the healing from blindness of Bertulf's daughter by his second wife. In 1084 her remains were exhumed and formally identified before being enshrined in the church. Pilgrims used to drink the water of a local well, which became known as St Godeleva's well, as a protection against sore throats—presumably because she had been strangled. The cult was popular around Boulogne and in parts of Belgium.

A contemporary account was written by a priest named Drogo; this and another Life are in *AA.SS.*, July, 2, pp. 409-36; Drogo's Life may also be found in *Anal. Boll.* 44 (1926), pp. 102-37. A later deed containing a copy of the authentication of the remains was found when the shrine was opened in 1907; see *Anal. Boll.* 62 (1944), pp. 292-5. See also *Bibl. SS.*, 7, 70-5, with numerous illustrations.

For a saint with only a regional cult Godeleva has a surprisingly rich iconography. Sixteenth- and seventeenth-century pictures in Louvain and Bruges depict her death very realistically, while a Bruges polyptych of *c.* 1480, now in the Metropolitan Museum of Art in New York, shows seven episodes from her life and death.

Bd Thomas Alfield, *Martyr* (1552-85)

Thomas Alfield (or Aufield, or Hawfield) was born in Gloucester in 1552, the son of a master at Gloucester School. He was brought up a Protestant and educated at Eton and King's College, Cambridge, where he was a fellow from 1571 to 1575. He became a Catholic about the year 1575 and visited the English College in Douai for a few months in 1576. He returned there in 1580 to study for the priesthood and was ordained at Châlons in 1581; very shortly afterwards he was sent to England, where he used the alias Badger. He was responsible for reconciling Bd William Dean (28 Aug.) to the Catholic faith and was present at the execution of St Edmund Campion and his companions at Tyburn in December 1581 (1 Dec.), but he was arrested in April the following year, perhaps betrayed by his own father. After being tortured in the Tower he gave up his Catholicism and was released from prison in September 1582. The events of the next three years are not clear; the former edition of this work says that he returned to Reims and repented, returning to England shortly afterwards, but neither Challoner nor Anstruther mention this or his apostasy, just saying he was known to be back in Gloucester in 1583. William, later Cardinal, Allen wrote in March 1583: "A priest, Thomas Alfield, who once wavered a little from fear of tortures and death, is on his way to us" (*i.e.,* to the college at Reims), so the lapse was a short one.

Thomas returned to England and was arrested and imprisoned again, this time in Newgate gaol, in June 1585. After being tortured he was brought to trial on 5 July under the statute that forbade the publishing or importing of any ballad or tract derogatory to the queen or her government; the charge against Thomas was that he had distributed copies of Cardinal Allen's book, *A True, Sincere and Modest Defence of English Catholics,* an answer to Lord Burghley's *The Execution of Justice,* which had argued that Catholics were being persecuted for treason and not their religion. During the trial he claimed that the book was loyal to the queen and admitted bringing in five or six hundred copies. The judges concluded that he had "no skill" in either the Old or New Testaments and was "bold, stout and arrogant"—more arrogant, indeed, than any prisoner they had ever met before. Also in court on the same charge was Thomas Webley, a dyer from Gloucester. After refusing an offer of freedom if they accepted the queen's headship of the Church in England, both were found guilty and hanged, drawn, and quartered at Tyburn on 6 July. For some reason a reprieve was granted to Thomas Alfield, but it arrived too late to stop the execution. He was beatified in 1929; Thomas Webley was declared Venerable in 1889. Alfield was the author of *A true report of the death and martyrdom of M. Campion Jesuit and priest, and M. Sherwin, and M. Bryan priests . . . 1582.*

Thomas had a brother, Robert, who had been converted to Catholicism by the Jesuit Fr Persons and employed by him as a servant on Thomas' warm recommendation. He later gave up the Faith and "did great harm," according to Persons, presumably as an informer.

M.M.P., pp. 105-6; C.R.S., 5, pp. 106-8, 112-20; *B.T.A.,* 3, pp. 27-8; Anstruther, 1, p. 3. See also the general entries for the English and Welsh Martyrs under 4 May and 25 October.

Bd Mary Teresa Ledóchowska, *Foundress* (1863-1922)

Maria Theresia von Ledóchowska was born in Loosdorf in Austria on 29 April 1863. Her father was a Polish count and her mother was Swiss. The family had a strong tradition of service to the Church: her uncle was Cardinal Ledóchowski, her brother Vladimir became general of the Jesuits, and her sister Ursula went on to found the Sisters of the Sacred Heart of Jesus in Agony. In 1873 she went to Sankt Pölten, where she attended the college of the "English Dames," and then she moved with the family to Poland. She fell dangerously ill with smallpox in 1885 but recovered and moved to Salzburg to become a lady-in-waiting at the court of the grand duchess of Tuscany and, later, a close companion of the duchess.

Her interests in the foreign missions seems to have come from a meeting in

1886 with some Franciscan Missionaries of Mary; she consulted her uncle who was cardinal-prefect of Propaganda at the time, and he encouraged her to use her considerable literary ability in the service of the Church. Three years later a meeting with Cardinal Lavigerie convinced her of the need for missionaries to work in Africa and that she herself should become a religious. She began to organize lay groups to support the work of the missions and to become active in the anti-slavery movement. She contributed articles to a number of journals and edited others herself, including *The Echo of Africa*, which she founded in 1889 and which by 1913 was appearing in nine different languages. Her writings were marked by detailed analysis and were without the sentimentality common to most missionary publications of the time. Eventually she left the court and went to live with the Sisters of Charity at Solnogrod.

In 1893 she drew up the rules for a missionary association, the Sodality of St Peter Claver; Peter Claver had been canonized in 1888 and in 1896 was to be declared patron of all those working for the evangelization of peoples of African descent (9 Sept.). The sodality, formally approved in 1899, was dedicated to work for the African missions and supported them with alms, prayer, and religious publications; although it was a religious Institute—she made her own vows as a member in 1895—Mary Teresa stressed the importance of lay involvement. She also realized the importance of the press, initiating the production of bibles, catechisms, and periodicals in various African languages and becoming actively involved in literacy programmes, both as a help in evangelization and as a way of improving the conditions of the African peoples. She attended conferences, lectured, and was a tireless correspondent on behalf of the sodality, inspired in all she did by a love of God and a belief in the unique value of each individual human being. In 1900 she organized an international anti-slavery conference in Vienna. Whatever success she had she attributed to God's goodness and mercy. All who met her were struck by her sincerity, her self-control, and her childlike enthusiasm for any good cause. She died on 6 July 1922 in Rome, where she had established the generalate of the sodality; her remains were moved there in 1934, and she was beatified in 1975.

The sodality is active in about twenty countries and runs printing presses, catechetical centres, and hostels for university students.

A.S.S. 67 (1975), pp. 214-6, for details of two cures obtained through her intercession, and pp. 594-6 for her beatification. See also T. Walzer, *Su Nuove Vie: Della vita e dell'attività della Ven. M.T.L.* (1974); M. Winowska, *Allez dans le monde entier—L'Appel de M-T. L.* (1975); *Diz. Ist. Perf.*, 5, 569-71; *Bibl.SS.*, 7, 1169-71, with photo of her as a young nun.

7

St Pantaenus (*c.* 200)

Pantaenus was a native of Sicily. A convert to Christianity and a former Stoic philosopher, he taught at the famous catechetical school of Alexandria, where one of his pupils was the famous theologian Clement of Alexandria, who succeeded him as head of the school. Clement clearly held Pantaenus in higher esteem than all his other teachers, and it was probably from him that Clement learned the art of combining in a single system of thought whatever he thought was best in other schools or writers. He says that Pantaenus' learning and effective teaching raised the reputation of Alexandria above all other centres of scholarship and "the lectures which he read, gathered from the flowers of the prophets and apostles, conveyed light and knowledge into the minds of all his hearers." Pantaenus' nickname "the Sicilian bee" may refer to the sweetness of his teaching or character and his place of origin, but it may also be a reference to the eclectic nature of his teachings. None of his writings has survived, and there is no evidence of whether he wrote any formal treatises or not. There are two direct references to his teachings: St Maximus the Confessor (*c.* 580-662; 13 Aug.) says that he taught that God's will and not the divine knowledge was the creative principle at work in the world; and Clement tells us that Pantaenus taught that the prophets used the present tense in their utterances in an indefinite sense and so might always be referring to the future as much as to the present.

According to the historian Eusebius (*c.* 260-340), Pantaenus had preached the gospel in India and had met Christians there who had received St Matthew's Gospel in Hebrew from the apostle St Bartholomew (24 Aug.); it is possible that "India" in this context refers to Ethiopia and Yemen, but Eusebius' statement has been used to support the view that the Church in India had apostolic foundations. St Jerome (30 Sept.) claims that Pantaenus was sent to India by Bishop Demetrius I of Alexandria (189-231) and that he brought back a copy of the Hebrew Gospel; this seems to be unlikely since he became head of the school in Alexandria about the year 180, after his travels.

E.E.C., 2, p. 639, discusses the references in Eusebius and others. See also *Coptic Encyc.*, 6, p. 1881; S. Lilla, *Clement of Alexandria* (1971), and "Pantaeno," in *Dizionario patristico e di antichità cristiana* (1984).

St Felix of Nantes, *Bishop* (*c.* 513-82)

Felix came from a noble family in Aquitaine. Traditional accounts say that he was married and that when he was chosen to be bishop of Nantes in 549 or 550 his wife entered a convent and he was ordained. The fact of his marriage, however, is not certain, and he could have been ordained in 540. As bishop he formed groups of young missionaries to evangelize the area, and the regulations he laid down for the diocese showed that he was determined to instill a sense of discipline in his clergy and impose order throughout the diocese. He was noted for his charity to the poor, his learning, and his eloquence. Unfortunately, little is known for certain about his personal life or his work as bishop. St Gregory of Tours (17 Nov.) is one of the main sources of information, but he did not always agree with Felix, his suffragan, on matters of policy and sometimes complained about his conduct. It seems that Felix supported Gregory's rival, Riculf, and Gregory refused to accept Felix's nephew as his successor as bishop of Nantes when Felix nominated him toward the end of his life. Gregory, however, still praised Felix's sanctity. The writer Venantius Fortunatus (*c.* 530-610; 14 Dec.) spoke very highly of Felix and especially of his public works, and both he and Gregory stressed Felix's work in converting the remnants of paganism to Christianity.

Felix was a political as well as an ecclesiastical figure, as bishops had to be in the unsettled days of Merovingian Gaul. He seems to have played an important role in stopping Breton invasions of the Nantes area in 579, and he intervened with King Clotaire I in favour of the king's rebellious son, who had taken refuge in Nantes. In return Clotaire put Felix in charge of the city and its surrounding area. He fortified the city and re-routed part of the Loire to provide a natural barrier. He also completed the building of a cathedral (a few traces of which have been found). As bishop he attended a number of councils in Tours and Paris. He died on 6 or 8 January 582, but his feast-day has traditionally been celebrated on 7 July, the date of the translation of his relics. He was invoked against plague, war, and famine.

AA.SS., July, 2, pp. 470-7, gives the relevant extracts from Gregory of Tours and Venantius Fortunatus. See also *Catholicisme*, 4, 1154; *Bibl.SS.*, 5, 548.

St Hedda, *Bishop* (705)

Hedda (or Haeddi) was a pupil of St Hilda (17 Nov.) at the great abbey of Whitby. He was ordained and later referred to as "abbas"—not "abbot" in our sense but a title of respect more like "father", though also implying that he held some important rank. In 676 St Theodore of Canterbury (19 Sept.) consecrated him bishop of the West Saxons. At first Hedda resided at Dorchester-on-Thames, but he later moved his see to Winchester in line with the shift of political power among the West Saxon people. He was one of the first benefactors of Malmesbury Abbey, and King Ine consulted him when he was drawing up his famous laws. He translated the relics of Birinus, the first bishop of the West Saxons, to Winchester. Bede tells us that he was a "good, just man, who carried out his duties as bishop guided by an inborn love of goodness rather than by anything learned from books." He was bishop for about thirty years, dying in 705. Miraculous cures were reported at his tomb, and local people took dust from his grave, mixed it with water, and sprinkled it on sick people or animals, or gave it to them to drink. He was venerated in a number of Wessex monasteries and at Croyland Abbey, which he is said to have visited and to have ordained St Guthlac (11 Apr.) there. His relics are still in Winchester Cathedral.

Bede, *H.E.*, 4:12, 5:18; *G.P.*, p. 159; *O.D.S.*, pp. 224-5.

Bd Benedict XI, *Pope* (1240-1304)

Niccolò Boccasino was born in Treviso in 1240, the son of a notary of humble family. He went to Venice for his education and entered the Dominicans at the age of seventeen. In 1268 he was appointed lecturer in theology and preacher at Venice and Bologna. He wrote commentaries on a number of biblical books, published a volume of sermons, and seemed fully at home in the world of scholarship. In 1286 he became provincial of the Dominicans in Lombardy and ten years later master general of the Order. This was an important position, and Nicholas inevitably became involved in the ecclesiastical politics of the day. He was a strong and vocal supporter of the controversial Pope Boniface VIII (1294-1303) against the dissident Colonna cardinals and the Franciscan Spirituals, and in 1297 he acted on the pope's behalf in peace negotiations between England and France. The following year Boniface made him a cardinal and subsequently bishop of Ostia, and in 1301 he sent him to Hungary as legate to back the claims of Carobert to the throne. This was unsuccessful, but Nicholas' attempt to help was appreciated by Carobert's grandfather, King Charles II of Naples, who occupied Rome during the conclave held in October 1303 following the unexpected death of Boniface after the indignities he had suffered at Anagni. The cardinals unanimously elected Nicholas as pope, and he took the name Benedict, the baptismal name of his hero Pope Boniface.

The situation he inherited was complex and confusing. In addition to the divisions among the cardinals—the powerful Colonna had been excluded from the conclave on the grounds that Boniface had excommunicated them—there was a serious quarrel with King Philip IV of France (1285-1314), whom Boniface had put under censure and who was demanding a general council to "try" the pope, another with Frederick III of Sicily (1296-1337) over the payment of church taxes, and civil war in Florence and Tuscany. "Weak, peace-loving, and scholarly (he felt at ease only with Dominicans), Benedict did what he could to promote conciliation at a time of acute crisis" (*O.D.P.*). He pardoned the Colonna cardinals, but this caused such opposition among their enemies in

Rome that he had to leave the city for Perugia. He was more successful with the king of Sicily but achieved nothing in Florence and Tuscany. He revoked his predecessor's measures against Philip of France and so gained a short period of peace, but he insisted that the French leaders of the attack on Boniface at Anagni (who included the king's chief adviser) should appear in Rome for trial, under threat of excommunication. His illness and death prevented him from having to carry out the threat.

Apart from these political involvements, Benedict lifted Boniface's order restricting the right of the Mendicant Orders (chiefly the Dominicans and Franciscans) to preach and hear Confessions, and he continued to take action against the Franciscan Spirituals. He created three Dominican cardinals (two of whom were Englishmen) and showed in his own way of life that he remained a friar at heart, following an austere régime and "abating none of his humility and moderation" (*B.T.A.*). One might question the Roman Martyrology's judgment that "he wonderfully promoted the peace of the Church, the restoration of discipline, and the increase of religion," but these were certainly his aims, and given the shortness of his reign and the difficulty of the situation, it is not surprising that he achieved little that lasted.

His death on 7 July 1304 was caused by dysentery and not, as was widely thought at the time, by poisoning. He was buried, appropriately, in the church of San Domenico in Rome, and a cult started soon afterwards, with miraculous cures being reported at his tomb. The cult was approved in 1736.

Various short Lives of Benedict are mentioned in *B.H.L.*, nn. 1090-4. See A. M. Ferrero, *Benedetto XI papa domenicano* (1934); *D.H.G.E.*, 8 (1935), 106-16; *O.D.P.*, pp. 210-2.

Bd Oddino of Fossano (1334-1400)

Oddino (or Odino) Barrotti was born into a well-known local family in Fossano, Piedmont, in 1334. After ordination he was appointed parish priest of the church of St John the Baptist in his native town. He earned a reputation for his care of the poor and the austerity of his life; it is said that his bishop had to order him to eat meat for his health's sake and to keep some of the tithes for his support and the upkeep of the church—Oddino was in the habit of giving everything away to the needy. In 1374 he was appointed provost of the collegiate chapter of Fossano and rector of the parish administered by the canons, but four years later he resigned to become spiritual director of a religious confraternity. He became a Franciscan tertiary, turned his house into a shelter for the destitute, and in 1381 went on pilgrimage to the Holy Land. He was held prisoner by the Turks for a short time and was reported to have worked miracles while in prison. On his return he was appointed governor of the Guild of the Cross, a pious association for the care of the sick and the provision of hospitality to pilgrims. He built a free hospital with a hospice attached, which was said never to have turned away a poor person or a pilgrim; it lasted into the nineteenth century.

He was so obviously successful as an organizer and builder that his successor as provost asked him to take on the responsibility of building a new church for the chapter. Many miracles are recorded to show that he worked on the project with divine support: he was given superhuman strength to move great loads single-handedly, for example, and raised from the dead a mason who had fallen from the tower—miracles that are familiar in the Lives of other builder-saints. In 1389 or 1396 he was elected provost for the second time. When plague struck the town in 1400 he was fearless in comforting the sick and taking the sacraments to the dying; he caught the infection himself and died on 7 or 21 July, "a fitting end in this world for one who had given the whole of his life to the pastoral care of others" (*B.T.A.*). He was buried in the collegiate church in Fossano, and the strong local cult was approved in 1808.

AA.SS., July, 5, pp.180-4; *Bibl.SS.*, 2, 830.

BB Roger Dickenson, Ralph Milner, and Laurence Humphrey, *Martyrs* (1591)

Roger Dickenson came from Lincolnshire. He entered the English College at Reims in 1582, was ordained at Laon a year later, and left for England in May 1583. While working as a priest he used a number of aliases: Richard Johnson, Kinson, Lacey, and Welby. He was arrested at the end of 1583 and examined on three occasions but not brought to trial; he may have been exiled in 1585. He is next heard of in Winchester helping Fr Thomas Stanney and working mainly among the poor and helping the Catholics who were in prison in the city. It was here that he met Ralph Milner (or Miller), an illiterate Catholic farm labourer who lived in nearby Slackstead with a large family of nine or ten children. Ralph had become a Catholic as an adult and had been arrested on the day of his First Communion; he seems to have been in gaol in Winchester on a number of occasions because of his Catholicism. He assisted Fr Roger in his work among the prisoners and gave him shelter at Slackstead. In January 1591 they were both arrested and taken to London for examination; they were lodged in the Clink for a time before being sent back to Winchester for trial. During the trial Ralph asked the judge to look after his wife and children, but the judge told him, "Go to church, fool, and look to thy children thyself." According to Challoner, Ralph replied, "Would your lordship then advise me, for the perishable trifles of this world, or for a wife and children, to lose my God? . . . I cannot embrace a counsel so disagreeable to the maxims of the gospel." Fr Roger was condemned for being a seminary priest working in England, Ralph for giving him shelter and assistance; both were executed in Winchester on 7 July 1591. Eight or nine Catholic women were condemned to death at the same trial for allowing Fr Roger to say Mass in their houses, but they were reprieved and returned to gaol.

Laurence Humphrey (or Humphreys) was a young layman who had converted to Catholicism, apparently through discussing matters of religion with Fr Stanney of Winchester. Fr Stanney wrote a short memoir about him, praising his piety and the energetic work he did instructing the poor and helping prisoners. Laurence fell ill and in a delirious fever apparently shouted out that the queen was a whore and a heretic. This was reported, and he was brought to trial for having called the queen a heretic—a treasonable offence according to the anti-Catholic statute of 1571. Despite his protestations of loyalty and denials of ever having spoken disrespectfully of the queen, he was condemned to death and hanged, drawn, and quartered in Winchester in his twenty-first year. The precise date of his execution in 1591 is not known, and he does not seem to have had any direct connection with Roger Dickenson or Ralph Milner, although their work in Winchester may well have overlapped. The three were beatified in 1929.

M.M.P., pp. 168-9, for Dickenson (or Diconson) and Milner; pp. 592-6 for Fr Stanney's memoir on Humphrey and Milner. Fr Stanney's memoir covered three lay martyrs who died in 1591: Ralph Milner, Laurence Humphrey, and St Swithin Wells (10 Dec.); it seems that he was spiritual director to all three. According to Challoner the alias Kinson attributed to Dickenson was a mistake and originated in his name being given in Latin as *De Kinsonio*. See also Anstruther, 1, p. 103, for Dickenson and Milner (whom he calls Miller).

Note: The new Roman Martyrology celebrates the feast of St Willibald, bishop (*c.* 700-86), today. An entry for him will be found under 7 June; this will be moved to today's date in the next edition of this work.

8

SS Aquila and Prisca (First Century)

Aquila and Prisca (or Priscilla) were disciples of St Paul (29 June). When Paul left Athens for Corinth "he met a Jew named Aquila whose family came from Pontus." Aquila and his wife Prisca had had to leave Italy a short time before because of an edict of the emperor Claudius, issued in the year 49 or 50, prohibiting Jews from living in Rome. Paul visited them in Corinth and found that Aquila was a tentmaker like himself, so "he lodged with them, and they worked together" (Acts 18:1-3). It is not clear whether they had already become Christians or were converted by Paul during his stay with them. When Paul left Corinth Aquila and Prisca went with him but stopped at Ephesus while he went on to Syria; in his absence they instructed Apollos, a Jew from Alexandria, "an eloquent man, with a sound knowledge of the scriptures," who had heard of Our Lord and received baptism from disciples of John the Baptist (Acts 18:18-19, 24-6).

Paul clearly held them in high regard. When he wrote to the Christians in Rome he sent special greetings to them as his "fellow workers in Christ Jesus, who risked death to save my life"; it is not clear what incident Paul is referring to here, but it could have been in Ephesus during the riot there (Acts 19:23-41). Paul added that he was not the only one to owe Aquila and Prisca a debt of gratitude: "all the churches among the pagans do as well." He ended by sending his greetings also "to the church that meets at their house" (Rom. 16:3-5). At some stage the couple left Rome again and moved to Ephesus; when Paul wrote from there to the church in Corinth around Eastertime in the year 57, he included "warmest wishes" from Aquila and Prisca and "the church that meets at their house" (1 Cor. 16:19). Finally, when he wrote to Timothy from prison in Rome, Paul sent them his greetings (2 Tim. 4:19).

Nothing for certain can be added to this picture of a devoted couple, willing to risk their lives for their faith and all the time giving practical support to the infant Church. The Roman Martyrology added that they died in Asia Minor, and this would fit in with their living in Ephesus, but there is also a tradition that they were martyred in Rome, a late legend linking them with what is now the church of Saint Prisca on the Aventine, which was known as *titulus Aquilae et Priscae*. Others have linked Prisca with the Priscilla of the catacombs on the via Salaria. It is perhaps surprising that such a couple, with their undoubted New Testament pedigree, did not feature more prominently in legend.

Their supposed *acta* date from the seventh century. See *Bibl.SS.*, 2, 326-8, and also *O.D.S.*, p. 407, for the Prisca who probably gave her name to the church on the Aventine.

St Procopius, *Martyr* (303)

An account of the *passio* of Procopius, the protomartyr of the persecution under the emperor Diocletian in Palestine, is given by Eusebius of Caesarea, a contemporary, in his *The Martyrs of Palestine*. According to this, Procopius had been born in Jerusalem and lived a life of extreme austerity devoted to the study of the Bible and to meditation. When he moved to Scythopolis (modern Bethsan) he worked as a reader and interpreter in Syriac and as an exorcist. He was arrested in Caesarea and ordered to sacrifice to the gods; when he refused on the grounds that there was only one God he was beheaded on 7 July in the year 303.

The previous edition of this work comments: "It is hardly believable that this simple and impressive narrative should have been the seed of the incredible legends which afterwards grew up around the name of Procopius: astonishing and absurd fables and trimmings that eventually transformed the austere cleric into a mighty warrior, and even spilt him into three people, the ascete, the soldier, and a martyr in Persia."

How these developments came about is of major interest to students of early hagiography. See H. Delehaye, *The Legends of the Saints* (4th ed., 1955), ch. 5, and for the Greek text of the *passio*, his *Les légendes grecques des saints militaires* (1909), pp. 75-89, 214-33. See also *Bibl.SS.*, 10, 1159-66, for the development of the legends.

A ninth-century fresco in S. Maria Antiqua in Rome, now badly damaged, is probably the oldest image of Procopius. A thirteenth-century fresco in the Palatine Chapel in Palermo shows him holding a cross in his left hand. In both these pictures he is depicted as a very young man with boyish features.

St Disibod, *Bishop* (*c.* 674)

Very little is known for certain about this Irish saint. St Hildegard of Bingen (17 Sept.) wrote a Life in 1170, but this contains few biographical details and is padded out with moral and scriptural observations of her own. The few facts come from the traditions of his monastery, but even these are not entirely reliable. He is said to have been born and brought up in Ireland, where he eventually became a bishop. Although he worked extremely hard as a preacher, he was not successful, and in the middle of the seventh century he abandoned Ireland in favour of Germany. With his three companions he founded a monastery in the hills overlooking the Nahe valley, near Bingen. This became known as Disibodenberg or Diessenberg (from Mons Disibodi), and was the base from which he and his companions carried out a fruitful apostolate among the local people. The monastery was rebuilt during the twelfth century by Benedictines from Hirsau, and an adjoining building was occupied by a community of nuns whose abbess was St Hildegard. It was not until after she had moved her community to the Rupertsberg, near Bingen, that the abbot of Diessenberg asked her to write a Life of the founder. Disibod is first mentioned in the martyrology of Rabanus Maurus (4 Feb.), who was archbishop of Mainz from 847 to 856. But he does not feature in the *Félire* of Oengus, the martyrology of Tallaght, or the Roman Martyrology.

Hildegard's Life is in *P.L.*, 197, 1095-1116. For Rabanus Maurus' martyrology see *P.L.*, 110, 1167. See also *Bibl.SS.*, 4, 666; L. Gougaud, *Les Saints Irlandais hors d'Irlande* (1936); H. Büttner, "Studien zur Geschichte von Disibodenberg," in *Studien und Mitteilungen zur Geschichte des Benediktinerordens*, 52 (1954), pp. 1-64.

St Kilian, *Bishop*, and Companions, *Martyrs* (*c.* 689)

Kilian was born in Ireland, perhaps in Mullagh in the diocese of Kilmore, whose church is one of the very few in Ireland dedicated to him. Nothing is known about his life until he left Ireland with eleven companions to work as a missionary in Germany; he may already have been a bishop. The group landed at the mouth of the Rhine and travelled up the river until they reached the mouth of its tributary, the Main; they then sailed up this as far as the town of Würzburg. Kilian succeeded in converting the local pagan chief, Gozbert, and then went to Rome, perhaps to obtain papal approval for his missionary work. He arrived during the pontificate of Pope Conon (686-7) and remained for about two years; some accounts say that he was given a formal brief from the pope to evangelize Thuringia and part of Franconia, but this does not seem likely. On his return to Würzburg he found that Gozbert had married his widowed sister-in-law; when Kilian denounced the marriage as against the church's law she had him and two companions, Colman (or, possibly, Colotan) and Totnan, murdered, probably in 687 or 689. It may be that she feared that Gozbert was about to leave her, or it may be that she and Gozbert planned the murder together. That he was murdered may be taken as historically established, but the occasion and the details are less certain.

Kilian's cult seems to have developed after the translation of his relics to the cathedral in Würzburg by the Anglo-Saxon St Burchard (2 Feb.), the first bishop of the city, in 752. The first *passio* probably dates from this time, and the cult was part of the deliberate development of the city into an important political and cultural centre from which Frankish influence could be spread into other parts of Germany. For this reason the translation of the relics was supported by King Pepin and the subsequent cult encouraged by Charlemagne. Kilian was listed in the Godescalc calendar (*c.* 780) as second only to St Boniface (5 June) in the work of evangelizing the region. His martyrdom was recorded in the ninth-century Irish martyrology of Tallaght, although with different names for his companions and in different circumstances, but there is no evidence of any strong cult in Ireland. Links between Würzburg and Ireland remained until the fifteenth century, and there was usually a house of Irish monks in the city.

The heads of the three martyrs were enshrined in the cathedral of Würzburg, while Kilian's tomb was in the crypt of the New Minster. A new golden reliquary was made for his remains in 1987, and in 1991 a relic was given to the church in Mullagh, Ireland. St Kilian featured on the seals and coins of Würzburg in the Middle Ages, when he became the city's principal patron. His feast-day is still celebrated annually with the *Kilianfest*, during which a modern mystery play about the saint's life is performed. A number of old Latin and German hymns and folksongs in his honour survive.

The Irish Saints, pp. 200-2; *O.D.S.*, pp. 282-3. A number of articles appeared in 1952 to mark the twelve-hundredth anniversary of the translation of the relics: see especially the collection *Herbipolis Jubilans* (1952); J. Hennig, "Ireland and Germany in the tradition of St Kilian," *I.E.R.*, 78 (1952), pp. 21-33; A. Gwynn, "New Light on St Kilian," *I.E.R.*, 88 (1957), pp. 1-16.

St Withburga (*c.* 743)

Withburga (or Witburh, or Wihtburg)) was the youngest daughter of Anna, king of the East Angles, and sister of St Etheldreda (23 June). Little is known about her except that she lived as a hermit near Holkham in Norfolk and later, on the death of her father, moved to East Dereham. There she may have established a community of nuns, but she died before the convent buildings were completed and was buried in the nearby churchyard. The date of her death is given as 17 March, probably in the year 743. Her body was exhumed fifty years later and found to be incorrupt; it was enshrined in the parish church.

In 974 Brithnoth, abbot of Ely, arranged for the body to be stolen from East Dereham in a well-organized "relics raid" and taken to Ely, on the specious grounds that Withburga would have wanted to be buried next to her more famous sister. In 1102 her relics were moved to the new part of the abbey church, and four years later those of SS Etheldreda, Sexburga (6 July), and Ermengild (13 Feb.) were moved close by. The church at East Dereham is dedicated to her, and Withburga's well is said to mark the place where her body was first exhumed. She features on a number of church screens in Norfolk accompanied by a tame doe that was supposed to have provided her with milk while she lived as a solitary. 8 July is the date of the translation of her relics; the new Roman Martyrology commemorates her on 17 March, and this will be followed in the next edition of this work.

AA.SS., Mar., 2, pp. 603-6; *O.D.S.*, pp. 502-3. For the translation to Ely see E. O. Blake (ed.), *Liber Eliensis* (1962), pp. 120-3, 228-36.

St Adrian III, *Pope* (885)

Adrian (or Hadrian), by birth a Roman, became pope in 884 during what the previous edition of this work called "a troubled period in the history of the papacy," while his election took place "in circumstances which remain obscure" (*O.D.P.*). Very little is known about his brief reign, and it is not at all clear why he was regarded as a saint. He had a high official of the Lateran palace named George blinded because he had been a bitter opponent of Pope JohnVIII (872-82), and tradition says that he had the wife of another official whipped naked through the streets; as Kelly suggests, Adrian seems to have continued the bloody vendettas that had prevailed at the time of John's assassination. He adopted a conciliatory approach to the Eastern Church, in line with the policy of his immediate predecessors.

In 885 the emperor Charles the Fat (881-8) summoned the pope to attend a diet at Worms in order to legitimize the emperor's bastard son so that he could be his official heir. This may be evidence that a pact had been struck between the emperor and Adrian at the time of the papal election offering imperial support in return for later papal favours. Adrian set out for Germany but died on the way at San Cesario sul Panaro, near Modena, in September 885. The fact that his body was not taken back to Rome added strength to the rumours that he was murdered. He was buried in the abbey of San Silvestro at Nonantula, and a local cult grew up around his tomb that has lasted ever since; it was approved in 1891. Later accounts credited him with averting the worst effects of a famine in Rome while he was pope, and Flodard, historian of the church in Reims, praises him for his kindness to other bishops.

L.P., 2, p. 225; *O.D.P.*, pp. 112-3.

St Grimbald (*c.* 825-901)

Grimbald was born in Thérouanne in north-eastern France about the year 825 and became a monk at Saint-Bertin in the present-day town of Saint-Omer. He was ordained about the year 870 and gained a reputation as a scholar. He went to Reims in 886, and it may have been through Fulk of Reims that he was invited to England by King Alfred in 886 or 887. Some accounts say that he had met the future king when Alfred had called at Saint-Bertin on his way to Rome and that Alfred later remembered him and wrote to the monastery to ask for him, but this is almost certainly no more than legend; in any case, Alfred was only four years old at the time of his visit to Rome and could not have remembered Grimbald so many years later. Alfred was looking for suitable monks to head the monasteries that he wanted to set up in England as part of his reform and almost certainly wrote to Fulk, archbishop of Reims, to ask for Grimbald. Fulk replied, deploring the ignorance, worldly living, and lack of chastity of the English clergy and agreeing to send Grimbald to help in their reform, for he was a monk and a priest, one of Fulk's most valued assistants, destined for high office and most suitable in every way to become a bishop. It appears that Grimbald became a court-scholar instead, settling in a small monastic house in Winchester and helping Alfred with his translations of Latin works into Anglo-Saxon. After Asser, he was the most important of the scholars who came to England during Alfred's reign. He may have brought a number of manuscripts with him from France, including a ninth-century one of Prudentius (now in Corpus Christi College, Cambridge), and less certainly, the well-known Utrecht Psalter. Alfred refers to him as "my Mass priest" in the introduction to his translation of St Gregory's (3 Sept.) *Pastoral Care.*

The king clearly held him in high regard, for when Eldred, the archbishop of Canterbury, died in 889 Alfred tried to persuade Grimbald to become archbishop, but he refused and remained in Winchester. Alfred's son, King Edward, built the New Minster there and made Grimbald superior of the canons who served it, apparently in an attempt to persuade him not to return to Saint-Bertin. We know nothing of his later life except that he had a reputation as a fine singer and led a blameless life. He died on 8 July, probably in the year 901, and was buried in the New Minster; his remains were moved on three occasions, the last being when the whole community moved from Winchester to Hyde. He was venerated in a number of Benedictine abbeys, and his cult was widespread in the tenth and eleventh centuries. A thirteenth-century Life provides the earliest legendary account of the founding of the university of Oxford by King Alfred in 886 as the result of a council convened in London the previous year to welcome Grimbald; the Life contains a wholly imaginary sermon delivered by the saint on that occasion.

The sources for Grimbald's life are few. A twelfth-century Life is lost and is only known through a sixteenth-century analysis. The monastic breviary from Hyde is now the most reliable source; see P. Grierson, "Grimbald of St Bertin's," *E.H.R.*, 55 (1940), pp. 529-61. See also *O.D.S.*, pp. 218-9.

Bd Eugene III, *Pope* (1153)

Pietro Pignatelli was born at Montemagno, between Pisa and Lucca. The previous edition of this work gave his surname as Paganelli and claimed that he came from a noble family, but more recent work suggests the form given here and concludes that he was "of unidentified but humble parentage" (*O.D.P.*). We know nothing of his early life; he may have been prior or abbot of the monastery of Saint Zeno in Pisa in 1128, although this is difficult to reconcile with other evidence, including St Bernard's (20 Aug.), that he was a canon and held important office in the church in Pisa. A meeting with St Bernard in 1137 or 1138 persuaded him to become a monk at Clairvaux, taking the name Bernard in religion, and he went on to become abbot of the Cistercian monastery of SS Vincenzo and Anastasio outside Rome. It was from there that he was unexpectedly elected pope in February 1145, taking the name Eugene III. St Bernard was astounded at the election of such an inexperienced person and wrote to the cardinals to rebuke them, saying "May God forgive you for what you have done!" Eugene, however, although he continued to wear the Cistercian habit as much as possible and followed a monastic régime, proved to be more resolute and capable than many had expected.

Eugene's predecessor, Pope Lucius II, had died from wounds received in trying to storm the Capitol in an attempt to restore papal control over the city. Eugene refused to recognize the Roman senate's authority and had to be consecrated at Farfa, north of Rome; he set up the papal court at Viterbo. In 1145 he issued a papal Bull proclaiming the Second Crusade and in March 1146 appointed St Bernard to preach it throughout France, while he himself went there to help in the preparations. The crusade set out in 1147, and Eugene hoped that it would help to improve relations with the Eastern Church. It was a complete failure, however, and Eugene wisely refused to follow St Bernard's advice to launch it again and to include the conquest of Constantinople in its aims.

The pope was a keen reformer and used the occasion of his stay in France to hold synods at Paris, Trier, and Reims. These dealt with doctrinal issues as well as matters of discipline and, among other questions, examined the visions and teaching of St Hildegard of Bingen (17 Sept.)—on the advice of St Bernard, Eugene gave these guarded approval but warned her against pride, urging that her spiritual message be "set out with caution." The pope also became involved in the quarrel between Archbishop Theobald of Canterbury and St William of York (8 June), deposing the latter in 1147 on St Bernard's advice, perhaps unfairly; the issues involved were complex and the quarrel was part of the larger disputes arising out of the civil war between King Stephen and Queen Matilda, and St Bernard was not always impartial in his views. In 1148 Eugene approved the Rule drawn up by St Gilbert of Sempringham (16 Feb.) for the English Order of Gilbertines.

Eugene was a strong supporter of the power of the papacy. When he invited bishops to attend the synod at Reims in 1148 he declared that through St Peter Christ had given the popes supreme temporal and spiritual authority. He reorganized the Church in Ireland, succeeded in strengthening the links between it and the papacy, and in 1152 sent a legate (Nicholas Breakspear, the future Adrian IV) to Scandinavia to reform the Church there and, again, to link it more firmly to Rome. In all this Eugene was following the line of the reforming popes that went back to the reign of St Gregory VII (25 May) in the previous century. St Bernard had high hopes of what Eugene might achieve and on his accession had written that the Lord would allow him before he died to see "the Church of God as in the days of old, when the apostles let down their nets for a draught, not of silver and gold, but of souls." To help the pope in his task Bernard wrote the treatise *De consideratione*, urging him to keep a balance between his necessary involvement in worldly matters, his main spiritual concerns, and his own interior development. Despite being "watchman over all" and "chief of ministers," the pope must not lord it over others or attempt to use the sword when spiritual weapons failed; the things of God must be always directly sought after, but by prayer rather than by argument. Clearly, Eugene was fortunate in having such a counsellor as Bernard, but the extent of the latter's influence can be exaggerated: while often openly dependent on his great master—and some at the papal court complained that Bernard, not Eugene, was pope—Eugene not infrequently acted independently, or even disregarded his advice (*O.D.P.*).

Eugene returned to Italy in 1148 and was able to enter Rome in December 1149 with military help from Roger of Sicily. His troubles with the people of Rome were still not over, however; he soon had to leave again, and it was not until 1153 that he was able to settle there. In the same year he signed a treaty with Frederick I Barbarossa (1152-90) safeguarding the rights of the Church and promising the king the imperial crown, but he died shortly afterwards, on 8 July. He was buried in St Peter's next to Pope St Gregory III (11 Dec.). An English chronicler, Roger of Hoveden, wrote: "He was worthy of the highest dignity of the papacy. His mind was always kindly disposed, his discretion always to be relied on, his looks always not only cheerful but even joyous." Peter of Cluny wrote to St Bernard about him: "Never have I known a truer friend, a more trustworthy brother, a kinder father. . . . There is in him no arrogance, no domineering, no royalty: justice, humility, and reason claim the whole person." Miracles were attributed to his intercession, and a cult soon started; this was approved in 1872.

Nearly six hundred of Eugene's letters survive; see *P.L.*, 180, 1013-1642. A contemporary Life by Cardinal Boso is in *L.P.*, 2, 386-7, and see also John of Salisbury's *Historia Pontificalis*, ed. R. L. Poole (1927), pp. 5-90. See also G. del Guerra *et al.*, *Il beato Eugenio III* (1954); *O.D.P.*, pp. 172-3. For St Bernard's treatise see J. D. Anderson and E. T. Kennan (eds.), *St Bernard of Clairvaux: Five Books of Consideration: Advice to a Pope* (1976).

9

St Agilolf, *Bishop* (*c.* 751)

There is some confusion about the life of Agilolf (or Agilulf). According to one tradition he was a monk in the monastery of Stavelot-Malmédy, where he had been educated. He later became abbot and then, about the year 747, archbishop of Cologne. A few years later, in 751 or 752, he was murdered while on a diplomatic mission, apparently at the instigation of Charles Martel, the illegitimate son of the Frankish king Pepin, because Agilolf had previously tried to persuade the king to disinherit him. According to this tradition Agilolf was a martyr, having died trying to do his duty as archbishop.

A Life of Agilolf, written by a monk of Stavelot-Malmédy toward the end of the eleventh century, gives another story. According to this, the monk Agilolf was the not the same person as the archbishop Agilolf, nor did he become abbot of the monastery, for the same abbot was in office when Agilolf was studying there as in 751. Agilolf remained a simple monk and was murdered at Amblève, perhaps as early as 717. In 1065 Annon, archbishop of Cologne, received the martryr's body from the monks and enshrined it in the church of Our Lady of the Steps in Cologne; this may have led to his being regarded as a former bishop of the city.

D.H.G.E., 1 (1912), 959-60; *Bibl.SS.*, 1, 362-3.

Bd Joan of Reggio (1428-91)

Giovanna Scopelli was born at Reggio Emilia in 1428. She wished to become a nun, but her parents forbade it, so she lived an austere life at home and wore a religious habit about the house. When her parents died she set about founding a Carmelite convent in the town, but she refused to use the money that she had inherited, preferring instead to rely on divine Providence. A widow offered her a house and joined Joan with her two daughters, so the four lived together for the four years it took to raise sufficient funds through alms and bequests. When the convent of Our Lady of the People eventually opened in 1485, with about twenty members, it joined the Mantuan Congregation of Carmelites with Joan as its first prioress.

Joan added long periods of private prayer to the daily routine and fasted all the year round, taking nothing but bread and water from September to Easter and subjecting her body to extreme mortification. She had a particularly strong devotion to Our Lady. Several miraculous cures were attributed to her prayers, and she gained a reputation as an effective spiritual healer and counsellor; other miracles included the filling of the empty convent larder within minutes of her praying for some food for the hungry nuns. Joan died on 9 July 1491, urging her Sisters to the last to keep to a rigid observance of the rule to love God and one another. Her cult began the following year when her body was exhumed for public veneration and was approved in 1771. Shortly after the Carmelite convent was suppressed in 1797 her remains were moved to the cathedral.

AA.SS., July, 2, pp. 728-35, gives a Latin version of a sixteenth-century Life by Fr Benedict Mutti of Reggio. See also *Bibl.SS.*, 11, 749-50.

St Nicholas Pieck and Companions,

The Martyrs of Gorkum (1572)

In June 1572, in the early years of the long struggle for Dutch independence from Spain, the anti-Spanish and Calvinist "Sea Beggars" (or *Les Gueux*) captured the town of Gorkum, near Dordrecht in The Netherlands. They rounded up the local Catholic clergy, secular and regular, who had led the resistance against their siege, and ill-treated them, partly, it seems, to find out where the church treasures had been hidden and partly out of contempt for their Catholicism. The priests were then taken to Briel for official interrogation by the *Gueux* admiral and long disputations with Calvinist divines about the Blessed Sacrament and the papal primacy. They were offered their freedom if they would denounce the Catholic doctrine of the Blessed Sacrament, but they refused. Meanwhile, the magistrates of Gorkum complained officially about their illegal detention, and the Prince of Orange, the leader of the anti-Spanish forces, sent a letter ordering their release. Unofficial attempts were also made by two brothers of Nicholas Pieck, the guardian of the Franciscans, to make him change his mind and give in to the Calvinists. A final offer of freedom was made by the admiral on condition that the the priests denied the primacy of the pope; when they refused, they were taken to a deserted monastery at Ruggen, on the outskirts of Briel, and hanged; four priests denied their faith and accepted freedom. They were buried in two ditches nearby, but in 1616 their remains were moved to the Franciscan church in Brussels. The martyrs of Gorkum were canonized in 1867.

There were nineteen martyrs in all. Eleven were Franciscan friars of the Observance, led by Fr Nicholas Pieck, the guardian of the friary, and Fr Jerome van Weert, its vicar; two other friars were Antony van Willehad, who was ninety years of age, and Nicasius van Heeze, who suffered the longest after being hanged. The other Franciscans were Theodore van der Eel, Antony van Weert, Antony van Hoornaert, Francis van Roye, Godfrey van Melveren, Peter van Assche (lay brother), and Cornelius van Wijk Bij Duurstede (lay brother). Four were secular priests: Frs Leonard Vechel, the parish priest of Gorkum,

Nicholas Janssen, Godfrey van Duynen, and Andrew Wouters, the last of whom had led a very irregular life up to the time of his capture. John Lenaerts van Oosterwyk was a Canon Regular of St Augustine and a very old man at the time of his martydom. A Dominican, John van Hoornaert, went to the assistance of the Franciscans when they were first captured and died with them. Finally, there were two Premonstratensians, Adrian van Hilvarenbeek and James Lacops; the latter had been irregular in his religious observance and had been a cause of some scandal.

An account of the martyrs was written by William Estius, a nephew of Nicholas Pieck and a native of Gorkum; see *AA.SS.*, July, 2, pp. 736-835. See also Hubert Meuffels, *Les Martyrs de Gorcum* (1922); D. De Lange, *De Martelaren van Gorcum* (1954).
   There are vivid portrayals of their deaths in paintings by Jan van Sande and Cesare Fracassini.

Bd Adrian Fortescue, *Martyr* (*c.* 1480-1539)

Adrian was born into an old Devonshire family; on his mother's side he was a cousin of Anne Boleyn. The date of his birth has traditionally been given as 1476, but that is too early: he was not born before 1480. He married twice—first, Anne Stonor of Stonor, and twelve years after she died, Anne Rede of Boarstall. There were two daughters from the first marriage and three sons and two daughters from the second. He lived the life expected of a well-connected and well-to-do gentleman of his day, becoming a justice of the peace for Oxfordshire, attending the court, and fighting in the king's campaigns in France in 1513 and again in 1523. He was part of Queen Catherine's entourage when she visited France for the famous "Field of Cloth of Gold," attended Anne Boleyn at her coronation in 1533, and was appointed a knight of the Bath.
   What sources exist "show us a man of exemplary if entirely conventional piety" (Rex). He gave alms regularly to the poor and other causes, became a *confrater* of the Dominicans in Oxford, made a collection of extracts from English devotional writings, and carefully annotated his copy of the *Pilgrimage of the Life of Perfection*—annotations that show that at least at some stage he was a firm believer in the papal supremacy. When the royal supremacy became an issue in the early 1530s, Sir Adrian seems to have conformed, outwardly at least, and to have avoided taking sides over the royal divorce; he took the Oath of Succession, which included recognition of Henry's marriage to Anne Boleyn. He was imprisoned in the Marshalsea prison in August 1534, not for any religious reason but almost certainly because of his family connection with the Irish earls of Kildare—Frances, his daughter, had married the tenth earl, who led the revolt against England in 1534. Adrian was released sometime in 1535, probably after the earl's surrender in August, and in 1536 was required to raise troops for the suppression of the Pilgrimage of Grace, a sure sign that his loyalty to the Crown was no longer in doubt.
   He remained at liberty until he was arrested in February 1539 and sent to the

Tower. Parliament passed an act of attainder against him and others in April on the charge that he "not only most traiterously refused his duty of allegiance, which he ought to bear to your Highness, but also hath committed divers and sundry detestable and abominable treasons, and put sedition in your realm." This was an unusually vague charge, containing nothing of substance and not relating to any specific event. Cardinal Pole was one of those included in the act. He was not resident in England but had certainly been involved in "traiterous activity" in support of the Pilgrimage of Grace in 1537, and again in 1539 when he tried to rally France and Spain against Henry; there is no evidence at all, however, that Sir Adrian assisted him or even agreed with his aims. It is not at all clear what the treasons were or why the act was rushed through Parliament so quickly. Among those who were attainted with him, besides Cardinal Pole, were Thomas Goldwell (later a bishop under Queen Mary and in Italy with Pole at this time) and Friar Peto (a future cardinal, also connected with Pole and abroad at this time), and this led the former editors of this work to argue that it was his religious views that were the issue; the most recent writer on the subject agrees "that the underlying reason or motive was indeed religious" (Rex). It is most likely that it was his connection with the Pole family that caused Sir Adrian's downfall, for they were the main target of the act, and Henry was determined to destroy them, including the aged countess of Salisbury, mother of Cardinal Pole, to whom Sir Adrian was related by marriage. This would explain the absence of any specific charge of treason against Sir Adrian.

There is another possibility: news of the papal excommunication of Henry in December 1538 reached England in the middle of January 1539, and this definite action by the pope might have convinced Sir Adrian that he could no longer hide his views about the royal supremacy. A public comment to the effect that he could not accept the king's position could no doubt have led to his arrest in February (Rex), although in that case one would expect that the charges against him would have included denial of the royal supremacy as the easiest way to justify his execution.

Sir Adrian was beheaded on Tower Hill on 9 July, along with the Ven. Thomas Dingley. There was no cult among the early English recusants, but he was venerated as a martyr by the Knights of Malta, and this was the basis of his beatification in 1895. Tradition has strongly maintained from the seventeenth century onward that he was a Knight of Malta, though as a married man he could only have been a "knight of devotion" and not a full member. Recent research, however, has failed to find any evidence of his membership, and "knights of devotion" were not allowed for in the Order's sixteenth-century statutes. There was a form of "confraternity" or "associate" membership, but again, there is no evidence that Sir Adrian enjoyed this. "It therefore becomes very hard to believe that Sir Adrian had, in his lifetime, any affiliation with the Order of Knights Hospitallers of St John of Jerusalem" (Rex).

Sir Adrian's eldest son, John, held high office under Elizabeth I and King James and was a friend of the founder of the Bodleian Library in Oxford; among the books he gave to Bodley were a manuscript in Sir Adrian's hand containing part of *Piers Plowman*, a treatise on *Absolute and Limited Monarchy*, and a set of proverbs and sayings. His youngest son, Antony, was involved in a Catholic plot against Elizabeth I in 1561 but was allowed to escape and leave the country.

John Morris, S.J., collected a large amount of information about Sir Adrian in *The Month* 60 (1887), pp. 153-70, 340-62; these articles make use of his notebooks and account books. See also *L.E.M.*, 1, pp. 413-61; *D.N.B.*, 20, pp. 36-7. But the traditional accounts have been strongly and tellingly criticized in R. Rex, "Blessed Adrian Fortescue: A Martyr without a Cause?" in *Anal.Boll.* 115 (1997), pp. 307-53.

There are three known portraits of Bd Adrian, none of them contemporary, all in Malta: two are in the church of St John in Valetta, and the third, a copy of an earlier Madrid portrait of him in the robes of a full Knight of Malta, is in the Wignacourt Museum in Rabat.

St Veronica Giuliani, *Abbess* (1660-1727)

Orsola Giuliani was born in 1660 into a middle-class family in Mercatello in Urbino. Her father later held public office in Piacenza, and Orsola was particularly pleased with the added affluence and dignity that this brought to her and the family; when she was older she reproached herself for the pride she had taken in her family and the ease of life it had allowed her, although from an early age she seemed also to be unusually devout and particularly moved by accounts of Our Lord's passion. In 1677, as the result of a vision of Our Lady but very much against her father's wishes because three of his daughters had already become nuns, she became a Capuchin at the convent of Città di Castello in Umbria, taking the name Veronica in religion. She had a difficult novitiate, dealing with her own spiritual trials and the harshness of her superiors, who thought she was ambitious and who had, understandably, reacted against the bishop, who at her clothing had spoken of her as a future saint.

After her profession her devotion to the passion began to dominate her life more and more, and a number of visions of the suffering Christ led to her experiencing something of those sufferings herself. In 1681 the imprint of a crown of thorns appeared on her head; in 1694 she experienced a mystical marriage with Our Lord, and two years later Jesus seemed to pierce her heart with an arrow, leaving a wound that bled frequently; on Good Friday 1697 the marks of the five wounds of Our Lord appeared on her body, and she carried the stigmata for the rest of her life. The convent superiors ordered her to undergo medical treatment and, when this had no effect, reported the case to the bishop, who in turn reported it to the Holy Office in Rome. He then made a close examination of the wounds, had them bound up, and ordered Veronica to wear gloves sealed with his personal seal so that nothing could be done to interfere with them. He also forbade her to receive Holy Communion, to mix with the other nuns, or to be alone—she was constantly watched and accompanied by a lay sister. When the physical phenomena continued despite these measures Veronica was eventually allowed to resume a normal community life, but she regained her full rights as a Sister only in 1716. These physical phenomena were spectacular in their number and duration. They were so well attested by witnesses and confirmed by a post-mortem examination that they cannot be doubted, while the rest of her life was so balanced and obviously holy that they can hardly be explained as the result of hysterical neurosis. It is interesting that Veronica exhibited none of the other phenomena sometimes found alongside the stigmata, especially that of prolonged abstinence from food. A long time before she died Veronica had told her confessor that the instruments of Our Lord's passion were imprinted on her heart and had drawn a plan to show where in her heart this was. A post-mortem examination in the presence of clerical and lay witnesses showed a number of minute objects in the right ventricle of her heart corresponding to the plan that she had drawn. Fr Herbert Thurston, an expert on the physical phenomena of mysticism, thought that the evidence of mystical phenomena in Veronica's case was "perhaps the most remarkable known to Catholic hagiology" (*B.T.A.*).

In 1688 she had became novice-mistress, a post that she held for over thirty years and continued to exercise even when she was elected abbess in 1717; she was re-elected abbess at three-year intervals until her death. She combined a high degree of contemplation with common sense and practical ability as an administrator; she would not allow her novices to read any mystical works, insisting instead on ordinary lessons in charity and obedience as the foundation for the religious life. While abbess she had piped water laid on for the nuns' use and enlarged the convent buildings; over two hundred of her letters to the local bishop survive, dealing with the affairs of the community, which she left in excellent economic condition.

Veronica died of apoplexy on 9 July 1727 and was canonized in 1839. A number of international conferences over the last twenty years have examined particular aspects of her spirituality and mysticism, and there have been suggestions that she should be declared a Doctor of the Church because of the richness of her insights and the value of her writings. She has been called the "most representative figure of baroque mysticism," with her spiritual life determined by "a loving contemplation and physical experience of the passion of Christ, the mystery of the cross, and the uncontrollable desire for self-immolation and expiatory suffering" (*Dict.Sp.*). She did not write any formal treatise on spirituality but left an account, or diary, of her life and spiritual experiences, written by order of her confessor, and this was used in the process of beatification—the process was a lengthy one, as the account ran to 22,000 handwritten pages, and there were also over five hundred letters to be examined. This material has become a prime source for the modern study of mysticism, since it is the fullest account that we have from any canonized mystic and covers a longer biographical period than any other such account. It is descriptive and introspective, as Veronica tries to analyze and express her experiences, but also contains surprising theological insights. All her life Veronica was a voracious reader, and her writings were influenced by those of St Gertrude of Helfta (16 Nov.), St Catherine of Siena (29 Apr.), St Teresa of Avila (15 Oct.), St John of the Cross (24 Nov.), and St Francis de Sales (24 Jan.).

Basic to her spirituality is a continual tension between the human and the spiritual, similar to St Paul's conflict between the flesh and the spirit; no accommodation is possible between these two elements in our make-up. She describes the steps by which the soul rises to union with God, ending in what she calls a "vision" of God in which God communicates directly and without words; she never claimed, however, to receive any revelations from God in the ordinary sense of being a visionary. The love shown her by God in these encounters demanded in return, she believed, a life dedicated to suffering: this was "the key to love," the "school of love," the "entrance to pure love." She was also inspired to share in Christ's redemptive love through her own suffering and to undertake sometimes extreme penances, not out of hatred of her body but to be united with him, driven "like a silly person," as she put it, "not knowing what else to do" in the face of his love for her. In addition to experiencing Christ in her moments of "vision," or union, she experienced him in the Eucharist, "that great invention of Love," as she called it, and the occasion for intense communication with God and extraordinary graces.

Earlier editions of St Veronica's works have been supplanted by Oreste Fiorucci (ed.), *Il Diario di S. VG.*, 5 vols. (1969-74); a revised fifth volume, ed. by L. Iriarte and A. De Felice (1987), includes her poems and other pieces, while vol. 6, *Le Lettere,* ed. by M. Cittadini and L. Iriarte (1989), is the only complete edition of her letters. The most useful volume of extracts from her writings is L. Iriarte (ed.), *S. V. G: Esperienza e dottrina mistica* (1981). There is a full account of her life and spirituality in *Dict.Sp.*, 16 (1994), 473-83, with an extensive bibliography; recommended Lives are those by F. M. da S. Marino (1973); C. Miglioranza (1981); F. da Riese (1985). See also L. Iriarte, *S. Véronique Giuliani: Le vertige de l'amour divin* (1989); *O.D.S.*, pp. 206-7.

The Martyrs of Orange (1794)

At the time of the French Revolution there were two convents in the small town of Bollène in the Comtat-Venaissin region of France, one of Ursulines and the other of Perpetual Adorers of the Blessed Sacrament, also known as Sacramentines. When the nuns were asked to take the Republican oath in April 1794 they refused on the grounds that it was anti-religious; they were arrested and imprisoned in the town of Orange. There they did what they could to organize a communal religious life for themselves and other nuns who were in the same jail.

The first of the prisoners to be condemned to death for attempting "to destroy the republic by fanaticism and superstition" was a Benedictine nun,

Mary Rose Deloye, executed on 6 July. On the next day Iphigenia de Gaillard de Lavaldène, a Sacramentine, was executed, and on 9 July two of the Ursulines met the same fate, Melania de Guilhermier and Angela de Rocher. There were executions on most days to the end of July, and in all thirty-two nuns were guillotined, sixteen of them Ursulines, thirteen Sacramentines, two Bernardines, and one Benedictine. Witnesses told how the dwindling group left in prison said prayers for the dying and sang the *Te Deum* each day, and the prison guards commented on how the nuns died so joyfully—one of them, Pelagia Bès, even shared out a box of sweets to celebrate "her wedding." The thirty-two martyrs were beatified in 1925.

After the fall of Robespierre the tribunal at Orange, which had gained a reputation for its ferocity, was itself condemned, and two of its judges and the public prosecutor were reconciled to the Church before their execution.

See the general entry under 2 January for The Martyrs of the French Revolution and the bibliography given there. See also *Vies des Saints*, 7, pp. 209-15.

Bd Pauline of the Suffering Heart of Jesus, *Foundress* (1865-1942)

Amabile Wisenteiner was born in Vigolo Vattaro in what is now the Trentino region of northern Italy on 16 December 1865. At the time the area was part of South Tyrol and ruled by Austria. In 1875 the family emigrated to Brazil, along with many other people from South Tyrol, and settled in the province of Santa Catarina in the south of the country on land allocated by the Brazilian government. Amabile's family was poor, and she worked at home and in the fields to help her parents support their large family. She found time to teach catechism classes to young girls and to visit the sick with a friend from the nearby town of Nova Trento. She was encouraged by the Jesuit missionaries in the area to think about entering the religious life, and in 1890 she and her friend left home to live in a small cottage near the chapel of St George of Vigolo. There they looked after a woman with cancer and so began their new life dedicated to the care of the sick and the foundation of the Little Sisters of the Immaculate Conception.

In 1895 Amabile moved to Nova Trento and received episcopal approval for the new Congregation, making her own religious vows and taking the name Pauline of the Suffering (*Agonizante*) Heart of Jesus. When her Jesuit director moved to Sao Paolo in 1903, Pauline moved there as well, and the Congregation flourished so much that a number of houses were opened. She remained superior until 1909, when due to a misunderstanding by the local archbishop, she was required to step down. From then until her death on 9 July 1942 she lived humbly as a simple Sister, caring especially for poor old people. In 1933 her Congregation received papal approval, and at the time of her death it numbered forty-five houses throughout Brazil; by 1980 it had 105 houses and over six hundred members. Hers was a perfect example of a life dedicated to the service of the gospel, first in a simple undertaking of parish work and then through caring for the sick and elderly. Her spiritual life was based on Ignatian principles. She was beatified in 1991.

J. L. da Costa Aguiar, *Madre Paulina do Coração Agonizante de Jesus* (1962); F. Dalcin Barbosa, *A Coloninha* (1981); *Bibl.SS.*, Suppl. 1, 1460-2; *Diz. Ist. Perf.*, 6, 1638, on the Congregation.

10

SS Victoria and Anatolia, *Martyrs* (date unknown)

These two sisters lived in or near the Sabine hills, north-east of Rome. The first mention of Anatolia is in a document of the late fourth century that describes her as a worker of miracles. She and Victoria are mentioned together in the *Hieronymian Martyrology* (about the middle of the fifth century) under today's date. An early *passio* contains extravagant accounts of their resistance to the demands of their suitors and final execution as Christian martyrs, but this is inconsistent and of no historical value; there are grounds for believing that the two sisters were martyred, but nothing is known of the circumstances. The *passio* was known to St Aldhelm (23 May; d. 709), who used St Victoria as an example in his work *De laudibus virginitatis*. The *passio* includes a third martyr, St Audace, whom Anatolia is supposed to have freed from a dragon. St Bede (25 May) praised all three saints in his *Martyrology* but puts Victoria under 23 December. What were claimed to be the remains of St Victoria were moved in 827 to protect them from Saracen raiders and are still venerated in the parish church of Santa Vittoria in Metanano. Those of SS Anatolia and Audace were said to be have been moved to Subiaco about the middle of the tenth century, and a plaque below the altar in the basilica of St Scholastica marks where they were re-buried. Their feast-day used to be 23 December.

P. Paschini, *La passio delle martire Sabine Vittoria et Anatolia* (1919); P.B., pp. 420-1; *C.M.H.*, pp. 364, 654; H. Delehaye, *Etude sur le légendier romain* (1936), pp. 59-60. See also *Bibl.SS.*, 1, 1074-82, under Anatolia, Audace, and Victoria, with illustrations.

They are represented among the twenty-two outstanding virgin martyrs in the mosaics on the north wall of Sant'Apollinare Nuovo in Ravenna, where they are shown offering their crowns of martyrdom in an act of homage to Christ. Anatolia also features alongside St Benedict (11 July) in a fifteenth-century fresco in the convent of St Scholastica in Subiaco. This shows her holding a martyr's palm and with a dagger or sword through her breast.

SS Rufina and Secunda, *Martyrs* (Mid-Third Century)

Very little is known for certain about these two martyrs beyond the fact of their existence, martyrdom, and early cult, since their *acta* are on the whole historically unreliable. They probably suffered for their Christianity during the reign of the emperor Valerian (253-9), who changed from being sympathetic to Christians to being one of their severest persecutors. According to legend the two martyrs were Roman sisters (a common relationship for pairs of martyrs in early *acta*) who refused to follow their fiancés into apostasy when the persecution broke out. Instead, they fled from Rome but were denounced by their former suitors (another common feature in such *acta*), captured, tortured, and then beheaded. They were buried at the tenth milestone from the city on the Cornelian Way by a sympathetic pagan named Plautilla. The martyrs had appeared to her in a dream to indicate where their bodies were, and she later became a Christian. The place where they were buried had been known as the *Silva Nigra*, or the Dark Wood; its name was changed to *Silva Candida*, or the White Wood, in their honour.

A church built over their tomb was almost certainly in existence by the fourth century—it may have been built by Pope Julius I (341-53)—and a town grew up around it named Silva Candida, or Santa Rufina; it later became an episcopal see. The early church was restored by Pope Adrian I (772-95). What were claimed to be the bodies of the two martyrs were moved in 1154 to the baptistery of the Lateran basilica; the original church over their tomb fell into disrepair, and its site is not known with any certainty. According to legend the church dedicated to them in Rome was built over the house where they lived.

The earliest mention of the two martyrs is in the *Hieronymianum*, which records their death on the via Cornelia; see *AA.SS.*, July, 3, pp. 30-1; *C.M.H.*, p. 364; *Bibl.SS.*, 11, 460-4, discusses the historical evidence.

St Amalburga (*c.* 770)

Amalburga was a native of the Ardenne region and at a young age became a nun at Munsterbilzen in modern Belgium. She was given the religious habit by St Willibrord (7 Nov.), the apostle of the Frisians, who died in 739. Legend has it that she was very beautiful and that Pepin, king of the Franks, had sought her hand in marriage for his son Charles, the future Charlemagne. She resisted all overtures, however, and even suffered a broken arm in resisting Charles' attempts to carry her off from a church in which she had taken refuge. She died about the year 770; a charter of the year 870 mentions that her relics were in the keeping of the monks of Saint Peter in Ghent, and in 1073 they were solemnly enshrined in the abbey church there. Her cult is very old and fairly widespread.

There has been confusion between this Amalburga and two others. One of these was also venerated on today's date; legend says that she became a nun after her husband Count Witger entered a monastery, and her three children were also venerated as saints. All we can be sure of is that she died as a nun in the convent of Maubeuge toward the end of the seventh century. The other source of confusion was a St Amalburga of Susteren, who was probably responsible for the tradition of praying to St Amalburga for the healing of bruises.

The Latin Life in *AA.SS.* for today is entirely fictitious; it was probably written at the abbey of Saint Peter in Ghent in the eleventh century. An earlier, tenth-century, homily by Radbod contains some historical references; see *Anal.Boll.* 31 (1912), pp. 401-9. See also *Bibl.SS.*, 1, 913-4, for the three saints and a surprisingly extensive bibliography.

SS Antony and Theodosius Pechersky, *Abbots* (1073 and 1074)

These two holy abbots were key figures in the establishment of Russian Orthodox monasticism. They share a common name but were not related, as the
name comes from the monastery of the Caves of Kiev, or Kiev-Pecierskaya
Lavra, of which they were abbots in the eleventh century. Theodosius is sometimes referred to as Theodosius of Kiev.

Antipa was born in 983 at Lubech, near Tchernigov, and at an early age
began to live a solitary life devoted to God on the lines of the Egyptian desert
solitaries. Realizing that he needed some training to be successful in such a way
of life, he went on pilgrimage to the famous Mount Athos in Greece, the home
of Byzantine monasticism. He spent some years there, changing his name to
Antony in honour of the great St Antony of Egypt (17 Jan.), and was unwilling
to leave, but his abbot ordered him to return to his native land with the words
"The Lord has strengthened you in the way of holiness and you must now lead
others. . . . You will be a father of many monks." Antony then tried to live in
one of the Russian monasteries but found it lacked the austerity and solitude
that he required, so he moved to a cave in a cliff above the river Dnieper at
Kiev. As disciples gathered around him further caves were excavated, including larger ones for use as a chapel and communal refectory, and then a proper
monastery and church were built on the hill above the cliff and dedicated to
the Dormition of the All-Holy Mother of God. Antony soon handed the rule of
the monastery over to a monk named Barlaam and retired for a time to
Tchernigov, where he founded another monastery. He eventually returned to
Pecierskaya-Lavra and died there in his cave, most likely in the year 1073, at
the age of ninety.

One of those who had been an original disciple of Antony in the caves was
Theodosius. Born into a wealthy family at Vasil'evo, near Kiev, about the year
1002, Theodosius had tried to make a pilgrimage to the Holy Land while still
very young. Later, he upset his mother by working as a baker among the poor,
and when she tried to stop him from becoming a monk he fled to the caves in
1032. He succeeded Barlaam as abbot in 1063 and began to re-organize the
monastery according to the Rule of St Theodore the Studite (11 Nov.). His
approach to the monastic life was different from Antony's, laying much less
emphasis on personal asceticism and preferring to stress the virtues of a communal life and the necessity of works of charity both inside and outside the
monastery. A hospital for the sick and disabled and a hostel for travellers were
attached to the monastery, and a cart-load of food was sent to the nearby prison
every week. The monks helped to evangelize Kiev and the surrounding areas,
and Theodosius played an important role in local affairs. "He saw his monastery as wholly integrated with the society of his time, a City of God towards
which the earthly city should tend" (*O.D.S.*). He was the typical *Staretz* of
Russian monasticism, a spiritual father in whom God dwelt in a special way
and who was able to counsel laypeople as well as his monks and reprove princes

and others in public life when necessary. He "sought to harmonize the contemplative and the active life, just as he sought to harmonize the needs of men as they are (and not as they ought to be) with the call to bring about the kingdom of God on earth" (*B.T.A.*). He was not always successful, however, in his efforts to persuade the monks to be more observant.

Theodosius died in 1074 and in accordance with his request was buried in one of the original caves of the monastery. In 1091 his remains were moved to the main church, and in 1108 he was canonized by the bishops of the province of Kiev. The monastery was sacked by invaders in 1240, 1299, and 1316 and in later centuries lost some of its original spirit as it grew in wealth and importance. In the twentieth century it suffered at the hands of the Communists and the Nazis, and Theodosius' church was destroyed, but after a period as a museum and scientific research centre it was restored as a monastery and is still a place of pilgrimage.

A few of Theodosius' homilies and extracts from some of his sermons are extant and show the richness of his approach. Some writers have seen in his gentleness and humility and his involvement with God's creation a foretaste of St Francis of Assisi (4 Oct.). "Christ's love is overflowing upon us, unworthy as we are," he taught, and we must meet that love with love and let it flow beyond the cloister. "Mindful of the commandment of the good Lord," he declared to his monks, "it is good for us to feed the hungry and the tramps with the fruits of our labour. . . . If God's grace does not uphold and nourish us through the poor, what should we do with all our works?" He felt the overpowering force of God's love: "What good have we done to God that he should choose us and rescue us from this transitory life? Have we not, all of us, erred and become useless for God's service? . . . He sought us out, found us, carried us on his shoulders, and set us at the right hand of the Father. Is he not merciful and the lover of mankind? It was not we who sought him, but he who sought us." It comes as no surprise to learn that Theodosius insisted on doing his share of manual work and the menial daily round in the monastery; as abbot he was the servant of his monks as well as their superior.

Antony and Theodosius do not feature in the new Roman Martyrology.

An early Life of Theodosius was translated by G. P. Fedotov; see his *Treasury of Russian Spirituality* (1950). See also C. de Grunwald, *Saints of Russia* (1960); D. Attwater, *Saints of the East* (1963), pp. 130-6; *O.D.S.*, pp. 454-5. For Antony see *Bibl.SS.*, 1, 221-3.

St Cnut of Denmark (1086)

This Cnut (or Canute) was an illegitimate son of Svein Estrithson, the nephew of King Cnut of England (1016-35). He became king of Denmark in 1080 and passed a number of laws in support of the infant Danish Church, imposing tithes for the upkeep of the clergy, restraining the power of the *jarls* (earls), and making some of the bishops into powerful temporal rulers in their place. He built a number of churches and endowed the monasteries that had been established by the English missionaries. He regarded the Norman invasion of England as a usurpation and on a number of occasions tried to break William's hold on the country so that Denmark and England could be united again. In 1069 or 1070 he sailed with the Viking fleet to help the English rebels, and in 1075 he raided York as part of King Svein's invasion but had to withdraw when the English side of the rebellion was defeated. In 1085 he began preparing another expedition but had to call it off when his own people, led by some of the disaffected *jarls*, rebelled against him because of the heavy taxation and tithes he had imposed. The rebels besieged him in Odense, where he took refuge in the church of St Alban. After receiving Holy Communion he and eighteen of his followers were murdered; the king was kneeling in front of the altar when he was killed. A modern historian comments that anarchy in Scandinavia had saved England once again, "and the northern calendar had gained another dubious saint" (Barlow). Cnut has traditionally been regarded as a martyr, but there seems to be little in the events surrounding his death to justify this, even though the rebels were objecting, at least indirectly, to his policies in favour of the Church.

A cult started almost immediately, and miracles were reported at his tomb. His body was enshrined in the church, where it still rests, and his cult was approved by Pope Paschal II in 1101. His feast-day used to be 19 January, the date when Evesham, the motherhouse of Odense, celebrated it, but the date of his death was 10 July 1086.

A Life written by an English monk, Aelnoth of Canterbury, is the main source for the miracles that were reported at Cnut's tomb; see *AA.SS.*, July, 3, pp. 118-49. See also C. Gertz, *Vitae Sanctorum Danorum*, pp. 27-168, 531-58; *O.D.S.*, p. 84. On relations between Denmark and England see F. Barlow, *The Feudal Kingdom of England 1042-1216* (4th ed., 1988).

Bd Emmanuel Ruiz and Companions,
The Martyrs of Damascus (1860)

After the Crimean War the Turkish government was required to treat its Christian subjects more fairly, and in 1856 the sultan issued a decree declaring that all inhabitants of the Turkish Empire should be treated equally with regard to taxation and the holding of public office. This caused resentment among many Muslims and was one of the causes of the terrible massacre of Christians that occurred in Syria four years later. In particular the Druse, an ancient Syrian Muslim sect, took exception to what they regarded as the spread of Christianity into traditionally Islamic areas, and in the spring of 1860 a number of petty incidents and attacks by both sides led to open conflict. The Christians had been disarmed and were unable to defend themselves properly. Christian villages were sacked, and thousands of Christians were murdered; the Turkish authorities seemed willing to allow the trouble to take its own course. Five Jesuit priests were killed at Zahleh, and at Dair al-Kamar the abbot of the Christian Maronite monastery and his twenty monks were also murdered. On 9 July the trouble reached Damascus, and a massacre of the large Christian population began. The governor of the city did nothing to prevent the killing, looting, and burning, but an Algerian emir, Abd el Khader, gave shelter to several hundred Christians, Syrian and European, whom he rescued from around the city; he risked his life to refuse the demands of the mob that he should hand them over. A modern estimate is that up to fourteen thousand died throughout Syria, two thousand of them in Damascus. There was an international outcry over the massacre and hundreds of those who had taken part in it were executed.

Eleven of the murdered Christians were beatified in 1926. Eight of these were Franciscan Friars Minor and three were Maronite laypeople. Seven of the friars were Spaniards: Emmanuel Ruiz, the guardian, had been born in 1804; when the mob broke into the house on the night of 9 July he ran to the church to consume the Blessed Sacrament; when ordered to adopt Islam or be killed he replied, "I am a Christian and will die a Christian" and was immediately cut down at the altar. The other Spaniards were Carmel Volta; Nicanor Ascanio; Pedro Soler; Nicolás Alberca; and Francisco Pinazo and Juan Jaime Fernández, both lay brothers. The eighth friar was an Austrian, Engelbert Kolland; he almost escaped by dressing as a Syrian woman, but his Franciscan sandals gave him away; he refused to apostatize and was killed. While most of the laypeople sheltering in the friary were spared or escaped, three brothers were murdered: Francis, Abdul-Muti, and Raphael Masabki. These three were not included in the beatification process, started in 1885, until 1926, but a complete dossier of their case had been kept by the Maronite bishop of Damascus, and this enabled their cause to be completed in less than six months.

The *Annals of the Propagation of the Faith*, 21 (1860), pp. 308-26, gives a general account of the massacre and some letters from eyewitnesses that bring out its horror. See also *Vies des Saints*, 7, pp. 235-43. A vivid eyewitness account of the massacre in Damascus is given in Mary S. Lovell, *A Scandalous Life, The Biography of Jane Digby el Mezrab* (1995), ch. 18.

ST BENEDICT
Sword and inscription for the Rule, with play on words
Benediciti (bless) / Benedicti (of Benedict).
Gold, white and red on black field

11

ST BENEDICT, *Abbot and Founder* (*c*. 480–*c*. 550)

The little recorded of the life of Benedict of Nursia, patriarch of Western monasticism, comes from the *Dialogues* of Pope St Gregory (3 Sept.). He was born in Nursia (present-day Norcia, near Spoleto in central Italy) about the year 480 and studied in Rome, where he was so upset by the immorality of society that he gave up his studies and retired to Subiaco to live as a hermit about the year 500. Several disciples gathered around him, and he organized them into twelve "deaneries" of ten monks each; they seemed to have followed a largely eremitical way of life. He stayed at Subiaco for about twenty-five years, but local jealousies disturbed the peace, and he took a small group of monks with him to Monte Cassino, near Naples. There he wrote, or at least finalized, his famous Rule, borrowing from previous monastic writers such as St Basil (2 Jan.), St John Cassian (23 July), St Augustine (28 Aug.), the Desert Fathers, and most of all, the anonymous author of the *Regula Magistri,* or "Rule of the Master." Benedict remained at Monte Cassino for the rest of his life; he did not become a priest, nor, probably, did he think of himself as founding a new Order. He was buried alongside his sister, St Scholastica (10 Feb.); the *Dialogues* describes how they used to meet to discuss spiritual matters and gives a moving account of their last meeting three days before Scholastica's death. There is no doubting that Gregory held him in the highest possible esteem: he wrote, "Benedict possessed the spirit of one man only, the Saviour, who fills the heart of the faithful"; he was the *vir Dei*, the man of God, before all else, "whose virtues have made him so like Christ that the wonders and signs of the life of the new Adam flow again in the world through his life and actions" (Ward).

The lasting fame of Benedict, however, rests on the greatness of his Rule, which in time became *the* monastic Rule throughout western Europe. As we have seen, it was a compilation of what he thought best in other Rules, but it was much more than just a compilation: it was "a taut, inclusive, and individual directory of the spiritual as well as of the administrative life of a monastery" (*O.D.C.C.*). It had three principal strengths: it was eminently practical; it was physically moderate and flexible at the same time as being spiritually uncompromising; and it was unique among monastic Rules in containing in a few pregnant paragraphs "a fund of spiritual and human wisdom that could guide abbot and monks in all the vicissitudes of life" (Knowles). For Benedict the monastery was "neither a penitentiary nor a school of ascetic mountaineering, but a family, a home of those seeking God" (*ibid.*). The family was presided over by an abbot elected by the monks, who should "so temper all things that the strong may wish to follow, and the weak may not draw back" (*Rule*, ch. 64). The family's principal occupation was the performance of the divine office in common, the rest of the day was taken up with private prayer, reading and study, and manual work.

At first Benedict's Rule was only one of several available in the West for those who wished to follow a monastic way of life. By the seventh and eighth centuries it was being followed widely in France, England, and Germany, but there still was not any union or federation that could be termed a "Benedictine Order." When Charlemagne and Louis the Pious embarked on a reform of monasticism they chose Benedict's Rule as the most suitable, and Louis imposed it on all monasteries in his territories. The emperor was assisted in this reform by St Benedict of Aniane (750-821; 11 Feb.), who presided over the Council of Aachen in 817. Even then, however, there was no uniformity in detail; rather it was the spirit of the original Rule and its stress on poverty, obedience to a monk-abbot, and celibacy that were important for the reformers. Gradually greater importance was attached to the liturgy, and its celebration became more solemn, while manual work diminished. There was a tension between the autonomy claimed by each monastery and the need that reformers saw for joint action to ensure proper observance; the development of large groups of houses affiliated to major centres such as Cluny and Gorze in the tenth century was an important advance, but attempts to impose general chapters and centralized visitation were only partially successful. Other reform movements led to the establishment of new Orders such as the Cistercians, whose members sought to follow a stricter interpretation of the Rule without losing the essence of Benedict's approach, while the Camaldolese focused on the eremitical elements in the Rule and set up congregations of hermits who met only for the liturgy and occasional communal meals.

Evidence of communities of nuns following Benedict's Rule goes back to at least the seventh century, and many of the monastic reform movements were parallelled by developments among the nuns, so that a flourishing spirituality and wide general culture developed under the guidance of distinguished abbesses. There are nowadays communities of Benedictine sisters, founded mainly in the nineteenth and twentieth centuries, who follow Benedict's Rule but are less bound by rules of enclosure, and who have an apostolate based on active charitable work. Twentieth-century developments include the establishment of Anglican Benedictine houses in England and Lutheran ones in Sweden. The rich variety that marks Benedictinism, male and female, contemporary and historical, is itself a tribute to Benedict's wisdom and to the balance that he achieved between the different monastic legacies that he had to draw on. As St Gregory remarked in the *Dialogues*, the author of such a Rule could not have been anything else but a living example of its spirit.

His cult was slow to develop until the growth of Cluniac influence in the tenth century. The abbey of Fleury claimed his relics from the seventh century, but this was hotly disputed by Monte Cassino. The date of Benedict's death was 21 March; the date of the translation of his remains was 11 July, and since 1969 the Roman Calendar has fixed this as his feast-day, so that it can be celebrated outside Lent.

St Gregory's *Dialogues* are in *P.L.*, 77, 149-430, and with French trans., in S.C., 260 (1979), pp. 120-249. For the Rule see *C.S.E.L.*, 75 (2d ed., 1977), and the English trans. of J. McCann, O.S.B., (1952); see also G. Holzherr (ed.), *The Rule of Benedict: A Guide to Christian Living* (1982; Eng. trans. by the monks of Glenstal, 1994), which gives the Latin and English texts. On the debates about the origins of the Rule see bibliography in *O.D.C.C.*, p. 183; D. Knowles, "The *Regula Magistri*," in *Great Historical Enterprises* (1963), pp. 139-95; Adalbert de Vogüé, *Etudes sur la Règle de Saint Benoît, Nouveau recueil* (1996). On the development of Benedictine monasticism see D. Knowles, *Christian Monasticism* (1969); *O.D.C.C.*, pp. 186-7, with full bibliography; D. H. Farmer (ed.), *Benedict's Disciples* (1980); E. R. Elder (ed.), *Benedictus: Studies in Honour of St Benedict of Nursia* (1981), including Benedicta Ward, S.L.G., "The Miracles of St Benedict," pp. 1-13; M. Schmidt and L. Kulzer (eds.), *Medieval Women Monastics: Wisdom's Wellsprings* (1996). For Anglican Benedictinism see P. Anson, *The Call of the Cloister* (4th ed., 1964). On St Benedict in art see Murray, pp. 51-2; *O.D.S.*, pp. 45-6.

The oldest representation of St Benedict is an eighth-century painting in the catacomb of Hermes, Rome; there is also a tenth-century one in San Crisogono. Monte Cassino has an illuminated manuscript of his life from the eleventh century, and there are frescoes at Subiaco (thirteenth century) and in the sacristy of San Miniato, Florence (late fourteenth century). There is an extensive series of scenes from his life by Signorelli and Sodoma (1497-1505) at Monte Oliveto Maggiore, near Siena. The commonest episodes depicted in art are taken from the *Dialogues*: the attempt to poison him, when the beaker broke and the poison spilled out as a snake, and a second attempt, when a raven took away the poisoned bread; also, how he rolled naked in a thorn-bush to overcome sexual temptation. In single pictures he usually wears a monastic habit and carries either the Rule or a rod for corporal punishment; sometimes he is shown with a broken cup or a raven.

St Pius I, *Pope (c. 142-55)*

According to the *Liber Pontificalis*, Pius was an Italian from Aquileia, the son of Rufinus. The second-century Muratorian Canon says that he was the brother of Hermas, the author of the popular *The Shepherd*; if this is true, as Hermas had been a slave it is possible that Pius had been one also. We know nothing directly of his reign but during it a number of leading Christian Gnostic thinkers, including Marcion of Pontus and Valentinus, were teaching in Rome, and in July 144 a synod expelled Marcion from the orthodox community; Pius would have presided over such a synod. He would also have been in touch with the Christian apologist and philosopher St Justin Martyr (1 June), who was teaching in Rome at the time and who was beheaded about the year 165. Pius himself has traditionally been regarded as a martyr, but there is no early evidence to suggest that he died for the Faith, and the first mention of him as a martyr is in the martyrology of Ado of Vienne, which was compiled in the mid-ninth century. Some early lists give a different date for his reign, putting him after his successor Anicetus.

O.D.P., p. 10. On the Gnostics see *O.D.C.C.*, pp. 683-5, 1033-4.

St Drostan, *Abbot (c.* 610)

Drostan was the first abbot of the monastic foundation at Deer, near Peterhead in Aberdeenshire. He may have belonged to the Cosgrach family in Ireland and so have been of royal descent. He became a monk under St Columba (9 June) and was later appointed to the new monastery at Deer. Other sources say that he went to Glenesk in Angus and lived there as a hermit, attracting disciples by his holiness and kindness to the poor; miracles were attributed to his intercession while he was still alive. When he died about the year 610 his body was transferred to a shrine at Aberdour, in Fife, on the Firth of Forth.

The only sources for the life of Drostan are the ancient *Aberdeen Breviary* and the *Book of Deer*, but these disagree in the detail they give. See *AA.S.S.*, July, 3, pp. 198-200; *K.S.S.*, pp. 326-7; *Bibl.SS.*, 4, 841.

St John of Bergamo, *Bishop (c.* 683)

The little that is known about John's personal life and his episcopate in Bergamo is that he became bishop about the year 670 and probably attended the Council of Milan in 678. One of his main concerns as bishop was to rid his diocese of the last remnants of Arianism (the heresy that held that Christ had only one, human, nature), and a charter of 873 relates that he converted a number of Arians. These may have included Grimoald, king of the Lombards; what is clear is that the king granted John jurisdiction over the church in Fara and its estates and that John transferred some of these to the cathedral in Bergamo. Further conversions followed under Grimoald's successors. He attended the important synod held in Rome in 680 by Pope St Agatho (10 Jan.) to agree a response to the Eastern emperor on the question of Monothelitism (the heresy that only one, divine, will operated in Christ), and signed the subsequent dogmatic letter, "John, the unworthy bishop of the church of Bergamo." He died between 680 and 691, probably in 683. There is no evidence for the claim in the former Roman Martyrology that "he was slain by the Arians for defending the Catholic faith," the reason for his former veneration as a martyr. He does not feature in early martyrologies nor in Bergamese calendars of the eleventh to the thirteenth centuries. Early accounts, however, do speak of his miracles, and one of the four bodies unearthed in 1291 in the ancient basilica of San Alessandro in Bergamo was identifed as his. His relics were moved to the cathedral in 1561.

John is referred to in Paul the Deacon's reliable *History of the Lombard People*, written about the year 790. See *Bibl.SS.*, 6, 624-7.

St Hidulf, *Abbot and Bishop* (*c.* 707)

Hidulf (or Hildulf) may have been born at Regensburg in Bavaria, and some accounts say that he was abbot of the French monastery of Saint-Dié before being consecrated bishop of Trier about the year 666. The French connection is unlikely, and he was probably not a diocesan bishop but a *chorepiscopus* attached to the monastery of Saint Maximin in Trier. This type of bishop was common in the missionary parts of Germany in the eighth century and fulfilled an important role in the evangelization of the country. At some stage Hidulf felt called to a more secluded way of life and retired to the Vosges mountains to live as a hermit. Soon afterwards, about the year 676, he established a monastery at Moyenmoutier, so called because it was situated between a number of other monasteries that formed a cross (*moyen* = middle; *moustier* = monastery). At first he followed a Rule based partly on that of St Benedict (11 July, above) and partly on that laid down by St Columban (23 Nov.) for the great abbey of Luxeuil in the same area. As was usual in that group of monasteries, Hidulf stressed the importance for his monks of manual work and was said to have always done some himself each day, despite his advanced years. He died on 11 July, probably in the year 707. His remains were translated a number of times and, from 1854, have been venerated in a side chapel of the monastery. Moyenmoutier remained an important foundation throughout the Middle Ages and in the sixteenth century became the second house of the Benedictine reform movement of Saint-Vanne at Verdun; the Congregation took the name of Saints Vanne-and-Hidulf.

The principal sources for Hidulf's life are in *AA.SS.*, July, 3, pp. 212-24, but much of the material printed there is legendary. See *Bibl.SS.*, 7, 645-6.

SS Placidus, *Martyr*, and Sigisbert, *Abbot* (Early Eighth Century)

Sigisbert was probably of Frankish origin and a monk of the great abbey of Luxeuil in what is now eastern France. He went to work as a missionary in the area of the upper Rhine and then founded a hermitage at Disentis in modern Switzerland. Placidus was an influential friend and supporter of Sigisbert; later accounts made him out to be a leading lawyer at the local court. The hermitage seemed destined to become a monastery as disciples gathered around Sigisbert, but the local ruler of Chur, who was opposed to any Frankish influence in his territory, prevented this happening and at the same time had Placidus murdered. His murder took place about the year 720, and Sigisbert died some time later. A monastery was established about the year 750 on the site of Placidus' murder; it became an important Benedictine abbey in the Middle Ages and still exists today.

The cult of these two saints became very popular and surprisingly long-lasting. Their remains were soon transferred to a new tomb in the crypt of St Martin's church; the tomb was surrounded by a grille, through which it was possible to touch the tomb and place objects on it for a blessing. 11 July was celebrated with a solemn procession in honour of St Placidus, and this custom was well documented throughout the Middle Ages and continues today. In 940 the monks of the Benedictine abbey that had been built in Disentis in the mid-eighth century moved the relics to Zurich to protect them from Saracen raids, and this helped to spread their cult more widely. Bd Notker (6 Apr.) wrote a sequence in their honour, which still survives, and a twelfth-century breviary from Naples contains a hymn to them. In the thirteenth century a *passio* of St Placidus appeared, which made Sigisbert an immediate disciple of the great Irish missionary, St Columban (23 Nov.), the founder of Luxeuil, but this does not tally with what little evidence we have about Sigisbert's dates. The remains of the saints were rediscovered in 1498 but almost completely destroyed during the French invasion of 1799. Their cult is still strong today locally.

Bibl.SS., 11, 1041-3. On the abbey of Disentis, see *Diz. Ist. Perf.*, 3 (1976), 719-20.

St Abundius of Córdoba, *Martyr* (854)

The years from 850 to 859 witnessed a severe outbreak of anti-Christian persecution by the Moorish rulers of Córdoba. The reasons for this attack by what were mainly tolerant authorities were not simply religious and to some extent had been provoked by the extremism of some of the local Christians. These were inspired to some extent by racial and nationalist attitudes as well as by fears that the Church was losing its hold on the people as these began to adapt to the culture of their conquerors and even to apostasize. In 852 the Council of Córdoba had to forbid Christians to seek voluntary martyrdom by provoking the civil authorities to take action against them. Whatever the cause of their deaths, those who died in the persecutions have always been regarded as martyrs throughout Spain, and the martyrs of Córdoba are venerated as a group on 11 March. Abundius was executed on 11 July 854.

See the bibliography for the Martyrs of Córdoba under 11 March. See also *Bibl.SS.*, 4, 173-6.

St Olga (*c.* 879-969)

Olga (or Helga) belonged to the Varyags, one of the Norse peoples that had invaded the lands along the Volga River in the ninth century. She was the wife of Prince Igor of Kiev, a Slav and the ruler of the new Russian kingdom that had resulted from the Norse conquest of Kiev in 882. This had led to the destruction of the Christian community in Kiev, and Igor and Olga were both pagans. When Igor was assassinated in 945 Olga ruled in his place and was ruthless in the pursuit of his murderers and their followers, many hundreds of whom were murdered. She proved to be an able and just administrator, however, and did much to stabilize the new Russian State. One of the issues she had to deal with was the relationship between Kiev and Constantinople: there had been trading links between them for many years, but the destruction of the Christian community in Kiev and an attack by Igor on the imperial city in 941 had upset the relationship. Olga saw the political value of closer links and decided to become a Christian; how far this was a purely political move and how far she was sincere in adopting her new religion is not easy to determine, but her subsequent loyalty to Christianity and her attempts to support and spread it show that her conversion, once made, was followed conscientiously, and she was a devoted Christian for the rest of her life. She was baptized in the year 957. Tradition has it that she was the first Russian person to be baptized, but this is certainly wrong; it is also said that her Baptism took place in Constantinople, and this is quite possibly true. It seems certain that she was at least instructed by Byzantine missionaries who had returned to Kiev, and she went to Constantinople herself in 957.

She was largely unsuccessful in persuading her people to adopt her new religion (she did not use force to compel them) and even failed to convince her own son to become a Christian. In 959 she sent a deputation to the German emperor, Otto I, requesting the help of missionaries to evangelize the country. This led to the abortive mission of St Adalbert of Magdeburg (20 June) in 961, when all his companions were slain and he was forced to return without achieving anything. The links she had created with Germany were, however, to prove important and showed that she appreciated the need to keep a balance between East and West. The move toward Germany may also have resulted from her disappointment when the Byzantine court refused to allow her son to marry one of their princesses, something that Olga had set her mind on. It was her grandson, St Vladimir (15 July), who succeeded where she had failed; they have traditionally been linked together as responsible for the conversion of Russia, and an eleventh-century chronicler referred to them as "the new Helen and the new Constantine, equals of the apostles." Olga had taken the name Helen at her Baptism; if this had taken place in Constantinople, where the emperor was Constantine Porphyrogenitus and his empress was Helen, the symbolic implications of choosing her new name must have been clear.

When her son was old enough to rule in his own right Olga retired from public life but continued her missionary efforts. She had a number of churches built, including one in Pskov and another in Kiev. She died in the year 969, and her popular cult began in 996 when Vladimir transferred her remains to a new church that he had built for the purpose. Kiev was totally destroyed by Mongol invaders in 1240, and her relics were not discovered again until the seventeenth century; meanwhile her cult was officially confirmed by the Russian Council of 1574. Her relics disappeared again at the beginning of the nineteenth century and have not been found.

O.D.S., p. 366; *Bibl.SS.*, 9, 1149-52. F. Dvornik, *The Making of Central and Eastern Europe* (1949), esp. pp. 67-9.

12

St Veronica (First Century)

The legend of Veronica has become one of the most popular in the Western Church, especially since its regular inclusion in the Stations of the Cross in the nineteenth century: as Jesus was carrying the cross on the way to Calvary a woman in the crowd took pity on him and wiped his face with a cloth, and an exact image of his face was left imprinted on the cloth. The woman's name was Veronica. The cloth became an object of great veneration, especially in the later Middle Ages, when devotion to the humanity and passion of Our Lord increased and, with it, devotion to the Holy Face. Viewing the face of Christ on the cloth was an anticipation of seeing him in glory—Petrarch for example, in one of his poems, makes an old man set out on pilgrimage to Rome "since yearning bade him look upon the likeness of him he hoped soon to behold in heaven," while Dante's pilgrims go to Rome "to see this miraculous image that Jesus Christ has left behind for us as evidence of his beautiful face, which my lady Beatrice contemplates in glory" (Belting). Thousands of copies of the image were made, and pilgrims to Rome had them sewn onto their hats (Chaucer describes his pardoner as wearing one); the occasions when the cloth was displayed for veneration were among the most popular times to visit the city, and the practice continued down to the nineteenth century.

Various attempts have been made to give Veronica a personal history by identifying her with women mentioned in the New Testament. The *Acts of Pilate*, for example, which contain the earliest version of the legend and date from the fourth or fifth century, identify her as the woman whom Jesus cured of an issue of blood (Matt. 9:20-2), while a French tradition makes her the wife of Zacchaeus (Luke 19:2-10) and claims that she evangelized the south of France after her husband had become a hermit there. Others have identified her as Martha, the sister of Lazarus, or a daughter of the woman of Canaan in St Matthew (15:22-8), or a Syrian princess, or the wife of a Roman (or Gallo-Roman) army officer on duty in Jerusalem at the time of Our Lord's death. Veronica's name has also caused debate. It has long been taken popularly to be a composite of the two words *vera* (Latin for true) and *eikon* (Greek for image), and applied from the object to its bearer, but it is interesting that in the East the woman with the issue of blood was named Berenike before there was any suggestion of her being linked with a miraculous image of Our Lord, and it is possible that Berenike became Veronica in later Western versions.

Images of Our Lord's face became known as veronicas or, in Old English,

84

vernicles. A large number of them existed in the Middle Ages, but most have now disappeared or been shown to be simple paintings on cloth; some were attributed to St Luke (18 Oct.), who was also supposed to have painted Our Lady's portrait. The most famous early example was the *mandylion* (a towel or handkerchief) from Edessa in Syria. According to legend, Jesus himself gave this image to Abgar, the king of Edessa; earlier versions of the legend say that it was a painting done by Abgar's messenger while waiting for a reply to a letter inviting Jesus to go to Edessa to cure the king. Later accounts change this human image to one miraculously produced by Jesus by pressing the cloth to his face and sending it to the king. It certainly existed at the end of the sixth century and was moved to Constantinople in the tenth; many copies of it were made, but nothing is known about its whereabouts after the sack of Constantinople in 1204, though the Eastern Church still claimed to possess it. The apologetic purpose of the two legends about its origin is clear enough: a live portrait of Christ was evidence of his life and genuinely human nature, while his giving of the image to the king showed that he wished images of himself to be circulated and venerated (Belting).

One version of the Veronica legend, given in the *Acts of Pilate*, relates how Veronica, the woman healed of the issue of blood, went to Rome and cured the emperor Tiberius by using an image of Christ that she had had painted out of gratitude for her own healing; when she died she left the cloth to Pope St Clement (23 Nov.), who died about the year 100. It was not until the thirteenth century, however, that what became known as "Veronica's veil," with a miraculous image, was spoken of in Rome. This was kept in St Peter's and originally had been an image-less handkerchief or small towel said to have been used by Christ in Gethsemane or on the way to Calvary. Later, no doubt to match accounts brought back from Constantinople of the *mandylion*, it was said to contain an image and was linked to the legend of Veronica, combining the idea of a non-human image with a historical event. It was also important for St Peter's to have its own sacred image, to equal the one kept in the Lateran basilica and said to have been painted by St Luke; the English chronicler Matthew Paris (*c.* 1199-1259) reported that Rome had two true images of Christ, one painted by St Luke, the other that given to Veronica. A Mass and Office of the Holy Face was authorized by Innocent III in 1216. Other Roman churches also claimed to have true likenesses—San Silvestro in Capite, for example, claimed to have an *abgarus*, which still exists today in the Vatican as a very ancient (possibly third-century) silver-framed icon—Belting suggests that this may even be the original of the Abgar legend. Copies and supposed originals proliferated throughout Europe, one of the most famous being in a convent at Laon, which remained the centre of pilgrimages and Holy Face confraternities until the French Revolution. When Rome was sacked in 1527 some Lutheran soldiers are said to have auctioned the St Peter's veronica in a tavern, and it disappeared. In the seventeenth century it was rediscovered in a relic chamber that Bernini had built into one of the piers supporting the dome of St Peter's. The veil kept in St Peter's today has no image on it.

Veronica herself does not feature in any of the early martyrologies and was not mentioned in the Roman Martyrology; St Charles Borromeo (4 Nov.) suppressed her feast and Office in sixteenth-century Milan. It is safe to assume that she was not a historical person but a fiction created to explain the relic. The former edition of this work concluded that Christians should think more about the love and the indifference to human respect that would have prompted the offer of help to Our Lord in his suffering than about the authenticity or otherwise of the relic or the historicity of Veronica herself.

The most comprehensive modern coverage is Hans Belting, *Likeness and Presence: A History of the Image before the Era of Art* (1994). See also *O.D.S.*, p. 477; *O.D.C.C.*, p. 1688-9; H. Thurston, *The Stations of the Cross* (1906); *D.A.C.L.*, 15, pt. 2 (1953), 2962-6. For the *Acts of Pilate* in English see J. H. Elliott, *The Apocryphal New Testament* (1993). See also Michael Walsh, *A Dictionary of Devotions* (1993), pp. 250-2, 267-8. For a modern feminist interpretation see E. Kuryluk, *Veronica and Her Cloth* (1991), which contains very useful historical information.

St John the Iberian, *Abbot* (*c.* 1002)

The Church in Iberia (better known as Georgia, in the Caucasus region east of the Black Sea) developed a rich vernacular Christian literature and a strong monasticism that spread beyond its immediate borders. John was born into a noble family in the region and at first pursued a military career with considerable success. When he reached middle age, however, he gave up this way of life, left his wife and family, and entered the monastery on Mount Olympus in Bithynia (present-day northern Turkey). He visited Constantinople to free his son, St Euthymios (15 May), who had been taken hostage, and returned with him to the monastery. After a time, however, about the year 970 they left for the greater seclusion of Mount Athos and joined the *laura* of St Athanasius the Athonite (5 Jul.), where John worked as a cook for two years. When he was joined by his brother-in-law, John Thornikios, a successful military commander, the three Iberians were allowed to build their own cells and a chapel. John Thornikios was, however, called back by the emperor to help in the war against the Bulgars; when he returned with a large amount of booty it was agreed that there should be a separate monastery on the holy mountain to meet the needs of the Iberians who were attracted by the presence of John and Euthymios. Building started about the year 980, but when John Thornikios died John took his son and a few companions and tried to flee to Spain to avoid the noise and the fame. He was prevented from doing so by command of the emperor and returned to Mount Athos to rule the new monastery, dedicated to Our Lady and St John the Baptist, and named Iviron.

John was bed-ridden for the last years of his life but ruled as abbot even when his son officially took over the running of Iviron. On his death-bed he exhorted the monks: "Let no one distract you from our holy work and from the love of God, that is, from humble obedience and a close unity and harmony of souls; so you will be saved in this mortal life and gain for the future eternal life by the love which Our Lord Jesus Christ bears toward humankind. . . . Never fail to receive guests well and share with the poor, according as you are able, those things that God in his goodness has given to you." He died about the year 1002, and his biographer likened him to Abraham, who had "gone forth from his country, to lead a life of exile and poverty." The monastery became famous, and Euthymios made it an important centre of scholarship by his translation of a large number of Greek texts into Iberian; it still exists.

There is a Life by a monk of Iviron who was almost contemporary with John; a Latin translation of this with notes is in *Anal.Boll.* 49 (1922), pp. 8-68, while a French trans. is in *Irénikon* 6 (1929) and 7 (1930). See also D. Attwater, *Saints of the East* (1963), pp. 109-17, on John and Euthymios.

St John Gualbert, *Abbot and Founder* (*c.* 990-1073)

Giovanni Gualberto was born in Florence toward the end of the tenth century and was a member of the noble Visdomini family. We know nothing of his early life except for the story that he met the murderer of his brother one Good Friday and was about to take revenge, as honour dictated, when the murderer crossed his arms on his breast and begged for mercy. John was moved by the act and by the remembrance of how Christ had prayed for his persecutors, so he let the man go. Shortly afterwards he entered the Benedictine monastery of San Miniato in Florence.

About four years later, after a disputed abbatial election, John left San Miniato with a companion to seek a more austere way of life. He visited St Romuald's hermitage at Camaldoli, near Arezzo, and while there decided to set up his own monastery. He chose Vallombrosa, about twenty miles east of Florence, and built a simple monastery there on land given by a local abbess. As the community grew he developed for it a modified form of the primitive Benedictine Rule, stressing silence, poverty, and strict enclosure. This Rule was approved in 1055. John did not want the monks to do manual work, regarding this as a distraction from a life of prayer and contemplation, and so he developed the use of lay brothers; his was the first monastery to use lay brothers in an organized way and to integrate them into the life of the monastery, though they existed in other Benedictine houses at that time.

John established a number of other monasteries on the model of Vallombrosa, insisting always that they should follow a simple model without costly or imposing buildings. Some of them had hospices for the sick and the poor, and John himself was noted for his generosity and almsgiving; there were stories of the miracles that he worked to feed the poor who crowded around the monastery gates in time of famine. He was also noted for his powers of prophecy and healing, and he was involved in some of the reform movements of the day, particularly in the efforts to end simony among the clergy—he was, for example, a strongly outspoken opponent of the bishop of Florence, Peter Mezzabarba, whom he condemned for his simoniacal excesses. Pope St Leo IX (19 Apr.) consulted John on a number of issues, and Popes Stephen X and Alexander II held him in high regard.

Out of humility John refused to become a priest. He died on 12 July 1073, "the only certain date in his history" (*B.T.A.*), and was canonized in 1193. His Order expanded during the Middle Ages: it had over fifty houses by the end of the twelfth century and more than eighty in 1500, almost all of them in Italy. The Order was reformed by St John Leonardi (9 Oct.) in the late sixteenth century. It still exists today, but with very small numbers; since 1966 it has been part of the Benedictine Confederation.

The earliest Life of John was written by Bd Andrew of Strumi (10 Mar.), who died in 1097 and had been abbot of Vallombrosa; another, by Bd Atto, dates from within fifty years of his death. Both are in *AA.SS.*, July, 3, pp. 343-82; that by Andrew of Strumi is also in *M.G.H., Scriptores*, 30 (pt. 2, 1934), 1080-1104. For modern Lives see those by E. Lucchesi (1959) and A. Salvini (1961). See also *O.D.S.*, pp. 262-3; *Bibl.SS.*, 6, 1012-29. On the Vallombrosan Order see *O.D.C.C.*, p. 1678.

An altarpiece in Santa Croce, Florence, shows scenes from John's life, and there is a fresco of him in S. Salvi, also in Florence.

Bd Leo of La Cava, *Abbot* (1239-95)

Leo was born in 1239 and became a monk at a very young age in the ancient abbey of the Holy Trinity at La Cava dei Tirreni, near Salerno. In 1268 he was elected abbot and carried on the reforming work of his predecessor. While attending the Council of Lyons in 1274 he took the opportunity of visiting the abbey of Cluny, once one of the great monastic reform centres in western Europe. At the council Bd Gregory X (1271-76; 10 Jan.) confirmed all the rights and privileges of La Cava. Leo built a new church at the abbey and a fine cloister, and under his care the work of the scriptorium developed and a number of important manuscripts were copied and preserved. He died on 19 August 1295 and was buried before the high altar in the abbey church. In 1675 his remains were moved to a side wall.

Bibl.SS., 7, 1282-3; *Vies des Saints*, 8, pp. 344-5.

Bd David Gonson, *Martyr* (1541)

David Gonson (or Gunston) probably came from a well-to-do English family and was born toward the end of the fifteenth century. He became a knight of the Order of St John of Jerusalem (the Knights of Malta) and may have spent some time in Malta. On 8 October 1540 he was brought before the Privy Council in London and questioned about his attitude to the king's supremacy.

He was imprisoned in the Tower until July of the following year, when he was found guilty of high treason for refusing to acknowledge the supremacy—it is not clear whether he was attainted by act of Parliament or not. He was taken from the Marshalsea and executed in Southwark on 12 July 1541. He was one of the large group of English and Welsh martyrs beatified in 1929.

Bibl.SS., 7, 103. *A.A.S.* 22 (1930), pp. 34-7, lists him among the newly beatified but gives no details. See the general entries on the English and Welsh Martyrs under 4 May and 25 October.

St John Jones, *Martyr* (1598)

John Jones was born at Clynnog Fawr in Gwynedd, north Wales, in 1559. He was brought up a Catholic and went abroad to study for the priesthood. He joined the Friars Minor of the Observance at Pontoise in France about 1590, taking the names Godfrey Maurice in religion. We do not know when or where he was ordained. Challoner states that he was listed among the secular priests kept prisoner in Wisbech Castle in 1587, but Challoner may have been confusing him with a Benedictine priest named Robert Buckley who was in Wisbech. There is further confusion in Gillow's statement that John had joined the Franciscans in Greenwich, withdrawing to the Continent in 1559 when Elizabeth I dissolved the Marian monasteries; this would mean that he must have been born several years before 1559. Whatever the root of these confusions, we know that he made his final profession in Rome in 1591 and in the following year asked to be sent to work on the English mission.

He lodged for a time in London in the house of Bd Anne Line (27 Feb.) before going to work in various parts of the country, using the alias Robert or Herbert Buckley. He was arrested in 1597 and tortured severely before being kept in prison while evidence against him was obtained. The Jesuit superior, Fr Garnett, described how "he had laboured hard for three years in tilling the vineyard of Christ with no small profit . . . (in prison) the quantity of good he did was incredible"; it was during this time that he reconciled St John Rigby (21 June) to the Faith. On 3 July 1598 he was brought to trial on a charge of being a priest ordained overseas but working in England. He protested that he had never been guilty of treason and asked to be tried by the conscience of the judges rather than by an ignorant jury. When the judge pointed out that his offence was treason by statute, John replied, "If this be a crime I must own myself guilty, for I am a priest and came over into England to gain as many souls as I could to Christ." He was hanged, drawn, and quartered on 12 July outside the church of St Thomas Waterings in the Old Kent Road in London, which had been a favoured stopping place for pilgrims going to Canterbury. There had been a delay of about an hour before his execution because the hangman had forgotten to bring a rope; while he was waiting on the scaffold he preached to the people and answered their questions. His head was displayed in Southwark and other parts of his body in Lambeth and Newington; two young men were imprisoned for trying to rescue these relics, but other Catholics managed to do so, and a part of them was kept at Pontoise. John was beatified in 1929 and canonized in 1970.

M.M.P., pp. 234–5; Gillow, 3, pp. 657–60; J. E. Paul, *Blessed John Jones* (1960); *O.D.S.*, pp. 267–8. See also the general entries on the English and Welsh Martyrs under 4 May and 25 October.

St Ignatius Delgado and Companions, *Martyrs* (1838)

Various groups of martyrs who suffered for the Faith in what is now Vietnam have been beatified and canonized, and a general entry for these will be found under 2 February. The martyrs venerated today died during the persecution of Christians that lasted from 1820 to 1841; seventy-seven of them who were beatified in 1900 were among the 117 canonized in 1988.

Clemente Ignazio Delgado y Cebrián was a Spanish Dominican. He had been born near Zaragoza in 1761 or 1762 and had arrived in Tonkin in 1790 along with Domingo Henáres, also a Dominican, who had been born near Córdoba in 1765. Ignatius was appointed coadjutor bishop in 1794 and became vicar apostolic of East Tonkin in 1799. He worked in the country for almost fifty years. Domingo Henáres became his coadjutor in 1803. When anti-Christian persecution broke out again, the two bishops went into hiding in 1838 but were captured with Bishop Dominic's Vietnamese catechist, Bd Francis Chien. They were imprisoned in small cages, and Bishop Ignatius died from exposure and ill-treatment before the sentence of beheading could be carried out; Bishop Dominic and Bd Francis were beheaded on 25 June 1838.

Three secular priests were also among those beatified in 1900: Peter Tuan, Bernard Due, and Joseph Nien. There were also four laymen: Joseph Canh, a doctor; Thomas De, a tailor; and two peasants, Augustine Moi and Stephen Vinh. Another catechist, Thomas Toan, twice gave way under torture and gave up his Faith but in the end died in prison from starvation on 27 June 1840. Three others, all soldiers, apostatized for a time but were later martyred: they were Augustine Huy, Nicholas The, and Dominic Dat. All these and twelve others among the beatified were Dominican friars or tertiaries.

The *Annals of the Propagagtion of the Faith*, 11 (1839), and 12 (1840), give the first eyewitness accounts. See *Bibl.SS.*, 3, 1234, on Francis Chien; 4, 542–3, on Ignatius Delgado, and 7, 586–7, on Domingo Henáres. For the social and political context see the principal entry on the Martyrs of Vietnam under 2 February.

13

ST HENRY II (972-1024)

Henry was born in 972, the son of Henry the Quarrelsome, duke of Bavaria, and his wife, Gisela of Burgundy. He was educated by St Wolfgang, bishop of Regensburg (31 Oct.), and in 995 succeeded his father as duke. On the death of his cousin, Emperor Otto III, in 1002, he became emperor. He had a rival for the imperial crown in Arduin of Ivrea, who had himself crowned king of Italy in Milan, but Henry crossed into Italy with an army and defeated him. He went to Rome in 1014 to be crowned by Pope Benedict VIII (1012-24).

Henry was in many ways a benefactor of the Church, repairing and endowing the sees of Hildesheim, Magdeburg, Strasburg, and Meersburg. In 1006 he founded the see of Bamberg and built a cathedral and monastery there as a means of strengthening his power in that part of Germany. He was opposed in this by the bishops of Würzburg and Eichstätt, who had to give up part of their dioceses and also objected to his high-handed treatment of them, but Henry obtained papal approval, and Benedict consecrated the new cathedral in 1020. In general Henry supported the Cluniac reform and in particular assisted St Odilo of Cluny (1 Jan.) and Richard of Saint-Vanne, but he was a strong ruler set on extending his power and influence; as the previous edition of this work put it, perhaps too delicately, "some of his politics look equivocal when examined from the point of view of the welfare of Christendom." He reversed his predecessors' policy toward the East, and for the first time "the imperial head of Western Christendom crossed swords with a Christian country [Poland], the Christian character of which had been so openly and solemnly blessed by his predecessor" (Dvornik). To further his ends he allied with some of the pagan tribes and allowed them to practise their religion openly and carry their banners and gods into battle—a far cry, it seemed to many contemporaries, from the emperor's traditional duty to convert the pagan. One of his critics was St Bruno (Boniface) of Querfort (19 June), who was himself a missionary to the pagan lands; he wrote to Henry: "Is it right to persecute a Christian nation and to admit a pagan nation to friendship? How can Christ have truck with Belial? How can we compare light with darkness? . . . Is it not better to fight the pagans for the benefit of Christendom than to wrong Christians for worldly honours?"

For these and other reasons his early biographers seem to have had a problem in portraying him as a saint: edifying legends were invented about him, especially in Bamberg, and some of these made him out to be a reluctant ruler and at heart a monk, following an ascetic way of life and living celibately with his wife St Cunegund (3 Mar.). These were all exaggerations, though it does appear that his personal life was mainly above reproach and that his generosity to the Church and his support for reform were genuine. If his canonization seems a little strange, especially in view of the fact that his predecessor, Otto III, seems to have been a much stronger candidate for that honour, we should remember that Henry had none of Otto's grand imperial vision: he was not interested in establishing an imperial position in Rome, and he granted the papacy political control over the so-called Patrimony of St Peter in Italy, in practice supporting the papacy's claim to political supremacy.

Henry was in Italy again in 1021 on an expedition against the Greeks in Apulia; he was taken ill at Monte Cassino on his way back, where it was claimed he was miraculously cured by praying to St Benedict, but he remained lame for the rest of his life. He died on 13 July 1024 and was canonized in 1152 (some authorites say 1146). Pope St Pius X (26 Aug.) made him patron of Benedictine oblates. His feast used to be celebrated on 15 July.

There are two early Lives, attributed to Adalbold of Utrecht and Adalbert of Bamberg; see *M.G.H., Scriptores,* 4, 679-95 and 789-816. Henry features in all the general histories of the period; see F. Dvornik, *The Making of Central and Eastern Europe* (1949), pp. 185-222. See also K. Pfaff, *Kaiser Heinrich II, sein Nachleben und sein Kult* (1963); *O.D.S.*, p. 227.

St Silas (First Century)

Silas is known through the New Testament. He is first heard of in the Acts of the Apostles, when he was chosen with Judas as one of the "leading men in the brotherhood" to take a letter from the apostles and elders gathered in Jerusalem to the Gentiles in Antioch, Syria, and Cilicia and "confirm by word of mouth what we have written in this letter." When they arrived in Antioch Judas and Silas, "being themselves prophets, spoke for a long time, encouraging and strengthening the brothers." They spent some time there and then returned to Jerusalem (Acts 15:22-34). For St Luke (18 Oct.), the author of the Acts, Jerusalem played a central part in the plan of salvation: it was from the Holy City that the evangelization of the world must start. In this context the use of Silas, a Jew, to take the teaching of the apostles to the Gentile world in Antioch, and to do so very effectively, fitted in with Luke's overall theological scheme. Luke portrays him as "a Jewish Christian in good standing in the leadership of the Jerusalem church . . . an approved representative . . . open to the gentile mission . . . and effective in a gentile church" (Kaye).

Later, when Paul quarrelled with Barnabas and they went on their separate missionary journeys, Paul chose Silas to accompany him into Syria and Cilicia (15:40). They were imprisoned together in Philippi, accused of causing a disturbance in the city, and flogged; during the night they were freed from prison miraculously. It is clear from this account that Silas, like Paul, was a Roman citizen (16:19-40); as such they should have been exempt from the penalty of flogging. When the party reached Beroea there was further trouble, and Paul left secretly for Athens, leaving Silas and Timothy to follow on as soon as they could; they met up again in Corinth (17:13-15; 18:5). It was from Corinth that Paul wrote both his letters to the Thessalonians, and in these he referred to Silas under his Roman name, Silvanus (1 Thess. 1:1; 2 Thess. 1:1; and see 2 Cor. 1:19). It has been suggested that Silas may have been a familiar form of Silvanus, but it is more likely that it was a separate Jewish name. St Peter also uses the Roman name when he chooses Silvanus, "who is a brother I know I can trust," to take his letter to the churches (1 Pet. 5:12), although it is possible that Peter is referring here to a different person. Overall, Silas was a distinguished early Christian missionary, held in high esteem by both St Peter and St Paul.

According to tradition, Silas died in Macedonia. Some of the Eastern Churches keep his feast-day on 26 November or 30 June and make him a bishop of Corinth. Some of the Fathers distinguished between Silas and Silvanus, and made Silas bishop of Corinth while Silvanus was bishop of Thessalonika.

O.D.S., p. 436; B. N. Kaye, "Acts' Portrait of Silas," *Novum Testamentum* 21 (1979), pp. 13-26; F. F. Bruce, *The Pauline Circle* (1985), pp. 23-8.

St Eugenius of Carthage, *Bishop* (505)

Eugenius, who may have been of Eastern origin, became bishop of Carthage in 481. The see had been vacant for twenty-four years because of the severe persecution of the Catholics in North Africa by the Arian Vandals, initiated by their king, Genseric. The latter died in 481, and his successor, Huneric, allowed the Catholics a limited freedom to re-open their churches and elect new bishops. Eugenius set about restoring the Church in Carthage and soon gained a reputation for his works of mercy and the effectiveness of his preaching. When advised to spend some money on his own needs instead of giving everything to the poor, he replied: "If the good shepherd must lay down his life for his sheep, can it be excusable for me to trouble about the passing needs of my body?" His success, however, brought him to the notice of the king, and he was ordered not to preach in public, not to perform any episcopal duties, and to refuse any Vandals admission to the Catholic churches throughout his diocese. It was the start of another wave of persecution. Huneric ordered the Catholic bishops to meet their Arian counterparts in a conference in Carthage in 484 with the idea of converting them to Arianism; when this failed and they drew up a *Liber Fidei Catholicae* to prove their orthodoxy, they were given four months in which to apostatize. Those who refused were exiled, and the Catholic laypeople were excluded from public life and business unless they could show a certificate of conformity to Arianism. Eugenius wrote to his people from exile in Tunisia: "If I return to Carthage I shall see you in this life; if not, I shall meet you in the other. Pray for us, and fast; fasting and almsdeeds have never failed to move God to mercy. Above all things, remember that we are not to fear those who can only kill the body." He also warned them against accepting re-baptism from the Arian clergy: "Keep the grace of baptism and the anointing of chrism. Let no one born again of water return to the water."

The persecution continued after Huneric's death later in 484 but began to slacken about 487, when Eugenius was allowed back into Carthage. Churches were gradually re-opened and the clergy allowed to minister to the people. The peace was short-lived, however, and when Trasimund became king in 500 persecution began again. Eugenius was condemned to death, but the sentence was not carried out; instead he went into exile in the south of France, where he died in a monastery near Albi in 505. The liturgical books of Albi put his feast on 6 September, which may have been the date of his death.

The main source for Eugenius' early years as bishop is Victor of Vita's reliable *History of the Persecution of the African Province*, written in exile about 485; this includes the *Liber* of the Catholic bishops. Eugenius' letter is preserved in Gregory of Tours. See *E.E.C.* 1, p. 296; V. Saxer, *Saints anciens d'Afrique du Nord* (1979), pp. 194-9.

St Mildred, *Abbess* (*c.* 700)

Mildred (or Mildrith) was the daughter of King Merewalh of Mercia and Domne Eafe, a Kentish princess. She was educated at the convent of Chelles, near Paris, where she was harassed by an unwelcome suitor. She returned to England and became a nun at Minster-in-Thanet, an abbey founded by her mother on land donated by King Egbert of Kent. The reason for the donation was the king's remorse at having murdered his two nephews, Aethelred and Aethelberht.

Mildred succeeded her mother as abbess sometime before 694, when she attended a council in Kent, but nothing is known about her rule as abbess. She died after a long illness about the end of the seventh century. Her biographer says of her, "She was merciful to widows and orphans, and a comforter to all the poor and afflicted, and in all respects of easy temper and tranquil"— conventional enough virtues that tell us nothing except the regard in which she was held. At first she was buried in the abbey church, but then her incorrupt body was moved by her successor to a new church dedicated to SS Peter and Paul, sometime before the year 748. Her tomb there was a popular place of pilgrimage until her relics were removed to St Augustine's Abbey, Canterbury, in 1035, a move that the local people resisted fiercely because of their devotion both to her and to relics that she was supposed to have brought back from Paris. These included a nail from the true Cross and a strange piece of rock that was said to have the imprint of her foot from when she had landed in England on her return, which had developed healing powers. At Canterbury, according to William of Malmesbury (*c.* 1090-1143), Mildred's remains were venerated above all the relics in that holy place, but a rival set of relics were said to have been given by Archbishop Lanfranc to the hospital of St Gregory he founded in Canterbury. Goscelin, a monk at St Augustine's from 1090 to around 1107, wrote a strong defence of the authenticity of the original remains, but at least the rival claims may be taken as further proof of the saint's popularity and the belief in her powers. Later, a portion of the relics from St Augustine's was given to the church in Deventer in The Netherlands; in 1882 Deventer presented a small relic to the Catholic church in Minster. In 1937 Minster Court, on the site of the successor of St Mildred's abbey, was occupied by Benedictine nuns from the abbey at Eichstätt in Germany.

The earliest surviving references to Mildred are in a late-tenth- or early-eleventh-century account of the killing of the two princes, written at Ramsey Abbey and based on an earlier version certainly composed in the second quarter of the eighth century. Goscelin's *Vita Mildrethae* used early material from Thanet. The fullest modern treatment is D. W. Rollason, *The Mildrith Legend: A Study in Early Medieval Hagiography in England* (1983). See also *O.D.S.*, pp. 340-1.

Bd James of Voragine, *Bishop* (*c*. 1230-98)

Jacopo da Voragine was born in the village of Voraggio (present-day Varazze) near Genoa about the year 1230. When he was fourteen he joined the Dominicans and later developed a reputation throughout Lombardy as a powerful preacher. He taught theology and scripture in a number of the Order's houses, became prior at Genoa, and in 1267 was elected prior provincial for Lombardy, a post he held for nineteen years. Such was his reputation that in 1286 the cathedral chapter in Genoa chose him as their bishop, but he refused to accept. Then two years later the pope, Nicholas IV (1288-92), entrusted him with the task of lifting the interdict and other censures that had been laid on that city for its support of the Sicilian revolt against Naples, and in 1292 he was again chosen as its bishop. This time his reluctance was overruled and he was consecrated bishop in Rome. His six years in charge of the see were largely unsuccessful, and he failed to bring about peace between the warring Guelphs (the pro-papal party) and Ghibellines (the pro-imperial party), whose quarrels divided the city. On the other hand, he endowed a number of hospitals and monasteries and repaired the churches damaged or neglected in the civil upheavals. He was generous to the poor and worked to restore clerical discipline. He died in 1298, and his cult, which had begun straight after his death, was approved in 1816.

James' fame, however, does not rest on his achievements in high office but on his literary masterpiece, the *Legenda Sanctorum* or, as it is better known, the *Legenda Aurea*, or *Golden Legend*; it was sometimes referred to as the *Lombardica Historia*. James wrote this between 1255 and 1266, and it comprises mainly the Lives of the saints, with short pieces on the main festivals of the Church's liturgical year. This "engagingly written narrative, full of anecdotes and curious etymologies" (*O.D.C.C.*), became the most popular and the most influential collection of saints' Lives in the Middle Ages—a thousand manuscript copies of the Latin text alone have survived—and James achieved his aim of producing a "book which people would read and whose message of love for God and hatred for sin they could not misunderstand" (*B.T.A.*). He gave six reasons for venerating the saints, including the honour such veneration gave to God, for whoever honours the saints honours him especially who has made them saints. He went on: "Their bodies, having been the temples of the Holy Spirit, were sources of power, the alabaster box of spiritual ointment from which healing flows" (Duffy). The advent of printing increased the book's circulation: the first printed edition of the Latin version appeared in Basle in 1470, to be followed by German, Italian, French, and Czech editions over the next ten years; the first English translation was printed by Caxton in 1483, with later editions incorporating new saints. No other book was reprinted more often between 1470 and 1530, by which date over a hundred different editions had been published, justifying the claim that it was easily the first printed bestseller.

His aims, however, were not quite as straightforward as the references quoted above might imply. His book was not meant to be read by laypeople but to be used by the clergy as a sourcebook for their sermons, and he produced it by borrowing from earlier collections; from that point of view, there is very little that could be called original in it. He did not, however, just borrow: he altered and abridged and was highly selective, and his aim in doing so was to lend weight to a particular view of the spiritual life. This was in tune with a change in attitude that was taking place more widely in the Church and which can be seen in canonizations after about 1270. There was a move toward more monastic saints, a greater distancing from the world and from active charity as an indication of holiness, a greater stress on the learned, the contemplative, the mystical, and the supernaturally heroic. Saints are more likely to be portrayed as being "holy from birth"; there were fewer "ordinary" people and, interestingly, fewer penitents. Pope Innocent IV (1243-54) had declared that to be canonized a person needed to have led a life of continuous and uninterrupted virtue. *The Golden Legend* was not the best medieval collection of saints' Lives, and it is not easy to see why it became the most widely used, but it seems that preachers found it "exceptionally useful" in the fourteenth and fifteenth centuries (Reames), perhaps because it upheld the regular clergy as superior to the laity (and, of course, to the secular clergy) and chose just those elements that fitted in with the new thinking.

The work was altogether unhistorical and uncritical and was strongly criticized by later humanists and reformers for the credulity it encouraged in the minds of the faithful—in their view it stood for much that was wrong in medieval religion. Its popularity wilted in the sixteenth century under Protestant attacks—Bishop Jewell used it to prove his accusation that Catholic priests preached "stark lies and fond fables"—but some Catholic scholars of the fifteenth and sixteenth centuries had already adopted a critical approach and wanted to get rid of the obviously superstitious elements: Nicholas of Cusa, for example, in 1455 forbade his clergy to teach the superstitious elements in *The Golden Legend*'s accounts of SS Blaise, Barbara, Catherine, Dorothea, and Margaret of Antioch, because those accounts promised that acts of devotion to the saints in question would magically guarantee deliverance from such evils as illness, poverty, and even damnation (Reames); it is not surprising that some people in the later Middle Ages, when its fame was at its greatest, preferred the more sober appeal of *The Imitation of Christ*. The most important question that these early Catholic critics asked was whether a particular work was likely to edify its readers, not whether it was historically true in our modern sense.

There have been some modern attempts to rehabilitate the *Legend*, and they have followed a similar line. Even the scholarly Bollandist Delehaye defended it on the grounds that it was a work of devotion and so ought not to be judged by the standards of historical criticism: "Legend, like all poetry, can claim a higher degree of truth than history"; he admitted that it often brought a smile to his lips, "but it is a sympathetic and friendly smile, which does not at all disturb the religious response aroused by the picture of the goodness and heroic deeds of the saints" (quoted in Reames). Without denying its literary merits and the pious intentions of its author, however, one may ask how wise it is to allow the claims of "devotion" to justify the portrayal of the plainly incredible and even ridiculous as the truth.

James also wrote a number of other works, among which are the *Chronicon Genuense*, a history of Genoa down to 1296 and still valuable for its local detail; a set of sermons for the Church's year; a *Defensorium contra Impugnantes Fratres Praedicatores* (a Defence against those who attack the Dominicans), and a *Summa Virtutum et Vitiorum Guillelmi Peraldi* (a Summa of the Virtues and Vices [in the teachings of] William Peraldi), a Dominican who died about 1250. He was also responsible for a series of sermons on Our Lady, arranged according to her titles and attributes. He used to be credited with translating the Bible into Italian; if he did so it is very surprising that no copies have survived.

There is, surprisingly, no modern critical edition of the text of *The Golden Legend*, but see the modern English trans. from the Latin by G. Ryman and H. Ripperger (1941, rp. 1969). A modern edition of the *Chronicon*, with a good biographical survey, was published by G. Monleone in *Fonti per la storia d'Italia* (1941). See also E. C. Richardson, *Materials for a Life of Jacopo da Voragine* (1935), although this is severely criticized in Sherry L. Reames, *The Legenda aurea: A Re-examination of its Paradoxical History* (1985). See also *O.D.C.C.*, pp. 689 and 861; *Dict.Sp.*, 8 (1974), 62-4. On Caxton and the *Legend* see N. F. Blake, *Caxton and His World* (1969), pp. 117-23. For an appraisal of the role of the *Legend* in medieval devotion see Eamon Duffy, *The Stripping of the Altars* (1992), esp. pp. 79, 169, 351-3.

Bd Thomas Tunstal, *Martyr* (1616)

Thomas Tunstal was born in Whinfell, near Kendal. He entered the English College at Douai in 1606 using the alias Helmes, was ordained priest, and was sent to work on the English mission in 1610, where he used a different alias, Dyer. He was arrested almost immediately and spent the rest of his life in various prisons. One of these was Wisbech Castle, which he managed to escape from and go into hiding in King's Lynn. Unfortunately, he had injured his hands in his escape and had to seek medical help when they turned septic; this brought him to the notice of a local magistrate, and he was arrested once again. He was put in Norwich goal and brought before the next session of the assizes. A false witness gave evidence that Thomas had reconciled two Protestants to Catholicism and had tried to convert him; when the two Protestants were called to support this evidence they said that they were still Protestants and that Thomas had only urged them to lead a holier life. The judge then offered Thomas the Oath of Supremacy, and when he refused to take it he was condemned to be hanged, drawn, and quartered. At the scaffold he was asked if he were a Jesuit and replied that he was a secular priest who had made a vow to join the Benedictines; for this reason he requested the sheriff if his head could be displayed on the city's St Benet's gate. Before he died Thomas asked what the time was; on being told it was eleven o'clock he said, "Then it is near dinner time. Sweet Jesus, admit me though most unworthy to be a guest this day at thy table in Heaven." He was allowed to hang until he was dead, and his head was displayed on St Benet's gate as he had requested. There is some uncertainty about the exact date of his execution. He was beatified in 1929.

M.M.P., pp. 353-8. Some confusions in Challoner's account were cleared up by Bede Camm in his *Nine Martyr Monks* (1931), pp. 238-57. Birt's *Obit Book of the English Benedictines 1600-1912* (1913) claimed that Thomas received the Benedictine habit while on the mission in England. See also the general entries for the English and Welsh Martyrs under 4 May and 25 October.

Bd Clelia Barbieri, *Foundress* (1847-70)

Clelia Barbieri was born in 1847 in Le Budrie, Bologna. Her family was poor but devout, and Clelia showed early signs of unusual piety. When her father died from the plague in 1855 the family's poverty became acute, and Clelia did not complete her elementary education; she learned to read in her teens.

Under the guidance of the parish priest she began to help out in the parish, teaching other children the catechism, and with the help of Teodora Baraldi she formed a circle of prayer among her sisters and friends. The parish priest, Gaetano Guidi, became her spiritual adviser and was struck by her continuous awareness of the presence of God and her intense life of prayer. In 1868 Clelia and three other young women began to live communally in a house next to the church that was already being as a school. They dedicated themselves to Our Lady of the Seven Dolours and St Francis of Paola (2 Apr.), and this was the beginning of the Congregation of the Minims of the Addolorata (Our Lady of the Dolours). Clelia is regarded as one of its founders, along with Ursula Donati, one of the original four. The Congregation became involved in parish work, education, and the care of the sick and the elderly. It faced opposition from the civil authorities and had to wait a long time for ecclesiastical approval, which was granted initially in 1905 but fully only in 1934. In 1951 it merged with the Servants of Mary.

Clelia died of tuberculosis at the age of twenty-three on 13 July 1870. At her beatification in 1968 the pope praised her "interior innocence," which both resulted from and nourished a continual awareness of God and an intimate communication with him: from this flowed her simple, affectionate, and attractive goodness.

The basic Life was G. Gusmini, *C.B. e le Minime dell'Addolorata* (1917). See also L. Gherardi, *La beata Clelia Barbieri (1847-1870)*, (1969); *Diz. Ist. Perf.*, 1 (1974), 1043, with bibliography; *N.S.B.* 1, pp. 107-8.

14

ST CAMILLUS DE LELLIS, *Founder* (1550-1614)

Camillus de Lellis was born in 1550 in Bucchianico di Chieti in the Abruzzi region of Italy. His father, a nobleman, had a distinguished military career in the service of Spain, and at the age of seventeen Camillus joined the Venetian army to fight against the Turks. He was exceptionally tall, being 6 feet and 6 inches in height, and very large, with a quick temper and an addiction to gambling—in the end he lost everything, including the proverbial shirt from his back, taken from him in the streets of Naples in 1574. Before that he had contracted a painful and repulsive disease in his leg (probably open ulcers) and had spent some time in the San Giacomo hospital for incurables in Rome as patient and servant as well as another spell as a soldier.

When his gambling had reduced him to poverty he remembered a vow he had once made to join the Franciscans and so went to work as a labourer at the new Capuchin friary in Manfredonia. The guardian of the house converted him to a life of penance for his previous sins, and in 1575 he applied to become a Franciscan novice. His disease prevented his acceptance, and so he returned to San Giacomo in Rome to devote himself to the care of the incurably sick. As well as being a devoted nurse he became an efficient administrator and was eventually appointed bursar of the hospital. He was shocked by the generally low level of care provided by the so-called nurses and by their immorality and felt that the patients needed spiritual as well as physical care. With the approval of his adviser, St Philip Neri (26 May), and with support from a wealthy patron he broke away from San Giacomo and set up on his own with two like-minded helpers. He wanted to establish a company of "men of good will who would consecrate themselves to the sick purely out of love of God and would wear a cross as their badge." They worked every day in the hospital of Santo Spirito in Rome and gained a reputation for their diligence in caring for the patients and for their own humility and prayerfulness. Meanwhile, Camillus also studied at the Roman College and was ordained priest in 1584.

In 1585 Camillus rented a larger house. He had been joined by other helpers, and so he drew up a simple Rule for them that included an undertaking to serve those suffering from the plague, prisoners, and those suffering in private houses. He obtained provisional approval of this Rule in 1586 and two years later opened a new house in Naples, where the Ministers of the Sick, as his brothers were beginning to call themselves, cared for those suffering from the plague; two of them died from it, the first "martyrs of charity" of the new

Congregation. In 1595 and 1601 some of his brothers went to Hungary and Croatia to nurse the wounded on the battlefield, the first recorded instance of a medical field unit. Pope Gregory XIV gave formal approval to their way of life in 1591 as an Order dedicated to the care of the sick and allowed its members, comprising priests and lay brothers, to call themselves clerks regular. In the same year Camillus and twenty-five others made their solemn profession, adding to the three usual vows a fourth of "perpetual physical and spiritual assistance to the sick, especially those with the plague." They wore a black habit with a large red cross on the breast and on their capes.

Camillus pioneered modern methods in the Order's hospitals, insisting on proper ventilation, suitable diets, and the isolation of those with infectious diseases. In the training of his nurses he stressed that while they should see in the sick person the figure of Christ, they should practise "old-fashioned charity but with up-to-date technical skill." He was genuinely interested in seeking cures for sickness and disease and not just in caring for patients until they died or happened to get better. His practical approach affected the spiritual training of the nurses too: he was suspicious of any claimed mystical experiences, writing, "I don't like this talk about mystical union . . . although it is the height of perfection, (we should) do good and help the poor . . . since we'll have plenty of time to contemplate God in heaven"; what he wants from us now are "works and charity." Camillus also insisted that his nurses should not become involved in the administration of the public hospitals in which they worked, as that would take them away from nursing the sick and leave it to the ill-trained and immoral nurses whom he had known at San Giacomo. His own spirituality was coloured by his personal knowledge of sin and illness and by the mystical experiences he had of the crucified Christ. His guiding principle was the words of Jesus, "Whenever you did this to the least of my brethren, you did it to me" (Matt. 25:40), and he would prostrate himself before a sick person as before the crucified Jesus. The red cross on the habit was to remind him and his followers of the only motive they should have in their work: to follow Christ in his redemptive sacrifice by spending themselves in the service of the sick.

Camillus suffered from a number of severe long-term illnesses but continued to nurse the sick personally. He resigned from being superior general in 1607 but was involved in a visitation of its hospitals when he fell dangerously ill in 1614. He died in Rome on 14 July in the Maddelena, the motherhouse of the Order. He was reputed to have worked miracles during his life, and many were attributed to his intercession after his death. He was canonized in 1746 and, with St John of God (8 Mar.), was made patron of hospitals and the sick by Pope Leo XIII and patron of nurses by Pope Pius XI. At the time of his death the Order had established fifteen houses and eight hospitals. It spread rapidly throughout Europe and abroad, and two female branches were established in the nineteenth century, with a Secular Institute of Missionaries to the Sick being set up in 1948.

A large number of Lives exist. See C. C. Martindale, S.J., *The Life of Saint Camillus* (1946); M. Vanti, *S. Camillo de Lellis e i suoi Min. degli Infermi*" (3d ed., 1964), and *Lo spirito di S. C. de L.* (3d ed., 1959). The saint's writings have been edited by M. Vanti, *Scritti di S. C. de L.* (1965). See also *Bibl.SS.*, 3, 707-22 (with a long section on the iconography of the saint); *Diz. Ist. Perf.*, 2, 5-10 (on Camillus) and 912-24 (on the Order).

Two elements dominate paintings of Camillus: his care of the sick, often graphically portrayed in heroic terms, and his mystical experiences with the crucified Christ. In addition, a large number of commmemorative busts and pictures were produced for the Order's hospitals and houses, as well as popular pictures and prints. All of these representations were carefully controlled by the Order to give only the approved impression of the saint, usually shown working in the Santo Spirito hospital in Rome. The large statue of him in St Peter's shows him holding the Order's Rule, while a large painting dating from 1743 by Torelli in the church of St Gregory, Bologna, shows Christ on the cross conversing with the saint, who is being supported by angels.

St Deusdedit, *Bishop* (664)

Frithona (or Frithuwine), who took the name Deusdedit when he became archbishop of Canterbury, was consecrated in March 655 by Ithamar, bishop of Rochester. There had been a delay of several months before his election, which may have been due to the fact that he was the first native Anglo-Saxon—he was from Wessex—to become archbishop after the five archbishops of the Augustinian mission. Bede mentions him several times but gives no detail about his life or activities except that he consecrated Damian, a native of Sussex, as bishop of Rochester and that he died of the plague that swept the country in 664, the year of the Synod of Whitby. He seems to have had some share in the founding of the abbey of Peterborough in 657, and he founded a nunnery on the Isle of Thanet.

The appointment of Anglo-Saxons as bishops shows that the Church was taking root in the country, but the lack of evidence about Deusdedit has led to the conclusion that he was "a man of mediocre qualities (who) does not seem to have exercised any authority outside his own diocese" (Godfrey), although this may be an unduly harsh judgment on his abilities as a bishop. The scarcity of information about him may rather be a sign of the relative insignificance and isolation of Canterbury at the time (Brooks). Deusdedit was buried with his five predecessors in the special tomb-chapel dedicated to St Gregory in the monastic church of SS Peter and Paul in Canterbury. His shrine survived until the Reformation, but his cult was never widespread.

Bede, *H.E.*, bk. 3, chs. 20, 27; bk. 4, chs. 1-2; *O.D.S.*, p. 132; C. J. Godfrey, *The Church in Anglo-Saxon England* (1962), pp. 101, 127, 167; N. Brooks, *The Early History of the Church of Canterbury, 597-1066* (1984, 1996), pp. 67-71.

St Vincent Madelgarius (*c.* 677)

Madelgarius was of wealthy Frankish origin and was born at Strépy (in modern Belgium). He married St Valdetrude, and they had four children, Landeric, Aldetrude, Madelberta, and Deutelinus, all of whom were venerated as saints.

Once their children were old enough to be left, both husband and wife decided to separate and dedicate themselves to God as religious. Valdetrude retired to Mons, while Madelgarius founded a monastery in Hautmont and became a monk there, taking the name Vincent in religion. After some time, in 653, he moved to Soignies, where he was the local lord, and established another monastery there. Shortly before his death he handed the monastery over to his son, Landericus, bishop of Metz. Vincent died on 14 July, most probably in the year 677. He became the principal patron of the town of Soignies, where there is a fine romanesque basilica that bears his name. A thirteenth-century casket containing his head was destroyed during the French Revolution, but it is possible that the relic itself was saved; it is said to be in a replacement casket made in 1803. His cult is still strong today and is marked by two major processions held in Soignies each year, one on 14 July, the other on the Monday after Pentecost. Elsewhere his feast-day was kept on 20 September.

There are no grounds for accepting the various legends that grew up around him, including his supposed Gascon origin, a visit that he made to Ireland, and the story that he was forced into marriage by his father; these seem to have originated in the earliest Life, which dates from the beginning of the eleventh century. See *Bibl.SS.*, 12, 1177-8.

St Marchelm (Mid-Eighth Century)

Marchelm, or Marculf, was one of the English missionaries who followed St Willibrord (7 Nov.) to work among the Frisians. It appears that he worked under St Gregory of Utrecht (25 Aug.) to begin with and may have accompanied him and St Boniface (5 June) to Rome. He then worked for about fifteen years in Friesland and Guelderland before being sent to evangelize Overyssel, a dangerous area to the east of Friesland, with St Lebuin (12 Nov.). It is not clear how far Marchelm was associated with Lebuin in building a church at Deventer and making it the centre of missionary work to the Saxons as well as the Frisians. He died about the year 760 at Oldenzaal, and his relics were later moved to Deventer. He is not named in any of the early martyrologies, and there was only a limited medieval cult. In the fourteenth century it was claimed that Marchelm, renamed Marcellinus, was the author of the (false) *acta* of St Suitbert, apostle of the Frisians. These make out that Marchelm was one of the eleven missionaries who accompanied St Willibrord in person. Neither of these claims is true, but they helped to increase devotion to Marchelm in the Low Countries and Germany, and as a result he was included in the sixteenth-century Roman Martyrology, under the name Marcellinus.

There is considerable uncertainty about Marchelm and it is difficult to work out a chronology of his missionary activities; see *Bibl.SS.*, 8, 681-2.

Bd Hroznata, *Martyr* (*c*. 1160-1217)

Hroznata was born about the year 1160 at Teplá, in western Bavaria, and became an important figure at the court of Ottokar I in Prague, apparently set for a successful military and political career. Suddenly his young son died, shortly followed by his wife, and Hroznata was so overcome by sorrow that he left the court. After building and endowing a Premonstratensian abbey in his native Teplá he made a vow to go to the Holy Land. He took the cross as a Crusader, but when the Crusade did not take place, he was released from his vow by the pope on condition that he found another religious house. This led to the foundation of an abbey for Premonstratensian Canonesses at Chotesov about the year 1200. The following year he joined the Premonstratensians himself and went to live as a lay brother at Teplá. At first, it seems, he fell out with a rather lax abbot there and left for a while to live elsewhere until the abbot promised to reform. Some time later he was given charge of the abbey's temporal affairs and properties, and it was while he was away trying to regain some of the lands taken by brigands that he was captured and imprisoned at Alt-Kinsburg, near Eger. His captors demanded a ransom for his release, but before this could be paid he died from the ill treatment that he had received. It was claimed, perhaps rather dubiously, that his death was due to his defence of ecclesiastical immunities from lay interference, and so he has traditionally been regarded as a martyr. He was buried in the abbey at Teplá, which remains a Premonstratensian house and where his body is still venerated. His cult was approved in 1897.

A thirteenth-century *Vita* and an account of his miracles, both by an abbot of Teplá, are printed in *AA.SS.*, July, 3, pp. 804-10. See also *Bibl.SS.*, 7, 606-8.

Bd Boniface of Savoy, *Bishop* (1207-70)

Boniface was a member of the ducal family of Savoy, the grandson of Bd Humbert of Savoy (4 Mar.) and uncle to Eleanor of Provence, wife of Henry III of England. Two altogether different assessments of his character and achievements have dominated accounts of his life and career as archbishop of Canterbury, depending on whether historians have looked at Savoyard or English sources. Contemporary Savoyard writers commented on his outstanding physical beauty—"the Absalom of Savoy" was one of his nicknames—and praised his wide range of accomplishments and virtues, treating him as a saint and justifying a long-lasting cult. English chroniclers, on the other hand, and later English historians, have mostly denounced him for his worldly interests, violent temper, and general failure as archbishop of Canterbury. Even recent accounts have not been complimentary: "one of the most disliked archbishops of Canterbury ever" (*O.D.S.*) and "essentially a secular figure" dominated by family ties and interests (Carpenter). The modern hagiographer must tread warily, but it appears that Boniface has not deserved the bad English press he has received, although the Savoyard tradition has also been too uncritical of a complex figure.

As a young man Boniface entered the Grande Chartreuse as a novice but left "in tears" after some time for reasons unknown; Hugh, the prior general of Chartreux, wrote of Boniface's reputation for virtue "over an extended period of time." At some stage he was appointed prior of the monastery at Nantua in south-eastern France, a post he retained for the rest of his life. In 1232 he was appointed by the pope to be procurator of the diocese of Belley, in Burgundy, and in the following year was elected bishop by the cathedral chapter; it could well have been this appointment to Belley that caused him to leave Chartreux unwillingly. Seven years later he was also appointed procurator of Valence. He was still in minor orders; such a collection of ecclesiastical offices by a member of the higher nobility was not unusual at the time, and Boniface took steps to administer them properly, earning himself a reputation as a determined upholder of his own and the Church's rights.

When St Edmund, archbishop of Canterbury (16 Nov.), died in 1241 Boniface was elected as his successor. The circumstances of his election by the Canterbury chapter are not altogether clear, but there is no doubt that it was due, at least partly, to the influence of Queen Eleanor and that the king, Henry III, was also pushing for Boniface's election to be approved by the pope. This approval was granted in 1243, and Boniface arrived in England in the following year. He attended the Council of Lyons in 1245, where he was consecrated archbishop by Pope Innocent IV. Whatever Henry and Eleanor had hoped to achieve from his appointment, they should have known that this independent-minded churchman would defend his rights and exercise his full powers as leader of the Church in England.

The main problem facing the new archbishop was financial. His holy predecessor had left the see in a precarious financial position, and Boniface quarrelled with his suffragan bishops and the king when he tried to collect money to pay his debts. The archbishop also caused great resentment by insisting on his right as metropolitan to visit the dioceses of his suffragan bishops, including a number of abbeys that claimed exemption from episcopal visitation. His motivation in doing so was his desire for reform, and he was accompanied by carefully-chosen Dominican and Franciscan friars. He met resistance from the dean and chapter of St Paul's, London; the prior of St Bartholomew's, Smithfield; and the abbot of St Albans. According to Matthew Paris' account, Boniface was involved in a fight at Smithfield when he knocked the subprior down and was discovered to be wearing chain mail under his robes. This story has been widely used to show Boniface's violent temper and unholy treatment of his opponents but is almost certainly a malicious fabrication. There were, indeed, fierce quarrels, and Boniface issued a number of excommunications to try to enforce his claims, including one against the bishop of London. Appeals and counter-appeals to Rome followed, and while he was allowed by the pope to continue his visitations, they were restricted in scope, and he was required to withdraw the excommunications. On the other hand, when he visited St Albans in 1253 the monks were impressed by his moderation and civility, in contrast to the behaviour of other foreigners at Henry III's court. It is also a fact that throughout his time as archbishop Boniface remained on good terms with the Canterbury chapter, and the picture that emerges of him from Canterbury sources is positive: "a man of simplicity; although not well-educated he lived soberly, humbly, and chastely, and was a most generous helper of the poor" who paid off the debts of his predecessors, built and endowed a hospital in Maidstone, and enlarged the episcopal palace.

The archbishop also quarrelled with the king. As soon as he arrived in England in 1244 he refused to confirm the king's choice as bishop of Chichester and installed his own candidate instead. This was the start of his campaign to free the Church from undue royal interference. The other English bishops were fighting the same battle, and together they tried to win protection for the Church's rights in return for payments to Henry for his planned Crusade. At first the king agreed, but the bishops' grievances continued, and Boniface, without consulting the king, called a meeting of church leaders in 1257. Henry reacted strongly and forbade the bishops to attend, but the meeting went ahead. Boniface urged the bishops to use spiritual censures to enforce their rights, and at another meeting in the following year a long series of provisions spelled out the rights of the Church and the proper relationship of the government to it. While this quarrel was developing the king was also increasingly involved in disputes with his lay lords, who were demanding reform of the government in return for their continued financial support of the king's policies. It is now clear that Boniface, far from being "the king's creature," sided with the magnates against Henry, and when a Parliament at Oxford in 1258 elected a new Grand Council to advise the king, he was its titular head. Finally, in May 1261, he called a provincial council to meet at Lambeth and used the occasion to restate the bishops' grievances against the king. The meeting issued the famous Constitutions of Lambeth, listing the grievances and restating the Church's rights against lay interference; these were to be Boniface's last official legislation and the "focus of continued conflict over the reform of the Church" for several centuries (Wilshire). Henry appealed to the pope against them, bitterly attacking Boniface's usurping of the royal prerogative and general presumptuous behaviour, and the pope agreed in 1262 not to confirm the council's decrees—Urban IV needed Henry's political support in his conflict with the emperor.

This defeat persuaded Boniface to leave England in 1262, since there seemed to be no way in which reform of the Church in England could be achieved as long as the king could appoint unworthy bishops and interfere in ecclesiastical matters. He remained in voluntary exile in France until 1266 but continued to carry out his episcopal duties. His conflict with the king also continued; matters did not improve when a group of young nobles invaded the archbishop's lands, sacking a number of manors and churches and abusing some of the clergy. Boniface excommunicated those involved, but they claimed royal protection—some of them were members of the king's council. Other quarrels arose from Boniface's refusal to confirm royal candidates to ecclesiastical posts if he thought them unworthy, and conflict also continued over royal taxation of the Church even when this had been approved by the pope. Despite these quarrels, during these years Boniface was a loyal supporter of the king against Simon de Montfort and his followers; his earlier support of the magnates against the king ceased when they started a civil war.

By 1268, however, he had all but retired from public life; in that year, with royal letters of protection for the journey, he left England for Savoy, where he died on 14 July 1270 and was buried at the Cistercian monastery of Hautecombe. There was never any cult of Boniface in England, but a long-lasting one developed quickly in Savoy, and in 1838 King Charles-Albert persuaded Pope Gregory XVI to approve this and declare Boniface beatified. His most recent biographer concludes that "the major impression that one gathers is that Boniface was a man who through his public life, especially as Archbishop of Canterbury, became deeply involved in what he saw as the reform of the Church" (Wilshire), while the contemporary Carthusian prior general spoke of Boniface's reforming zeal but urged him to mitigate his enthusiasm with love and understanding.

Although the registers for his time as archbishop have been lost, there are ample sources for his Life. On the whole, English chroniclers of the time were unfavourable to foreign prelates, and the main English source, the *Chronicle* of Matthew Paris, a monk of St Albans, vilified the archbishop. For example, on the occasion of the London quarrels he has a street mob calling Boniface "an impious and bloody aggressor of our priests . . . illiterate and married as he is . . . whose foul infamy has already infected the city." It is important to note, however, that Matthew Paris himself, when he revised his chronicle shortly before his death sometime between 1258 and 1261, altered or deleted many of the references to Boniface and wrote, "It is most confidently hoped that the archbishop might be gifted with strength from above, and following in the footsteps of St Thomas . . . do battle with those who attack the Church." Furthermore, Matthew Paris died not later than 1261 and so was unable to cover the last years of Boniface's life, years that are crucial in assessing his achievements. The general English neglect or condemnation of Boniface was based on Matthew Paris' vilification—a major nineteenth-century study, for example, noted: "Of the principles of Boniface we can say nothing: indeed, he seems to have had none." A few more recent English writers, aware of the favourable accounts of Boniface in the Canterbury sources, have tried to give a more balanced view (e.g., Powicke calls him "in his way a great man and a successful prelate") but have still been coloured by Matthew Paris' condemnation. For modern accounts and judgments see especially L. E. Wilshire, *Boniface of Savoy, Carthusian and Archbishop of Canterbury, 1207-1270*, (*Analecta Cartusiana* 31 [1977]), the most favourable English interpretation of Boniface to date, based on the widest range of original sources. See also F. M. Powicke, *King Henry III and the Lord Edward* (1947); Edward Carpenter, *Cantuar, The Archbishops in their Office* (2d ed., 1988), pp. 68-9; *O.D.S.*, pp. 61-2. For the general historical background see A. Harding, *England in the Thirteenth Century* (1993), and J. R. Maddicott, *Simon de Montfort* (1994).

Bd Caspar de Bono (1530-1604)

Caspar de Bono was born in 1530 into a poor family in Valencia in Spain. As a young man he joined the Dominicans but had to leave soon afterwards to help support his family. He tried his hand at his father's silk trade but was unsuccessful and took to soldiering instead, enrolling in the army of the emperor, Charles V. He was in Italy until 1560, when he was badly wounded in a battle near Florence and vowed to Our Lady to become a religious again if he survived. Back in Spain he joined the Minims, a reformed and austere branch of the Franciscans, taking his final vows in 1565 and being ordained priest the following year. He became prior of Valencia and was elected provincial of the Order in Spain about 1580. He gained a reputation for the prudence with which he encouraged its members to the strictest interpretation of the Rule, while living an extremely austere life himself. He died in Valencia on 14 July 1604 and was beatified in 1786.

G. M. Roberti, *Il beato Gaspare de Bono* (1904); *D.H.G.E.*, 9 (1937), 1085; *Encic. Catt.*, 4, 1257.

St Francis Solano (1549-1610)

Francisco Solano was born in Montilla, Córdoba, in 1549, to well-to-do parents. He joined the Franciscans of the Observance when he was twenty and was ordained priest in 1576. Five years later he became master of novices and gained a reputation as a popular and effective preacher, working throughout southern Spain for many years and helping the victims of the plague in Montoro in 1583, when he was struck down by the disease himself for a short time. He thought of going to Africa as a missionary but in 1589 was instead ordered by his superiors to Peru, following a request from King Philip II, as there was a shortage of missionaries there compared with the more accessible Mexico. On the way their ship ran aground in a storm, and passengers and crew took to the single lifeboat, leaving behind a group of African slaves because there was not enough room for them. Francis had been instructing them in the Faith and refused to leave the sinking ship; he stayed on the wreck, baptized the slaves, and when some of them were drowned as the ship finally broke up, stayed with the rest on a sandbank until they were rescued.

Francis worked for twenty years ministering to the native population and the Spanish settlers in various parts of Peru and what is now Argentina and Paraguay. By the time he arrived the initial evangelizing commitment of the missionaries had notably diminished, despite the reforms ordered by St Turibius of Mogrovejo (23 Mar.). Francis was one of the missionaries determined to put these reforms into practice. He made a number of dangerous journeys through uncharted territories and learned the local language wherever he stayed for any length of time. He spent many years in the distant province of Tucumán (in modern north-west Argentina), then a remote area, being on the far side of the

Andes from Lima, and in Paraguay. Tucumán had suffered from a bishop opposed to Turibius and a source of scandal. Francis undertook mass Baptisms and made Christianity apparently acceptable in the province (though, as elsewhere, the "converted" Indians continued to practise their own traditional religion side by side with Catholicism). It is claimed that he also defended the Indians against bad treatment by their Spanish overlords, intent on extracting the maximum profits from their forced labour in the nearby silver mines of Potosí, and that he took a primitive form of violin into the jungle and played music and danced with the tribes living there. He would also play this instrument in private devotions to Our Lady far into the night. He was appointed "guardian" in 1592, responsible for supervising the scattered missions he had founded on his travels. But precise information about his years in this "wild" region is scant, replaced by legends of miraculous healings and tamings of wild animals.

He was then transferred back to Lima, possibly in 1594 or 1595, and seems to have spent some seven years travelling widely throughout the viceroyalty of Peru. His health declined, and he was appointed guardian of the friary in Lima and, for a time, of that in Trujillo. Turning his attention to the Spaniards in the city and other towns brought out another side of his character—his puritanism. He was said to have frightened the people so much with his sermons about the end of the world and his processing through the streets holding a crucifix that the viceroy had to intervene and ask him to moderate his preaching. The wealthy élite of Lima probably had good reason to fear his strictures: he would rush into theatres and gaming houses to berate them for their vicious way of life. He was credited with the gifts of prophecy and of tongues, and his reputed miracles won him the title "Wonderworker of the New World," while the preacher at his funeral called him "the hope and edification of all Peru, the example and glory of Lima, the splendour of the Seraphic Order." Over 200,000 Baptisms were attributed to him. Stories of his sense of humour also abound: he would say he was going to serenade a beautiful lady when on his way to pray at a shrine of Our Lady; he made a greedy friar carry a heavy box, telling him it was full of treasure when in fact it contained the body of an Indian child he was setting out to bury.

He was confined to the infirmary from 1608 until he died on 14 July 1610. His coffin was carried by the viceroy, the archbishop, and other notables of Lima, and his cult spread rapidly in South America and Spain. He was beatified in 1675 and canonized in 1726; he deserves to be numbered among the great missionary figures of New World colonization. He is the patron saint of many cities in South America.

There are a number of early Lives and accounts. See *Bibl.SS.*, 5, 1241-4, and L. J. Plaudolit, *El Apóstol de América, S. F. Solano* (1963); Stephen Clissold, *The Saints of South America* (1972). For the background see D. A. Brading, *The First America* (1991); E. Dussel (ed.), *The Church in Latin America: 1492-1992* (1992), esp. pp. 285-9.

Bd Richard Langhorne, *Martyr* (1679)

Richard Langhorne was a barrister of the Inner Temple in London and was called to the bar in 1654. When the so-called Popish Plot was revealed by Titus Oates in 1678, Richard, as a prominent Catholic layman, was one of the first to be accused of complicity in it. He was imprisoned in Newgate for eight months and then brought to trial at the Old Bailey in June 1679, accused of plotting to kill the king. Oates himself gave evidence against him and was supported by another false witness; Richard called witnesses to rebut their evidence and pointed out some glaring inconsistencies in their statements, but he and five Jesuits who had been tried the previous day were condemned to death. He was spared from execution for about a month, as the authorities hoped that he would implicate others; on the scaffold at Tyburn Richard told the people how offers of land and preferment had been made to to persuade him to give up his Catholicism, but he had refused to change. He professed his loyalty to the king, and as the hangman was placing the rope around his neck Richard took hold of it and kissed it, praying, "Blessed Jesus, into thy hands I commend my soul and spirit; now at this instant take me into paradise. I am desirous to be with my Jesus." He was hanged, drawn, and quartered on 14 July 1679 and beatified in 1929.

Richard left two works, both published after his death: *Mr Langhorn's Memoires, with some Meditations and Devotions . . . and his Speech at his Execution* (1679); and *Considerations touching the great question of the King's right in dispensing with the penal laws . . .* (1687).

M.M.P., pp. 538-41, is based on the printed account of the trial and last speech. See also *D.N.B.*, 32, pp. 102-3. For the Jesuit martyrs tried with Richard see the entry for 20 June. See also the general entries on the English and Welsh Martyrs under 4 May and 25 October.

15

ST BONAVENTURE, *Bishop, Cardinal, and Doctor* (1221-74)

Giovanni di Fidanza was born in the year 1221 in Bagnoreggio, near Orvieto. He joined the Franciscans in 1243, taking the name Bonaventure in religion, and was sent to Paris to study, where the English Franciscan Alexander of Hales was an important influence on him. He gained his teaching licence five years later and in 1253 became master of the Franciscan school there. In 1257 he was elected minister general of the Order and began the work that earned him the title of "second founder of the Franciscans." Although St Francis (4 Oct.) had died only thirty years earlier, in 1226, his Order was already facing a crisis: different factions within it claimed to be the true interpreters of the founder's mind—there was disagreement in particular about his strict attitude to poverty and the presence of friars in the universities; the loose administrative structure was failing to cope with a huge increase in numbers, and critics pointed to a falling off in apostolic zeal. Bonaventure adopted a balanced approach in dealing with these issues: he was keen to keep as far as possible to the original spirit of St Francis, but he rejected what he saw as the extremism of the Spirituals, who insisted that poverty was the single most important feature of Franciscanism and that the corporate ownership of either buildings or books should not be permitted. Bonaventure supported attendance at the universities and the building of specialist friaries in university towns, because for him study and learning were key elements in the apostolate of the friars, to preach and give spiritual direction to the people.

He wrote a commentary on the Rule, and his Life of St Francis, the so-called *Legenda Maior*, was approved in 1263; a general chapter in 1266 accepted it as the only official biography, ordering the destruction of all other Lives and "legends," as part of the campaign against the Spirituals and others who were claiming that the founder's life supported their interpretation of the Franciscan spirit. Not everyone has agreed that he was correct in his interpretation of Francis' mind, and some have argued that at times he contradicted Francis' express commands. Others have argued that his treatment of his holy predecessor, Bd John of Parma (20 Mar.), and some of the conservative friars was unduly harsh and that his method of exercising authority would have made the founder frown. Yet he presented a *via media* and did more than anyone else to make "the Franciscan ideal viable for a great order" (Knowles). He was largely successful in re-invigorating the Order and in confirming its new orientation, because he showed in his own life how the simplicity, frugal poverty, and

111

personal imitation of Christ preached by St Francis could be combined with intellectual eminence, great learning, and the holding of high office.

Pope Clement IV (1265-8) wanted to make him archbishop of York, but Bonaventure refused. He was involved in the doctrinal disputes that shook the university of Paris in the early 1270s, and his attacks on the errors of those who followed Averroes and especially his *Collationes in Hexaëmeron* were important in defining the borders of orthodoxy. Bonaventure was instrumental in having Gregory X elected pope in 1271, and when the new pope nominated Bonaventure as cardinal-bishop of Albano in 1273, he took care to include in the appointment a command forbidding Bonaventure to refuse. It is said that when the papal messengers arrived at Mugello, near Florence, with the news of the appointment Bonaventure was washing the dishes; he asked the visitors to wait until he had finished the task. The new cardinal-bishop took a prominent part in the Council of Lyons, called by the pope in 1274 to bring about reunion between East and West, to liberate the Holy Land, and to bring about a general moral reform in the Church. The council was attended by a very large number of bishops, theologians, and saints, including St Albert the Great (15 Nov.), St Philip Benizi (23 Aug.), and the future pope Bd Innocent V (22 June); St Thomas Aquinas (28 Jan.) died on his way to it. Bonaventure supported the moves for reunion and preached at the Mass of Reconciliation to mark the agreement reached between the two Churches (unfortunately repudiated a few years later). He died while the council was still in session, on 15 July 1274, and was buried in Lyons. There was no early cult, but Bonaventure was canonized in 1482 and declared a Doctor of the Church in 1588—he is usually referred to as the "Seraphic Doctor," after the name sometimes given to the Franciscan Order in memory of St Francis' vision on Mount Alverna. His feast used to be celebrated on 14 July.

Bonventure is remembered today chiefly as one of the outstanding spiritual and theological writers of a prolific century—one of the "twin summits of medieval theology" (Knowles). His main theological work was his commentary on the *Sentences* of Peter Lombard, while his influential spiritual writings were the *Itinerarium Mentis in Deum* ("The Journey of the Mind toward God") and his *Breviloquium*. It is perhaps inevitable that comparisons should be made between him and St Thomas Aquinas, especially as they stand as the founders of the influential Franciscan and Dominican schools of thought. Bonaventure was the more conservative of the two, teaching a theology firmly based on St Augustine (28 Aug.) and St Anselm (21 Apr.) and suspicious of the fresh insights that the thirteenth-century study of Aristotle was bringing and which Aquinas was happy to employ in his great work of systematization. Bonaventure was happy to use Aristotle's logic and his philosophical terminology, but for him theology could never be a purely theoretical study; it had to be of benefit to those seeking to live a Christian life; knowledge without faith was worthless, and there was for him, as for Augustine, only one worthwhile pursuit: progress toward union with God; any help that pagan philosophy might offer to the seeker was limited to being, at most, a useful tool. Bonaventure stressed the importance of the emotions in this search for God without denying the power of human reason to examine and understand divine revelation. All human knowledge and wisdom, however, were as nothing when compared with the divine illumination that God can give to the human mind, and this mystical approach has led some authors to argue that Bonaventure should be seen more as a mystical or spiritual writer than as a systematic, dogmatic theologian. This may be true, but he had a mind of great clarity and creative power, and his was the first great synthesis of thought and doctrine, drawing together all the strands of his learning to give an account of God, creation, the angels, the nature of the soul, grace, the virtues, the gifts of the Holy Spirit, and the progress of the soul toward perfection: he was able to organize and illuminate every topic (Knowles).

While Bonaventure wrote some specific works on spirituality, it is no exaggeration to say that all his writings are shot through with spiritual teaching. The perfect spiritual exemplar for him was St Francis of Assisi; the aim of the person following a spiritual way of life should be the union with God experienced by Francis on Mount Alverna. Bonaventure offers guidance on every stage of that progress, from the conversion of the sinner to the ecstatic experience of the contemplative. The parts played by God's grace, the sacraments, study of the scriptures, devotion to the passion of Our Lord, bodily mortification and penance, prayer—on all these he has much to say that is illuminating and also comforting, for he was writing and preaching as a pastor inspired by the same ardent commitment to the individual's salvation as fired his mentor, St Francis. Those seeking God pass through three stages—Bonaventure's famous "three ways"—active purification from sin that brings the "calm of peace," the peace of a clear conscience; then the way of illumination, based on the imitation of Christ and leading to what Bonaventure calls the "splendour of the truth"; and finally union with God, which leads to the "sweetness of love." The calm of peace, the splendour of truth, and the sweetness of love: by enjoying these both the individual and the Church on earth come closest to resembling the state of the blessed in the heavenly Jerusalem. For Bonaventure the purpose of human knowledge—and that includes theology—is not to speculate but to love. As Gilson wrote, in reading Bonaventure's theology we might imagine that St Francis has become a philosopher and is teaching at the university of Paris.

Bonaventure's works were published by Franciscan editors in a critical ten-volume edition (1882-1902) and a five-volume *Opera Theologica Selecta: editio minor* (1934-64); an English trans. by J. de Vinck appeared in five volumes (1960-70). See also E. Cousins (ed. and trans.), *"The Soul's Journey into God," and other short works*, in Classics of Western Spirituality series (1978). An early Life, probably dating from 1300, is no longer extant; subsequent Lives have not always been free of the particular biases shown by the factions in his lifetime. There is a huge bibliography; see, for example, *Dict.Sp.*, 1 (1937), 1768-1856; *N.C.E.*, 2 (1967), pp. 658-64; *O.D.C.C.*, pp. 222-3. See also E. Gilson, *The*

Philosophy of St Bonaventure (Eng. trans., 1938); C. H. Tavard A.A., *Transiency and Permanence: The Nature of Theology according to St Bonaventure* (1954); D. Knowles, *The Evolution of Medieval Thought* (1962), esp. pp. 236-48; Z. Hayes, O.F.M., *The Hidden Centre: Spirituality and Speculative Christology in St Bonaventure* (1981). For iconography see Murray, pp. 59-60.

In art Bonaventure was often shown in the grey habit of a friar but with the red hat of a cardinal; sometimes the hat is shown hanging on a nearby tree to illustrate the legend of his telling the messengers to wait. A painting by Zurbarán, unfortunately destroyed in Berlin in 1945, showed a legendary meeting between the saint and Thomas Aquinas in Paris; according to legend, when Thomas asked Bonaventure the source of his learning and wisdom, Bonaventure drew back a curtain to reveal a crucifix. A large fresco in Santa Croce in Florence, attributed to Taddeo Gaddi (*c.* 1330), shows Bonaventure seated at the foot of the cross composing his meditation on the passion, the *Lignum Vitae*; this was probably the earliest representation of him. Interest in painting him increased after he was declared a Doctor; Zurbarán executed a series of paintings for the Franciscan house in Seville (1619). He features as the equal of Aquinas in Raphael's *Disputa* (and also in Dante's *Paradiso*).

St Felix of Thibiuca, *Bishop and Martyr* (303)

As part of the persecution of Christians under Diocletian decrees were issued ordering the destruction of the scriptures and liturgical books. Felix was bishop of Thibiuca (present-day Zoustina), near Carthage in North Africa, at the time, and he resolutely refused to hand over the sacred books to the authorities even though other Christians had found excuses to do so. He was sent to Carthage for trial and executed there on 15 July 303; according to his *passio* he was fifty-six years of age. His body was buried in the basilica of Faustus in Carthage. Some martyrologies give 24 October as his feast-day.

This is a straightforward story that may be accepted as fundamentally true. What is strange about Felix's cult, however, is its strength in southern Italy, and especially in Venosa, and the additions to his biography that seek to explain his transfer from North Africa. According to these Felix was not executed in Carthage but sent to Italy for trial, travelling through various cities such as Agrigento, Catania, and Messina before reaching Venosa in Apulia, where he was executed on 30 August. Another version of the Italian legend has Felix being sent to Rome and then executed at Nola on 29 July. According to these accounts his relics were taken back to Carthage. His cult in southern Italy is ancient and well attested and was probably started by the presence in Venosa and Nola of relics belonging to an African martyr, probably Felix. The Venosa account mentions some companions of Felix who are said to have been executed with him, including Gennarus, Fortunatus, and Septimius; these may well have been other African martyrs whose relics were in southern Italian churches.

Bibl.SS., 5, 585-7. H. Delehaye examined the legends in detail in *Anal.Boll.* 39 (1921), pp. 241-76.

St James of Nisibis, *Bishop* (338)

James, a Syrian monk, became the first bishop of Nisibis in Mesopotamia about the year 308, and St Ephraem (9 June), his disciple, tells us how important his work was for the Church in the area. Among other things he built a fine basilica and may have been responsible for starting the city's first theological school, although the school that later became famous was founded only in 457. He was present at the Council of Nicea in 325, and St Athanasius (2 May) and the historian Theodoret both relate that he was an uncompromising opponent of Arianism. When the Persian king Sapor II made his first attack on Nisibis in 338 James was still alive, but there is good evidence that he died later that same year during the siege—hence his burial in the walls of the city of which he was the defender. His remains were later taken to Constantinople by the emperor John Tzimisces, although another tradition relates that they were taken to Amida when Nisibis was ceded to the Persians in 363.

Nothing else certain is known about James. It used to be believed that he was the author of substantial theological works, and Alban Butler claimed that these had won for him a place among the Doctors of the Church, the equal of St Ephraem himself. These writings were wrongly attributed, and nothing that can be attributed with certainty to James survives. His cult was widespread in the East from an early date, and he is recognized liturgically in practically every Eastern Church.

The unravelling of the legends about St James and the subsequent doubts cast on the traditional accounts were fully covered by P. Peeters in *Anal. Boll.* 38 (1920), pp. 285-373. See also *D.T.C.*, 8, 292-5; *Bibl.SS.*, 6, 411-2.

St Donald (Eighth Century)

All that is known about Donald (or Domhnall) is that he lived at Ogilvy in Forfarshire in the eighth century, was married, and had nine daughters. When his wife died he and his daughters lived together as a religious community under his spiritual direction. On Donald's death the daughters entered a monastery founded by St Darlugdach and St Brigid at Abernethy. They are commemorated in various natural Scottish features named "The Nine Maidens." The popularity of the Christian name Donald in Scotland seems to be due to the spread of the Clan Donald and not to this saint.

The *Aberdeen Breviary* is the only source for knowledge of Donald. See *K.S.S.*, pp. 324-5, 395-6; *Bibl.SS.*, 4, 806-7.

St Joseph of Thessalonika, *Bishop and Martyr* (*c.* 760-832)

Joseph was born in Constantinople about the year 760. His mother was a sister of St Plato (4 Apr.), abbot of Symboleon on Mount Olympus. It was his example that persuaded all the family to take up the religious life: Joseph's

mother and sister entered a monastery in Constantinople, while the three brothers and their father retired to their estates in Bithynia and founded a monastery
there at Sakkoudion. The family became involved in the quarrel between Plato
and the emperor Constantine VI over the latter's adulterous marriage;
Sakkoudion was closed and the monks driven away. They returned in 797, only
to face attacks from the invading Arabs, and so they left for Constantinople,
where they settled in the monastery of Saint John the Baptist. This had been
founded in the fifth century by the consul Studius—hence its name Studios—
and was to become a model of Eastern monasticism under Joseph's brother, St
Theodore (11 Nov.). Because he was a member of this community for some
years, Joseph is often referred to as "Joseph the Studite."

Joseph became bishop of Thessalonika in 806 or 807. In 809 a new patriarch,
St Nicephorus (13 Mar.), was appointed, but Joseph and his monk-relatives
refused to recognize him as he was not yet ordained. Nicephorus had them
imprisoned and then called together a council on the new emperor's orders to
reinstate the priest who had blessed Constantine VI's marriage. When Theodore
and Joseph refused to celebrate the liturgy with this priest they were banished
to the Princes' Islands in the Sea of Marmara, where they remained for two
years. In the meantime another bishop was appointed in Joseph's place. Whether
Joseph returned to his diocese or not on his release in 811, he had to spend
another period in exile from 815 to 821 during the Iconoclast persecution—he
and his brother were firm upholders of the value of images in Christian worship and devotion. He died on 15 July 832. Twelve years later his remains were
re-buried close to those of his uncle, Plato.

Joseph's extant writings consist of two homilies on the cross of Our Lord,
one on St Demetrius (8 Oct.), a panegyric on St Nestor (26 Feb.), and much
religious poetry. He collaborated with Theodore in composing the *Triodion*
and *Pentecostarion*, two series of liturgical hymns for the Sundays of the year,
and he also wrote a number of Canons. In addition, he wrote long poems
against the Iconoclasts, but these have not survived. The fact that he wrote
hymns has led to some confusion between him and St Joseph the Hymnographer
(3 Apr. in the East), who died in 886.

Bibl.SS., 6, 1309-10. Joseph's liturgical works have been published in Greek by E.
Eustratiadès in *Makedoniká* 2 (1952), pp. 25-88.

St Athanasius of Naples, *Bishop* (*c.* 832-72)

Athanasius was the son of Sergius I, duke of Naples, and became bishop of the
city in 849, when he was not yet twenty years old; his election was received
with acclaim by the clergy, the people, and the nobles—such was his reputation for holiness. He was consecrated in Rome by Pope Leo IV. As bishop he
continued to lead a life of austerity and prayer, and he was particularly involved in providing a proper training and education for his clergy. He intro-

duced the Roman custom of having a group of his priests sing Mass in the cathedral every day and also arranged for the staffing and upkeep of churches and chapels throughout the diocese. Other ecclesiastical works included the restoration of the monastery of the Most Holy Saviour and the founding of a new one attached to the basilica of Saint Januarius outside the walls of the city, the decoration of the cathedral, the establishment of a hospice for pilgrims, and a scheme for ransoming Christians who had been captured by the Saracens. He attended the Lateran Council of 863.

Athanasius was also heavily involved in political matters. He frequently attended the court of Emperor Ludovic II, who was campaigning against the Saracens in southern Italy, and became a respected imperial counsellor, but the good relations he had enjoyed with the dukes of Naples deteriorated when his nephew, Sergius II, became duke. Sergius proved to be "an ambitious and troublesome tyrant, whose private life was as unscrupulous as his public politics" (*B.T.A.*). Athanasius attacked him openly for his way of life, for his simoniacal appointments to ecclesiastical offices, and for his organized theft of church treasures. Sergius replied by imprisoning the bishop in Sorrento and continued to harass him when the people had forced his release. In 871, to avoid further trouble, Athanasius left Naples and took up residence in a monastery on a nearby island. Sergius tried to persuade him to resign altogether and become a monk and sent troops to arrest the bishop when he refused to do so. The emperor intervened, however, and Athanasius was given protection by the duke of Amalfi. Sergius ransacked the episcopal palace in Naples, using violence against the bishop's supporters, and was excommunicated by Pope Adrian II. Ludovic set out to restore Athanasius to Naples by force, but the long-suffering bishop died before this could happen, on 15 July 872 at Veroli, near Monte Cassino.

A strong cult developed, and Athanasius is still regarded as one of Naples' most important bishops, who restored religious and civil life in the city after the destruction and disruption brought about by the Saracen incursions and defended the rights of the Church against political control. In 877 his remains were solemnly transferred to the basilica of Saint Januarius; in the thirteenth century they were transferred again to the cathedral in Naples, where they were placed under the altar in the chapel of the Most Holy Saviour; his head is kept in a reliquary in the cathedral treasury.

The account by Athanasius' contemporary John the Deacon is largely reliable; there is also an anonymous tenth-century Life. See *Bibl.SS.*, 2, 553-5.

St Edith of Polesworth (? Tenth Century)

There is considerable confusion over the identity of this St Edith (or Eadgith), and some have argued that there were a number of holy women with "of Polesworth" in their title. One is mentioned in the Lives of St Modwenna (formerly 6 July), herself a shadowy figure, probably of the seventh century. According to this tradition Edith was a daughter of King Egbert and was entrusted to Modwenna by her brother, who later built an abbey at Polesworth for her; she became its abbess and was buried there. The chronicler Goscelin, however, writing his Life of St Edith of Wilton (16 Sept.) in the late eleventh century, says that she had a holy aunt, Edith of Polesworth, who was the sister of King Edgar. Unfortunately there is no evidence of such a person in the royal genealogies, and Goscelin himself removed the reference to Edith when he revised his account—he may have been confusing two aunts of King Edgar, one of whom was named Edith. She married the emperor Otto the Great in 930, died in 946, and had no connection with Polesworth. Another suggestion, given in the thirteenth-century chronicle of Matthew Paris, is that she was the sister of King Athelstan and married Sihtric, the Viking leader, at York in the year 925; such a marriage did take place, but we do not know the name of the lady involved. According to this tradition, Edith was eventually buried at Tamworth, a few miles from Polesworth, having died "in the odour of sanctity."

All that can be said with any certainty is that in the later Middle Ages there were two convents dedicated to St Edith, one at Tamworth (Staffordshire) and the other at nearby Polesworth (Warwickshire). It has been suggested that both Goscelin and Matthew Paris took the liturgical cult of St Edith of Wilton, observed at Polesworth, and created from it another Edith in order to provide a saintly foundress for the convent (*D.H.G.E.*).

Stanton, pp. 337-8. See also *Anal. Boll.* 56 (1938), pp. 5-101, 265-307; *D.H.G.E.*, 14 (1960), 1437-8.

St Vladimir of Kiev (*c.* 960-1015)

Vladimir, the illegitimate son of Svyatoslav and so the grandson of St Olga (11 July), was born about the year 960 and educated under his grandmother's supervision. After his father's death he quarrelled with his elder brother and spent some time in voluntary exile in Scandinavia, returning in 978 with an army of adventurers. He captured Kiev and became its duke, thus making himself the effective ruler of Russia. In 981 he launched a campaign against the Poles and captured a number of their important towns. This was the start of the long struggles between the Poles and the Russians, but the immediate result was to turn Russian eyes westward again and bring them into contact with Christian States, although there seemed to be little chance of an effective evangelization of the Russian people. St Olga had already attempted to convert them but with little success, and during Svyatoslav's reign German missionaries had been killed in Kiev—only St Adalbert of Magdeburg (20 June) survived—as the result of a pagan reaction against these attempts to introduce Christianity. In this context Vladimir's conversion to Christianity, after a period during which he was an active supporter of the pagan revival, was unexpected.

The Russian annals of the time explain the conversion as a considered choice by Vladimir between the competing envoys from various religions who went to Kiev to win him over: Jews, Muslims, German (i.e., Western) Christians, and Byzantine Christians. Once the choice was some form of Christianity, the annals claim, he made the decision to adopt the Byzantine model rather than the Western one on the basis of the excitement of the Greek liturgy compared with the pedestrian German celebrations, for his envoys reported on what they had seen in Greece: "We knew not whether we were in heaven or on earth, for on earth there is no such splendour or such beauty and we are at a loss how to describe it" (Dvornik). In reality, of course, Vladimir's decision was influenced far more by political considerations than by liturgical ones. For some years there had been links between Kiev and Constantinople, and according to the treaty of 971 the emperor could ask for Russian military help. When Basil II did so in 987, Vladimir was happy to oblige but only on condition that he be allowed to marry the emperor's sister. Such a suggestion caused horror in the imperial court, but Vladimir's military intervention was decisive, and it seems that he threatened to invade the empire if his condition was not met. He was baptized about 987 at Kherson in the Crimea and married Princess Anne at the same time; Dvornik comments that at least she had the consolation of knowing that for her sake Vladimir put aside his five wives and eight hundred concubines. The link with Constantinople added tremendously to Vladimir's prestige, ensured preferential trading agreements, and enabled him to break with the troublesome Scandinavians who had helped him against his brother. His conversion also helped to develop links with the West, especially Germany.

Once converted, Vladimir was a sincere and faithful Christian for the rest of his life and determined to have his people converted. He supported the work of the Greek missionaries sent from Constantinople and backed up their efforts by making it an offence to refuse Baptism. It is not clear how much force was used to persuade people adopt the new religion, but its acceptance became a test of personal loyalty to Vladimir. He built and endowed churches and monasteries, setting aside a tenth of his income to support the church of Our Lady in Kiev, and personally accompanied the German bishop St Boniface (Bruno) of Querfort (19 June) into the lands of the Pechenegs, whom he was hoping to convert. During his reign links with Rome were established through the exchange of diplomatic messengers by both sides; as a result, Constantinople, frightened of Vladimir's becoming too pro-Western to escape its rigid control, gave the Church in Kiev more autonomy and allowed it to have its own metropolitan archbishop.

Revolts led by two sons of his former wives troubled the end of Vladimir's reign, and he died in 1015 while on campaign against them. Traditionally he has been revered as the "apostle of Russia," and the conversion of the country to Christianity is dated from his reign. The speed of that conversion has been exaggerated, however, and by his death the new religion had probably not penetrated much beyond Kiev itself and even there may have been limited to the nobility and wealthier merchants. Vladimir had been a politically astute ruler, strengthening the new Russian State by his alliances and keeping a careful balance between East and West, ecclesiastically and politically.

F. Dvornik, *The Making of Central and Eastern Europe* (1949); *Bibl.SS.*, 12, 1323-9.

St David of Munktorp, *Bishop* (*c.* 1080)

David (also known as David of Sweden and David of Västerås) was an English monk who volunteered to work on the English mission to Sweden; he may have been at a Cluniac house on the Continent at the time. The occasion was the murder of St Sigfrid's (15 Feb.) three nephews, and David seems to have been motivated by a desire for martyrdom. Sigfrid was bishop at Växjö, and he sent David to work in Västmanland. There he evangelized the people and built a monastery at a place later known as Munktorp, where he is said to have baptized the local people in a spring. He was credited with the gift of miracles, and his missionary work was successful. Tradition claims that he was the first bishop of Västerås, and Davö, where he lived for a time, is named after him. Swedish sources refer to him as the "apostle of Västmanland." He lived to a great age and died peacefully about the year 1080. Miracles were reported at his tomb in Munktorp. His relics were moved to the cathedral there in 1463, but the shrine was destroyed at the time of the Reformation and his bones reburied in the local cemetery.

C. J. A. Oppermann, *English Missionaries in Sweden* (1937), pp. 112-7; *Bibl.SS.*, 4, 516.

Bd Ceslaus of Breslau (*c.* 1180-1242)

Tradition says that Ceslaus (or Czeslao) came from the family of the counts of Odrowatz in Silesia and suggests that he was the brother of St Hyacinth (17 Aug.), but there is no historical foundation for the latter statement. He was born about the year 1180 and educated at Cracow, Paris, and Bologna. He became a priest and gained a reputation for piety and learning before becoming a canon at Cracow and provost of St Mary's in Sandomir; he is said to have used the income from these posts to help the poor. He accompanied the bishop of Cracow and St Hyacinth to Rome in 1220 and was so impressed by St Dominic (8 Aug.) that he became a Dominican friar, receiving the habit at the same time as St Hyacinth.

He was sent to preach and open Dominican houses in Poland; on the way he founded a house in Prague, and from there he moved to Cracow, where he was based for some years. After this he moved to Wroclaw and in 1232 became Polish provincial. He spent a short time back in Bologna before returning to

Poland to make further foundations. He was a successful spiritual adviser: among those whom he is said to have guided in the spiritual life were St Hedwig (17 July) and Bd Zdislava Berka (1 Jan.). In 1240, while Ceslaus was prior of Wroclaw, the Tartars invaded the region and appeared to be unstoppable as they advanced on the city. The Christian forces that went out to meet them, however, won an easy victory, and this was attributed to Ceslaus' constant prayers on their behalf. He died in 1242 and was buried in the church of Saint Adalbert; his remains were translated in 1330. The popular cult was approved in 1713.

Bibl.SS., 3, 1159-60.

Bd Bernard of Baden (1428-58)

Bernard was born in the year 1428 to Margrave James I of Baden and his wife, Catherine. He seemed destined for a brilliant career as he was both well educated and an able military leader, and on the death of his father in 1453 he succeeded him as Bernard II. At some stage he seems to have been espoused to Madeleine, the daughter of Charles VII of France, but no marriage appears to have taken place. Bernard had already been in the service of the emperor Frederick III, and when Constantinople fell to the Turks in 1453 Frederick sent him as his envoy to various European courts to arouse interest in and collect money for a new Crusade against the Turks. He became so attracted to this mission to save Christendom that he gave up his position as margrave and handed over the government of Baden to his brother Charles so that he would be free to pursue it more effectively. In 1458 he set out for Rome to meet Pope Callistus III (1455-8), who was himself trying to drum up support for a Crusade with great enthusiasm but little success. Shortly after leaving Turin, however, Bernard caught the plague and died in the Franciscan monastery at Moncalieri, still less than thirty years of age. He already had a reputation for sanctity and for his special devotion to Our Lady, and a number of miracles were reported to have taken place at his tomb. His cult spread quickly in Piedmont and neighbouring areas of France and Germany, and he became the patron of Fribourg and of Vic, near Nancy. The former edition of this work says that he was beatified in 1479 by Pope Sixtus IV (1471-84), but this is a mistake: Sixtus set up an inquiry into Bernard's life as the normal preliminary to beatification, but it was only in 1769 that Pope Clement XIV approved the unofficial cult and at the same time declared Bernard to be the patron of Baden. In 1958 the Sacred Congregation of Rites agreed to the introduction of the cause for his canonization.

AA.SS., July, 4, pp. 110-8; *Bibl.SS.,* 3, 70-1.

Bd Ignatius Azevedo and Companions, Martyrs (1570)

Ignazio Azevedo was born into a wealthy family in Oporto in 1527 or 1528 and joined the Jesuits when he was twenty years old. As a novice his self-imposed physical penances were so severe that he had to be rebuked by his superiors. At the early age of twenty-five he was appointed rector of the college of St Antony in Lisbon, a post he held for ten years with just a short break when he was vice provincial of Portugal; he then went to be rector of the college in Braga. While in Lisbon he also worked as unofficial chaplain to two hospitals and a number of prisons, finding this work of ministering to the unfortunate more to his taste than his duties as rector. He had had for some years a desire to serve as a missionary, inspired, it seems, by a Japanese student, a convert of St Francis Xavier (3 Dec.) who was studying in Lisbon, and eventually in 1566 he was sent as visitor to inspect the Jesuit missions in Brazil. After two years he returned, and in 1569 he went to Rome to recommend that more missionaries be sent to South America to help with the work of evangelization and to protect the native people from the cruelty of the settlers. He was commissioned to choose suitable priests from the Portuguese and Spanish provinces and go with them as superior to Brazil, and the party set out on 5 June 1570. The missionaries were divided into three groups: thirty-nine sailed with Ignatius in a merchant ship, while the two other groups travelled separately in other ships. The intention was to use the voyage to instruct the orphans who were being transported to provide young settlers in the colonies.

They sailed with a military escort as far as Madeira, but then the merchant ship went on ahead on its own. As they left Madeira Ignatius addressed his companions on the dangers that lay ahead of them in South America and on the glory of martyrdom. Off the Canary Islands five French privateers, manned by Huguenots from La Rochelle, caught up with the merchant ship after apparently following it deliberately on account of its Jesuit passengers. The ship was captured, and the Huguenot commander, Soury, ordered the missionaries to be killed, while sparing the crew and other passengers. Ignatius and his thirty-nine companions were massacred in cold blood, Ignatius himself being thrown overboard holding a picture of Our Lady that had been presented to him by Pope St Pius V (30 Apr.)—a rare copy of the picture supposed to have been painted by St Luke. Nine of those killed were Spanish, the remainder Portuguese; all were beatified in 1854. They are sometimes referred to as "The Martyrs of Brazil" or "The Protectors of Brazil," and their cult was particularly strong in that country.

There were a number of contemporary accounts of the massacre, one of which was sent to Bd Ignatius' brother and another to St Teresa of Avila (15 Oct.), whose relative, Bd Francis Godoy, was among the martyrs. See J. Brodrick, S.J., *The Progress of the Jesuits* (1946), pp. 220-30. *Bibl.SS.*, 3, 388-91, gives the names of all the martyrs.

St Pompilio Pirrotti (1710-56)

Domenico Pirrotti was born in 1710 in Montecalvo Irpino in Campania, Italy. He came from a well-to-do and ancient family and received a good education. When his father objected to his decision to enter religion, Dominic wrote: "I am determined to stick to my decision to serve God and not to change my idea of doing God's will, abandoning the world if that is what he wants and putting up with the loss of relatives and friends." He had already decided to devote himself to teaching in an attempt to remedy the lack of educational provision, especially for the poor. He left home and joined the Clerks Regular of the Religious Schools (also known as "Piarists" or *Scolopini*) founded by St Joseph Calasanz (25 Aug.); he was professed in 1728 with the religious name of Pompilio Maria. He taught for some years in a number of schools, gaining a reputation for sanctity and learning.

After ordination to the priesthood in 1732 he worked as a roving missioner in various parts of Italy, concentrating on preaching and hearing Confessions; he earned the title "apostle of the Abruzzo" because of the outstanding work he did in that region. While he was working in Naples, a campaign of slander organized by some local clergy who objected to his zeal and obvious success caused the archbishop to withdraw his confessional faculties; the main accusations laid against him were that he was too ready to absolve penitents and too lenient in imposing penances on them. Pompilio's enemies also denounced him to the king on the grounds that he courted public popularity and so was politically dangerous; as a result he was exiled from the city. A public outcry at the injustice of the sentence forced the king to recall him.

Pompilio did all he could to spread devotion to the Sacred Heart throughout Italy. He founded a pious confraternity in its honour in Montecalvo and composed a novena of prayer to promote the devotion. He also had a strong devotion to Our Lady and was credited with having saved a town from the effects of an earthquake by his prayers to "la Mamma Bella." This was one of a number of miracles attributed to his intercession during his lifetime. Throughout his missionary activities he stressed the necessity of constant prayer: "The more you find yourselves in the dark, the more you must persist in holy prayer, because it is in prayer that God gives his light to suit our needs; I assure you that the devil will achieve nothing as long as you do not give up prayer, but take that away and everything collapses and every virtue is in ruins, just as plants wither if they are not properly watered."

In 1765 he was sent to the Congregation's house in Campi Salentina, near Lecce, where he died the following year on 15 July. He was buried in the Congregation's church, where his remains are still venerated. He was beatified in 1890 and canonized in 1934.

A selection of the saint's letters has been published: L. Picanyol, *Lettere Scelte* (1934). See also *A.A.S.* 27 (1935), pp. 223-34; *Bibl.SS.*, 10, 1007-11.

Bd Anne Marie Javouhey, *Foundress* (1779-1851)

Anne Marie Javouhey was born in 1779 in Jallanges, Burgundy, the fifth of
nine children of Balthazar Javouhey, a well-to-do farmer, and his wife, Claudine.
She was a forceful child and seems to have dominated her brothers and sisters,
organizing them under a Rule to keep periods of silence and recite the Hours.
In 1792, when the anticlerical revolutionaries were particularly active in Burgundy, she rescued people from a chapel that had been set alight, warned
priests about the spies operating in the neighbourhood, and misdirected the
mob when they came to hunt them out. She taught local children the catechism
and prepared them for Holy Communion, which they had to receive secretly in
one of her father's barns. This early experience led to her decision to devote
her life to the education of the poor. In 1798 she made a private vow of
virginity, and as soon as religious Orders were allowed to operate again in
France she joined the Sisters of Charity at Besançon. The convent had been
chosen for her by her parents, however, and she realized that it was not for her,
leaving it the evening before she was due to take her vows.

She started a small school for girls in a house bought for her by her father,
but it was not a success, as the local community saw litle point in educating its
daughters. She tried her vocation again, this time at the Trappist house at La
Val-Sainte in Switzerland, but found the way of life alien to her active temperament and again left before taking any vows. During this period of uncertainty about her future she was troubled by a vision (or perhaps just a dream,
or her imagination, as she herself wondered) that she had had first at Besançon:
there was a crowd of poor, sick, and crying children, and especially a large
number of black men, women, and children, all calling her "Dear Mother."
She and her three sisters started another school, this time in Chamblanc, but
were forced to live at almost starvation level because they had so little support.
Then in 1805 they had an audience with Pope Pius VII, who stopped at nearby
Chalon on his way back from Napoleon's coronation in Paris. He gave them his
blessing and told Anne Marie to persevere in her vocation. Encouraged by this
meeting, she went to see the mayor of Chalon, who let them use the buildings
that had been the seminary, while the town council voted them an annual
grant. Within a short time her brother and a colleague were running a school
for eighty boys while she and eight colleagues had a school for 123 girls, of
whom thirty-four were boarders. They obtained permission from the civil
authorities for a "religious association formed in the diocese of Autun and
called by the name of St Joseph, with the purpose of forming children of either
sex for work, good morality and christian virtue." In May 1807 Anne Marie,
her sisters, and five other women were clothed in their blue and black habits by
the bishop of Chalon.

Anne Marie was a very capable organizer and before long had opened workshops, a hostel for the poor, another boy's school, a preparatory seminary, and

new houses in other dioceses. This expansion, however, overextended the re-sources of the Congregation, and only Balthazar Javouhey's intervention saved it from bankruptcy; he paid its debts and in 1812 bought a former Franciscan friary at Cluny to be its motherhouse—hence its subsequent name, the Con-gregation of St Joseph of Cluny. Two years later Anne Marie opened a school in Paris and began to use the English "Lancastrian" system, in which the teacher taught a group of monitors who then taught the rest of the children. She was heavily criticized for doing so, mainly, it seems, because it was Eng-lish and had been pioneered by a Quaker; to Anne Marie it just seemed a practical way to deal with a shortage of teachers. The Parisian authorities, however, supported her, and the minister of the interior introduced her to the deputy-governor of the French island of Réunion, who saw in her work the potential for developing a system of education for the French colonies and especially for their newly-emancipated slave populations.

Four Sisters left for Réunion early in 1817 and started a school on the island. When they were joined by four more Sisters they were able to open a second one, and news of their success persuaded the authorities to ask them to work in Senegal in West Africa. Anne Marie's sister Rosalie led the group, and her brother Pierre went as escort. Gradually Anne Marie came to the conclusion that the Congregation should concentrate on this missionary work, which seemed to tie in with her early vision or dream, and so she set up teams of sisters to work in Réunion, Senegal, Guadeloupe, and Guiana; in 1822 she went to Senegal herself. She obtained some land and built a settlement, introducing some cows and teaching the Senegalese how to plant maize, rice, and beans. At the request of the British governor of Sierra Leone and The Gambia she went to work there as well, in particular helping to run the hospitals.

Repeated illness forced her to return to France. There she had to deal with a move by the Réunion community to choose their own superior and break away from the Congregation. This developed into a bitter and lengthy quarrel, dur-ing which the rebel superior gained papal approval for a time and declared all the other houses of the Congregation to be irregular. Appeals and counter-appeals followed until the matter was eventually settled in Anne Marie's favour by the archbishop of Paris. Meanwhile, by 1828 eight new houses had been opened in France and missionary settlements in Martinique, Saint-Pierre and Miquelon, and India. Anne Marie concentrated her own efforts in Guiana, sailing with an expedition of forty Sisters, twelve lay male assistants, a doctor, a chaplain, and her brother Pierre, to colonize and Christianize the Mana district at the request of the French government, which was frightened that the large number of freed slaves would cause trouble. She organized and carried on the work in the face of increasing hostility from the French planters.

The growth of the Congregation in these years is amazing and was due to Anne Marie's energy and determination; she had a clear grasp of the essentials of any new project, a mind free of any of the prejudices of the time, and a simple and humble faith in God's providence. At the same time some people found that her determination could become an inflexible stubbornness, and she made enemies, especially among some of the French settlers who thought she was doing too much for the ex-slaves in educating them. Nor did she always listen to wiser counsels; she insisted, for example, on sending some young Guianians to train for the priesthood in French seminaries. As she had been warned, the cultural gap was too great for most of them, and of the few who were ordained only one returned to Guiana. Here she was ahead of her time; it could be argued that the maturity of nineteenth-century missionary enterprises, Catholic and Protestant, is best judged by their attitude to the establishment of a native clergy and that most failed to meet this criterion.

Anne Marie's trials increased in the 1830s. A new bishop of Autun had strong views on religious Congregations, believing they needed "a man's hand, and that hand was his" (Martindale). He declared himself superior general of Anne Marie's Congregation and appointed a priest as superior at Cluny. On her second visit to Guiana he sent a priest to be superior of the settlement; he refused to give her the sacraments for two years, and the bishop wrote threatening her with excommunication if she did not obey him. In this connection Anne Marie wrote: "The Cross is found wherever there are servants of God, and I rejoice to be reckoned among them." In 1845 the bishop threatened to close Cluny altogether, and it seems that it was only the efforts of the papal nuncio that prevented this happening. In the end Anne Marie was confirmed as superior general by a commission set up by the archbishop of Paris. Before she died she ordered all the papers concerning her quarrel with the bishop to be destroyed, and there is no account of the long drawn-out struggle in the official account of her life.

She had left Guiana in 1843 to supervise the work of the Congregation and arrange for new foundations in Tahiti, Madagascar, and elsewhere. Toward the end of her life she decided to go to Rome to obtain full papal approval for the Congregation, which now had 118 houses, but she died before she could set out, on 15 July 1851. She was buried in the Congregation's chapel at Senlis, north of Paris, and beatified in 1950, by which time the Congregation was working in thirty-two different countries. In 1986 it had 3,406 members in 378 houses across the world.

Anne Marie was a woman of great faith and great vision; her treatment of the black population of the colonies was surprisingly advanced, and her administrative ability and courage were outstanding. She is another proof of the extraordinary flowering of spirituality in the late eighteenth and nineteenth centuries that produced so many new Congregations devoted to putting into practice Our Lord's command to us to love one another as he had loved us.

Jean Hérbert and Marie-Cécile de Segonzac, *Anne Marie Javouhey: Lettres*, 4 vols. (1994); André Merland, *Anne Marie Javouhey, audace et génie* (1996); F. Delaplace, C.S.Sp., and

P. H. Kieffer, C.S.Sp., *Blessed Anne Marie Javouhey* (new ed. and Eng. trans., 1998). See also the older English Lives: C. C. Martindale, S.J., *Mère Anne-Marie Javouhey* (1953), and G. D. Kittler, *The Woman God Loved* (1958). On the Congregation see *Diz. Ist. Perf.,* 8, 504-7.

ST BONAVENTURE (p. 111, above)
Gold cross and chalice, white host, on blue field

16

St Athenogenes, *Bishop and Martyr* (*c.* 305)

The former Roman Martyrology had two entries relating to Athenogenes. One, under 18 January, described him as "an old theologian," who, before being executed at the stake, "sang a hymn of joy, which he left in writing to his disciples." The other entry, under today's date, said that he died at Sebaste in Armenia with ten disciples during the persecution under the emperor Diocletian (284-305); since that persecution started only in the year 303, and the emperor died two years later, this would mean that Athenogenes' death occurred between 303 and 305. He was probably a *chorepiscopus* rather than a full diocesan bishop. Mention of the martyr's name in the ancient Syriac martyrology and in the *Hieronymianum* is proof that an early cult existed. St Basil (2 Jan.), in his treatise on the Holy Spirit, praised Athenogenes' hymn, which had expressed the bishop's belief in the true divinity of the Holy Spirit, and tells us that he had been burned alive; other sources say he was killed by a blow from a sword. St Gregory the Enlightener (30 Sept.), who died about the year 330, is said to have established a feast-day in the Armenian Church in honour of St Athenogenes and John the Baptist and to have built a church in their honour at Achtichat on the ruins of a pagan temple, and at Bagavan, where their feast-day replaced a pagan festival. Athenogenes was also venerated in Egypt and Constantinople.

H. Delehaye, *Les Origines du culte des martyrs* (1911), pp. 177-8. *D.H.G.E.*, 5 (1931), 44-6, separates this Athenogenes from the author of St Basil's hymn.

St Helier, *Martyr* (Sixth Century)

Little certain is known about Helier. Tradition says that he was from Tongres, in Belgium, where he was converted as a boy to Christianity by a priest named Cunibert, who was then murdered by Helier's non-Christian father. Helier fled to the Cotentin region of Normandy and sought refuge in the monastery at Nanteuil, where St Marculf (1 May), who died about the year 558, was abbot. A different tradition says that he was converted to Christianity by Marculf. After spending some time at Nanteuil, Helier went to the island of Jersey to find greater solitude, perhaps following the example of his master Marculf, who had spent some time as an island hermit before founding Nanteuil. He led a life of fasting and prayer, living in a cave and working to convert the local people. He was murdered by some robbers or pirates to whom he had preached the gospel. The main town of Jersey is named after him, and his cult was also popular along the Normandy coast.

A Life of limited historical value is in *AA.SS.*, July, 4, pp. 145-52. See also Stanton, pp. 342, 661.

St Reineldis, *Martyr* (*c.* 680)

Reineldis (or Renelde) was the daughter of St Amalburga (10 July). Her place of birth is disputed and was either Kontich, just outside Antwerp, or Condé-sur-Escaut in present-day northern France; Kontich seems to be the more likely. Tradition says that after her parents and her sister, St Gudula (8 Jan.), embraced the religious life, she followed her father to the abbey of Lobbes, hoping that there could be some way for her to join him there and giving the abbey most of her wealth and possessions. When this proved to be impossible she went on pilgrimage to the Holy Land, where she stayed for seven years (some sources say only two years), and returned with a large number of relics. On her return she lived at Saintes, near Hal, south-west of Brussels, until she was murdered there by raiding barbarians. Her servant, Gundulf, and a subdeacon named Grimoald were killed with her, and all three were venerated as martyrs—the presence of the remains of the three martyrs explains the place name.

A cult seems to have started fairly soon after her death, and in 866 the bishop, St John of Cambrai, raised the relics and had them re-buried in a solemn ceremony. The first Life of St Reineldis probably dates from this time. The relics were authenticated on a number of occasions down to 1811, and Reineldis was invoked especially in cases of eye diseases. A twelfth-century document describes the translation of her relics to Lobbes, probably in 1170, and their authentification by the local bishop. This document seems to have been a sermon by a monk of Lobbes on an anniversary of the translation and is more hagiographical than historical, but at least it is reliable evidence that Reineldis' cult was strong around Saintes and in the abbey of Lobbes. Doubts have been thrown on the story of her visits to Lobbes and the Holy Land on the grounds that these may have been invented to justify the abbey's holding of certain estates and to lend authenticity to its collection of relics.

Bibl.SS., 9, 92-5. On the translation of her relics see *Anal. Boll.* 22 (1903), pp. 439-45, and on the place of her birth and the Life, *ibid.*, 69 (1951), pp. 348-87.

St Fulrad, *Abbot* (784)

Fulrad was born in Alsace of wealthy parents. He became a monk at the abbey of Saint-Denis, near Paris, and sometime before 751 was elected its abbot. He was responsible for increasing the abbey's lands, especially by reclaiming those confiscated by Charles Martel, and endowing it with his own family estates. In addition he won important privileges of exemption and built a new abbatial church, consecrated in 775. He visited Rome in 763 to obtain the relics of SS Vitus (15 June), Alexander (3 May), Hippolytus (13 Aug.), and others, which he distributed among various churches and monasteries, especially Saint-Denis and the abbey of Lièpvre in Alsace. As abbot of Saint Denis, Fulrad was a leading figure at court; he was a member of the royal council under three kings, Pepin (d. 768), Carloman (d. 771), and Charlemagne (768-814), and head of the court clergy, a post that enabled him to have a major influence on the appointment of reforming bishops throughout the kingdom.

Fulrad was necessarily involved in politics. He had been part of the delegation, along with St Burchard of Würzburg (14 Oct.), that had gone to Rome in 751 to ask Pope St Zachary (15 Mar.) to settle the disputed succession to the Frankish throne. The pope decided in favour of Pepin, who from then onward was a keen supporter of the papacy. In 756 Fulrad was again in Rome, this time to hand over to the pope the keys of Ravenna and the cities of the Pentapolis, taken by Pepin from the Lombards. This was important for the development of the Papal States in Italy and for the move of the popes away from dependence on the Eastern emperors for temporal support. When Pepin died in 768 Fulrad worked for the unification of the Frankish kingdom under Charlemagne (Pepin had divided it between his two sons, Carloman and Charlemagne), and this was achieved on the death of Carloman in 771.

Fulrad died at an advanced age in 784 and was buried at Saint-Denis; Alcuin and Dungal composed the epitaphs for his tomb. He had been an important figure in the development of the Frankish State and Church. His remains were later moved to the abbey of Lièpvre, which he had founded and where his cult remained popular until the eighteenth century. He is not named in early martyrologies.

There is no early Life of Fulrad, but references to him in various documents are plentiful. See *Bibl.SS.*, 5, 1316-7.

Bd Ermengard, *Abbess* (*c.* 832-66)

Ermengard was born about the year 832, the daughter of King Louis the German and his wife, Emma, and granddaughter of Charlemagne. She is listed in the book of the Confraternity of Saint-Gall with her mother and three sisters. At her own request, Louis appointed her abbess of the monastery of Buchau and then of the royal abbey of Chiemsee in Bavaria. She gained a reputation for virtue and penance and for her care of the members of the houses that she ruled. A local abbot wrote of her: "She led her flock to the Lamb, giving to him many pure [virginal] companions, and she was dear to God because of her holy merits, [and was] full of outstanding good works, a spouse dedicated to God her spouse." She died on 16 July 866 and was buried in the abbey church. Her cult was strong locally and continues today; Pius XI confirmed it in 1928 at the request of the German bishops.

Ermengard has sometimes been confused with Bd Irmgard or Ermengard, venerated in Cologne on 4 September, who died about the year 1100.

A.A.S. 21 (1929), pp. 24-6, gives the decree confirming the cult and a brief Life.

St Mary-Magdalen Postel, *Foundress* (1756-1846)

Julie Françoise Catherine Postel was born in the small French port of Barfleur, near Cherbourg, in 1756, the daughter of Jean Postel and his wife, Thérèse Levallois. She was educated in a local school and then in the Benedictine convent in Valonges, where she decided to devote herself to God's service and made a private vow of virginity. The nuns wanted her to stay on as a postulant, but when she reached the age of eighteen she returned to her home town and opened a school for girls. The Revolution (1789) saw the church in Barfleur pass into the hands of the constitutional clergy, and Julia was one of those who refused to recognize their authority or accept the sacraments from them. She made a secret chapel under the stairs in her house so that Mass could be said there and the Blessed Sacrament reserved, and she was trusted so much by the clergy who served her chapel that she was allowed to carry Communion to the sick—St Pius X (26 Aug.) was to call her a "maiden-priest" at her beatification. In 1798 she became a Franciscan tertiary

After the concordat of 1801 Julia worked for four years to rebuild the faith of the people and restore parish life in the town: she taught, prepared children and adults for the sacraments, and organized works of mercy. There were some local difficulties, and so she moved to Cherbourg, where she had heard that the authorities needed teachers, and explained to a local priest, Abbé Cabart: "I want to teach the young and to inspire them with the love of God and a liking for work. I want to help the poor and relieve some of their misery. These are the things I want to do, and for long I have seen that I must have a religious Congregation to do it." He was supportive and found her a house, which she dedicated to Our Lady, Mother of Mercy; three other teachers joined her, and in 1807 the four of them made their religious vows. Julia took the name Mary-Magdalen in religion. Within three years she could report to the civil commissioners that they were educating two hundred young girls, teaching them their religion and handicrafts, rescuing others from the streets, and giving out large sums of money to help the poor.

In 1811, however, she and her Sisters left Cherbourg to make room for the Sisters of Providence, who had worked there before, and for the next few years failed to find a settled home where they could continue their teaching. At one stage matters were so desperate that Abbé Cabart urged them to disband, but Mary-Magdalen replied: "I am so certain that Our Lord wants me to succeed in achieving my dreams that I shall not cease pursuing them with the greatest ardour. He who has given my daughters to me and who watches over the birds of the air can easily provide me with the means to support them."

Another two years of extreme poverty were to pass before her trust was rewarded and they were able to settle in Tamerville and open a school. The Community began to grow in numbers and in 1832 they took over the dilapidated abbey of Saint-Sauveur-le-Vicomte. In 1837, however, Mary-Magdalen was required to give up the Rule she had been using for twenty-eight years, when the authorities in Rome insisted that she adopt that approved for the Brothers of the Christian Schools—hence the name of the Congregation became the Sisters of the Christian Schools of Mercy. After the Second Vatican Council they renamed themselves Sisters of St Mary-Magdalen Postel.

Expansion continued: the abbey was rebuilt, and the number of Sisters and schools increased, so that at the time of Mary-Magdalen's death on 16 July 1846 they numbered 150 Sisters in thirty-seven houses. Their work expanded to include the nursing of the poor and elderly at home as well as teaching. Their Constitution received provisional approval in 1901 and full approval in 1925, the year of Mary-Magdalen's canonization. In 1986 the Congregation numbered 636 Sisters in seventy-five houses throughout the world.

Mgr G. Grente, *Une sainte normande* (1946); J. Gautier, *La véritable vie héroïque de ste M-M. Postel* (1971); *Diz. Ist. Perf.*, 5, 963-4, and 8, 724-5.

17

St Speratus and Companions, *Martyrs* (180)

These martyrs, sometimes known as the Scillitan Martyrs, suffered during the last year of the persecution started by the emperor Marcus Aurelius, although the year of their death was the first of his successor Commodus' reign. There were twelve Christians in the group, seven men and five women, and they came from Scillium, somewhere in present-day Tunisia. When they were arrested they were taken to Carthage for examination by the proconsul, who offered to pardon them if they would worship the Roman gods and swear by the divine spirit of the emperor. Speratus replied: "I do not recognize the empire of this world. Rather, I serve that God whom no man has seen, nor can see, with these eyes. I have not stolen, and on any purchase I pay the tax, for I acknowledge my lord who is the emperor of kings and of all nations." The proconsul asked if they needed time to think the matter over, but Speratus spoke for the others when he said, "In so just a matter there is no need for deliberation." They all stressed their loyalty to Caesar, but their overriding duty was to obey and serve God. In passing sentence, the proconsul said that they were being condemned for "having acknowledged themselves as Christians and having refused an opportunity of returning to the Roman customs." Their names are given as Speratus, Aquilinus, Cittinus, Donata, Felix, Generosa, Januaria, Laetantius, Nartzalus, Secunda, Vestia, and Veturius. They were beheaded outside the city. The fact that they were not tortured and were executed by beheading may well indicate that they were Roman citizens. Their *acta* are considered authentic; they are the first dated Latin document from the Western Church and the first to mention the existence of a Latin Bible.

A.C.M., pp. xxii–xxiii, 86-9, from which the quotations above are taken.

SS Justa and Rufina, *Martyrs* (? 287)

According to an ancient tradition, Justa and Rufina were Christians who lived in Seville in Spain in the second half of the third century, earning a living by selling earthenware pots. When a procession in honour of the pagan gods passed their house one day, they refused to sell pots to be used in it, and the angry crowd destroyed their stock-in-trade; the two women retaliated by smashing the pagan statues. They were arrested and tortured to make them give up their Christian beliefs, but they persevered in refusing to honour the pagan gods. Justa died on the rack, Rufina was strangled or beheaded, and then their bodies were burned. The year of their death is given as 287, but there seems to be no evidence to support this.

There was a strong cult of the two martyrs in Spain, and they became the patron saints of Seville and other cities. Their names feature in early martyrologies, although the *Hieronymianum* does not mention Rufina, and in some lists Justa appears as Justus, a man. An account of their martyrdom that exists in a tenth-century manuscript may date back to the fifth century; its sober style and exact description of pagan rites and other historical detail would indicate that it was based on a strong oral or written tradition.

Bibl.SS., 6, 339-43.

The martyrs were a favourite subject for Spanish painters. A painting by Murillo, in Seville, shows them holding palms and a miniature of the large tower of Seville Cathedral, with a number of pots lying on the ground. Goya portrayed them with the cathedral in the background, a lion at their feet, and palms in their hands (in the Prado). A similar painting by Zurbarán is in Paris.

St Marcellina (*c.* 330-400)

Marcellina was the elder sister of St Ambrose (7 Dec.) and was probably born in Trier about the year 330, when their father was prefect there. She went to Rome with the family and in the year 353 consecrated herself to God's service before Pope Liberius in St Peter's. In his sermon on that occasion Liberius exhorted her to love only Our Lord Jesus Christ, to live in perpetual recollection and mortification, and always to behave in church with the utmost respect and awe. St Ambrose reports the sermon, adding to the pope's eloquence where he thought it insufficient for the occasion (*B.T.A.*). He dedicated his own work on the excellence of virginity to Marcellina. When he became bishop of Milan she used to visit him there and advise him on spiritual matters, continuing the work she had started when she had been entrusted with his early care and education. Three letters he wrote to her, in which he deals with the problems he was facing, have survived. Her own life was marked by great austerity, and toward the end of her life St Ambrose urged her to moderate her fasting and penance. She did not live in community but in a private house in Rome with a single companion. She died some time after Ambrose, who died in 397, and an ancient Life says that she died while St Simplician (15 Aug.) was bishop of Milan, which was from 397 to 401. When Ambrose preached a funeral sermon for St Satyrus (17 Sept.), their younger brother, he referred to Marcellina as "a holy sister, worshipful for her innocence, equally so for her uprightness, and no less so for her kindness to others." She was buried in the basilica of St Ambrose in Milan, near to her brother; in 1812 her relics were moved to a special chapel built in her honour from donations given by the faithful.

The main source for Marcellina's life are the writings of St Ambrose and a panegyric about her preserved by Mombritius. See *Bibl.SS.*, 8, 646-8.

St Ennodius of Pavia, *Bishop* (*c.* 473-521)

Magnus Felix Ennodius was born in Arles about the year 473 and brought up in Pavia (or possibly Milan). He married but then decided to enter the Church and so was ordained as a deacon, while his wealthy young wife became a nun. He taught rhetoric in Milan for some time before becoming bishop of Pavia in 514. He had already been involved in controversy, writing a defence of Pope St Symmachus (498-514; 19 July) against the antipope Laurence. Ennodius was a firm upholder of the rights of the papacy and wrote against those who challenged the papal synod of 502, arguing that of its nature the papal office was exempt from any control by the secular powers: "God certainly ordained that men should settle the affairs of men, but the passing of judgment on the pontiff of the supreme see God reserved to himself." Along with Dioscorus of Alexandria, Ennodius played a key part in settling the bitter disputes that followed the synod and lasted until 506, persuading King Theodoric to confirm the synod's findings in Symmachus' favour.

Pope St Hormisdas (514-23; 6 Aug.) sent Ennodius on two missions to the patriarch of Constantinople to try to bring about reconciliation between the two Churches, but neither mission was a success. As bishop of Pavia he gained a reputation for his work in converting sinners, relieving the poor, and building and decorating chuches. It is as a writer, however, that he is principally remembered today. His output was prolific and included an account of his own religious experiences (his so-called *Eucharisticon*, or *Thanksgiving*), a long panegyric of King Theodoric, Lives of St Antony of Lérins (28 Dec.) and of St Epiphanius of Pavia (21 Jan.), several discourses on various subjects, hymns (including two for the lighting of the paschal candle), and many poems, letters, epigrams, and epitaphs. His style is often turgid and tiresome and occasionally unintelligible, but his works are particularly valuable for the incidental light they throw on the events and culture of his age, and "his work reflects an attempt to combine a fundamentally pagan culture with the profession of the Christian creed" (*O.D.C.C.*). He died in 521, and his epitaph survives in the church of San Michele in Pavia. Early sources do not usually give him the title "saint," but he is included in the Roman Martyrology for today.

The main source for Ennodius' life is his own *Eucharisticon*. For his writings see *P.L.*, 63, 13-364. See also G. Bardy, *Le Christianisme et l'Occident barbare* (1945), pp. 229-64; *O.D.C.C.*, p. 547.

St Kenelm (Early Ninth Century)

Various calendars and liturgical books from about 975 onward include the name of St Kenelm (or Cynhelm) on 17 July and list him as a martyr. William of Malmesbury, writing in the first half of the twelfth century, says that it was St Dunstan (19 May; d. 988) who sanctioned his veneration as a martyr. There is no doubt that he was a historical person: he was the son of Kenulf (or

Coenwulf), king of Mercia from 796 to 821, and his sister was Quendreda (or Quoenthryth), at some stage abbess of Minster in Kent. In 798 Pope St Leo III (12 June) confirmed Kenelm's ownership of Glastonbury, and his name is found on charters from 803 to 811 with the titles *princeps* (prince) or *dux* (general or leader). As it is unlikely that he witnessed charters before he was sixteen years of age, he was probably about twenty-four in 811. We know nothing else about him except that he died in 812 or, possibly, 821 and was buried in Winchcombe, a leading Mercian centre and royal burial place. It is possible that he died at a relatively young age in battle. His father, whom he probably predeceased, was also buried in Winchcombe.

According to legend, however, Kenelm was only seven years old when he succeeded his father as king, and after ruling for just a few months he was murdered by his tutor at the instigation of his jealous sister; she was later punished by her eyes falling out as she practised her witchcraft by reading the Psalter backwards. This story is first found in the eleventh-century chronicle of Florence of Worcester. As the former edition of this work says, it was the sort of simple tale that attracted our ancestors and, decked out with astonishing details, made Kenelm widely venerated in England in the Middle Ages; as William of Malmesbury reported, "The little saint's body is solemnly revered, and hardly anywhere else in England is venerated by a greater throng of people attending a festival" (quoted in Bassett). Later versions of the legend describe how the boy's body was buried secretly by the murderer but discovered when a letter fell from a dove's beak onto the altar in St Peter's, Rome, and was translated by some English pilgrims who then found the grave. A blood-stained knife was found beside the body, and a spring of healing water gushed from the grave once the body had been removed. Kenelm's innocence as a young boy and the injustice of his death were sufficient for him to be venerated as a martyr.

The chapel of St Kenelm at Clent, near Stourbridge, was said to be the site of the murder, and the blocked arches under the east end of the church show where pilgrims used to approach the holy spring. Excavations at Winchcombe in the early nineteenth century unearthed two stone coffins, one holding the bones of an adult man, the other the bones of a child and a knife. The bones crumbled away but the coffins remain in the parish church and may well have been those of Kenulf and Kenelm (Anderson). Recent work has suggested that the crypt of the former church of St Pancras in Winchcombe may have been the original mausoleum of the royal pair, before their remains were moved to the nearby abbey church. The cult seems to have been in decline from the thirteenth century. Overall, one may agree with the verdict that "the Legend of Kenelm is a good example of how a writer with a vivid imagination and some half-understood historical data produced a completely fictitious account of a prince who certainly existed but of whom virtually nothing is known" (*O.D.S.*).

A short version of the legend is in *N.L.A.*, 2, pp. 110-3. See S. R. Bassett, "A probable Mercian royal Mausoleum at Winchcombe," *Antiquaries Journal*, 65 (1985), pp. 82-100; M. D. Anderson, *History and Imagery in British Churches* (1971, 1995), pp. 44-5 and plate; *O.D.S.*, pp. 279-80.

There is a statue of St Kenelm in Wells Cathedral, which shows him wearing a crown and standing on the body of a woman who has fallen forward onto a book, presumably a reference to the fate of his sister. A modern window in St Kenelm's church in Clent illustrates the legend.

St Leo IV, *Pope* (855)

Leo was Roman by birth but probably of Lombard descent. He was brought up in the Benedictine monastery of San Martino, near St Peter's, where he became a monk. His first official post was as a curial subdeacon under Gregory IV (827-44). Gregory's successor, Sergius II (844-47), made him a cardinal priest of SS Quattro Coronati (the church of the Four Crowned Martyrs; 8 Nov.), and he was elected pope unanimously on Sergius' death, without the required reference to the emperor, apparently on the grounds that the Saracen raids that were threatening Rome made it imperative to have a strong leader in the city. Leo set about strengthening the walls and defences to prevent a repeat of what had happened the previous year when the Saracens had sailed up the Tiber and raided the city, desecrating the tombs of SS Peter and Paul. With financial help from the emperor, Lothair I, he had new walls built around St Peter's and the Vatican hill, creating what became known as the "Leonine city," whose massive walls and towers can still be seen—"both a demonstration of independent papal vigour, and an organizational triumph" (Duffy). Meanwhile, he organized the fleets of Amalfi, Gaeta, and Naples and defeated the Saracens in a decisive sea battle off Ostia in 849. In 854 he set about rebuilding the town of Centumcellae on a safer site and named the new town Leopolis (present-day Civitavecchia). Finally, as part of these comprehensive defences he garrisoned Porto with Corsican refugees. Leo was hailed as the saviour of the city, and the personal respect he enjoyed helped to restore papal authority.

In ecclesiastical matters Leo was just as decisive and strong-minded. He denounced Hincmar, archbishop of Reims, and John, archbishop of Ravenna—both powerful prelates—and excommunicated Anastasius, cardinal of San Marcello, despite the emperor's support of him. He backed the Breton bishops against the duke of Brittany and refused the emperor's requests to have Hincmar made apostolic vicar and the bishop of Autun given the *pallium*. He annulled the decrees of the Synod of Soissons (853) and ordered it to be held again, this time with papal legates in the chair. His relations with the western emperors were marked by a sensible balance: he sought their approval of episcopal appointments, and he crowned and anointed Lothair's son, Louis II, in Rome in 850, but as the examples already given show, he refused to let them dictate ecclesiastical policy or interfere in important appointments. He ordered the execution of three imperial agents who had murdered a papal legate, despite the strain that this put on his relations with Lothair. With the Eastern Church and emperor he was equally unbending: he objected when the patriarch deposed a Sicilian bishop without consulting him and summoned both prelates to Rome so that he could settle the matter.

The list of Leo's benefactions to churches takes up twenty-eight pages in the *Liber Pontificalis*, and he was as keen on restoring church discipline as he was on making sure that the liturgy was performed in suitable surroundings. In 849 he replied at length to a list of questions on disciplinary matters submitted by the bishops of England; four years later he reminded a North African bishop that the ancient penitential code had to be enforced. A council that he held in St Peter's in 853 upheld the reforming decrees of his predecessor Eugene II on such issues as clerical education, Sunday observance, simony, and marriage. His liturgical reforms were concerned mainly with the proper observance of what he referred to in a letter to an erring abbot as "the sweet chant of St Gregory . . . [in use among] all those who use the Latin tongue to pay their tribute to the King of Heaven." He also established the observance of an octave for the feast of the Assumption of Our Lady.

An outstanding organizer and firm believer in the universal jurisdiction of his office, Leo was also a saintly person untouched by the least breath of scandal or corruption, and this personal integrity served to add weight to the revival of papal prestige brought about by his secular and ecclesiastical leadership.

O.D.P., pp. 104-5; *O.D.C.C.*, p. 968; Eamon Duffy, *Saints and Sinners, A History of the Popes* (1997), pp. 78-9.

A ninth-century fresco in San Clemente in Rome shows Leo with a halo and holding a book. A dangerous fire in the Borgo district of Rome was said to have been extinguished by Leo's prayers, and this forms the subject of a painting by a pupil of Raphael in the Sala dell'Incendio di Borgo in the Vatican.

St Hedwig of Poland (1374-99)

Hedwig (or Jadwiga) was born in 1374, the daughter of Louis Angevin, king of Hungary and Poland, and his wife, Elizabeth of Bosnia. She was barely a year old when she was bethrothed to Wilhelm, Habsburg heir to the grand duchy of Austria and four years her senior. The two children met in 1378 and exchanged solemn vows by proxy, after which Hedwig was sent to the Habsburg court in Vienna to be educated for her future role as grand duchess. She was soon back in Buda, however, as her eldest sister Catherine died, and Hedwig was chosen by her father to succeed him as queen of Hungary in place of Catherine. He died unexpectedly in 1382, when Hedwig was only eight years old, but the Hungarians rejected her as queen in favour of her sister Maria, who had already been accepted by the Polish nobility as their future queen. After considerable diplomatic activity and political intrigue, Hedwig was chosen by the Poles as their queen in place of Maria and arrived in her new country in the summer of 1384. She was crowned that same year, and it remained only for her to marry so that the succession could be secured. Despite her earlier vows, the Polish nobles decided that she should marry Jagiello, the grand duke of Lithuania and Ruthenia, who was not yet a Christian—he promised to be baptized if the marriage went ahead. The Habsburgs tried to persuade the young queen to accept Wilhelm as her husband, and he travelled to Cracow to claim his bride, but she refused and, perhaps reluctantly, agreed to the choice of her advisers. Jagiello, his brothers, and the leading Lithuanian nobles were baptized in February 1386 in Cracow Cathedral, and the royal wedding took place later that month; Hedwig was twelve years old (the age of maturity at the time), he was thirty-six. The union of Poland, Lithuania, and Ruthenia promised to make a powerful State capable of resisting the expansionist designs of both Germany and Moscow.

The Habsburg court did not allow the matter to rest, and malicious reports were circulated that Wilhelm and Hedwig had consummated their marriage when he had visited her and that he had been crowned king. Hedwig was declared an adulteress and a bigamist and Jagiello a usurper, false convert, and a bride snatcher. While these reports were malicious and politically motivated there were some legal grounds for the Habsburg case in the official betrothal ceremony that had taken place in 1378, which normally created a barrier to marriage with another person. Presumably the Habsburgs added the story of the consummation of the marriage because the legal case was very much weakened by Hedwig's young age at the time of the betrothal. The charges did considerable damage to the young queen's standing outside Poland, especially when they were repeated in the chronicles of the Teutonic Knights, who had their own reasons for disliking Jagiello. They received even wider dissemination in the works of Enea Silvio Piccolomini (the future Pope Pius II) in the following century, and the high regard he enjoyed as a writer added weight to them. The slanders continued even after a papal statement in 1388 praised the royal couple, called Jagiello "a most Christian prince," and rejoiced in his Baptism; a later pope, Boniface IX, agreed to stand as godfather to the child Hedwig was expecting.

Meanwhile, Jagiello turned to the task of Christianizing Lithuania in accordance with the promise he had made at his wedding. He went there in 1386 with teams of missionaries and personally took part in the destruction of the pagan temples and sacred groves. Force was not used to compel the people to be baptized, but royal decrees insisted on it, and the people were baptized in groups after fairly minimal instruction—apparently none of the missionaries spoke Lithuanian. A diocese was set up in the capital, Vilnius, and both Jagiello and Hedwig sent chalices, pictures, and vestments for the new cathedral and churches. Later she endowed a college in Prague for the education of Lithuanian priests.

The queen wished to unite the Latin and Orthodox Christians in her territories. She admired the beauty of the Byzantine liturgy and brought in from Prague some monks who used a Slavonic rite to help build bridges between the two groups, and Jagiello founded a monastery of Slavonic Benedictines outside Cracow. She also turned her attention to the liturgy in Cracow Cathedral. She wished to make it a centre of perpetual adoration, in return for the graces that God had granted her, and so founded a "college of psalmists," a group of sixteen priests who took it in turns to sing the psalms in the cathedral twenty-four hours a day, only stopping if a service was in progress.

During her reign she had to deal with a number of revolts and with an invasion of Lithuania by the Teutonic Knights. The politics involved were complicated, but Hedwig always tried to find a peaceful solution and even succeeded in defeating the powerful Knights through careful negotiation and compromise. Early in 1399 she retired from public life since she was expecting a child. A daughter was born prematurely in June but died after three weeks; Hedwig herself died four days later, on 17 July. She was buried in Wawel Cathedral. Her will asked for all her personal possessions to be sold and the proceeds used to help in the restoration of Cracow University. Her cult spread rapidly, and an account of the miracles worked through her intercession was kept in a special register. She was usually referred to as "Blessed" and the cause for her canonization was opened in 1426. In later centuries, as Poland was partitioned, she became the ideal of Polish nationalism: "This life, so short, but entirely devoted to a great cause, marks, like the life of Joan of Arc in the history of France and the west, the most decisive turning point in the destiny of Poland and eastern Europe" (Halecki). She was not beatified until 1986. Pope John Paul II canonized her in Cracow in 1997.

The most recent work in English is B. Przybyszewski, *Saint Jadwiga, Queen of Poland (1374-1399)* (Eng. trans. by Bruce MacQueen, 1997). See also Oscar Halecki, *History of Poland* (2d. ed., 1983), pp. 65-74; T. Silnicki, "Queen Jadwiga, 1374-1399," in J. Braun (ed.), *Poland in Christian Civilization* (1985), pp. 211-44.

The Martyrs of Compiègne (1794)

The first victims of the French Revolution to be beatified (in 1906) were a group of Carmelite nuns from Compiègne and a layman, Mulot de la Ménardière, who had helped them. The nuns had left their convent and were living in private houses, wearing secular dress but doing their best to continue their Carmelite way of life. They were arrested in June 1794 on the charge of continuing to live their religious life and plotting against the Republic; Mulot de la Ménardière was arrested at the same time and charged with helping the nuns in their crimes. They were imprisoned at first in the Visitation convent in Compiègne, along with the English Benedictine nuns from Cambrai, and while there they retracted the Oath of Allegiance to the Republic that they had taken in 1790. They were then taken to Paris, tried, and condemned to death for having made themselves "enemies of the people by conspiring against its sovereign rule." Sixteen nuns and Mulot de la Ménardière were guillotined on 17 July 1794. Three other members of the community were spared the guillotine through infirmity or prior death.

The group comprised ten choir-nuns, a novice, three lay Sisters, and two externs. They were Marie Madeleine-Claudine Lidoine, in religion Sr Thérèse de Saint-Augustin, prioress, aged forty-one; Marie-Anne Françoise Brideau, Sr Saint-Louis, subprioress, aged forty-two; Marie-Anne Piedcourt, Sr de Jésus-Crucifié, aged seventy-eight; Anne-Marie Madeleine Thouret, Sr Charlotte de la Résurrection, aged seventy-eight; Marie-Claude Brard, Sr Euphrasie de l'Immaculée Conception, aged fifty-eight; Marie-Françoise de Croissy, Mère Henriette de Jésus, aged forty-nine; Marie-Anne Hanisset, Sr Thérèse du Coeur de Marie, aged fifty-two; Marie-Gabrielle Trézel, Sr de Saint-Ignace, aged fifty-one; Rose Chrétien de Neuville, Sr Julie-Louise de Jésus, aged fifty-two; Marie Annette Pelras, Sr Marie-Henriette de la Providence, aged thirty-four; Angélique Roussel, Sr Marie du Saint-Esprit, aged fifty-one; Marie Dufour, Sr Sainte-Marthe, aged fifty-two; Elisabeth Juliette Vérolot, Sr Saint-François-Xavier, aged thirty; the novice Marie-Geneviève Meunier, Sr Constance, aged twenty-nine; and two externs, the sisters Catherine and Thérèse Soiron, aged fifty-two and forty-six.

See the general entry on the Martyrs of the French Revolution (1792-4) under 2 January, and the bibliography given there. One member of the Carmelite Community, the former prioress Mère Josephine, left in the spring of 1794 but re-entered the Carmel at Sens in 1823; she wrote a valuable account of the events up to June 1794, which was published in 1836 after her death.

Bd Peter ToRot, *Martyr* (1912-45)

Peter ToRot was born in 1912 in Rakunai, a village on the Melanesian island of New Britain, today an eastern province of Papua New Guinea. His parents, Angelo ToPuia, the village chief, and Maria IaTumul, had been baptized as adults and belonged to the area's first generation of Catholics. A local priest thought that Peter had a vocation to the priesthood, but his father refused to give permission on the grounds that none of his people were yet mature enough in the Faith to be ordained. He agreed, however, that his son could become a lay catechist, and so in 1930 Peter enrolled at a mission school to begin his training. A contemporary account spoke of his lack of vanity with regard to both his background and his abilities; he seems to have become the unofficial leader of the catechists while still comparatively young. He was effective as a teacher, basing his approach firmly on the scriptures and developing a sensitivity to other people's problems. In 1936 he married Paula IaVarpit, one of his former pupils.

In 1942 the Japanese imprisoned all the missionaries but allowed Peter to continue his work. He organized prayer services and the distribution of Holy Communion, baptized adults and children, and cared for the poor. The Japanese had destroyed the church in Rakunai, and Peter put up a makeshift building to replace it on the outskirts of the village. He appeared to be on reasonably good terms with the occupying authorities until the Japanese armies began to suffer reverses in other parts of the Pacific; then the military police took over and imposed a much more rigorous régime. They forbade all Christian worship, public or private, and tried to re-introduce the practice of polygamy. Finally, in April or May 1945, they arrested Peter and sentenced him to two months' imprisonment. The main charge against him seems to have been his opposition to the decree on polygamy—as he put it himself, "I am here because of those who broke their marriage vows and because of those who do not want the growth of God's kingdom." He even broke off relations with his own brother when he took advantage of the new decree to divorce his wife and take a different partner. Peter was kept in prison after his sentence was over and on 17 July 1945 was given a lethal injection by one of the prison doctors; he died after a few hours of severe physical suffering.

A very large crowd attended the funeral, and local people had no doubt that Peter had been murdered for his faith and his defence of the Christian ideal of marriage. His cult continued after the end of the war. He was beatified in January 1995 by Pope John Paul II at a special Mass in Port Moresby, New Guinea. In his sermon the Pope praised Peter for his refusal to take the "easy way of moral compromise," and quoted his statement: "I have to fulfil my duty as a Church witness to Jesus Christ."

The above is based largely on the account of the beatification by Renato Simeone, M.S.C., in *L'Osservatore Romano* (English ed.), 25 January 1995. Use has also been made of the account of the Pope's visit to New Guinea in the Port Moresby *Post-Courier*, 13 January 1995.

ST MARY MAGDALEN (p. 164, below)
Identified by iconographers with the penitent who anointed Jesus
with precious ointment.
White pot with gold cover and base, teardrops on divided
purple and black field

18

St Philastrius, *Bishop* (Late Fourth Century)

According to tradition, Philastrius (or more correctly, Filaster) travelled through many provinces of the empire in the fourth century and made a reputation as a seeker-out of heretics, especially the Arians. St Gaudentius (25 Oct.) likened him to Abraham, who left his family and native land to follow God's word. He is said to have been scourged and to have suffered other injuries at the hands of the heretics, and in Milan he opposed the activities of Auxentius, who was trying to lead the people there into error, while in Rome he held public disputations with the heretics. How much of this is true is difficult to say, but we do know that he became bishop of Brescia sometime before the year 381, for he attended the Council of Aquileia in that year. In order to warn his people and clergy against false teachers he wrote his *Catalogue of Heresies*. This is a refutation of twenty-eight Jewish and 128 Christian heresies and disputed opinions; it suffers from "clumsy arrangement and a certain lack of proportion" (*O.D.C.C.*), including, for example, the "heresy" of those who gave the days of the week pagan names, or refused to believe that God re-positioned the stars in the sky every night. It has little value in theological terms but does throw some light on the views of other writers, such as Hippolytus, and was used by St Augustine (28 Aug.), who met Philastrius with St Ambrose (7 Dec.) in Milan in 384. In his panegyric on Philastrius, St Gaudentius, who succeeded him as bishop of Brescia, praised his modesty, quietness, and "sweetness toward all," which included helping tradespeople who asked for his assistance to establish or carry on their businesses. He died some time before Ambrose, who died in 397 and who had appointed Gaudentius as Philastrius' successor. He was buried in the cathedral of St Andrew in Brescia, which he may have built. In 838 his remains were moved to the church of Santa Maria and finally, in 1674, to the new cathedral.

The main source is the panegyric written by St Gaudentius for the fourteenth anniversary of Philastrius' death; its authenticity has been questioned, but it is reliable enough in outline, although most of it is very generalized. The *Catalogue* is in *P.L.*, 12, 1111-1302. See *Bibl.SS.*, 5, 684-5; *O.D.C.C.*, pp. 1273-4.

St Pambo (*c.* 390)

Pambo (or Pamo) was an Egyptian, born about the year 303. As a young man he may have been a disciple of St Antony (17 Jan.); he was one of the first to join St Ammon in Nitria in Lower Egypt, and he is considered to be one of the founders of the Nitrian monasteries. He was ordained about the year 340, and we are told that St Macarius of Alexandria (2 Jan.) was present at his first Mass. His life was typical of the desert monks: hard manual labour, long fasts and physical penance, and sustained periods of prayer. Pambo was especially noted for his silence and a reluctance to speak any more than was necessary, seeing in control of the tongue a basic first step toward a deeper spirituality; he is said to have meditated on this verse from the Psalms for six months: "I will watch how I behave, and not let my tongue lead me into sin" (Ps. 39:1). On the other hand, he had a broader outlook than many of his colleagues in the desert and did not believe that their way of life was necessarily the best; he settled an argument between two monks as to which was more perfect, becoming a monk or staying in the world and doing works of mercy, by saying: "Before God both are perfect. There are other roads to perfection besides being a monk."

His constant theme in teaching others was "Guard your conscience toward your neighbour, and you will be saved." He was held in high regard by St Athanasius (2 May), who invited him to Alexandria. He was visited by St Melania the Elder while she was in Egypt, and she gave him three hundred pieces of silver. Pambo did not examine the gift, merely saying "May God reward you." Melania expected to be thanked more effusively and pointed out how large her gift was, to which Pambo replied, "My child, he who measures the mountains knows better the amount of silver. If you are giving it to me, you spoke well; but if you are giving it to God, who did not overlook the two obols, then be quiet."

As he was dying he said to his disciple Palladius, "Since I came to this place of the desert and built my cell and dwelt here, I do not remember having eaten bread which was not the fruit of my hands and I have not repented of a word I have said up to the present time; and yet I am going to God as one who has not yet begun to serve him." Pambo is said to have died about the year 390, and Palladius gives his age at death as seventy. He stood out among the Egyptian solitaries as a defender of Nicene orthodoxy (Meyer).

Most of what is known about Pambo comes from Palladius' *Lausiac History*, written about the year 420; Eng. trans. by R. T. Meyer (1965); see especially pp. 44–7. See *Coptic Encyc.*, 6, pp. 1877–8; B. Ward (trans.), *The Sayings of the Desert Fathers* (1975), pp. 164–6, and *The Lives of the Desert Fathers* (1981), from which the quotations above are taken.

St Arnulf of Metz, *Bishop* (*c*. 582-640)

Arnulf (or Arnoul) was born about the year 582, served at the court of Theodebert II, king of Austrasia (present-day eastern France and western Germany), and gained a reputation for his skill as a royal counsellor and his military exploits. He married a woman named Doda, and they had two sons, Clodulf, a future bishop of Metz, and Ansegisel, the father of Pepin of Héristal. After some years he wished to retire to the monastery of Lérins, but the clergy and people of Metz asked for him as their bishop; he was consecrated about the year 610. There is no information about his activities as bishop except that he attended two councils, at Clichy in 626 and at Reims in 630, but he continued to play a part in politics and was one of the nobles who on Theodebert's death invited Clotaire to become king of Austrasia as well as Neustria (present-day western France). Ten years later Clotaire divided the kingdoms again and made his son Dagobert king of Austrasia, with Arnulf as his chief counsellor. Soon after this, however, Arnulf resigned from the court and his diocese and retired to a hermitage in the Vosges mountains with his friend St Romaric (8 Dec.). He died there about the year 640. His remains were later moved to the church in Metz named after him. Under Romaric the hermitage developed into the monastery of Remiremont.

A contemporary Latin Life is in *M.G.H., Scriptores Merov.*, 2, pp. 426-46. See *Bibl.SS.*, 2, 446-7.

St Frederick of Utrecht, *Bishop and Martyr* (838)

Frederick was a priest in Utrecht, where he was put in charge of instructing converts. The English chronicler William of Malmesbury calls him Fridericus Cridiodunus (that is, from Crediton in Devon, the birthplace of St Boniface) and makes him a nephew of St Boniface (5 June), but there is no reliable evidence for this; it is just possible that he was English, perhaps from Wessex, although it is much more likely that he was a Frisian. Whatever his country of origin, he became bishop of Utrecht about the year 825 and was responsible for sending missionaries, including St Odulf (12 June), to the northern parts of the Low Countries, including Friesland, where Boniface had been murdered in 754. He took part in the Council of Magonza in 829.

According to tradition, Frederick became involved in the quarrels between the emperor, Louis the Pious, and his sons, who resented the position of the empress Judith, their stepmother—it may be that Louis' first wife was still alive. They accused her of immorality, and Frederick felt obliged to remonstrate with her. She resented his assumption that the accusations were true and became his implacable enemy. He also became unpopular with the people of Walcheren, who objected to the evangelizing missions sent out by the bishop and, in particular, to any attempts to regularize their marriage customs; they were so difficult to deal with that Frederick himself went there as a missioner. He was murdered on 18 July 838. An eleventh-century Life and William of Malmesbury claim that the murderers were working for Judith, but this seems very unlikely and quite out of character. It is more likely that the murderers were disaffected inhabitants of Walcheren. Frederick was buried in the church of the Most Holy Saviour, Utrecht.

Frederick composed a hymn to the Trinity that was used for many centuries in the Low Countries. His cult owed a great deal to a poem in his honour by Rabanus Maurus (*c.* 780-856; 4 Feb.), abbot of Fulda, archbishop of Mainz, and one of the foremost theologians of his age; he also dedicated his commentary on the book of Joshua to Frederick. An eleventh-century Life by Oetbert has no historical value.

Bibl.SS., 5, 529-31; *D.N.B.*, 13, pp. 94-5.

St Bruno of Segni, *Bishop* (1049-1123)

Bruno was born into the family of the lords of Asti in Piedmont in 1049. After his studies in Bologna and Siena he was made a canon of the cathedral in Siena, and in 1079 he was in Rome to attend a council, although his name does not appear in its official documents, at which he seems to have defended the orthodox doctrine on the Blessed Sacrament against the teaching of Berengarius of Tours. The following year he was appointed bishop of Segni by Pope St Gregory VII (25 May) and "entered with fearless enthusiasm into all his [Gregory's] projects for the reform of the Church" (*B.T.A.*), especially in relation to lay investiture. Bruno accompanied Bd Urban II (29 July) to France in 1095, when the pope launched the First Crusade, and attended the Council of Tours. On his return to his diocese he was imprisoned for three months by one of Gregory's opponents, Count Ainulf, a strong supporter of the emperor, Henry IV, and later withdrew to Monte Cassino in the face of continued opposition to his reforms. He received the monastic habit, and when the people of Segni demanded his return the abbot persuaded the pope to allow him to remain in the monastery but at the same time to keep his post as bishop; Bruno became abbot of Monte Cassino in 1107.

He continued to be interested in reform, writing against simony and lay investiture, and as papal legate in France (1106) and Sicily (1110) was involved in reforming the clergy. When he rebuked Pope Paschal II (1099-1118), however, for making concessions to the emperor-elect in Germany, Paschal responded by ordering him to resign as abbot and return to his diocese, which he did, remaining there until his death in 1123. Bruno wrote extensively, including a life of St Leo IX (1049-54; 19 Apr.) and three liturgical works, and was the leading scriptural commentator of his age in Italy; in theology he maintained the erroneous view that sacraments administered by simoniacal clergy were invalid. He was canonized in 1183.

There are two early Lives of Bruno, one by Peter the Deacon, the other, and more reliable, by an anonymous comtemporary; see *Bibl.SS.*, 3, 578-80. Bruno's works are in *P.L.*, 164 and 165.

Bd Simon of Lipnicza (*c.* 1440-82)

Simon was born between 1435 and 1440 in Lipnicza Murowana, Poland. As a young man he showed signs of unusual piety, especially toward Our Lady, and while he was studying at Cracow University he came under the influence of St John of Capistrano (23 Oct.), who had set up the first house of Franciscan Observant Friars there in 1453. Simon wished to join them but was persuaded to finish his studies first. He then became a friar and was ordained priest sometime before 1465. His ability and devotion led to his promotion within the Order: from 1465 he was guardian of the house at Tarnow and a member of the provincial chapter in Cracow. He had been appointed official preacher in Wawel Cathedral two years earlier, the first Franciscan to displace the Dominicans from the post. It was for his preaching that he became famous, especially for his clear exposition of the scriptures, and many conversions were attributed to his skillful handling of difficult topics. In 1478 he was made definitor of the Order in Cracow and travelled to Pavia for a general chapter. From there he went on to Rome and the Holy Land, hoping, apparently, for a martyr's death at the hands of the Turks.

He was back in Cracow by 1482, when a terrible outbreak of plague struck the city. Simon and the other Franciscans were involved in caring for the victims, and Simon himself caught the infection. As he lay dying he asked to be buried under the entrance of the church so that those entering it would be trampling on his remains. He died on 18 July 1482 and was beatified in 1685. His feast used to be celebrated on 30 July.

Bibl.SS., 11, 1181-2; *Vies des Saints*, 7, pp. 423-4.

19

St Macrina the Younger (c. 330-79)

Macrina was the eldest of the ten children of St Basil the Elder and St Emmelia. She was born about the year 330 in Caesarea in Cappadocia and at the age of twelve was betrothed to be married. When her fiancé died suddenly, however, she vowed not to marry and remained at home to help in the education of her brothers, among whom were St Basil the Great (2 Jan.), St Peter of Sebaste, and St Gregory of Nyssa (9 Mar.). Later Basil established his mother and Macrina on an estate in Pontus, where they lived a communal life and were joined by other women. When her mother died, about the year 373, Macrina gave away all her possessions and lived on what she could earn by her own labours; when she died in 379 she was so poor that nothing could be found to cover her body but a coarse veil. She was buried in the church of the Forty Martyrs of Sebaste. At some stage she had become superior of a double monastery at Annesi, on the other side of the river from Basil and his community.

This account of Macrina is based on the Life written by her brother Gregory in the form of a letter to a solitary named Olympius. He also wrote a treatise, *De anima et resurrectione* ("On the soul and resurrection"), in the form of a dialogue between himself and Macrina as she lay dying. In the Life he describes a miracle that she worked to heal the diseased eye of a young girl, and he comments on other reported miracles: "Though they seem incredible, they are all believed to be true by those who have carefully investigated them. But they are judged by the carnally-minded to be outside the possible," and so he would not list them, "lest the unbeliever should suffer hurt by being led to disbelieve the gifts of God."

W. K. Lowther Clarke, *St Gregory of Nyssa: The Life of St Macrina* (1916); M. Kloeppe, *Macrina die Jüngere, eine altchristliche Frauengestalt* (1964); *Vies des Saints*, 7, pp. 444-8.

St Arsenius (c. 360- 450)

Arsenius (sometimes named the Great, or the Roman, or the Deacon) was born in Rome about the year 350. He was of senatorial rank and well educated, and according to tradition, when the emperor Theodosius I asked Pope St Damasus I (366-84) to suggest a suitable tutor for his two sons, Arsenius was the person he recommended. Arsenius spent about the next ten years at the imperial court in Constantinople without having much success in giving the young princes, Arcadius and Honorius, a Christian outlook on life or a responsible attitude to their calling. There is some doubt, however, about this traditional account, and Arsenius may just have been an official at the court. In any case, he retired to Alexandria in 394 to become a monk and put himself under the direction of St John Kolobos (17 Oct.) at Scetis in Lower Egypt. His learning and background did not endear him to the other monks, nor, initially, to St John himself, but Arsenius overcame a series of trials and was eventually accepted as having a genuine vocation to be a hermit. He lived as a solitary near Petra, about thirty miles from the main settlement, attracting very few disciples and gaining a reputation for austerity and silence. When asked why he avoided the other monks, he replied: "God knows that I love you, but I cannot live with God and with men. The thousands and ten thousands of the heavenly hosts have but one will, while men have many. So I cannot leave God to be with men." It is said that he would even stand behind a pillar in the church to avoid attracting any attention. After about forty years the settlement at Scetis was destroyed for the second time in barbarian raids, and so Arsenius moved to the mountain of Troë (modern Turah, about ten miles south-east of Cairo) and then to the island of Canopus, near Alexandria. Finding that he was too close to the city and its distractions, he moved back to Troë, where he died sometime between 440 and 450. He is named in the Canon of the Armenian Mass and is held in high esteem in the Coptic Church, as well as being venerated in the Greek Church.

Some writings attributed to him, including a letter in Georgian that is almost certainly authentic, survive. This shows his spirituality to have been strongly scriptural; for the monk he stresses attachment to his cell, perseverance, abstinence from sleep as well as food, and constant prayer.

A Greek Life was written by St Theodore the Studite (11 Nov.). A large number of Arsenius' sayings and teachings have survived; see B. Ward (trans. and ed.), *The Sayings of the Desert Fathers* (1975), pp. 7-17, from which the quotation above is taken. On his letter see M. Van Parys, "La Lettre de saint Arsène," in *Irenikon* 54 (1981), pp. 62-86. See also D. J. Chitty, *The Desert a City* (1966); *Coptic Encyc.*, 1, pp. 240-1.

St Symmachus, *Pope* (514)

Symmachus was Sardinian by birth and a convert from paganism. He was a deacon in Rome when he was elected in 498 to succeed Pope Anastasius II. He was the choice of a majority of the clergy who had objected to Anastasius' policy toward the East, because they believed that he had been willing to make too many concessions to heal the schism between the two Churches. On the same day as Symmachus was elected in the Lateran basilica, a group of pro-Eastern aristocrats and their clerical supporters in Santa Maria Maggiore elected Laurence, the archpriest of St Praxedes in Rome, as pope. Laurence had the support of most of the senate and especially of its leader, Festus, who was a supporter of the emperor, and the rival parties in Rome formed factions that caused serious breaches of the peace and threatened to disrupt both city and

Church. Symmachus and Laurence appealed to King Theodoric at Ravenna to resolve the dispute, and he decided in favour of Symmachus on the grounds that he had the larger number of supporters—and, no doubt, because Symmachus was sympathetic to the Gothic king and opposed any increase of imperial power in Italy. Symmachus straightaway held a synod in Rome, which banned all discussion of the papal succession while a pope was alive and decreed that a pope could name his own successor; if he had not done so when he died, the clergy should elect his successor, but the laity were barred from taking part. Laurence accepted the judgment and was appointed bishop of Nuceria in Campania.

Laurence's supporters, however, had not given up. They accused the pope of not celebrating Easter according to the new calendar, of being unchaste in his way of life, and of misusing church property. Theodoric called Symmachus to Ravenna to answer these charges, but the pope took fright and took refuge in St Peter's. The king took this as an admission of guilt and appointed a visitor to rule in Symmachus' place until an Italian synod had met to judge the issues. The synod ended in 502 and found in Symmachus' favour on the grounds that as he was pope "no human court could judge him and judgment must be left to God" (*O.D.P.*). Again Symmachus called his own synod without delay and issued a decree prohibiting any alienation of church properties by a pope; this, he hoped, would prevent laypeople being rewarded for their support and so reduce their interference and also show that Symmachus was innocent of the charges against him. The king, however, was unhappy with Symmachus' acquittal and was going through a pro-Eastern phase, so he encouraged Laurence to return to Rome, where he ruled for four years as pope from the Lateran, while Symmachus had to stay in St Peter's because of the rioting and bloodshed organized by his opponents. It was during this period that the so-called Symmachian Forgeries were produced, documents based on spurious precedents and aimed at showing that the pope was not subject to human judges. Eventually in 506 Theodoric ended the divisions in Rome by accepting Symmachus' innocence and ordering Festus and his supporters to hand control of Rome back to him. The king's change of heart was partly a result of his change of policy toward Constantinople and partly due to the diplomatic activity of St Ennodius (17 July) and the Alexandrian deacon Dioscurus.

Restored to power, Symmachus exercised his ministry vigorously, expelling the Manichaeans from Rome, sending generous gifts to victims of Arian persecution in Africa, and paying ransoms for prisoners taken in Italian wars (*O.D.P.*). He built or restored numerous churches in Rome and extended the buildings of St Peter's to include a papal residence and facilities for pilgrims. He was the first pope to send the *pallium* to a non-Italian bishop when he conferred primatial rights on St Caesarius of Arles (27 Aug.). In an effort to heal the breach between the two Churches, the emperor Anastasius I invited Symmachus to preside over a council in Heraclea to settle the doctrinal differences that were dividing the Eastern Church, but Symmachus had died, on 19 July 514, by the time the invitation reached Rome. An ardent supporter of the rights of the papacy and a fierce opponent of any lay interference in ecclesiastical matters, Symmachus was not always judicious in his actions, and the bitterness that had marked his reign in Rome (most of it, admittedly, not of his making) was "fuelled according to his critics by his own misconduct. . . . Many, including the saintly deacon Paschasius, never became reconciled to him" (*O.D.P.*). He was buried in the portico of St Peter's.

O.D.P., pp. 50-2; *O.D.C.C.*, p. 1567.

St Bernulf of Utrecht, *Bishop* (1054)

Bernulf (or, more correctly, Bernold) was appointed bishop of Utrecht by the emperor, Conrad II. Conrad's usual practice in making episcopal appointments makes it likely that Bernulf would have been an official of some sort at the imperial court and well known to the emperor, who always supported the bishops once they were appointed and remained on friendly terms with most of them. A good part of Bernulf's efforts as bishop was taken up with extending the lands of his see, and he was helped in this both by Conrad and by King Henry, who succeeded Conrad in 1046 as Henry III. Henry was a friend of Bernulf and granted him additional estates when he visited Utrecht in 1040 and again in 1042 after an expedition against the Hungarians, in which Bernulf probably took part. These and other donations angered the lay lords of Lorraine, and in 1046, when Henry was in Rome, they formed a league against him. Despite the league's support from the Saxons, the Danes, England, and even Pope St Leo IX (19 Apr.), Henry was able to defeat the rebels. He followed up his victory with a council at Aachen in 1049, presided over by the pope, at which he confirmed and increased the lands of the diocese of Utrecht.

Bernulf's other principal interest as bishop was reform. He attended a national synod at Frankfurt and supported Conrad when he reduced episcopal rights over the Benedictine abbey at Amersfoort, even though this had been an episcopal foundation and Bernulf lost some of his authority as a result. Bernulf promoted Cluniac reforms in the monasteries in his diocese and was active in reducing lay control over various churches. He was responsible for the building of three churches in Utrecht itself and a fourth in Deventer.

Bernulf died on 19 July 1054. His veneration as a saint dates back to at least the late fourteenth century. The Netherlands artists chose him as their patron when they set up their guild in 1917.

D.H.G.E., 8 (1935), 856-7; *Bibl.SS.*, 3, 79-80.

Bd Stilla (*c.* 1140)

Stilla was born into the family of the counts of Abenberg, near Nuremberg, toward the end of the eleventh century. What is known about her life is soon told: she may have been one of three sisters who helped to endow the convent at Heilbronn, and she lived at home as a nun. In 1136 she built at her own expense a chapel dedicated to St Peter, which she used to visit every day and where she may have made a vow of virginity in the presence of St Otto (2 July), bishop of Bamberg. Apparently she hoped to build a monastery nearby but died before it could be started.

Despite some opposition from her family, she was buried in her private chapel, and her tomb became a place of pilgrimage, but there seems to have been no early medieval cult, and a book listing the miracles at her tomb starts only in 1488 (and runs to 1771). An ancient tomb was discovered in the church of St Peter in 1884 with a bas relief of a woman holding the model of a church and what seem to be rosary beads; this dates from the period 1220 to 1250. Remains found during various excavations may possibly be hers; these are now in the church of St Peter (also known now as St Stilla's), the cathedral in Eichstätt, and the parish church of Abenberg. In 1897 the local bishop established that her cult dated back at least to the early sixteenth century, and this led eventually to its approval in 1927.

A.A.S. 19 (1927), pp. 140-2, gives a summary of her life and the decree approving the cult. There is a late sixteenth-century Life. See *Bibl.SS.*, 12, 33-4.

St John Plessington, *Martyr* (*c.* 1637-79)

John Plessington (or Pleasington) was born at Dimples Hall, near Garstang in Lancashire, probably in 1637. Challoner gives his Christian name as William and adds, "or, as others call him, John." He was educated at Scarisbrick Hall near Ormskirk and then at Saint-Omer in France before going to the English College in Valladolid in Spain to study for the priesthood. Ordained in 1662, he returned to England the following year and began his ministry at the shrine of St Winifred (3 Nov.) in Holywell, north Wales—a place of pilgrimage for English Catholics even during penal times. He used the alias William or John Scarisbrick. In 1670 he moved to Puddington Hall in the Wirral to take up the post of tutor to the Massey family's children. The 1660s and 1670s were relatively peaceful for Catholics, and John was able to minister fairly openly to the local Catholic population. As a result of the Popish Plot of 1679, however, there was a new outbreak of violent anti-Catholicism, and he was arrested and imprisoned in Chester Castle. He was charged with treason, condemned, and hanged, drawn, and quartered at Gallows Hill, Aldford, near Chester, on 19 July 1679. His speech from the scaffold was printed and distributed; in it he professed his loyalty and asked God "to bless the king, grant him a prosperous reign here and a crown of glory hereafter." He claimed that he had been condemned only because he was a priest and denied that Catholics believed that the pope could give them permission to assassinate rulers.

His quartered body should have been displayed around Puddington Hall, but the family buried the parts in Burton graveyard. What was thought to be his grave was opened in 1962, but the remains found in it could not be identified as belonging to the martyr. He was canonized in 1970 as one of the Forty Martyrs of England and Wales.

O.D.S., pp. 403-4. See also *M.M.P.*, pp. 541-3; Anstruther, 3, pp. 170-1 (does not mention the period in Holywell, but says John worked in Lancashire until 1669); M. Waugh, *Blessed John Plessington* (1961), and the general entries on the English and Welsh Martyrs under 4 May and 25 October.

20

St Joseph Barsabbas (First Century)

Joseph Barsabbas makes a very brief appearance in the Acts of the Apostles. After Our Lord's ascension the Christians in Jerusalem decided, on St Peter's prompting, to choose a replacement for the disgraced Judas Iscariot. After quoting from the Psalms, "Let someone else take his office" (Ps. 109:8), Peter went on: "We must therefore choose someone who has been with us the whole time that the Lord Jesus was travelling round with us, someone who was with us right from the time when John was baptizing until the day when he was taken up from us—and he can act with us as a witness to his resurrection" (Acts 1:20-22). Two candidates were chosen: "Joseph known as Barsabbas, whose surname was Justus," and Matthias. The assembled Christians (about 120 in number) prayed for guidance and then cast lots; Matthias was the one chosen and so he was numbered among the twelve apostles (*ibid.*, 23-6). It is possible that Joseph was related to the Jude Barsabbas of Acts 15:22.

So Joseph is said to have been a keen follower of Jesus, and it is probable that he had been one of the seventy-two disciples (Luke 10:1-20). Eusebius, who died about the year 340, states that Joseph definitely was one of them and that he later preached in various countries; among other miracles, Eusebius reports that Joseph drank poison without any ill effects, as Our Lord had promised that his disciples would be able to do (Mark 16:18). Eusebius relied on the writings of Papias (*c.* 60-130) for these traditions about Joseph. The apocryphal Acts of Paul (second century) say that Joseph was imprisoned during the reign of Nero, 37-68, but released when St Paul appealed to the emperor.

Bibl.SS., 2, 835-6.

St Aurelius of Carthage, *Bishop* (430)

Aurelius was a deacon in Carthage, North Africa, at the end of the fourth century. Almost nothing is known of his life before he became a bishop. St Augustine (28 Aug.) met him about the year 388 in Carthage, and they became friends; Augustine wrote later of Aurelius' great charity to the poor in these early years and of his zeal for the proper performance of the liturgy. About the same time as Augustine became bishop of Hippo (*c.* 396), Aurelius became bishop of Carthage, a position that made him the unofficial leader of the Church in North Africa and one of the foremost bishops in the West. For much of his thirty-seven years in charge he had to face the challenge of two powerful heretical movements, Donatism and Pelagianism, and he presided over numerous synods and councils dealing with the issues involved. In his own diocese he was keen to end the abuses in the celebration of feasts of the martyrs, and he required his priests to preach in the cathedral in his presence. He introduced the chanting of the psalms during Mass to encourage greater lay involvement in the celebration.

Aurelius' last years were disturbed by the Vandal invasions of North Africa. He died in 430, overshadowed by his great contemporary but worthy in his own right of veneration. Augustine held him in high regard and consulted him frequently; he dedicated a number of his works to him and also wrote a treatise on the monastic life in answer to Aurelius' complaints that some monks were using the pretence of contemplation to cover their laziness. Others who thought highly of him were Pope Innocent I (401-17) and St John Chrysostom (13 Sept.). The decrees of his councils and synods are a monument to his ability, and in relation to the serious issues dealt with he has been called the man of action, while Augustine was the thinker (*Bibl.SS.*). The African bishops referred to him as "*Sanctus senex, sanctus papa Aurelius*" ("Holy old man, holy pope Aurelius").

Four of St Augustine's letters to Aurelius survive (nos. 22, 41, 60, and 174, in *P.L.* 33), as do a few of his own writings, especially a circular letter of 419, *De damnatione Pelagii atque Caelestini*, and short addresses to various councils and synods: see *P.L.* 20, 1007-16. There is no early Life, but references in contemporary conciliar documents are numerous. See *Bibl.SS.*, 2, 609-11; *E.E.C.*, 1, p. 102.

SS Flavian II and Elias, *Patriarchs* (*c.* 520)

Flavian was a Syrian monk who had served at the imperial court in Constantinople as delegate of the patriarch of Antioch and in 498 was appointed by the emperor, Anastasius, to be patriarch of Antioch. He faced strong opposition from Xenaias (or Philoxenus), bishop of Hierapolis (Maboug), and his suffragans; they formed a group that was fanatical in its rejection of the Council of Chalcedon's teaching that there were fully human and fully divine natures in the single person of Christ. They tried to influence the emperor to pursue pro-Monophysite policies (the Monophysites taught that there was only one, divine, nature in Christ), and put pressure on Flavian to condemn known supporters of Chalcedon. Flavian had accepted the *Henotikon*, a compromise document of the emperor Zeno produced in 482, intended to reconcile the differences; this had been rejected in Rome, but many in the East saw in it a peaceful solution to a dangerously disruptive controversy. Anastasius was a man of peace and discouraged any controversy about Chalcedon, but tension was increasing between the two parties, and the compromise of the *Henotikon* was being increasingly rejected by both pro- and anti-Chalcedonians. Flavian presided over a council in Antioch that attempted to reach another compromise and condemned Chalcedon's "two natures" approach, though he refused to condemn the council itself. Eventually, however, Anastasius was won over to the Monophysite position, and after rival groups of monks had fought in the streets of Antioch Flavian was deposed by the Synod of Laodicea and driven into exile in 512, even though he had tried to prevent this final break by condemning Chalcedon. As was said at the time, for the supporters of Chalcedon "winter had descended on the empire" (quoted in Frend). Flavian died at Petra, in present-day Jordan; the date of his death is not known.

One of his strongest supporters in these controversies had been Elias, the patriarch of Jerusalem. Elias was an Arab, educated in an Egyptian monastery but later exiled from the country on the orders of Timothy, the Monophysite patriarch of Alexandria. He went to Palestine, founded a religious community at Jericho, and was ordained priest. When he became patriarch of Jerusalem in 494 he established a monastic community close to his house; its members dedicated themselves to the solemn recitation of the divine office and the liturgy. As patriarch he succeeded in winning over the majority of the Palestinian monks to pro-Chalcedonian views, but his offensive against those who would not agree with him helped to make the controversy more bitter and to persuade them that their only hope of survival lay in winning over the emperor. Elias accepted as many of the anti-Chalcedon synods and decrees as he could, but then a council at Tyre, presided over by Flavian's successor at Antioch, condemned Chalcedon and Pope St Leo's *Tome* outright in 515, and the governor of Palestine deposed and exiled the patriarch in 516. His work with the monks of Palestine proved effective, however, and they were among the leaders of the anti-Monophysite reaction. He died in exile at Elat, on the shore of the Red Sea, in 418.

Clearly, both men in the end suffered for their orthodox beliefs, but both had earlier supported the *Henotikon* and had perhaps gone further in accommodating the Monophysites than they should have done. The former edition of this work said that the two patriarchs acted "equivocally" in other ways, too, and added a note: "It must be admitted that the recorded conduct of both patriarchs has laid them open to much criticism." The issues were complex, however, and they seem to have been motivated throughout by a desire to avoid schism and the violence that often accompanied it. Their names were inserted in the Roman Martyrology by Baronius in the sixteenth century, but there does not appear to have been any earlier cult.

W. H. C. Frend, *The Rise of the Monophysite Movement* (1972), esp. ch. 5; *E.E.C.*, 1, pp. 268 (Elias), 325 (Flavian II).

St Vulmar, *Abbot* (*c.* 620-700)

Vulmar (or Wulmer) was born in the area around Boulogne in northern France. He was married but later entered the abbey of Hautmont in Hainault as a servant, looking after the cattle and cutting wood for the community. It is not clear why he left his wife, Osterhildam: it may be that she was already married and that her first husband persuaded the court to demand her return. After a time he was ordained and left Hautmont to live for some years in a hermitage near Mount Cassel. He then founded a monastery near Calais, subsequently known as the abbey of Samer (a corruption of the full name, Saint-Vulmar), which lasted until the French Revolution. He also founded a convent at Wierre-aux-Bois, about a mile from Samer. The West Saxon king, Caedwalla, passed through the area on his way to Rome in 688 and contributed to the endowment of the monastery. Vulmar was credited with many miracles during his life, and these continued at his tomb. His remains were moved first to Boulogne and then to the abbey of Mont-Blandin in Ghent, where they remained until they were destroyed in the sixteenth century.

An early Life was written around the year 850, based on rather doubtful oral traditions. See *Bibl.SS.*, 12, 1370-1.

St Ansegisus, *Abbot (c. 770-833)*

Ansegisus was born about the year 770, probably in the Lyonnais region of France. He became a monk in the abbey of Fontenelle and after a time was appointed by the emperor, Charlemagne, to administer two abbeys, those of Saint Sixtus at Reims and Saint Menge near Châlons. He then became abbot of Saint Germer-de-Fly in the diocese of Beauvais, where the buildings were in a state of collapse and the community in decline. Although he was still a young man, he became one of Charlemagne's advisers and trusted administrators, holding the office of supervisor of the royal buildings and finances, a trust that continued under the next emperor, Louis the Pious. In 817 Louis appointed him abbot of Luxeuil, a famous abbey that had suffered badly at the hands of the Vandals, and Ansegisus worked for five years to restore it to its former discipline and prosperity. Finally he became abbot of Fontenelle in 823. Under his care it became famous for its library and *scriptorium*, and he was responsible for putting together a collection of the decrees of the various Frankish rulers, the *Libri IV Capitularium*, which was used as an official source book or capitulary for several centuries. He died in the abbey on 20 July 833. His life had been that of an able administrator, but his success in restoring monastic discipline and learning argues that there was much more to him than that; he could not have inspired others to a more spiritual way of life if he had not shown the way by example.

The main source for Ansegisus' life are the chronicles of Fontenelle. See *D.H.G.E.*, 3 (1924), 447-8; *Bibl.SS.*, 1, 1339-40.

St Joseph Díaz Sanjurjo, *Bishop and Martyr* (1818-57)

Joseph Díaz Sanjurjo was born in 1818 at Santa Eulalia de Suegos, a suburb of Lugo in north-western Spain. He attended the university of Compostela, became a Dominican in 1842, and was ordained two years later. The rest of his life he spent as a missionary in Vietnam, first as rector of the seminary at Luc-Thuy. A popular uprising, inspired by the emperor Tu Duc's persecution of the missionaries, led to the closure and destruction of the seminary in 1847. Two years later Joseph became coadjutor bishop of a new vicariate in East Tonkin and bishop (of what is now Bui Chu diocese) in his own right in 1852. He founded a centre to look after abandoned children, which sheltered some two thousand children in its early years. Persecution continued, but it was possible to carry on missionary work cautiously until 1857, when the persecution became severe again. Heads of villages faced the death penalty if they or their people concealed foreigners; Joseph was denounced and arrested. Two months later he was condemned to death by the mandarin and executed on 20 July 1857; his body was thrown into the river at Nam-Dinh.

He and three other Spanish bishops were among the group of twenty-five martyrs executed between 1857 and 1862 who were beatified in 1951 and canonized in 1988. Twenty-three of the group were Tonkinese and nineteen of them laypeople.

The centre he founded is still in existence; it was renovated in 1975 after the Vietnam war and has a team of forty, who look after physically and mentally disabled children as well as elderly people who have no family support. News reports issued from Vietnam suggest that it is now acceptable to recognize the fact of the martyrdom of European missionaries as part of the community's history.

See *Annals of the Propagation of the Faith*, 29 (1857), pp. 63-75; 30 (1858), pp. 268-9; 31 (1859), pp. 74-5, for contemporary reports. See also *Bibl.SS.*, 4, 599-600, and the general entry on the Martyrs of Vietnam under 2 February. Internet UCAN report of 13 Apr. 1999.

Note: According to the new edition of the Roman Martyrology, today is the correct day for the veneration of St Frumentius, bishop (*c*. 380). His feast-day used to be celebrated on 27 October, and a full entry on him and his companion Aedesius can be found under that date.

21

ST LAURENCE OF BRINDISI, *Doctor* (1559-1619)

Giulio Cesare Russo was born in Brindisi in the kingdom of Naples in 1559, the son of well-to-do Venetian parents. When his parents died he went to Venice to be looked after by an uncle, a priest, and attended the college of Saint Mark; at the age of sixteen he became a Capuchin friar in Verona, taking the name Laurence in religion. Very quickly he developed a reputation as a scholar, and he was particularly good at languages, both modern and ancient, with an extraordinary knowledge of the texts of the scriptures. After his ordination in 1582 he preached successfully in Padua, Verona, Vicenza, and other northern towns until in 1596 he was called to Rome to be definitor general of the Order and was appointed by Pope Clement VIII (1592-1605) to take special responsibility for the conversion of Jews, a task in which he is said to have had considerable success. For the rest of his life, whatever official posts he might hold, preaching was his main apostolate.

His next posting was to Austria and Bohemia, with Bd Benedict of Urbino (14 May) and a team of Capuchin friars, to set up Capuchin houses as part of the Catholic Reformation. As well as making foundations in Vienna, Prague, and Gratz, they involved themselves in the care of the sick, especially the victims of the plague. In the general chapter of 1602 Laurence was elected minister general of the Order, a post that he carried out with energy and charity as he visited the different provinces. He was re-elected three years later but refused to serve a second term; in 1606, however, he became commissary general and in 1613 and 1618 definitor general.

Laurence's abilities were recognized in other areas as well. The emperor, Rudolf II, enlisted his help in persuading the German princes to unite against the Turks, who were threatening Hungary. He was successful and was appointed chaplain general of the army, leading it into the battle of Szekes-Fehervar (1601) in person, with a crucifix held aloft. The Christian success in the battle was attributed by many to Laurence's morale-boosting encouragement of the troops and his prayers. Rudolf then sent him to negotiate Philip III of Spain's membership of the Catholic League; while in Madrid Laurence took the opportunity to open a Capuchin house there. Finally he became papal nuncio in Munich, negotiating with Maximilian of Bavaria, the head of the League, administering two of the Order's provinces, and continuing his work of preaching and conversion.

He retired to the friary in Caserta in 1618, hoping to be free from distractions so that he could devote his time to prayer. Even then, however, he was required to go to Madrid again over troubles in Naples; when he arrived he found that the king had gone to Lisbon, so he followed him there although he was very unwell and the summer heat was oppressive. His negotiations with the king were successful, but Laurence died shortly afterwards, on 22 July 1619, and was buried in the cemetery of the Poor Clares at Villafranca del Bierzo in northern Spain. Beatified in 1783, he was canonized in 1881 and declared a Doctor of the Church in 1959. His cult was very popular, and great reverence was paid to his relics, including the everyday things he had used and especially the handkerchiefs with which he would wipe away his tears during Mass.

Laurence's writings consist mainly of his sermons (804 of them in total), but he also wrote a commentary on Genesis, a number of controversial works against Lutheranism, and an autobiographical account of his time in Germany and Austria, *De rebus Austriae et Bohemiae*, written at the request of his superiors; about eighty of his letters also survive. Very few of these works were printed until the twentieth century, which prevented a scholarly examination of his teachings. It is now clear that he had a strong devotion to Our Lady, and his *Mariale* has earned him the title of "the most important mariologist of his time" (*Dict.Sp.*). He was, in fact, ahead of his time in espousing Marian teachings that began to circulate more widely only much later, such as Mary's roles alongside Christ in the divine plan of creation and salvation, as the mediator and dispenser of every grace, the mother of the Church, and the repository of all sacred and profane knowledge (*ibid.*). This exaltation of Mary flowed from his worship of Christ: his spirituality was entirely christocentric, and his devotion to Christ's humanity was evident in the way he celebrated the Nativity, the passion, the Sacred Heart, and the Eucharist. The Mass was the focus of his devotional life; it sometimes took him three hours or more to celebrate it, and he experienced ecstasies, the gift of tears, and other physical phenomena while doing so. For the last thirteen years of his life he enjoyed the papal privilege of being able to say the votive Mass of Our Lady daily. As a spiritual writer he did not belong to any one school and, indeed, borrowed very little from others: his teaching was based almost exclusively on texts from the scriptures, which he took a delight in expounding in as many ways as possible. Some have seen similarities between his writings and those of St Francis de Sales (24 Jan.) because of his humanist background, his stress on the importance of the will and the emotions, and his optimistic belief in the potential of human beings to achieve perfection by imitating Christ.

The Capuchins of the Venetian Province have published the complete works in fifteen volumes (1928-56). See the definitive biography by Arturo da Carmignano, *San Lorenzo da Brindisi, Dottore della Chiesa*, 5 vols. (1960-63), and his *St Laurence of Brindisi* (Eng. trans. by P. Barrett, 1963). See also Fr Serafino, *S. Lorenzo da Brindisi: discorsi mariani* (1950); *Dict.Sp.*, 9 (1976), 388-92, with important bibliography; *Bibl.SS.*, 8, 161-80.

Representations of the saint are very numerous, and many copies of his image were made immediately after his death. His beatification in the eighteenth century saw the production of paintings by all the main Italian artists of the time; their principal themes were his celebration of Mass in tears and ecstasy and his writing about Our Lady, usually with divine inspiration. In the nineteenth century a third image became popular, that of the saint at the battle of Szekes-Fehervar, inspiring the Christian troops against the Turks.

St Victor of Marseilles, *Martyr* (Late Third Century)

The origins of Christianity in Marseilles are obscure but seem to have been relatively late despite the city's position as a port and its trading links with Italy and the eastern Mediterranean, and it is difficult to discover very much about St Victor, its principal patron. The sixth-century writings of St Gregory of Tours (17 Nov.) and Venantius Fortunatus (14 Dec.) show that his tomb in Marseilles was one of the most popular places of pilgrimage in France. He may have been of senatorial rank and perhaps a Christian officer in the Roman army who, when the emperor Maximian (284-305) visited Marseilles, encouraged the local Christians to stand firm in the face of persecution. The city was under siege in 287, and it may be that the persecution arose when the Christians refused either to fight or to sacrifice to the gods and recognize the divinity of the emperor. Victor was denounced, taken before the emperor, and tortured. According to the *passio* he succeeded in converting three of the guards to Christianity; these were immediately executed, and after further tortures and refusals to honour the pagan gods he was beheaded. The four bodies were thrown into the sea but recovered by friends and buried in a hollowed-out rock in what later became the city's cemetery.

Victor may have been one of the several Victors who were listed as martyrs in the *Hieronymianum*, but the first full mention of him is in the martyrology of Lyons (806). It is strange that such a popular cult did not result in any evidence such as inscriptions. St John Cassian (*c.* 360-435; 23 July), an Eastern monk, founded two religious houses in Marseilles, including the one dedicated to St Victor. Some have suggested that he was the author of Victor's *passio*, but others argue that this was written very much later and was based on the little information contained in the martyrologies. It is possible that Cassian adopted an Eastern martyr and translated him to Marseilles, re-writing his details to suit the new location, as there were no early "native" martyrs in Gaul who could serve as patrons and provide relics; it should be noted, however, that Victor is a Latin name, not Greek, as those of the martyr-patrons of other nearby Provençal towns are.

The *passio* has been generally dismissed as historically worthless, but recent research shows that it may have some value. Excavations in the crypt of Saint Victor's in 1963 unearthed a rocky necropolis with several burials and an altar underneath the remains of a sixth-century chapel. Under five or six superimposed tombs were two marble ones, containing the remains of two males and the remains of a paleo-Christian building similar to those often built over the tombs of martyrs originally buried in pagan cemeteries. This building can be dated to the early fifth century and the tombs to the early fourth century and are evidence of a cult going back at least to that date. It is probable that the tombs contained the remains of two martyrs, who could be Victor and a companion—though the name Victor could well have been an attempt to give a symbolic name to an unnamed martyr. Cassian could have written the *passio* to provide information about the patron of the new monastery and may have used an oral tradition as the source of at least some of the detail.

Bibl.SS., 12, 1261-73; *D.A.C.L.*, 8, pt. 2 (1932), 2211-4. For the most up-to-date examination of the texts of the *passio* see J-C. Moulinier, *Saint Victor de Marseille. Les récits de sa passion* (1993).

St Arbogast, *Bishop* (*c.* 600)

Both Ireland and Scotland have been put forward as Arbogast's country of origin, but it seems much more likely that he came from Aquitaine in France; his name would indicate a Frankish origin. He went to live as a hermit in Alsace, and tradition says that he came to the notice of King Dagobert (629-39) when the king's son was seemingly killed while hunting in the woods close to Arbogast's cell but recovered as a result of the hermit's prayers. Other accounts, however, put this story later in Arbogast's career, after he had become a bishop. It was the king who appointed him bishop of Strasbourg, and he built the first cathedral in the city and spent the rest of life looking after his people and giving an example of humility; it is said that he asked to be buried on a hillside where only criminals were buried. This was done, and a church was later built on the site. He may have died about the year 600. He is the principal patron of the Strasbourg diocese and a patron of other towns in the region. His existence and reputation as a builder have been established by the discovery of bricks stamped with his name.

   Great uncertainty surrounds the life of Arbogast, and it is impossible to disentangle the various traditions about him, some of which would seem to belong to other people. His second successor as bishop, Ansoald, attended the Council of Paris in 614, so presumably Arbogast was bishop before the end of the sixth century. This does not fit in with the story of his curing the king's son, above, but it is interesting in this context that the early Life just mentions "a certain Dagobert" and does not say that he was the king. The whole story of the cure could, of course, be a later invention to explain why Arbogast was appointed bishop.

A late and largely legendary Life by one of his successors, Uto III, seems to have some historical basis. Two twentieth-century biographies exist: A. Postina, *S. Arbogast, Bischof von Strasburg*(1928), and M. Barth, *Der heilige Arbogast* (1940). See also *Catholicisme*, 1, 758.

Bd Angelina of Marsciano, *Foundress* (1377-1435)

Angelina was born in Montegiove, near Orvieto, in 1377. Her father was Giacopo Angioballi, count of Marsciano, and her mother Anna, daughter of the count of Corbara; Angelina is sometimes referred to as Angelina of Corbara. When she was fifteen years old Angelina married the count of Civitella, Giovanni da Terni; he died two years later, and she was left in charge of the castle and estate of Civitella del Tronto. She decided to dedicate the rest of her life to the service of God—it appears that she had thought of becoming a nun before her marriage—and assumed the dress of a Franciscan tertiary. With a group of female companions she travelled around the country preaching repentance and the value of virginity and helping those in need, until she was arrested on charges of sorcery (because of her power over young women) and heresy (because of her supposed Manichean opposition to marriage). She defended herself before Ladislaus, king of Naples, who dismissed the charges against her but later, as complaints continued, exiled her and her companions from his kingdom.

She went to Assisi and in the church of Santa Maria degli Angeli had a vision in which God told her to found an enclosed monastery of the Third Order Regular of St Francis in the city of Foligno. The bishop approved these plans, which were in line with the type of enclosed religious life expected of women at the time and meant an end to the active ministry that she had been practising. In 1397 the convent, dedicated to St Anne, was opened with Angelina as superior of its twelve members. This was the first convent of regular tertiaries and was so successful that Angelina soon opened others in Florence, Spoleto, Assisi, and Viterbo; eleven other houses were founded before she died in 1435. Angelina was buried in the Franciscan church in Foligno, and her remains were moved to a proper shrine in 1492. Her cult was approved in 1825.

Angelina insisted on her communities remaining small so that it would be easier to insist on proper observance and, in particular, to prevent them from becoming too well endowed. They became very popular in the fifteenth and sixteenth centuries and opened a large number of houses. In 1428 Pope Martin V put them under the jurisdiction of the Friars Minor and gave them the specific task of educating and instructing young girls; in practice they continued a variety of apostolic work until required to observe strict enclosure from 1617, when their work became purely educational. In 1903 the requirement to observe papal enclosure was lifted and they were able to undertake a wider apostolate once again as the Franciscan Sisters of Bd Angelina. Currently they have eleven houses and about eighty members.

Bibl.SS., 1, 1231-2.

22

ST MARY MAGDALEN (First Century)

St Luke tells us that as Jesus made his way through towns and villages "preaching and proclaiming the good news of the kingdom of God," he was accompanied by the twelve apostles and by "certain women who had been cured of evil spirits and ailments: Mary surnamed the Magdalene, from whom seven devils had gone out," and others (Luke 8:1-3). This Mary Magdalen features prominently whenever the evangelists mention the women who ministered to Jesus: she heads the list of the women present at Our Lord's passion and burial in three of the Gospels and comes after Our Lady and her sister in St John's account (see, for example, Mark 15:40, Matt. 27:61, and John 19:25). The fact that she is usually placed first shows that she is "a reference point, a guide perhaps, for the others" (Ricci), and her importance is underlined by St John's moving description of her going to the tomb alone and of her grief when she finds the body of Jesus missing: in tears she says to the angels inside the tomb, "They have taken my Lord away and I do not know where they have put him." Then the risen Jesus appears to her in the garden before any of the apostles have seen him, addresses her simply as "Mary," and gives her the privilege of announcing the fact of his resurrection to the others (John 20:1-18).

Given her prominence in the Gospels it is not surprising that several traditions grew up around her. In the East it was believed that she accompanied St John and Our Lady to Ephesus and died there—*The Golden Legend* even has her betrothed to St John; her body was later taken to Constantinople and venerated there for many centuries. In the West tradition stated that she, Martha, Lazarus, and others were turned loose in an oarless boat from Palestine and drifted to the coast of southern France, where they preached the gospel and succeeded in establishing Christianity. One of the group was St Maximinus (8 June), supposedly one of the seventy-two disciples, who became the first bishop of Aix. Mary Magdalen was said to have lived her last years in a cave (in the twelfth century identified as being at La Sainte-Baume in the maritime alps to the east of Marseilles) and to have been transported miraculously just before she died to Saint-Maximin, where she was given the Last Sacraments by Maximinus. One of these Provençal legends borrowed elements from the story of St Mary of Egypt (2 Apr.) and had her living as a hermit and clothed only in her long hair. Other accounts had her preaching to the people in Marseilles and dying at Le Saint-Pilou, where she was given the Last Sacraments by Maximinus. These associated legends appear to date back to the ninth century but to have been developed in France mainly from the eleventh and twelfth centuries; despite their great popularity, however, they have no discernible historical basis, although it does now seem that parts of Provence were evangelized as early as the first century. From the eleventh century onward Vézelay in Burgundy claimed to have her relics and became a popular place of pilgrimage. In the late thirteenth century, however, the monks of Saint-Maximin "discovered" the body of the saint in their crypt, and pilgrimage attention switched to there. The French government in the seventeenth century discouraged the cult attached to La Sainte-Baume because of its association with certain guilds, and the writer Jean de Launoy wrote a book in 1644 against the Provençal legends of Mary Magdalen, but the cult remained popular, and pilgrimages to La Sainte-Baume and Saint-Maximin still take place (see below) despite the critical efforts of the Bollandists and other serious scholars to deny the legends' reliability.

According to Western tradition Mary Magdalen has been identified with the woman, a sinner, who anointed Jesus' feet, as described in Luke's Gospel in the verses immediately before the naming of Mary Magdalen (Luke 7:36-50). She has also been identified with Mary, the sister of Martha and Lazarus of Bethany (see John 12:1-8), who anointed Jesus' feet and wiped them with her hair. Because the woman in Luke's anointing was a "sinner" or, in the *Jerusalem Bible,* one "who had a bad name in the town" and Mary Magdalen had had "seven demons" cast out of her, it has been traditional to say that Mary Magdalen was a reformed prostitute, and this tradition has dominated Western thinking about, and artistic representation of, her for centuries—witness, for example, the name Magdalens given to homes for reformed prostitutes. Recent biblical scholarship, however, has rejected these identifications in favour of the view that the three women named Mary were different people. In support of this it has been pointed out that the naming of Mary Magdalen in Luke 8:1-3 could just as well have been to distinguish her from the woman of the anointing of the previous verses (who is not named, anyway). Nor need the "seven demons" indicate that the woman had been a prostitute, since there is no necessary connection between demonic possession and sexual sin: indeed, it seems to relate more to psychic disturbances that were otherwise inexplicable. We are not told when she had been cured by Jesus, but Magdala was a town on the west bank of the Sea of Galilee, and Jesus carried out much of his early ministry around its shores.

The anointing by a woman who was a sinner is described by Luke as having taken place in the house of Simon the Pharisee. Both Matthew and Mark describe a similar anointing by an unnamed woman (Matt. 26:6-13; Mark 14:3-9), in the house of Simon, a leper, in Bethany, shortly before the passion. John's Gospel also has such an anointing: it takes place in Bethany shortly before the passion in an unknown house but in the presence of Martha and Lazarus and presumably in their house, and the woman is Mary, the sister of

Martha and Lazarus (John 12:1-8). If these accounts are taken as referring to a single anointing, then it would follow that Mary of Bethany was the reformed sinner of Luke's account, but there would still be no need to identify her with Mary Magdalen. Tradition in the Eastern Church has kept the three women separate, with feast-days on 21 March (the unnamed sinner), 18 March (Mary of Bethany), and 22 July (MaryMagdalen). In the past most exegetes in the West supported the views of St Jerome (30 Sept.) and St Gregory the Great (3 Sept.) that the three women were in reality only one, Mary Magdalen—although St Bernard (20 Aug.) and other Cistercian writers rejected this in the twelfth century. Exegetes in the twentieth century, however, have moved away from this position and believe there were three separate women named Mary and more than one anointing; neither Mary of Bethany nor Mary Magdalen should be identified with the sinner in Luke's account of the anointing.

It is likely to be a long time, however, before the identification of Mary Magdalen as a reformed prostitute disappears from art, hagiography, and popular consciousness, despite its rejection by the Roman Calendar in 1969. It would be altogether more in keeping with the privileged position accorded to her by all the Gospel writers to stress her role as the bringer of good news, the herald of Christ's resurrection, a symbol of hope—a role that is highlighted in the ancient Easter sequence: "Tell us, Mary, what did you see on your way? I saw the tomb of the living Christ and his glory as he rose. . . . Christ my hope has risen." She was to carry this news to the others, who were still lamenting Jesus' death, "the mediatrix of the proclamation that life prevails over death, light over darkness" (Ricci).

A feast of Mary Magdalen has been kept in the West since the eighth century. Her popularity in England can by seen from the large number (187) of ancient church dedications in her honour and the fact that she appears in all the medieval calendars. Both Oxford and Cambridge Universities have colleges named after her.

The literature on Mary Magdalen is immense—see the bibliography in *Bibl.SS.*, 8, 1081-1104. See, for example, V. Saxer, *Le Culte de Marie Madeleine en Occident des origines à la fin du moyen-âge* (1959); Carla Ricci, *Mary Magdalene and Many Others* (1994)—a stimulating feminist approach with a very thorough and up-to-date bibliography. See also *O.D.S.*, pp. 329-30; *O.D.C.C.*, pp. 1049-50. All modern gospel commentaries deal with the questions of identification raised here. See also the entry for Mary of Bethany under 29 July. On Mary Magdalen in art see *Bibl.SS.*, 8, 1078-1107, and Murray, pp. 291-3.

Her participation in such events as the passion, the deposition, the resurrection, and, of course, the anointing of Jesus, ensured that Mary Magdalen became a favourite subject in Christian art from the Middle Ages onward—there appear to be no early mosaics or carvings of her, a testimony, perhaps, to the relative lateness of her cult. In the earliest Eastern depictions she appears as just one of the group of pious women. In general there are two contrasting images of her: she is either depicted in the rich dress of a prostitute (especially in Venetian and Dutch paintings), or in the rags of a penitent hermit; her symbol is the jar of ointment or oil which she used in the anointing, and her hair is usually long. There is a fourteenth-century fresco cycle in Santa Croce, Florence, in which Mary

Magdalen weeps at Christ's feet; Veronese's *Feast in the House of Simon* (before 1573; Louvre) shows the same scene, while Giotto's *Crucifixion* in the Arena Chapel, Padua, shows her weeping at the foot of the cross, as does Grünewald's Isenheim Altarpiece of about 1515. Fra Angelico shows her kissing the feet of the dead Christ in his 1436 *Deposition* in San Marco, Florence. Titian's *Noli me tangere* depicts the meeting in the garden after the resurrection (National Gallery, London), as does Rembrandt (1638; the Royal Collection). Titian also used the penitent imagery (1533, Pitti Gallery), as did Veronese (1583, Prado), but the most intense of these portrayals is the wooden statue by Donatello (Baptistery, Florence)—"a gaunt and haggard creature, moving in her very ugliness" (Murray).

At La Sainte-Baume there is a grotto in the face of the limestone cliff, where the penitent Magdalen is said to have spent her last days. St John Cassian (23 July) established a monastery there in the fifth century, but this was devastated by the barbarians and forgotten until the thirteenth century, when the grotto became a chapel and pilgrimages started. A recumbent statue (by Fossaty; eighteenth century) representing her was actually originally a statue of Hope on the tomb of the comte de Valbelle at Montrieux. There is another chapel on a rock high above the grotto, marking the spot where angels are said to have conveyed her every day to pray. At Saint-Maximin, her reputed burial-place, an oratory was built at an early date and a Benedictine abbey founded: this was destroyed by the Saracens in the eighth century, when the relics were hidden and reputedly transferred to Vézelay. The abbey was re-founded in the Middle Ages, and the body "discovered" in a cellar in the town. The present church was probably built by Dominicans, who succeeded the Bendictines in 1295. During the French Revolution Louis Bonaparte lived in Saint-Maximin and is said to have saved the church and relics from destruction. The relics are contained in a sumptuous bronze casket dating from 1860 in the crypt (Michelin, *Guide Bleu*).

St Wandregisilus, *Abbot (c. 600-68)*

Wandregisilus (or, in French, Wandrille) was born near Verdun in eastern France about the beginning of the seventh century. He was an official at court and married, but about the year 628 he and his wife agreed to separate and become religious. Wandregisilus became a monk under St Baudry at Montfaucon but soon retired to live a life of complete solitude at Saint-Ursanne in the Jura mountains. He seems to have been influenced by the ascetic practices of the Irish monks, especially St Columban (23 Nov.) and his disciple St Ursicinus (20 Dec.), who had worked in the area and established monasteries there. Wandregisilus gained a reputation for great austerity before leaving to spend some time at St Columban's monastery at Bobbio in northern Italy. From there he moved to the abbey of Romain-Moûtier, on the Isère, where he stayed for about ten years and was ordained by St Ouen (24 Aug.), archbishop of Rouen.

He put this varied experience to good use when he founded an abbey at Fontenelle in Normandy; its church was consecrated in 657. Under his guidance the monks followed the Rule of St Columban and laid the foundations for the subsequent growth of the abbey into one of the leading monasteries in France, important as a centre of learning and evangelization. Before his death in July 668 (or possibly 665) he assured his monks that if they were faithful to the traditions that he had given them, the house would prosper: "The Lord will always be amongst you, and will be your comfort and your help in every need."

As a safeguard against desecration by the Vikings, his relics were divided among a number of places, including the abbey of Mont-Blandin in Ghent; it was from here that the celebration of his feast-day spread to pre-Conquest England.

A Life composed by a monk of Fontenelle about 700 is of historical value; see *M.G.H., Scriptores merov.*, 5, pp. 1-24. Popular Lives of the saint were largely based on a later unreliable Life. See also *O.D.S.*, p. 489.

Bd Augustine of Biella (1430-93)

Agostino Fangi was born of noble parents in 1430 in Biella, Piedmont. He joined the Dominicans and lived a life of strict observance and patient acceptance of suffering brought about by long-term illness and unsuccessful surgery. He celebrated Mass with particular devotion, often in tears, and was well known for his devotion to Our Lady. He was prior of a number of friaries and where necessary restored them to a closer observance of the Rule. Successful as a preacher and confessor and with a reputation for working miracles, he shunned publicity and was eventually allowed to retire to the friary in Venice, where he spent the last ten years of his life. He died on 22 July 1493, with the words "Praise be to God! Praise be to the Most High!" on his lips. When his tomb was opened in 1496 his body was found to be incorrupt, and this was taken as a proof of his sanctity. Part of his remains were moved to Biela and Soncino, and in 1825 he was re-buried in the church of St Thomas, Venice. His cult was approved in 1872. Traditionally his feast-day has been celebrated on 24 July.

Procter, pp. 208-10; *Bibl.SS.*, 1, 425-6.

SS Philip Evans and John Lloyd, *Martyrs* (1679)

Philip Evans was born in Monmouth in 1645. He went abroad to study at the English College in Saint-Omer and became a Jesuit at the age of twenty. After ordination in 1675 he worked as a missioner in South Wales until 1678, when the so-called Popish Plot led to increased persecution of the Catholic community and £200 was offered as a reward for his arrest. Early in December he was taken in the house of Christopher Turberville at Sker (probably the modern Skewen) in Glamorgan. After refusing to take the Oath of Allegiance Philip was imprisoned in Cardiff Castle; he was not brought to trial for several months as the authorities found it difficult to find witnesses to testify against him.

John Lloyd came from Brecon in South Wales. He was born about the year 1630, studied abroad in Valladolid, and was ordained in 1653. He worked as a missioner in Wales from 1654 onward until his arrest at Penlline in Glamorgan in 1678, accused of having said Mass in Llantilio, Penrhos, and Trievor. He was in prison in Cardiff Castle at the same time as Philip Evans, and both were brought to trial on 3 May charged with having returned to work as priests in Wales after ordination abroad.

Both priests were condemned to be hanged, drawn, and quartered, and were executed in Gallows Field (present-day Richmond Road) in Cardiff on 22 July 1679. Philip Evans addressed the people in both English and Welsh, declaring during his speech, "I die for God and religion's sake; and I think myself so happy that if I had never so many lives, I would willingly give them all for so good a cause." John Lloyd spoke only very briefly, saying, "I never was a good speaker in my life," but he declared that he died in "the true Catholic and apostolic faith," and urged the Catholics present to "bear their crosses patiently, and to remember that passage of Holy scripture 'Happy are they that suffer persecution for justice, for theirs is the kingdom of heaven.'" Both priests were among the forty English and Welsh martyrs canonized in 1970.

M.M.P., pp. 544-7; Anstruther, 2, p. 201 (on John Lloyd); *O.D.S.*, pp. 171-2, 301-2. A broadsheet printed in 1679 describes the execution; a copy is in the British Museum. See also the general entries on the English and Welsh Martyrs under 4 May and 25 October.

Martyrs of the Spanish Civil War (1934-9)

The Spanish civil war lasted from July 1936 to April 1939. During that period 6,832 priests and religious were put to death by the forces of the revolutionary Left, for no other apparent reason than their profession of their faith. Many more Catholic lay men and women were also executed, but as one side in the war, the Nationalists, almost immediately adopted a Catholic banner, it must be impossible in the cases of most of them to say with certainty whether they suffered for their faith or for their political or military allegiance. To date (1999) some 230 victims have been beatified as martyrs, of whom the vast majority were priests or religious. They have been beatified in groups by Pope John Paul II, in 1987, 1989, 1990, 1992, 1993, 1995, and 1997, and in spring 1999 the nine martyrs of the Asturias uprising in October 1934 were canonized. There are a further 103 groups whose causes for beatification have been started, covering 1,268 individuals. In accordance with the stated policy of the new Roman Martyrology that the country of martyrdom is the unifying factor rather than the date of beatification, they are considered here as a group, with additional individual entries for those about whom more is known on the actual anniversary of their deaths.

The causes of the war are complex, and anything beyond a brief summary of the events leading up to it as they affected the Church is beyond the scope of this work. Throughout the nineteenth century Spain had oscillated, sometimes violently, between "liberalism" and "conservatism," the difference being often more of personality than of policy, but with an overall tendency—as elsewhere, including the rebelling former Spanish colonies—for the liberals to be anticlerical, either in the face of a conservative-dominated Church or forcing the

Church into an ultra-conservative position. The loss of the last colonies in 1898 produced a mood of national soul-searching led by writers and intellectuals known collectively as the "Generation of '98," who in general looked for secular and European remedies. This tendency, together with its opposite, which sought renaissance through restoration of the spirit of empire and saw the "ideal" Catholicism as the national Catholicism of the age of the conquest of Latin America, produced the changes of régime of the early years of the twentieth century.

In the 1920s a constitutional monarchy manipulated by conservative interests had been upheld under the generally benign dictatorship of General Manuel Primo de Rivera, from 1923 to 1930. When monarchist candidates were heavily defeated in municipal elections in April 1931, however, King Alfonso XII abdicated, and a democratic Republic came into being by default. It was the overall failure of successive democratically elected governments to resolve the economic, social, and political problems of the country over the next five years that led to a series of revolutionary outbreaks by radical forces on the Left and finally provoked the right-wing Nationalist uprising of July 1936, which in its turn sparked off the waves of persecution of clerics, at their peak in the early weeks of the war.

The earliest group of martyrs, however, met their deaths before the outbreak of war. In October 1934 the grouping known as CEDA (*Confederación Española de Derechas Autónomas*), a generally right-wing confederation of parties, though with its own "left wing" committed to the social teaching of the Church, was brought into the government in one of many attempts to stabilize the political situation and form an effective government. This provoked armed revolts by the Socialists, who saw the CEDA as "clerical fascist" and were convinced that its Catholic conservative influence in government would lead to fascism. The revolt held sway longest in the north-western mining province of Asturias.

One of the main causes of the general backwardness of Spain compared to other European countries was its lack of educational facilities, and one of the main grievances of the Left was the fact that education was largely in the hands of the religious Congregations. Without them the system would have collapsed, but they bred resentment, especially among the urban poor—effectively divorced from devotion or observance—partly on account of the culture of devotion they tried to impose on their charges and partly because the products of their schools and workshops competed with the work of the poor. "For teaching brothers intent on equipping their pupils with at least the rudiments of a trade in carpentry or joinery or metalwork, the only way to do it without charging fees the pupils could not pay was the sale of goods produced in the practical workshops. . . . From other perspectives, of course, this was all cheap labour, undercutting the local women who took in washing or sewing and the local men who made items of furniture and did household repairs" (Lannon, p.

170

76). In 1933 legislation had been passed banning Catholic education, though its implementation was haphazard. The Socialists in Asturias seized a group of De la Salle Brothers (pioneers of this type of "practical" education) in the town of Turón and executed eight of them—described at their beatification in October 1990 by Pope John Paul II as, in the eyes of their persecutors, "guilty of having dedicated their lives to the human and Christian education of youth in the Catholic school of Covadonga in that mining town." They and a Passionist priest who had been hearing the De La Salle Brothers' students' Confessions were shot—"like rabbits, with no previous accusation or judgment," according to the postulator of their cause—on 9 October and have an entry in this work as BB Cyril Bertrand (his names in religion) Tejedor and Companions on that date. The revolt was brutally suppressed by government troops after fifteen days with the loss of over one thousand lives. In spring 1999 they were canonized by Pope John Paul II, the first martyrs of the Spanish civil war to receive this honour, and in recognition of this fact their (civil) names are repeated here. The seven Spanish members of the community were José Sanz Tejedor, Filomeno López, Claudio Bernabé Cano, Vicente Alonso Andrés, Román Martínez Fernández, Manuel Seco Gutiérrez; Héctor Valdivielso Sáez came from Argentina and so becomes the first native-born Argentinian saint; the Passionist priest was Manuel Canoura.

Fresh elections in February 1936 resulted in a narrow win for the Popular Front, an alliance of Socialists, Communists, and left-wing Republicans, but the Socialists did not join the government, which lost control of the situation. With revolts in cities and the countryside producing increased violence, churches being burned, and other targets bombed, the "Right"—which still represented almost half the electorate—turned increasingly to support for a military coup. The assassination on 13 July of Calvo Sotelo, the leader of the authoritarian Right, who had consistently appealed to the army to "save" Spain, effectively removed all restraint from the army, but it was the revolutionary attack on the Church above all that united the conservative forces under the banner of a Catholic crusade. The civil war can therefore, with hindsight, be seen as "the last of the European religious wars" (Carr and Fusi), though the leaders of the uprising were "not primarily moved by sentiments of religious piety to take arms against an impious régime. . . . Issues of politics, economics, and institutional privilege dominated over those of religion" (Payne).

Between February and June 1936, 160 churches were totally destroyed and 251 partially wrecked. After the military uprising, which had the effect of producing revolts against the government from revolutionary forces of the Left throughout the country, destruction of church property increased, bringing with it slaughter of clergy. During this period 4,184 secular priests were killed, almost one out of seven in the entire country, plus 2,365 monks and 283 nuns, making a total of 6,832. The slaughter was generally greatest where the anarchists seized power: in the Aragonese district of Barbastro, overrun by Catalan

171

anarchists, 88 per cent of the diocesan clergy, including the bishop, were killed. Bishop Florentino Asensio Barroso had been born in the Castilian province of Valladolid in 1861 and ordained priest in 1901. He gained a doctorate in theology at the Pontifical University of Valladolid, where he taught until he was appointed priest of the metropolitan cathedral on the death of the archbishop, Cardinal Cos. He earned a great reputation as a spiritual director and as a preacher, and many of his homilies survive. He was appointed bishop and apostolic administrator of Barbastro early in 1936 and spent his short time there working for social justice and unity. He was, however, unable to overcome the hostility of the authorities, and three days after the military uprising, on 20 July, he was placed under house arrest. Accused of collaborating with "the enemies of the people," he was tortured and mutilated. In the early hours of 9 August he was loaded on to a "death truck" with twelve others, taken to the cemetery, and shot. His body was thrown into a common grave but was later exhumed and taken to the burial place of the bishops of Barbastro in the cathedral crypt. He was beatified on 4 May 1997, in the same ceremony as Ceferino Jiménez Malla (2 Aug.), "patron of Gypsies," also executed in Barbastro.

The entire community of the Missionary Sons of the Immaculate Heart of Mary (the Claretians, founded by St Antony Mary Claret; 24 Oct.) were rounded up and executed in the same wave of violence in Barbastro. Their house was surrounded by some sixty armed militia on 20 July; they entered and searched the house and imprisoned all its inhabitants. The superior, Fr Felipe de Jesús Munárriz, the spiritual director, and the procurator were separated from the others and taken before a firing squad at dawn the next day. The students were placed in a makeshift prison in the basement of a theatre; they were deprived of bedding and water, and the only visitors allowed were prostitutes sent in to tempt them. They expressed their thoughts on whatever materials were at hand—the walls, planks of wood, even the lid of a piano—asking that their fate should not give rise to vengeance. The twelve senior students were taken out and shot in the early morning of 12 August, followed by another group of twenty that night and a further group of twenty on 15 August. Two who had been in hospital were taken from there to the prison and executed three days later. All died singing hymns and shouting *"Viva Cristo Rey!"* ("Long live Christ the King!"). All were beatified on 25 October 1992, as Bd Felipe de Jesús Munárriz and his Fifty Companions.

At the same ceremony another large group was also beatified as BB Braulio María Corres, Federico Rubio, and their Sixty-Nine Companions. These were all religious belonging to the Hospitaller Order of St John of God (8 Mar.), later re-founded in Spain by Bd Benedict Menni (24 Apr.). They all worked in children's hospitals and psychiatric hospitals in different provinces of Spain: four in Talavera de la Reina, Toledo; fifteen in Calafell, Tarragona; forty-seven in three different places on the outskirts of Madrid—San Rafael,

Ciempozuelos, and Carabanchel Alto; four in Barcelona itself; and one in San Baudilio de Llobregat, Barcelona, where forty Brothers of St John of God looked after 305 male inmates, while fifty Sisters of the Sacred Heart cared for the 370 women inmates. The fact that they and so many others had joined religious communities largely "to perfom there all those corporal works of mercy that seemed certain otherwise to be left undone . . . did not expunge, in the eyes of their assailants, the offence of belonging to a religious community" (Lannon). They died at various times between July and December 1936, most in panic killings motivated by General Franco's advance on Madrid in November. Sixty-four of them were Spanish and the other seven from Colombia, in Spain to complete their religious and professional training. At the beatification ceremony the pope specifically linked the occasion to the "fifth centenary of the evangelization of America" and singled out these seven as the "first fruits of the Colombian Church." All were held up an an example to everyone but especially to those who devote their lives to the care and service of the sick.

In Barcelona, where the civil authorities were somewhat more successful in restraining the anarchists, 22 per cent of the secular clergy were killed. Religious Sisters were forced to leave their convents and take refuge in private houses. Among these was María Mercedes Prat y Prat. Born in Barcelona in 1880, she joined the Archconfraternity of Mary Immaculate and St Teresa in her teens and was active in the Sunday School movement, teaching servant girls and the children of the poor to read and write as well as giving them religious instruction. In 1905 she entered the Tortosa convent of the Company of St Teresa and Jesus, founded by St Henry de Ossó y Cervelló (27 Jan.), and she made her profession in March 1907, adding "of the Heart of Jesus" to her baptismal name. She taught in several schools in Barcelona and nearby and in 1915 was appointed provincial counsellor, moving to the Congregation's novitiate in Tortosa. She remained there until 1920, when she transferred to the convent of San Gervasio in Barcelona. There she acted as secretary to the superior general and worked on a teaching journal, "Jesus the Teacher," impressing everyone by her devotion to the ideals of the founder and her life of prayer. On 23 July 1936 she was making her way to another house with Sister Joaquina Miguel when they were recognized as teaching Sisters (the education issue counting against them) and taken as prisoners to a house where other religious were being held. During the night they were led out into the street and shot. María Mercedes did not die for some hours; in great pain she kept reciting the Our Father and other prayers until some other soldiers found her and shot her again; she died at about four in the morning of 24 July. Sr Joaquina Miguel, though wounded herself, nursed her in her last hours and survived to witness to the martyrdom when her cause was introduced in 1969.

María Mercedes was beatified on 29 April 1990 in the same ceremony as the martyrs of Turón in 1934 (above) and Jaime Hilario, a Brother of the Christian Schools killed in Tarragona in 1937. In his homily at the beatification ceremony, Pope John Paul II said of him: "The exceptional path of this religious, a model of the man of faith searching constantly for God's will, is shown in unsuspected ways. The fidelity which he learned from his parents . . . was constant in his life. . . . This is what he wrote, in Catalan, his native language: 'My father is a model Christian and an example of an honest citizen. His conduct, speech, and actions are beyond reproach. . . . My mother is a saint. She lived sowing seeds of sweetness and love everywhere.' In the light of these witnesses one understands better the importance that this teacher and outstanding catechist gave to the role parents play in the education of children and young people."

In areas controlled by the Socialists rather than the anarchists the terror was scarcely less. To the south of Madrid, nearly 48 per cent of the priests were killed in the province of Toledo, 40 per cent in the rural province of Ciudad Real. The great majority of these were "simple, poor parish priests of modest background, scarcely any wealthier or more privileged than the supposed 'class enemies' who killed them" (Payne). Ciudad Real was also the setting for the killing of twenty-six members of the Passionist Order.

Some were students still doing their training (sixteen were aged twenty-one or less), some were lay brothers, and some priests. Their leader was Vicente Nicéforo Diez Tejerina, in religion Fr Nicephorus of Jesus and Mary, the provincial, who happened to be on an official visit to the small Passionist house in Daimiel (in the province of Ciudad Real) when the war broke out. Daimiel was in the territory controlled by the Republican forces, and the Passionists were forced to leave their monastery. Before they left Fr Nicephorus gathered everyone together in the chapel, gave them Holy Communion, and encouraged them to endure the sufferings that would certainly be theirs in the near future: "Brothers," he said to them, "this is our Gethsemane! . . . Citizens of Calvary, take courage!" He then divided them into four groups, mixing the older with the younger so that they could help each other. They left the monastery during the night of 21 July 1936 and were taken by the soldiers to the cemetery, where they thought they would be shot; instead, they were led off to different places and were beaten and manhandled as they went. The first group was killed on the night of 22 July at Carabanchel Bajo, and the second on the next day at Manzanares (Ciudad Real)—six of this group were only wounded, and they spent some time in hospital before being killed on 23 October. The third group was put on the train for Madrid but was shot at Urdá station (Toledo) on the night of the 23-24 July; of the final group, two were shot in Ciudad Real on 25 September, but the other five managed to escape.

The names and dates of birth of the martyrs in each group were:

1. Fr Germanus of Jesus and Mary (Pérez), 1898; Fr Philip of the Child Jesus (Valcabado), 1874; Bro. Maurilio of the Child Jesus, 1915; Bro. Joseph of Jesus and Mary (Osés), 1915; Bro. Julius of the Heart of Jesus (Mediavilla), 1915; Bro. Joseph Mary of the Suffering Jesus (Ruiz), 1916; Bro. Laurinus of

Jesus Crucified (Proano), 1916; Ancharius of the Immaculate One (Benito), lay brother, 1906; Philip of St Michael (Ruiz), lay brother, 1915.

2. Fr Nicephorus of Jesus and Mary (Diez Tejerina), 1893; Bro. Joseph of the Sacred Hearts (Estalajo), 1915; Bro. Epiphanius of St Michael (Sierra), 1916; Bro. Abilius of the Cross (Ramos), 1917; Bro. Zaccharia of the Blessed Sacrament (Fernández), 1917—all martyred on 23 July; Fr Ildephonsus of the Cross (García), 1898; Fr Justinian of St Gabriel (Cuesta), 1910; Euphrasius of the Merciful Love (De Celis), 1913; Bro. Thomas of the Blessed Sacrament (Cuartero), 1915; Bro. Honorius of the Dolorous Virgin (Carracedo), 1916; Bro. Joseph Mary of Jesus (Cuartero), 1918; Bro. Fulgentius of the Heart of Mary (Calvo), 1916—all martyred on 23 October.

3. Fr Peter of the Heart of Jesus (Calvo), 1907; Bro. Felix of the Five Wounds (Ugalde), 1915; Benito of the Mother of God of Villar (Solano), lay brother, 1882.

4. Fr John Peter of St Antony (Bengoa), 1890; Paul Mary of St Jospeh (Leoz), lay brother, 1882.

All these martyrs were beatified in 1989.

To the north of Madrid, the mountainous province of Guadalajara was occupied by Republican forces on 22 July 1936, leading to the martyrdom of three Carmelite nuns from the convent of St Joseph in the provincial capital, the first of the martyrs of the civil war to be beatified, on 29 March 1987.

The eldest of the three was Sr María-Pilar of St Francis Borgia, born Jacoba Martínez García in Zaragoza in 1897. She became a Carmelite in Guadalajara in 1908 and led an uneventful life, happy to serve others in the community and especially devoted to the Blessed Sacrament. She was heard to say, two days before being forced to leave the convent, that she was ready to offer herself as a victim and that "if they martyr us we will go singing, like the Compiègne martyrs" (referring to the sixteen Carmelites martyred during the French Revolution).

Sr Mary of the Angels was born in Getafe, near Madrid, in 1905, the last of ten children born to Manuel Valtierra and his wife, Lorenza Tordesillas, and christened Marciana. She was inspired by St Thérèse of Lisieux' (1 Oct.) autobiography to enter Carmel but was prevented from doing so until she was twenty-four, as she had to care for her widowed father. She joined the convent in Gaudalajara in 1929, embracing the spirit of poverty and showing great devotion in praying for the Church, the pope, missionaries, and sinners. She faced the prospect of death as the chance to share in the sufferings of Our Lord; when the convent was threatened, she wrote: "My God, [grant] my life the pains of martyrdom and accept it as a testimony of my love for you, just as you have accepted so many who have perished for the very reason that they have loved you."

Sr Teresa of the Child Jesus and St John of the Cross was born Eusebia

García García in the small town of Mochales, Guadalajara, in 1909. She too was much influenced by reading *Story of a Soul* and, like St Thérèse, longed to enter Carmel while still too young to be accepted. She is described as having "a lively temperament and impulsive character," which she had to dominate in order to conform to the ways of the convent, which she was able to enter when she reached sixteen. She had a special devotion to Our Lady, was a caring infirmarian, and took as her motto "Charity above all." She seems to have anticipated martyrdom with unusual cheerfulness, saying at one of the last suppers they ate together in the convent: "We must eat a lot and have plenty of blood to shed for Christ the King."

Groups of militia arrived in Guadalajara in the morning of 22 July. Afraid that the convent would be set on fire, the Sisters abandoned it in the afternoon, going out two by two, in modest secular dress, to seek refuge in hotels or the houses of sympathizers. When twelve Sisters were gathered in a boarding house the following day, the landlady took fright and said she could keep no more than three. Sr Teresa suggested to the other two that they should follow her to another house. They were recognized as nuns by militia, were unable to gain entry to the house, had to come back to the street, and were shot at. Sr Mary of the Angels was killed immediately, Sr María-Pilar was badly wounded and taken to hospital, where she died later, but Sr Teresa escaped. A militia-man caught up with her and pretended he was going to protect her but in fact forced her to the cemetery, trying to make her say, "Long live Communism!" to which she would only answer, "Long live Christ the King!" She was shot against the cemetery wall. The three were buried in a common grave, but their bodies were exhumed in 1941, recognizable from their scapulars and the crucifixes on their breasts.

In Madrid itself two Sisters of Charity of the Sacred Heart of Jesus from the college of Santa Susana were dragged out, driven to a suburb, and shot on 20 July 1936. They were Rita Dolores Pujalte Sánchez, born in 1853 and so eighty-three years old, and Francisca Aldea Aruajo, aged fifty-five. They were beatified in May 1998 together with seven Visitandine nuns, all members of the Madrid house of the Order, killed in November 1936, and Sr María Sagrario of St Aloysius Gonzaga, prioress of the Carmel of St Anne and St Joseph, aged fifty-five, shot in the Pradera de San Isidro on 15 August.

In Almería, in the south-eastern corner of Spain, revolutionary committees were formed on the outbreak of war and imprisoned everyone they suspected of not supporting the revolution, concentrating particularly on priests and religious. Their victims included Bishop Diego Ventaja Milán of Almería and Bishop Manuel Medina Olmos of Guadix, the town consisting largely of cave-dwellings between Almería and Granada. Both bishops had showed pastoral concern for all their people and were noted for their tireless visitations of their dioceses. Bishop Ventaja had been given several opportunities to flee the war zone but had steadfastly opted to remain with his flock. They were taken out to be shot in the night of 29-30 August, Bishop Medina telling his executioners that "we have done nothing to deserve death, but I forgive you so that the Lord may also forgive us. May our blood be the last shed in Almería." This was not to be: their deaths were closely followed by those of seven De la Salle Brothers from the College of St Joseph in Almería: Aurelio María, José Cecilio, Edmigio, Amalio, Valerio Bernardo, Teodomiro Joaquín, and Evencio Ricardo. All were taken into custody on 22 July; three were executed during the night of 30-31 August, two on 8 September, and the last two in the night of 12-13 September. These nine martyrs were beatified on 10 October 1993, together with two other educators, Pedro Poveda Castroverde, the founder of the Teresian Association, and Victoria Díez y Bustos de Molina, a member of the Association: see the separate entry on 28 July.

In Motril, on the south coast, seven Augustinian recollects and a parish priest were shot between 25 July and 15 August 1936. They were Vicente Soler, Deogracias Palacios, León Inchausti, José Rada, Vicente Pinilla, Julián Moreno, José Ricardo Diez, and Manuel Martín Sierra. They were beatified in May 1999.

The eastern and central provinces of Valencia, Teruel, Toledo, and Ciudad Real produced a further forty-five martyrs, killed on various dates between July 1936 and the end of the war and beatified on 1 October 1995. They were, in order of their date of death: nine members of the Congregation of Diocesan Workers (1936); thirteen Piarists, one priest and twelve lay brothers (1936); three men religious teachers belonging to the Marianist Order (1936); seventeen women catechists, Sisters of Christian Doctrine (1936); one layman, Vicente Vilar (1937: see the separate entry under 22 Feb. in the supplement to the December volume); and the bishop of Teruel and his vicar general (1939).

The Diocesan Workers were members of the Congregation founded by Bd Emmanuel Domingo y Sol (25 Jan.), dedicated to the promotion and formation of aspirants to the priesthood. The general director of this community was Fr Pedro Ruiz de los Paños y Angel, born in Mora in the province of Toledo in 1881. A prominent churchman, he had taught at the seminaries of Málaga, Badajoz, and Seville, as well as being rector of Plasencia College and of the Spanish College in Rome. He also founded the Disciples of Jesus, a Congregation of Sisters dedicated to fostering vocations. He was seized in Toledo on the outbreak of the war and killed there immediately. His eight companions were killed on various dates, all in 1936.

The Piarists (Clerks Regular of the Christian Schools, the Congregation founded by St Joseph Calasanz; 25 Aug.) were led by Fr Dionisio Pamplona. Born in 1868 in Calamocha, Teruel, he had served as rector of the Congregation's school in Buenos Aires for a time but in 1936 was acting parish priest of Peralta de la Sal, Huesca, the founder's birthplace. He was arrested there with five members of the community and imprisoned. He escaped and went to the

177

parish church, where he consumed all the consecrated hosts to save then from profanation. He was captured again and taken to prison in Monzón. When he and twelve companions were dragged out to be shot, he stood out among them as he was very tall, and the executioners aimed most of the shots at him, shouting "Leave the priest to me!"

The three Marianists were lay brothers: Carlos Eraña Guruceta, born in the Basque province of Guipúzcoa in 1884; Fidel Fuidio; and Jesús Hita. They were imprisoned in Ciudad Real in the general outburst of anticlerical and particularly anti-Catholic educational feeling at the beginning of the war. Carlos Eraña, a distinguished member of the first generation of Spanish Marianists (a teaching Congregation founded in Bordeaux in 1817 by Ven. Fr Guillaume Joseph Chaminade), was principal of the Colegio N. S. del Pilar (School of Our Lady of the Pillar) in Madrid, which was requisitioned by the Republicans mounting the defence of the capital. He went to Ciudad Real to seek help from former pupils but found that the Congregation's two schools there had also been requisitioned and their communities scattered. He was arrested, imprisoned for a time, and shot at dawn on 18 September 1936; his two companions were killed a few days later.

The seventeen Sisters of Christian Doctrine were the superior general, Angeles de San José Lloret Martí, born in Alicante in 1875, and "her sixteen companions." They were forced to leave their generalate and came together as an emergency community. Arrested at the outbreak of the war and imprisoned for some four months, they were all executed together in late autumn 1936.

The bishop of Teruel was Anselmo Polanco Fontecha, born the son of modest farmers in Buenavista de Valdavia in the province of Palencia in 1881. He joined the Augustinians in Valladolid in 1896 and was later made prior, holding this office until he was appointed provincial councillor in the Philippines. He bcame provincial superior there in 1932, his duties taking him on journeys to the United States, China, Colombia, and Peru. In 1935 he was named bishop of Teruel and apostolic administrator of Albarracín. He appointed Felipe Ripoll Morata as his vicar general. Born in Teruel in 1878, he had been professor and spiritual director at the diocesan seminary. Teruel was the one region in which the Republican side made significant military gains in the later stages of the war, and it was during this offensive in early 1938 that the bishop and his vicar general were seized. They were held prisoner for thirteen months and were finally shot during the Republican evacuation of Catalonia in the closing days of the war in March 1939.

The only region in which the Church, or a significant part of it, sided with the Republican cause was the Basque Country, where many of the clergy were numbered among advocates of separate rule. Fourteen such priests were shot by the Nationalists, accused of subversive political activities, while over sixty more were imprisoned. The papal nuncio intervened on their behalf, and they were kept under armed guard in a monastery. Catholics were to be found in the ranks of the Republican forces, including Generals Miaja and Rojo, and the Republican government tried, for political reasons, to maintain diplomatic relations with the Vatican throughout the war. But the Church was massively identified with the Nationalist cause and the privileged castes this was seen by the revolutionary Left to represent, and as such it was an inevitable target for revolutionary violence. This in turn meant that popular Catholic support for the military revolt eventually became overwhelming, which, as Stanley Payne comments, "was hardly surprising; only a diametrically opposite response would have been remarkable." And, he concludes: "The savage persecution by the Spanish Revolution was possibly the most intense single trial suffered by Spanish Catholicism in its long and eventful history. Both the ordinary clergy and the faithful bore their sufferings with courage and stoicism. Scarcely a single apostasy was registered among the latter in the face of their tormentors. The courage with which both clergy and laity withstood the most intense persecution was, sad to say, not equalled by corresponding mercy, charity, and justice among the triumphant Catholics of Franco's Nationalist zone" (pp. 169-70). It was not until fifty years after the outbreak of the war that the Spanish bishops could attempt to draw a line under the tragedy: "Although the Church does not pretend to be free from every error, those who reproach her with having ranged herself on the side of one of the contending parties should bear in mind the harshness of the religious persecution suffered in Spain from the year 1931. Nothing of this kind, on either side, should ever be repeated. May forgiveness and magnanimity provide the climate for our times. We accept the whole heritage of those who died for their faith while pardoning those who put them to death, and so many who offered their lives for a future of peace and justice in Spain" (from the document "Constructors of Peace" issued by the Spanish bishops, July 1986).

Biographical material (in English) on most of the individual martyrs is scant. The above account relies largely on the brief biographies published in the weekly *Osservatore Romano*: see the issues of 28 Oct. 1992, 13 Oct. 1993, 4 Oct. 1995, 7 May 1997. For the 1934 martyrs of Turón see *The Pope Teaches* (1990), no. 5, pp. 141-3; *El Mundo*, 27 Dec. 1998, p. 9; for the Carmelites of Guadalajara, Jesús Pla Gandia, *From Carmel to Calvary* (1987); also *A.A.S.* 80, pt. 1 (1988), pp. 360-4; *N.S.B.* 2, pp. 106-7; on Nicephorus Díez Tejerina and companions, *D.N.H.*, 3, pp. 142-5; *Bibl.SS.*, Suppl. 1, 416-8. For the general background the most comprehensive source is Hugh Thomas, *The Spanish Civil War* (3d ed., 1977), with ample bibliography; see also R. Carr and J. P. Fusi, *Spain: Dictatorship to Democracy* (1979), intro. and ch. 1, with further refs. in the notes. Citations above from Stanley G. Payne, *Spanish Catholicism* (1984), pp. 165-73. Specifically on the persecution of the Church see Frances Lannon, *Privilege, Perscution and Prophecy: The Catholic Church in Spain 1875-1975* (1987); Antonio Montero Moreno, *Historia de la persecución religiosa en España 1936-9* (1961), generally regarded as the definitive work on the killings of clergy and religious; Vicente Cárcel, *Mártires españoles del siglo XX* (1966).

23

ST BRIDGET OF SWEDEN, *Foundress* (1303-73)

Birgitta was the daughter of Birger, the powerful governor of the Swedish province of Uppland, and his second wife, Ingeborg, and was born in 1302 or 1303. As a child she had two visions: in one she was crowned by Our Lady, and in the other she saw Christ on the cross and heard a voice saying that those who spurned his love were responsible for his death. This second vision affected her very deeply, and the sufferings of Our Lord became the focus of her spiritual life. At the age of thirteen or fourteen she married Ulf Gudmarsson and they lived happily together for twenty-eight years, having eight children, one of whom became St Catherine of Sweden (24 Mar.).

Bridget gained a reputation for her care of the sick in the neighbourhood, performing herself many of the nursing tasks usually left to servants and insisting that her children should accompany her on her visits. About the year 1335 she was called to the court of King Magnus II to become a lady-in-waiting to his new queen Blanche of Namur. She tried to change the behaviour of both king and queen, but without any success: they admired her obvious piety but refused to take her and her visions seriously. When her youngest son died in 1340 she went on pilgrimage to the shrine of St Olaf in Trondheim, Norway, and later, with her husband, to Compostela in Spain. Unfortunately, Ulf died shortly afterwards at the Cistercian monastery at Alvastra, and Bridget remained there for three years as a penitent—there is some evidence that husband and wife had planned to enter religious houses on their return from the pilgrimage. Her visions and revelations increased during this period and became so frequent that Bridget herself wondered if they were delusions inspired by the devil, but she was assured by a learned Swedish canon that they were genuinely from God. In one of them Our Lord told her that she would be his bride and his mouthpiece and would "hear and see spiritual matters and heavenly secrets." Shortly after this he said to her: "You are mine, therefore I shall do with you as it please me. Love nothing as you love me. Cleanse yourself hourly of sin . . . there is no sin so trivial or so trifling that it can be disregarded" (quoted in Andersson).

As a result of one of her visions, in 1346 she set about founding a monastery at Vadstena, on Lake Vättern—it was not finally established until 1369. In the vision Our Lord described how the monasteries of the time were in decline and continued, "I shall plant for myself a new vineyard, and to it you shall bear the vine branches of my words and there they shall take root" (*ibid.*), and this was the beginning of her Order of the Most Holy Saviour, or Bridgettine Order, as it is more usually referred to. Every detail of the Rule was revealed to her in a number of visions. There was to be a double monastery, for sixty nuns and twenty-five men, thirteen of them priests, four deacons, and eight laymen. Bridget as abbess was in overall charge of temporal matters, but the superior of the monks directed the spiritual life of both parts. Any surplus income was to be given to the poor, the buildings had to be simple, and the only additional belongings the nuns and monks could have were books for study—during the fifteenth century the monastery became the literary centre of Sweden. This Rule was approved only in 1370, and then as an addition to the Benedictine way of life imposed on the members by the pope; there were to be two separate houses next to each other. The Order eventually spread throughout Europe, reaching a peak of seventy houses.

Bridget's visions also involved her in the politics of the day, and, like her contemporary St Catherine of Siena (29 Apr.), she tried above all to persuade the popes to leave Avignon and return to Rome, but she had little hope of success with Pope Clement VI (1342-52), whom Christ in a vision had supposedly called "a destroyer of souls, worse than Lucifer, more unjust than Pilate, and more merciless than Judas" (1:41). On a later occasion her envoy to Avignon refused to read her letter to the pope because its language was so strong. Bridget was also worried about the war between France and England and the devastation that she had seen while travelling through France as a pilgrim. She wanted Pope Clement VI to bring about peace between King Edward III and King Philip IV and also sent envoys to the kings themselves. These efforts achieved nothing, however, and she was again disappointed when King Magnus went ahead with a so-called crusade against his pagan neighbours when what he wanted was their lands and not their conversion; Bridget had at first supported his plans, but he had refused to accept her idea of what a truly religious crusade should be. She was out of favour at the Swedish court, and although she had become more popular among the people by travelling around the country with a team of chaplains, helping to look after the poor and working inexplicable cures among them, the effect of her outspoken condemnations and prophecies was wearing off—given their language, this is hardly surprising: "The Son of God speaks: I have said before that I will scourge the knights of this kingdom with the sword, the spear, and my fury. But they answer, 'God is merciful. This evil will not come. . . .' Harken now to what I say! I shall stand up and I shall spare neither young nor old, rich nor poor, honest nor dishonest; instead, with my plough I shall tear out the stubble of the fields and the trees . . . the houses shall be without inhabitants. . . . Three sins abound in this kingdom, pride, voluptuousness, and greed" (*Extrav.* 74, in Andersson). Many of these early revelations and visions concentrate on the evils of sin, the corruption of the world, and the need for bodily penance. They were vivid and pictorial, at times even apocalyptic. The Virgin Mary features prominently in them, instructing Bridget on the spiritual life and especially on the need to meditate on Christ's sufferings. Other revelations were the result of people asking Bridget for advice on specific topics—the king on how he should rule, a pious bishop on how he should live his life—and go into precise detail on everyday matters.

Bridget always reported her visions and revelations to her confessors, sometimes writing them down herself in Swedish and taking considerable care to express them correctly; at other times it was her confessors who wrote them down for her; after this initial transcription, often done quickly to avoid her forgetting the detail, a revision and translation into Latin were made under her supervision. Only a few fragments of her original Swedish remain. There has been considerable debate about the accuracy of the accounts as we have them and a strong belief that her confessors altered her accounts to make them more acceptable. Alban Butler commented that a version by Bridget herself "would have been compiled with more simplicity and with greater life and spirit, and would have received a higher degree of certainty." We now know, however, that Bridget was very concerned about the accuracy of what her confessors wrote, having them translate their Latin back into Swedish for her, or reading it carefully herself to check it for accuracy—Bridget later learned enough Latin herself to read what they had written. Our Lord himself had told her that she was not capable of "recounting and writing sufficiently warmly of what you have felt without both weighing it in your memory and writing and rewriting it until you come to the true meaning of my words." Her main editors were Canon Mathias of Linköping (her first director), Prior Peter of Alvastra, Prior Peter of Skänninge, and the Spaniard Alfonso of Pecha, whom Bridget met on pilgrimage. The two Peters and, later, Alfonso were a constant part of her household once she moved to Italy and were responsible for the first Life, prepared within months of her death. A modern authority concludes: "The scribe-editors had very little scope for independent operation, (and) acted simply as faithful and accurate translators"; even where Bridget permitted them a more active role, to clarify doctrinal ambiguities or enhance the style, it was always done with her approval and only to help her express "the proper sense of the divine message" (Ellis).

Bridget became increasingly dissatisfied and frustrated in Sweden and in 1349 was directed by a vision to go to Rome, partly to gain the jubilee indulgence of 1350, partly to obtain papal approval for her new foundation, but principally in the hope of being more effective in her efforts to persuade the pope to return from Avignon. She arrived in Rome to find a city partly in ruins and divided into armed camps by rival factions. She and her small household took up residence in a house given them by a cardinal near San Lorenzo in Damaso. It was here that she wrote her famous *Sermo Angelicus,* the result of revelations dictated by an angel. These comprised twenty-one lessons, three of which were to be read at Matins each day of the week. Bridget tells how she sat in her room every morning for several days after her prayers, with pen and paper ready, awaiting the arrival of the angel, who proceeded to describe how the Virgin Mary in her perfection existed in God's mind before the beginning of time, how the prophets and patriarchs rejoiced over her coming, how she was born and grew to maturity, how her Son was born and how she shared in his suffering, and finally how she died and was received into heaven (Andersson). The whole is a long hymn in praise of Mary, showing the positive side of Bridget's revelations in contrast to the frequent denunciations they contained: for example, when Mary's soul left her body "it was gloriously raised by God above all the heavens, and God gave her the rank of Empress over the whole world and made her the everlasting sovereign of the angels. . . . Because she had proved to be the most humble among angels and men, she was raised above all that was created, and is most beautiful of all and more like God than any other can be." The images are sometimes unusual: Mary "can properly be called the Tree of Life," and if people venerate her devotedly and "with all their might strive to bend the branches of the tree," she will help them obtain the "fruit of the Tree of Life, namely Christ's most holy body . . . nourishment and life for you sinners here on earth, and for the angels in heaven" (*ibid.*). The overall theme of the revelations is the omnipotence of God, sovereign of the universe, who exercises justice tempered with mercy. Bridget's devotion to the humanity of Our Lord and to Our Lady is prominent throughout, and she also urged devotion to St Joseph and the angels (Hogg).

From Rome she visited the great monastery at Farfa to remonstrate with the abbot, who, in her words, was "a very worldly man, who did not trouble about souls at all." She had more success in Bologna, where she set about reforming a lax monastery, with help this time from her daughter Catherine, who returned with her to Rome and remained as her companion and helper. Later they made a tour of the Italian shrines; this lasted about two years and showed Bridget's intense devotion to the saints.

In 1367 Bd Urban V (19 Dec.) returned to Rome from Avignon, and Bridget was overjoyed. This did not last long, however, as Urban spent much of his time away from the city and was rumoured to be thinking of a return to France. Bridget had a vision in which Our Lord appeared to tell her to go to the pope, warn him that his death was near, and show him the Rule of her new Order. He approved the Rule but returned to Avignon in 1370, where he died four months later. Bridget wrote several times to his successor, Gregory XI, warning him to return to Rome, which he did four years after her death, but not as a result of her pleading. Again like Catherine of Siena, she did not understand the complexities of the issues involved in the church politics of the day or the strength of the vested interests. Neither did she realize that the different factions in the Church used her for their own advantage, claiming that her visions and prophecies supported their cause. This lost her considerable popularity in Rome, and her prophecies that the people would be severely punished if they did not reform did not help her; she had to leave her house and was seriously in debt, being reduced to begging for herself and her daughter.

Another vision directed Bridget to go on pilgrimage to the Holy Land, and she set out in 1371 with her daughter Catherine, two of her sons, and a group of followers. Her son Charles died while they were in Naples, after becoming scandalously involved with Queen Joanna "of unenviable reputation" (*B.T.A.*), and the party was almost drowned in a shipwreck off the coast of Palestine, but the pilgrimage went ahead, with Bridget experiencing a succession of visions of biblical events where they had happened; especially vivid were visions of the Nativity in Bethlehem and of the crucifixion on Calvary. (Some details are rejected by modern New Testament scholars.) On the way back they visited Cyprus, where Bridget denounced the wickedness of the royal family and the people: "People of Cyprus, if you do not wish to repent and mend your ways I shall destroy your race and your descendants . . . and I shall spare neither rich nor poor. I shall so thoroughly destroy this race that in a short space of time the memory of you will be obliterated from the minds of men as if you had never been born into this world." She did the same in Naples, where her condemnations and warnings were read out by the clergy from the city's pulpits, but to little effect. She arrived back in Rome in March 1373, already seriously ill, and died in the city on 23 July in the house on the corner of the Piazza Farnese, which is still a Bridgettine convent. Four months after her temporary burial in the church of San Lorenzo nel Panisperna her remains were taken in triumph through Dalmatia, Austria, and Poland to Sweden, where they were re-interred in the abbey at Vadstena, where they still rest. Bridget was canonized in 1391 and is the patron saint of Sweden. Her feast was formerly celebrated on 8 October.

Bridget was canonized for her virtues, not for her visions. Her austere way of life, her work as a foundress, her service to the poor and the sick, and her devotion in visiting shrines and helping pilgrims, were outstanding, but it was her revelations and visions that caught the imagination. The book of her revelations was translated into several languages; a partial translation by the English Bridgettine Richard Whytford was printed in 1531, but they had already been known in England long before that, the first English translation having appeared before 1415. They became a standard part of fifteenth-century works of devotion and were used in instructing people about the active and contemplative life. In England the cult seems to have been largely literary and devotional, with few of the ordinary signs of a popular cult such as dedications and pictorial representations, although Bridget does appear on some screens in East Anglia and Devon. The centre of her cult was the great Brigettine abbey of Syon, half-way between Windsor and Westminster. This was founded in 1415 by Henry V, who had a great devotion to her; he also had a highly-prized relic. English writers were to the fore in defending the orthodoxy of the revelations in the fifteenth century.

Today there are three branches of the female Brigettines with about thirty convents in all: one of these can claim an unbroken tradition from the medieval foundations and exists in The Netherlands, Germany, and England. The second is a Spanish branch, founded at the beginning of the seventeenth century and with subsidiary houses in Mexico, while the third is a Swedish branch founded in 1911, with its headquarters in Bridget's house in Rome and houses in England, Italy, Sweden, India, and the U.S.A.; this last branch concentrates on active charitable work. The English abbey at South Brent in Devon can claim unbroken continuity with Syon Abbey, dissolved under Henry VIII (and which produced one of the first of the English martyrs, St Richard Reynolds), for the nuns took refuge in Flanders, and after a brief spell back in Syon under Mary I, moved to Lisbon and then to Spettisbury in Dorset in 1861; they moved to Chudleigh in 1887 and to South Brent in 1925.

Alfonso Pecha prepared an official text of the *Revelations* for the canonization process in 1377: this consisted of seven books, the *Sermo Angelicus*, and four prayers; in 1380 he produced another version with an additional fourteen chapters, probably omitted previously because of their criticism of various clerics; Peter of Alvastra also added further chapters to Book 6, and by 1391 an eighth book had been added. Peter of Alvastra also collected the *Revelationes extravagantes*, taken from Bridget's notes and clarifying obscure points in some of the revelations. Copies of the *Revelations*, whole or partial, were circulating in Europe before Bridget's death, and they were translated into most European languages; they were first printed in 1492 (Hogg). The first complete modern edition, in Swedish, was by T. Lunden (1957-9); a critical edition is being prepared by the Royal Academy in Stockholm.

The earliest Life of St Bridget was written by Peter of Alvastra and Peter of Skeninge immediately after her death as the first step toward canonization; this was later revised by Alfonso, but it was not printed until 1871. Another Life was written before 1383 by Birger, archbishop of Uppsala, and at least three others in the first half of the fifteenth century. Much scholarly material exists in Swedish. I. Collijn, *Acta et Processus canonizationis beatae Birgittae* (1924-31), is the principal source and contains the early Life. For English biographies and studies see Helen Redpath, *God's Ambassadress* (1947); J. Jörgensen, *St Bridget of Sweden*, 2 vols. (Eng. trans., 1954); A Butkovich, *Revelations; Saint Birgitta of Sweden* (1972); Aron Andersson, *St Bridget of Sweden* (1980), based on her visions and revelations; A. R. Kezel, *Birgitta of Sweden. Life and Selected Revelations* (Eng. trans., notes, and ed. by Margaret Harris, 1990); James Hogg (ed.), *Studies in St Birgitta and the Brigittine Order*, 2 vols. (1993), in *Analecta Cartusiana* series, 35; this includes Roger Ellis, "The Divine Message and its Human Agents: St Birgitta and her Editors." See also Arne Jönsson (ed.), *St Bridget's revelations to the popes. An edition of the so-called Tractatus de summis pontificibus* (1997); F. R. Johnston, "The English Cult of St Bridget of Sweden," *Anal.Boll.* 103 (1985), pp. 75-93; *Dict.Sp.*, 1 (1937), 1943-58; *Bibl.SS.*, 3, 439-533; *Diz. Ist. Perf.*, 1, 1572-93.

It is generally agreed that the graphic nature of Bridget's visions, especially those of the Nativity and the cruxcifixion, influenced fifteenth- and sixteenth-century artists in their portrayal of these subjects, although it is not always easy to be definite about specific works of art. Paintings of the Nativity that show the Virgin in white and kneeling with her mantle and shoes beside her, with Jesus lying naked on the ground, probably owe a debt to Bridget's vision (Murray). Grünewald's famous Isenheim Altarpiece was also influenced by her. Bridget herself is represented in a number of ways, sometimes in the act of receiving her revelations from an angel, sometimes founding her Order—as in the Sogliani canvas in the Galleria dell'Accademia, Florence, which shows her looking up to the heavens and Our Lord, Our Lady, and the angels in glory. She is usually dressed both as a widow and a religious, in a black or grey habit and the white veil of widowhood over her head (the habit of her nuns), and carries either an abbess' crozier or a pilgrim's staff.

Her abbey at Vadstena, with her room overlooking the high altar of the church, has been extensively and tastefully restored.

St Apollinaris of Ravenna, *Bishop and Martyr* (date unknown)

According to tradition, Apollinaris was from Antioch and a disciple of St Peter the Apostle (29 June), who appointed him first bishop of the imperial city of Ravenna. This tradition, however, dates from the seventh century and has no historical support; it dates from the time of Archbishop Maurus (642-71), who was almost certainly its author—perhaps, it has been suggested, to give additional prestige to the city, which was beginning to lose its importance. In the early Church Apollinaris was certainly venerated as a martyr and his cult was strong, but there are no reliable details about his life or how he died. He is first mentioned in the fifth-century *Hieronymianum* under today's date, and St Peter Chrysologus (30 July), who became bishop of Ravenna about the year 433, also mentions him in his writings. The beautiful basilica of San Apollinare in Classe, dedicated in 549, contained his tomb and a fine mosaic of him in the vault of the apse. In the eighth century the basilica of San Martino in Ciel d'Oro was re-named San Apollinare Nuovo on the occasion of the translation of the relics to a new shrine. Popes Symmachus (498-511) and Honorius (625-38) were responsible for the development of the cult in Rome, while Clovis, king of the Franks (481-511), built a church dedicated to St Apollinaris in Dijon, further witness to the spread of the cult.

E. Will, *Saint Apollinaire de Ravenne* (1936); *D.H.G.E.*, 1, 957-9; *E.E.C.*, 1, p. 59. See also *N.C.E.*, 12, pp. 96-102, on Ravenna.

St John Cassian (*c.* 360-435)

John Cassian (often referred to simply as Cassian) was born about the year 360. Gennadius of Marseilles, writing in the second half of the fifth century, said that he was a "Scythian," that is, from Scythia Minor or Dobrogea, and he may have come from around the shores of the Black Sea in what is now eastern Romania. He went on pilgrimage to the Holy Land and became a monk in a monastery in Bethlehem, leaving after a short time to go to Egypt to study the monastic life of the Desert Fathers. He came under the influence of Evagrius Ponticus, a key figure in the development of monastic spirituality, and spent some time at Sketis living with the monks there. About the year 400 he was in Constantinople, where he became a disciple of St John Chrysostom (13 Sept.)

and was ordained deacon. When St John was deposed, John Cassian was part of the delegation sent to Rome to intercede with Pope St Innocent I on his behalf; it is possible that he was ordained priest at this time, perhaps in Rome.

As far as is known, John Cassian spent the rest of his life in the West. About the year 415 he founded two monasteries in Marseilles, one for monks built over the tomb of St Victor (21 July), the other for nuns. He wrote two important works on monasticism, the *Institutes of the Monastic Life* and the *Conferences of the Egyptian Monks*. The first of these set out in detail the rules for the living of the community monastic life and included what he saw as the main obstacles to monastic perfection. By way of preface he wrote: "I shall make no attempt to relate anecdotes of miracles and prodigies. For although I have heard of many unbelievable marvels from my elders and have seen some with my own eyes, I have wholly omitted them because they contribute nothing but astonishment to the instruction of the reader in the perfect life." This sober approach may have helped the work to become a standard reference for those interested in developing monastic rules in the centuries after his death; it was used extensively in the West and was one of the sources used by St Benedict (11 July). The *Conferences* is an account of his conversations with various Egyptian monks and was influential in introducing their ideas and practices into Western, and especially French, monasticism, although there is some debate about how accurately he reported the long speeches of the Desert Fathers—some of them embody elements from Evagrius Ponticus. "They became a classic without rival in the monastic west . . . and (they) were read every night before compline in early medieval monasteries. They were a *vade mecum* of saints as different as Thomas Aquinas and Teresa of Avila" (Knowles).

John Cassian also wrote *De Incarnatione Domini contra Nestorium* ("On the Incarnation of the Lord against Nestorius") at the request of St Leo the Great (10 Nov.) to warn the West against the view that there were two persons in Christ. He died about 435 and is regarded as one of the founding-fathers of Western monasticism. There was little or no cult of him in the West outside Marseilles although the Eastern Church regarded him as a saint, and he did not feature in the Roman Martyrology because he was taken to be the originator of the Semi-Pelagian heresy. This concerned the relationship between the human will and divine grace and maintained that the first steps toward the Christian life could be taken by the unaided human will, with grace intervening only later. This contradicted St Agustine's strict teaching on predestination and the inability of the human will to do anything good without grace, and John Cassian's teaching should be seen as part of the anti-Augustinianism that was strong in southern Gaul, especially in the monasteries, and which continued there for many years.

John Cassian's writings may be found in *P.L.*, 49 and 50. A French trans. of the *Conferences* was published by E. Pichery, O.S.B., in S.C. 42, 54, 64 (1955-9), and of the *Institutes* by J. C. Guy, S.J., *ibid.*, 109 (1965). See O. Chadwick, *John Cassian, A Study in Primitive*

Monasticism (2d. ed., 1968); *Dict.Sp.*, 1 (1953), 214-76; D. Knowles, *Christian Monasticism* (1969), pp. 15-36. On Semi-Pelagianism see *O.D.C.C.*, p. 1481.

Bd Joan of Orvieto (*c.* 1264-1306)

Giovanna was the daughter of a peasant family, born in Carnaiola and known locally as Vanna. When her parents died while she was still only five years old, she was adopted and brought up by relatives in Orvieto. In due time they arranged for her to marry, but Joan refused to accept this, ran away from home, and became a Dominican tertiary. The rest of her life she dedicated to serving God and looking after the poor, and she gained a reputation for praying especially hard for those who had offended her—so much so that it became a byword in Orvieto that anyone who wanted help from her should do her a bad turn! Her early biographer describes her as being "constant in her patience, tranquil in her obedience, and wonderful in her works." For some years she was under the spiritual direction of Bd James of Bevagna (23 Aug.), a local Dominican, and she made such progress that she frequently experienced ecstasies and other physical phenomena during her prayers, including bilocation and levitation. It was reported that for the last ten years of her life she spent from midday to evening on Good Friday in a trance-like ecstasy, stretched out on the floor as though crucified. She had a particularly strong devotion to the passion of Our Lord and to the angels, especially to her guardian angel. Joan died on 23 July 1306 and was buried in the local Dominican church; her remains were moved to a more obvious shrine the following year. They were authenticated in 1743 and her cult approved in 1754.

There is a fourteenth-century Life by James Scalza. See *Bibl.SS.*, 6, 556-7.

24

St **Declan,** *Bishop* (date unknown)

"There were in Ireland before Patrick came thither four holy bishops with their followers who evangelized and sowed the word of God there; these are the four: Ailbe, Ibar, Declan, and Ciaran. They drew multitudes from error to the faith of Christ, although it was Patrick who sowed the faith throughout Ireland and it is he who turned chiefs and kings of Ireland to the way of baptism, faith and sacrifice and everlasting judgment" (quoted in *The Irish Saints*). This extract from the early Irish Life of St Declan would seem to settle the debate as to whether he preached before or after St Patrick (17 Mar.), a debate that the previous edition of this work believed undecided; it does not, however, provide any clear indication as to the date of his birth or death.

Before Patrick's arrival in the fifth century Ireland had links with the Continent and with Wales, and people from the south-east of the country had already settled in Wales. These links would have led to the introduction of Christianity and probably also of monasticism as practised in Gaul, even though the majority of the Irish people remained pagan. We are told that Declan was born while his noble parents were visiting an uncle who lived between modern Cappoquin and Lismore among the Déisi people of Waterford. The site is marked today by a "very insignificant ancient graveyard with traces of the foundations of a church" (*ibid.*). A priest named Colman persuaded the parents to have the child baptized, and Declan later studied in some sort of cell with two or three others, but there is no reason to think of this as a monastic settlement. It appears that he then went to the Continent to continue his studies and to be ordained priest and perhaps consecrated as a bishop, though accounts of a journey to Rome and a meeting with Patrick in Gaul may be discounted. Nor could he have met St David (1 Mar.), as the Life states, but it is quite likely that he did visit Wales and some of his own people there. His choice of Ardmore in County Waterford is said to have been the result of a miraculous boulder that followed him from Wales—the boulder, in fact an ice-age erratic, is still on the beach at Ardmore and features in the annual pilgrimages in honour of the saint. Declan made Ardmore his centre and from there evangelized the areas around present-day Waterford and Lismore, although he failed to convert the king of the Déisi. In his old age he retired to a hermit's cell—marked today by the ruins of a large church and a holy well—but returned to the main settlement at Ardmore to die. The martyrology of Oengus (early ninth century) commemorates him: "If you have a right, O Erin, to a

189

champion of battle to aid you, you have the head of a hundred thousand, Declan of Ardmore."

Over the supposed site of his tomb stands the remains of an early oratory known as Declan's House. There are extensive remains at Ardmore, including a round tower and a twelfth-century cathedral built over the remains of an earlier church. His tomb was for centuries the focus of an annual pilgrimage, but since 1951 this has shifted to the holy well by his hermitage, which now has a bathing place and an oratory; modern cures are reported to have occurred there.

For the ancient Irish Life, see P. Power (ed.), *Life of St Declan of Ardmore* (1914). See also *The Irish Saints*, pp. 137-42, on which the above account is based and which includes an account of various miracles and the famous wonder-working bell of Declan.

SS Boris and Gleb, *Martyrs* (1015)

Boris and Gleb were two of the sons of St Vladimir of Kiev (15 July), who had been responsible for introducing Christianity as the official religion of the Russian State. They are among the best known of all Russian saints, but there are different accounts of their deaths, which makes it difficult to give a definitive version and to assess how far they should legitimately be regarded as martyrs. The most commonly accepted version is that Vladimir died suddenly before he could settle the inheritance to his kingdom. His son Svjatopolk took control and decided to exterminate his brothers in order to ensure that he became sole ruler. Boris, who was about twenty years old at this time, was returning from an expedition against the Pechenegs when he learned of these plans, but he refused to allow his soldiers to defend him against Svyatopolk, arguing that as the brother now stood in the place of Vladimir, Boris owed him the same respect and obedience as he had given to his father. After considering the matter and praying about it for some time, Boris decided to wait quietly for his murderers and was killed near the river Alta on 24 July 1015, only nine days after Vladimir's death. Later that year Gleb was returning to Kiev at Svjatopolk's invitation when a group of assassins sent by his brother met him on the River Dnieper. For a time he argued with his murderers, trying to persuade them to spare him, but then he submitted and was killed; the date was 5 September. Four years later Jaroslav, another of Vladimir's sons, overcame Svjatopolk and took possession of Kiev. He transferred the bodies of Boris and Gleb to the church of St Basil in Vyshgorod, honoured them as martyrs, and began the diffusion of their cult throughout Russia, where they became venerated as the proto-martyrs of the Russian Church. They were canonized by Metropolitan John I (1019-35).

There is some debate about how popular the two saints were in the years immediately after their death; their canonization could have been politically inspired and the cult imposed, as it were, from above by Jaroslav. Some have argued that they were venerated first as healers, because healing miracles were reported at their tombs, and that their cult was restricted to a small circle of relatives before a translation of their relics in 1072—which some see as the actual canonization. Perhaps a popular Christian cult could hardly be expected so soon after the conversion of the people, anyway, and probably the cult developed slowly, after Jaroslav had brought the bodies of his brothers together, miracles had been reported, and the bodies disinterred and found to be incorrupt. Their relics were translated on two occasions to new churches in Vyshgorod, and their cult spread only slowly into more outlying parts.

The two certainly did not fit into the normal categories of sainthood: they had not been missionaries or great teachers, neither had they been monks or bishops. It has been argued that they were the first examples of a peculiarly Russian category of sainthood: they had died unjustly in the cause of non-violence and so were "passion-sharers" with Christ and worthy of the title of martyr: they fulfilled Christ's prophecy that his followers would be betrayed by members of their own families (to some extent, St Wenceslaus [28 Sept.] could be regarded as the prototype of this model). One account says that, just before he died, Gleb thanked God in these words: "Glory to you, my Lord, for enabling me to escape from the allurements of this deceitful life. . . . For your sake I am led like a lamb to the slaughter. . . . I do not resist, I do not complain" (quoted in Attwater); it is unlikely these are Gleb's words, but they illustrate the outlook of those who regarded him as a martyr.

In the West Pope Benedict XIII approved their cult as martyrs in 1724—in Baptism Boris and Gleb had taken the names Romanus and David, and they were sometimes referred to by these names in the West. A number of Russian monasteries and villages were named Borisoglebsk in their honour.

Gail Lenhoff, *The Martyred Princes Boris and Gleb: A Socio-Cultural Study of the Cult and the Texts* (1989), is an important modern study in English, drawing mainly on Russian research. See also *Bibl.SS.*, 3, 356-9; *O.D.S.*, pp. 62-3; D. Attwater, *Saints of the East* (1963), pp. 125-9.

In art the two brothers are always shown together, almost like twins; they are usually carrying swords and holding Russian crosses in their hands; they are sometimes on horseback. They were among the commonest subjects for icon painters.

Bd Cunegund of Poland (*c.* 1224-92)

Cunegund (in Hungarian, Kinga) was the daughter of King Bela IV of Hungary and the niece of St Elizabeth of Hungary (17 Nov.). She was born about the year 1224 and brought up at court until she was sixteen years of age, when she was married to King Boleslaus IV of Poland. Tradition has it that on their wedding night she told her husband that she had vowed herself to God and wished to live a life of celibacy; he agreed to this for a year, and then together they took a vow of celibacy before the bishop of Cracow—hence his name Boleslaus the Chaste in Polish history. It is possible that this tradition grew out of the need to explain their childlessness.

Cunegund continued at court as queen but lived an austere life, wearing a hair shirt and giving what time she could to the care of the poor and sick. When her husband died in 1279 she refused to rule in his place and instead became a Poor Clare in the convent she had founded at Stary Sacz in the far south of the country. She built churches and hospitals, supported the Friars Minor financially, and paid for the ransom of Christian prisoners from the Turks. Later she reluctantly became prioress. In 1287 the Tartars invaded the country and the nuns had to take refuge in a castle; at first the invaders besieged it, but they then withdrew peacefully as a result of Cunegund's prayers. The final years before her death, on 24 July 1292, were marked by miracles and other supernatural manifestations, including an apparition of St Francis of Assisi (4 Oct.). Her popular cult was approved in 1690, and in 1715 she was declared patron of Poland and Lithuania.

Two medieval Lives exist, both originating in Cracow in the fifteenth century; see *Bibl.SS.*, 4, 400-1; *Vies des Saints,* 7, pp. 700-1.

Bd John of Tossignano, *Bishop* (1386-1446)

Giovanni Tavelli was born in Tossignano, near Imola, in north-eastern Italy, in 1386. He studied law at the nearby university of Bologna and then received the tonsure and minor orders with the intention of going on to ordination. For some reason he did not do so but joined the *Gesuati,* a lay Congregation dedicated to nursing and other works of charity, founded in the previous century by Bd John Colombini (31 July). In addition to this practical apostolate John translated parts of the Bible, some of St Gregory's (3 Sept.) *Moralia,* and a number of St Bernard's (20 Aug.) sermons into Italian and wrote several devotional works of his own. In 1425 he used his legal expertise to produce the *Capitula seu Regulae . . . Iesuatorum,* which became the official version of the Rule of the *Gesuati.* He also wrote a Life of John Colombini and a treatise on the religious life, *De perfectione religionis,* at the request of the monks of Santa Bonda in Siena. In 1426 the general chapter elected him rector of the community in Ferrara, where he was responsible for building their church, dedicated to St Jerome.

In 1431 he was appointed bishop of Ferrara, and he enjoyed a moment of universal attention when Pope Eugene IV (1431-47) transferred the Council of Basle to Ferrara in 1437: the council was to bring about union between the Eastern and Western Churches, and John was host to the pope, the emperor, and the patriarch of Constantinople until Eugene transferred the council to Florence early in 1439. As bishop John was a careful pastor and won the respect of his people and the clergy; accounts of his visitations and his letters reveal his zeal, deep spirituality, and wide learning. In 1444 he devoted the whole of a large legacy to building a hospital for the poor. He died two years later and was buried in the church of Saint Jerome; after the suppression of the

Congregation in 1688 his remains were moved to the Carmelite church. The fifth centenary of his death in 1946 saw a big increase in the popularity of his cult, originally approved in 1712, and his remains were moved again, to a separate side altar.

A Life was written about the year 1505 by one of the *Gesuati;* see *AA.SS.*, July, 5, 787-804. A Life by an anonymous contemporary was published in *Anal.Boll.* 4 (1885), pp. 31-42. See also *Bibl.SS.*, 12, 151-5.

Bd Louisa of Savoy (1462-1503)

Louisa was the daughter of Bd Amadeus IX of Savoy (30 Mar.) and his wife, Yolande of France. She was born in Geneva in 1462 and in 1479 married Hugh of Châlon-Arlay, lord of Nozeroy. The couple gave an excellent example of how to live a Christian life in courtly society. Hugh died in 1490, and two years later Louisa joined the Poor Clares at Orbe (Vaud), where she died on 24 July 1503. She was buried in the convent chapel, but in 1531, when there was a danger of her tomb being defaced by Protestants, her remains were moved to lie beside those of her husband in Nozeroy. The very popular cult was approved in 1839, and in 1842 her remains were moved again, this time to the royal chapel in Turin. Her feast used to be celebrated on 9 September.

There is a Life by Catherine de Saulx, one of Louisa's ladies-in-waiting, who followed her into the convent. This was published in 1860 by A. M. Jeanneret. See *Bibl.SS.*, 8, 297.

BB Robert Ludlam and Nicholas Garlick, *Martyrs* (1588)

Robert Ludlam was born in Radbourne in Derbyshire about the year 1551. He spent two years at St John's College, Oxford, but left without taking a degree. After teaching for some time he entered the English College in Reims in 1580, was ordained the following year, and left for England in April 1582. His ministry as a priest seems to have been back in his native county, and it was there that he was arrested at Padley in a house belonging to the Fitzherberts and inhabited at the time by a John Fitzherbert. The latter claimed that he did not know that Robert Ludlam and Nicholas Garlick, who was arrested at the same time, were seminary priests, and the two priests themselves supported his statement just before they died. Nevertheless, John Fitzherbert was kept in prison in Derby for two years and was then sent to the Fleet in London, where he died in 1590.

Nicholas Garlick was born near Glossop in Derbyshire about the year 1554. He spent a few months at Gloucester College, Oxford, in 1574, and then worked as schoolmaster at Tideswell, Derbyshire, for seven years. One of his pupils was Robert Bagshaw, who later became a seminary priest and wrote an account of his former teacher; another pupil was Bd Christopher Buxton (1 Oct.). Nicholas entered the English College in 1581, was ordained the following year, and returned to work in England in January 1583. He was betrayed by a Catholic prisoner who had lived in Tideswell, was arrested in London, and banished in 1585. After spending only two days in Reims he left again for England, but one of Walsingham's spies reported the following year that "father Garlick the demonite . . . laboureth with great diligence in Hampshire and Dorsetshire; would God he were intercepted." The term "demonite" probably indicates that Nicholas had been one of the priests engaged in the famous exorcisms in Hackney in 1585 and 1586 (Anstruther). He was soon back in Derbyshire, where he was arrested with Robert Ludlam in 1588.

Both priests were condemned at Derby for being seminary priests working in England and were hanged, drawn, and quartered on 24 July 1588, together with Fr Richard Simpson, who had for a short while wavered in his commitment as a Catholic but had then repented and been executed. Robert Ludlam and Nicholas Garlick were beatified in 1987.

M.M.P., pp. 129-31; Anstruther, 1, pp. 126-7, 215-6. See also the general entries on the English and Welsh Martyrs under 4 May and 25 October.

Bd Joseph Lambton, *Martyr* (1568-92)

Joseph Lambton was born in Malton in Yorkshire in 1568 and went to study at the English College in Reims in 1584. From there he went to Rome in 1589 and was ordained in 1592 with a dispensation for being under age. He left for England the same year to work in Westmorland but was arrested in Newcastle upon Tyne not long after landing. It was the town clerk who arrested him; having met him in the town and suspecting that he was a stranger, he examined him and had him put under house arrest as a possible priest. Bd Edward Waterson (8 Jan.), who had accompanied Joseph Lambton from Rome, was also arrested, this time when he applied to the mayor of Newcastle for a passport to travel by sea to London. Both arrests are vivid examples of the difficulties facing priests as they moved about the country. The two priests were brought to trial and condemned for being seminary priests working in England. Joseph Lambton was executed on 24 July 1592, being only twenty-four years old (Fr Waterson was not executed until the following January). The hangman made a hash of the hanging, drawing, and quartering, and the martyr was left in agony until someone else was brought in to finish it off. The sheriff then took part of the remains to Fr Waterson, hoping to frighten him into submission, but he only kissed it as a relic. Joseph Lambton was beatified in 1987.

M.M.P., pp. 189-90, mistakenly places the execution in 1593; Anstruther, 1, pp.204-5.

St John Boste, *Martyr* (*c.* 1543-94)

Today was formerly kept as the feast-day of the Durham Martyrs of 1594. This group of four comprised St John Boste, Bd John Speed, Bd George Swallowell, and Bd John Ingram. Only one of these died on 24 July, and so their feast-days will be found under the dates of their deaths: John Boste today, John Speed on 4 February, George Swallowell and John Ingram on 26 July.

John Boste was born at Dufton in Westmorland about the year 1543. He was educated at Queen's College, Oxford, and for a time was a Protestant minister. At some stage he became a Catholic and went to Reims in 1580 to study for the priesthood. Ordained in Châlons in March 1581, he returned to England the following month, landing at Hartlepool in County Durham. For the next twelve years he ministered in the north of England using the alias Harekley, with occasional visits to Scotland, and became the most wanted priest in the north. Eventually he was taken by Anthony Atkinson, a renegade Marian priest, in the house of William Claxton, near Waterhouses, in September 1593. He was sent to London for examination and was questioned by Topcliffe at Windsor (where the Privy Council was at the time) and then in the Tower, where he was so severely tortured that he was permanently crippled. During his examination he apparently told Topcliffe that he loved the queen and would take her side even if the pope himself sent an army against her; but "if the pope by his Catholic authority do proceed against her to deprive her as a heretic, then he cannot err, nor the Church, and Catholics must obey the Church." Topcliffe added to his report, "Full of treason, as ever wretch was." He remained in the Tower until the summer of 1594, when he was sent back to Durham for trial at the July assizes. He was condemned to death for being a seminary priest working in England and was hanged, drawn, and quartered on 24 July at Dryburn, outside the city. Bd Christopher Robinson (5 Apr.), who witnessed the execution, reported that the martyr recited the *Angelus* as he mounted the scaffold. Bd John Ingram and Bd George Swallowell were tried on the same day but executed two days later. John Boste was canonized in 1970 as one of the Forty Martyrs of England and Wales.

M.M.P., pp. 202-4; Anstruther, 1, pp. 43-4. C.R.S., 1, pp. 85-92, gives an account by Bd Christopher Robinson (5 Apr.) of the execution, while C.R.S., 5, pp. 215-23, gives details of the arrest and examination.

ST JAMES THE GREATER (over page)
Scallop shells for the pilgrimage to Santiago.
Gold shells on blue field

25

ST JAMES THE GREATER, *Apostle* (First Century)

James was the brother of St John (27 Dec.) and a son of Zebedee; he is called "the Greater" to distinguish him from the other, younger apostle of the same name. He was a Galilean and worked with his father and brother as a fisherman on the Sea of Galilee; he may have lived in Bethsaida, where St Peter (29 June) lived. Our Lord called the two brothers to be his disciples as they were arranging their nets in a boat; they immediately followed him, leaving their father with his hired men (Mark 1:16-20). James and John are specifically mentioned as being present at the cure of Peter's mother-in-law (Mark 1:29-31) and at the raising of Jairus' daughter from the dead, when Jesus "allowed no one to go with him except Peter and James and John the brother of James" (Mark 5:35-43; Luke 8:49-56). They were also chosen to witness the transfiguration on Mount Tabor (Mark 9:2-8; Matthew 17:1-8; Luke 9:28-36), and to watch during Jesus' agony in the garden of Gethsemane (Mark 14:32-42; Matt. 26:36-46). This privileged position of the three disciples in the Gospel narratives indicates, presumably, the special position that they held in the very early Church.

Other passages in the Gospels give some insight into James' character. He and his brother were nicknamed "Boanerges," or "Sons of thunder," by Jesus, presumably on account of their lively tempers (Mark 3:17); on one occasion, when a Samaritan village refused to welcome Jesus, James and John suggested that they should call down fire from heaven to destroy it (Luke 9:51-6). Matthew relates how their mother approached Jesus and asked him to allow her sons to sit one on his right, the other on his left, when he established his kingdom; Jesus answered by asking them if they could drink the cup that he was going to drink. They answered confidently that they could, and Jesus promised that they would do so (20:20-4). The other apostles were angry with the two brothers for putting themselves forward in this way, presumably because they felt that they were behind the mother's request; it is interesting that in Mark's account of the incident (10:35-40) there is no mention of the mother, and James and John make the request themselves.

We do not know whether James left Jerusalem after Pentecost to preach the gospel—the early Christian tradition says that none of the apostles did so until after his death. He may well have stayed in Jerusalem, but he is not mentioned as taking part in the early preaching of the gospel to the Jews, as Peter and John are. He was the first of the apostles to suffer martyrdom. King Herod Agrippa started persecuting some of the Christians and put James to death by the sword; when he saw that this pleased the Jews, he arrested Peter as well (Acts 12:1-3). This is all that is known about his death, which took place about the year 44. Tradition says that he was buried in Jerusalem.

Over the years "an immense controversy has raged over the connection of St James with Spain" (*B.T.A.*), a connection that rests on two traditions: one that he preached in Spain at some stage between Pentecost and his death, the other that his body was taken to Spain and buried there. The earliest reference to him visiting Spain is from the seventh century and originated in the East; it has nothing to commend it historically, and St Julian of Toledo (8 Mar.), who died at the end of the seventh century, did not mention it in his account of the journeyings of the apostles. Some authors have used St Paul's testimony to support the tradition: when writing to the Romans he said that he planned to visit Spain, but a few verses earlier he had claimed not to preach "where Christ's name has already been heard" (Rom. 15:20, 24). The second tradition, dating from about 830, holds that James' body was first moved to El Padrón in Galicia, and then to Santiago (*i.e.*, St James) de Compostela, where his shrine became one of the greatest pilgrimage shrines in medieval Europe, especially after he became the patron of Spanish military efforts to defeat the Moors. The earliest written evidence of such a translation is the martyrology of Usuard, dating from 865. The supposed relics are still there and were referred to as authentic in a Bull of Leo XIII in 1884. Again, this second tradition linking James with Spain wins no support from non-Spanish historians, and the genuineness of the relics is seriously questioned. They were lost for a time but were recovered, and the present ones may well be the same as those venerated in the Middle Ages, "but the authenticity of medieval relics is always difficult to establish and in this case it is more than dubious" (*B.T.A.*). It is, however, true that the shrine at Compostela is built over an early Christian cemetery that contained a *martyrium*, testifying to the cult of an early saint whose name is unknown. It is interesting that the church in Mérida in the south-west of Spain claimed to have James' (and other apostles') relics as early as 627, before the Moorish conquest; presumably a local cult was associated with the relics.

An apocryphal epistle of St James was discovered among the Nag Hammadi manuscripts in 1945. It purports to be the record by James of a conversation that Jesus had with James and Peter after the resurrection and seems to have originated in Jewish Christian circles (*O.D.C.C.*).

O.D.C.C., pp. 857 (James), 389 (Compostela); *O.D.S.*, pp. 250-1. On the Spanish connection, see T. D. Kendrick, *St James in Spain* (1960), for a critical account of how the legends developed over the centuries. R. A. Fletcher, *St James' Catapult: the life and times of Diego Gelmírez of Santiago de Compostela* (1985), deals with the deliberate development of the cult in the eleventh and twelfth centuries. In favour of the historicity of the tradition, see A. Castro, *La realidad histórica de España* (1954), and the detailed bibliography in *Bibl.SS.* On St James in art see Murray, pp. 248-9; *Bibl.SS.*, 6, 381-8.

James appears in art in three different guises, as an apostle, a pilgrim, and a mounted knight. As an apostle he was most often shown as dark-bearded, with a scroll or a book in his hand, and sometimes holding a sword as a symbol of his martyrdom. He features in this way on the façades and portals of many buildings, from Toledo to Lübeck, and in many Italian paintings of the fourteenth and fifteenth centuries. A fresco cycle in Padua by Mantegna (destroyed in the war) included pictures of James the apostle before Herod Agrippa and curing a paralytic on his way to execution. His connection with Compostela changed his symbols to those of a pilgrim—a floppy hat, water-bottle, pilgrim's staff, and scallop shell. This is the commonest Spanish image, and it appears all along the pilgrims' route to Compostela: in the great cathedrals in Burgos, Chartres, Amiens, and Reims, and in small village churches. Later Spanish depictions, using the legend that James appeared and fought alongside the Spaniards in a battle against the Moors, included paintings of him as a knight on a horse, not unlike St George (23 Apr.), and trampling a Moor underfoot— and Tiepolo also painted him like this (1729). In this guise he is known in Spain as Santiago *matamoros*, "kills Moors."

St Christopher, *Martyr* (? Third Century)

There undoubtedly was an early Christian martyr named Christopher whose cult was known in the East and the West. The Roman Martyrology says that he suffered in Lycia during the persecution of the emperor Decius (249-51) and that he died by being shot with arrows and beheaded after attempts to burn him had failed, but none of these facts can be verified. A church in Bithynia was dedicated to him in the year 452. Early legends say that he was exceptionally tall and of rather fearsome appearance and that while he was in prison attempts were made by two women to seduce him but he converted them instead and they were then martyred. His name, "Christ-bearer" in Greek, was explained in terms of his bearing Christ in his mind by devotion, in his body by his austerities, and in his mouth by his preaching to others.

These legends were developed and added to in the Middle Ages, especially in the famous *Golden Legend* of Bd James of Voragine (13 July). Christopher was said to have searched for a master to serve and chose the devil as being the most powerful; then he heard that Christ was even more powerful and so he learned about the Faith and became a Christian. The hermit who had instructed him gave him the task of helping travellers across a local river; one day he had to carry a child across on his shoulders and found the weight so great that he was bowed down under it. The child turned out to be Jesus, and the great weight was that of the world, which the child carried with him. To prove that he was Jesus, the child told Christopher to plant his staff in the earth, when it would bear flowers; this happened the next day. The preposterous accounts of the attempts by his gaolers to kill Christopher, which already existed in the early legends, were elaborated in these later accounts.

Christopher became one of the most popular saints and was included among the Fourteen Holy Helpers, those saints who had a special care for our everyday needs. His speciality was the care of travellers and a protection against sudden death. The custom arose of putting statues or wall-paintings of him in churches, usually opposite the south door where they would be seen easily, for it was believed that anyone who looked on Christopher would not die that day. This custom arose from the medieval belief that martyrdom with arrows conferred the power of protection against sudden death, caused, it was believed, by the shafts of angry spirits (Anderson). There were more wall-paintings of St Christopher in English medieval churches than of any other saint (*ibid.*). His name became, and has remained, one of the most popular Christian names, and despite attacks on the incredibility of his legend by sixteenth-century writers such as Erasmus, he remained the patron saint of travellers and in the modern age became the patron saint of motorists—a church in the part of Paris where Citroën cars are made is dedicated to him (*O.D.S.*). His feast was removed from the universal Calendar in 1969 but may still be observed locally.

B.T.A., 3, pp. 184-7, gives a long extract from Caxton's edition of *The Golden Legend.* Texts of the earlier legends are in *Anal.Boll.* 1 (1882), pp. 121-48, and 10 (1891), pp. 393-405. See also *O.D.S.*, pp. 97-8; M. D. Anderson, *History and Imagery in British Churches* (1971/1995), pp. 137-9.

In surviving paintings Christopher is shown as a very large figure carrying the child Jesus on his shoulders. As the legends developed other details were added, such as the flowering staff, the hermit, the river, and occasionally the two seducers. English examples may be seen in Aldermaston (Berkshire), Impington (Cambs.), Haddon Hall (Derbyshire), and many other places—186 such paintings have been identified; he also features in some stained-glass windows, for example in Great Malvern Priory church and at Thaxted in Essex. St Christopher was also a common subject in woodcuts; one of the earliest of these dates from 1423 and shows all the pictorial elements associated with him; they were produced in large numbers so that people could carry his image with them and so gain his protection (see the illustration in Anderson).

SS Thea, Valentina, and Paul, *Martyrs* (*c.* 308)

These three martyrs suffered in Palestine under the governor Firmilian during the severe persecution initiated by the emperor Diocletian (284-305). Thea was arrested at Gaza and threatened with detention in a local brothel if she did not give up her Christianity. She rebuked Firmilian for his injustice, and he was so outraged at her outspokenness that he had her tortured. Valentina, a Christian from Caesarea, was present at the trial and cried out in Thea's defence. She was arrested and taken to the pagan altar prepared for sacrifice; when she kicked this over she was severely tortured and then burned to death along with Thea. Paul was beheaded at Gaza on 25 July 308; just before his execution he prayed aloud for the spread of Christianity, for the judge, the emperor, and the executioner.

The above account is based on Eusebius (*c.* 260-*c.* 340), who was bishop of Caesarea. There is some debate about Thea's name, and in some Syriac accounts she is called Ennat(h)a. The cult of the three martyrs was stronger in the East than in the West, but Baronius introduced their feast-day into the Roman Martyrology in the sixteenth century under 25 July, the date given by Eusebius, but gave them two separate commemorations, one for Paul and one for "Valentina and companion."

Eusebius, *De Martyribus Palestin.*, 8, 5-12, in G. Brady (ed.), S.C. 55 (1958), pp. 145-6. See also *Bibl.SS.*, 10, 310-13, under Paul.

St Olympias (*c.* 361- 408)

Olympias was called by St Gregory Nazianzen (2 Jan.) "the glory of the widows in the Eastern Church." She was born into a distinguished family in Constantinople, probably in 361 and certainly not later than 368. She was left an orphan at an early age and brought up by her uncle, the prefect Procopius. He entrusted her education to Theodosia, sister of St Amphilochius (23 Nov.), a well-educated and very devout woman, who gave Olympias a detailed knowledge and love of the scriptures that remained with her for the rest of her life. In 384 Procopius arranged for her to marry Nebridius, a former prefect of Constantinople. St Gregory Nazianzen wrote to apologize that his age and bad health kept him from attending the wedding and added a poem on the ideal of the Christian wife: she should dress modestly, not wear make-up, and should love and be devoted to her husband, ignoring the pleasures of the world as she busied herself in looking after their home. Nebridius, however, died soon afterwards, and Olympias decided not to remarry, saying, "Had my king wished me to live with a husband, he would not have taken my first one away."

Her uncle wished her to make a prestigious re-marriage, and even the emperor Theodosius pressed her to accept one of his relatives. When she refused he put her fortune in the hands of the prefect and ordered him to act as her guardian until she was thirty years old. The prefect prevented her from going to church and from seeing the bishop, and so she wrote to the emperor, thanking him rather drily for relieving her of the burden of looking after her money and suggesting that it should be divided between the poor and the Church.

When she reached the age of thirty in 391 her estates were restored to her, and she offered her services to St Nectarius (11 Oct.), bishop of Constantinople. He was so impressed by her holiness and charitable works that he gave her the title of deaconess, a title usually reserved for widows over sixty years of age. She established herself in a convent with a number of other single women who wanted to devote themselves to God's service; the convent was attached to Santa Sophia and communicated directly with the narthex of the church by a special stairway. Enclosure was strictly observed, and only St John Chrysostom (13 Nov.) was allowed in to instruct the religious, whose numbers grew rapidly and apparently reached a peak of 250. Olympias' dress was said to be plain, her prayers assiduous, and her charity so generous that St John advised her to be more cautious in giving alms so that she would have some money for those who needed it most: "You must not encourage the laziness of those who live upon you without necessity. It is like throwing water into the sea." In 398 he became patriarch of Constantinople and took Olympias and her disciples under his protection. On his advice she founded a hospital and an orphanage, and when some monks who had been expelled from their monastery came to Constantinople to appeal she housed and fed them at her own expense.

When St John was exiled in 404 Olympias continued to support him and suffered in the persecution levied against his friends. She was accused of having set fire to the episcopal palace but defended herself so forcibly that the case was dismissed. She was ill all that winter and in the spring left the city; she was brought back and fined heavily for refusing to recognize the false patriarch Arsacius. His successor, Atticus, dispersed her household and put an end to her charitable works. She was troubled by frequent illness, slanderous accusations, and petty persecution and was exiled to Nicomedia. St John comforted her from exile and entrusted her with important commissions on his behalf; his letters, of which seventeen survive, describe his own and her troubles. The date of death is uncertain, but it seems to have occurred in or shortly after 408. Among her friends had been St Amphilochius (23 Nov.), St Epiphanius of Salamis (12 May), St Peter of Sebastea (26 Mar.), and St Gregory of Nyssa (10 Jan.). Palladius described her as "a wonderful woman . . . like a precious vase filled with the Holy Spirit."

Her convent was destroyed in the fire that devastated Santa Sophia in 532 but was rebuilt by the emperor Justinian (483-565); excavations outside Santa Sophia in 1963 uncovered rooms that probably belonged to the original building. Her remains were taken from Nicomedia to the church of St Thomas; when this was destroyed in the early seventh century they were moved to the convent, but nothing more is known about them.

Knowledge of St Olympias comes from several sources: the *Lausiac History* and the *Dialogue* on the Life of St John Chrysostom by Palladius of Helenopolis (*c.* 365-425); a Greek Life that uses Palladius and was written about the mid-fifth century; Sozomen's *Church History* (early fifth century); the letters of St John Chrysostom; and other contemporary writings. The Greek Life was published in *Anal.Boll.* 15 (1896), pp. 400-23. For an English trans. of the letters of St John see E. A. Clark, *Jerome, Chrysostom and Friends: Essays and Translations* (1979). See also J. Bousquet, "Vie d'Olympias la diaconesse," *Revue de l'Orient Chrétien*, 2d series, 1 (1906), pp. 225-50, and 2 (1907), pp. 255-68; *D.A.C.L.*, 12, 2064-71; *Bibl.SS.*, 9, 1154-8.

St Magnericus of Trier, *Bishop* (*c.* 595)

Magnericus (or Magnéric) was born about the beginning of the sixth century and educated in the household of St Nicetius (or Nizier; 5 Dec.), the last Gallo-Roman bishop of Trier. After ordination he became the bishop's confidant and accompanied him into exile when he was banished by the Frankish king, Clotaire I, whom Nicetius had excommunicated for his immoral way of life. They were recalled a year later when Sigebert succeeded to the throne, and six years after that, probably in 566, Magnericus succeeded to the bishopric of Trier. He had a great devotion to St Martin of Tours (11 Nov.) and built churches and a monastery in his honour; when he visited Tours he met and became friends with St Gregory of Tours (17 Nov.), who later testified to his sanctity. When Theodore, bishop of Marseilles, was exiled in 585, Magnericus took up his cause and pleaded for his re-instatement before King Childebert II, who held him in great esteem—Magnericus was godfather to the young Théodoret, Childebert's son. Overall, it appears that Magnericus played a fairly important role in political matters. St Venantius Fortunatus (14 Dec.) was another person who was greatly impressed by the saintly bishop of Trier, praising his "shining piety and sound learning" and extolling him as an ornament of the Church. Magnericus, who died in 595 or 596, attracted a large number of disciples whom he trained to serve the Church; one of these was St Géry (or Gaugericus; 11 Aug.), who later became bishop of Cambrai. Magnericus was buried in the church of Saint-Martin in Trier.

A fairly full Life was written in the eleventh century by Eberwin, abbot of Saint-Martin in Trier; see *AA.SS.*, July, 4, pp. 168-92. A letter of Venantius Fortunatus referring to Magnericus is in *M.G.H., Epistolae,* 3, p. 128. See also E. Ewig, *Trier im Merowingerreich* (1954), pp. 107-11; *Catholicisme,* 8, 163.

Bd John Soreth (*c.* 1405-71)

Jean Soreth was born in Normandy about the year 1405. At the age of sixteen he became a Carmelite and after ordination went to the university of Paris, where he gained a doctorate in 1438. Two years after this he was elected prior provincial of the Order in France. He had to deal with a number of difficult problems, including a serious dispute that had broken out between the university of Paris and the Mendicant friars and a schism in the Carmelite province of Lower Germany. He was successful and soon gained a reputation for his learning, wisdom, and energy. In 1451 he was elected prior general of the Order, a post he retained until his death, being re-elected in 1456, 1462, and 1468. At one stage Pope Callistus III (1455-8) wanted to make him a bishop and perhaps a cardinal, but John wanted to devote himself to his Order and so refused.

In the fifteenth century the Carmelites, like the other Mendicant Orders, were in need of reform. Pope Eugene IV (1431-47) had permitted an easing of the original very strict Rule, and the regulations concerning the personal ownership of property and the obligation to live in community had subsequently been relaxed, especially for those engaged in teaching. John's aim was to introduce reform without splitting the Order; his method was to establish in each province one or two houses of strict observance and to encourage as many friars as felt called to a stricter way of life to join them. In 1462 he published his *Expositio paraenetica in regulam Carmelitarum,* keeping what he believed was the original Carmelite ideal but modifying the Rule to suit the times. It was a practical guide for the new houses and drew on the writings of some of the established masters of the monastic life, such as St John Cassian (23 July) and St Bernard (20 Aug.), as well as the contemporary writers of the *devotio moderna.* He wished to go beyond external observance and mortification to concentrate on the chief Carmelite aim, which was to create an atmosphere conducive to prayer and contemplation. He was willing to accept the mitigations allowed by Eugene IV, arguing that these did not interfere with the basic obligation on the

Carmelite friar or nun to seek union with God through prayer. It was only in the context of this obligation, he argued, that such things as silence, mortification, solitude, and so on made sense.

John encouraged the development of a Carmelite Rule for nuns, and new convents came into existence when several communities of *béguines* in the Low Countries asked to be affiliated to the Order. The first of these convents was at Gueldre in The Netherlands, and others followed at Liège, Dinant, Namur, and elsewhere. He was helped in this work by Bd Frances d'Amboise (4 Nov.), and it was largely through her assistance that he was able to introduce the Carmelite nuns into France—she founded and endowed a convent at Vannes, which she later entered in 1468, receiving the Carmelite habit from John himself. By the end of the century the movement had spread to Italy and Spain, and a number of treatises on the Carmelite way had appeared modelled to a greater or lesser extent on John's work and, like him, using the *devotio moderna* approach.

John's attempts to reform the friars, however, met with only limited success. He travelled tirelessly from province to province, usually accompanied only by a single friar and a muleteer, and the hardships and obstacles that he faced were similar to those suffered by another Carmelite reformer of the next century, St Teresa of Avila (15 Oct.). A contemporary Benedictine praised him in these words: "He was a man deeply versed both in sacred science and in profane philosophy. But over and above such gifts, it was his religion and goodness that made him the glory and the most illustrious reformer of the Carmelite Order. By word and example he attained that high indifference to the vanities of the world that is only reached by chosen souls. He was a model of regular observance and of Christian virtues" (quoted in *B.T.A.*).

It seems that John was responsible for the formal institution of a Carmelite Third Order, although local fraternities had existed before his time. He drew up a short Rule for the tertiaries in 1455 that is still the basis of the Rule of Calced Carmelite tertiaries.

John died from cholera at Angers on 25 July 1471—there is no truth in the often-repeated story that he was poisoned by a disgruntled friar who objected to being reformed. His cult was persistent but not widespread; it was approved in 1865. His feast-day used to be celebrated on 30 July.

Diz. Ist. Perf., 2, 484-5. *B.T.A.*, 3, pp. 215-6.

Bd Peter of Mogliano (1442-90)

Pietro Corradini was born in Mogliano in the Marche region of Italy in 1442. After studying law at the university of Perugia he decided to join the Observant Franciscans in Ancona, a decision he reached after being greatly moved by the preaching of one of the friars. He was clothed in Assisi in 1467 and later ordained priest. His first posting was to be preaching companion to St James

Gangali ("of the Marche"; 28 Nov.), one of the outstanding helpers of St John of Capistrano (23 Oct.) in spreading the Observant reform throughout Italy. Peter proved to be an effective preacher and spiritual director and became the confidant of the duke of Camerino, whose daughter, Bd Battista Varani (8 June), owed much to his guidance. Peter served as vicar provincial of the Marche for three terms and also of the Roman province for a term, while in 1472 he went as commissary to Crete. He brought to these various offices a high degree of prudence, dedication, and understanding of people and business.

Bd Battista wrote an account of his last days and reported that for the last three years of his life he was known locally just as "the holy father"; people loved him so much, she went on, that a crowd followed him wherever he went and on one occasion nearly killed him by their overenthusiastic attentions. He died on 25 July 1490, murmuring the name of Jesus, and so left this world "with that dear name on his lips by whose strength he had worked so many wonders during his life" (Bd Battista). His cult was approved in 1760.

Much of what is known about Peter comes through his connection with Bd Battista. See *Bibl.SS.*, 4, 197-8.

Bd Rudolf Aquaviva and Companions, *Martyrs* (1583)

The five Jesuit martyrs venerated today are Rudolf (Rodolfo) Aquaviva, Alphonsus (Alfonso) Pacheco, Peter (Pietro) Berno, Antony (Antonio) Francisco, and Francis (Francesco) Aranha; the first four were priests, while Francis Aranha was a temporal coadjutor.

Rudolf Aquaviva was the son of the duke of Atri, in the kingdom of Naples, and the nephew of Claude Aquaviva, the fifth general of the Society of Jesus; his family was closely related to the Gonzagas. He was born in 1550, entered the Jesuits in 1568, and after ordination in Lisbon, was sent to work in Goa, in India. In 1579 the Great Mogul, Akbar, asked for missionaries to be sent to his court near Agra to discuss matters of religion. Fr Rudolf was appointed leader of the small group who went; they laboured without any noticeable success for about four years, although Rudolf seems to have impressed Akbar by his sincerity and austerity. Rudolf was recalled to take charge of the mission in Salcete, a province adjoining Goa.

Alphonsus Pacheco had been born in Castile in 1551, had become a Jesuit in 1567, and joined the mission in India in 1574. He worked for some years in Goa and in 1581 was appointed superior of the Salcete mission, a post he gave up to Fr Rudolf a few years later.

Peter Berno had been born, probably in 1553, in Ascona (Ticino), Switzerland. He joined the Jesuits in Rome in 1577 and left for Goa two years later, where he was ordained priest in 1580. He was sent to minister at the mission in Salcete. Little is known about the background of his companion there, Antony

Francisco. He had been born at Coimbra in Portugal in 1553; after joining the Jesuits he was sent to India, where he was ordained in 1583. The fifth member of the group, Francis Aranha, was also Portuguese. He had gone to Goa with his uncle, who was the first archbishop of the city, and had joined the Jesuits at the age of twenty-seven as a temporal adjutor, or lay brother. He was an able architect and was employed in building and repairing churches and mission buildings. He had been in India for about twenty-three years when he joined the Salcete mission in 1583.

Shortly before this Fr Pacheco and Fr Berno were involved in two punitive expeditions launched by the Portuguese against the village of Cuncolim, a centre of Hindu religion and culture close to the provincial capital of Salcete; both priests took part in the destruction of the village's sacred buildings, including the main temple dedicated to Shantadurga, the goddess of peace. This was in line with the royal decree of 1546 ordering the destruction of Hindu images throughout Portuguese territory and the suppression of Hindu festivals—while most sixteenth-century Catholic writers opposed the use of violence against people in making converts, they tended to support the destruction of non-Christian temples, shrines, and statues as part of the Christian State's duty to suppress idolatry. Moreover, while forcible conversions were officially condemned, the Portuguese exerted strong social and economic pressure on the local Hindus to persuade them to convert.

In July 1583 the five Jesuits, believing that Cuncolim was still the focus of Hindu opposition to their missionary work, decided to go there to launch a fresh missionary campaign. They set out with some other Christians to find a piece of land on which to erect a church and a mission cross, but the village leaders met them with force, determined to oppose them. One of the Christian laymen suggested that the missionaries should fire on the Indians, but Fr Pacheco stopped him, saying, "We are not here to fight"; since there were quite a number of Christians in the group and they had guns, this was a remarkable show of restraint on the Jesuits' part, as Christian writers at the time generally agreed that violence could be used legitimately to protect missionaries from attack, even if the missionaries were preaching in places where their presence was not welcomed. The four priests were killed straightaway. Brother Francis was found to be still alive the next day and was offered his life if he worshipped the statue of a Hindu deity; when he refused, he was killed by arrows.

A number of other Christians were killed at the same time as the Jesuits. We know the names of four of them who were Indians: Domingos, a Brahmin boy, was killed because he had shown the priests the pagodas they had destroyed; Alfonso, also a Brahmin boy, had his hands cut off before he was killed because he had carried Fr Pacheco's Breviary; Francisco Rodriguez had advised the priests on a number of matters, and Paulo da Costa had helped them in gaining converts. Another layperson was the Portuguese Gonçalo Rodriguez, who was killed so that he could not spread the news of the other deaths. Another Portuguese layperson, Domingo d'Aguiar, escaped with his life on a ship belonging to a friend. The archbishop of Goa omitted all the lay names from the list he drew up for the start of the martyrs' cause in 1600; we do not know what reasons he gave for doing so—the previous edition of this work adds, "From what is known of the methods of that prelate, they would probably be found unconvincing today."

The cause progressed very slowly, with the "devil's advocate" making the point that the original Portuguese attack on the village had created a state of war, and that the villagers were merely repelling an enemy, not attacking Christians as such. Such caution was typical of the reluctance often shown by the Roman authorities lest they seemed to be condoning deliberately offensive action against non-Christians. In 1741 Pope Benedict XIV, however, declared that the deaths did constitute genuine martyrdoms; even then, the formal beatification did not take place until 1893. They are sometimes referred to as "The Martyrs of Salcete," and their feast used to be celebrated on 27 July.

Josef Wicki (ed.), *Documenta India* (1972), 12, pp. 974-94, prints a report of 1609 from Fr Sebastian Gonçalves, S.J., which gives details of all the deaths. See also P. Suau, *Les BB. martyrs de Salsette* (1893); J. S. Narayan, *Aquaviva and the Great Mogul* (1946). See *Bibl.SS.*, 11, 597-600, for a detailed bibliography.

Bd Antony Lucci, *Bishop* (1681-1752)

Antonio Lucci was born in Agnone del Sannio (Abruzzo) in Italy in August 1681. He joined the Conventual Franciscans, was ordained in 1705, and devoted himself to teaching and preaching. He was professor and prefect of studies in Agnone and Naples, became minister provincial, and then, in 1718, rector of the college of Saint Bonaventure in Rome, a post he held for ten years. During that time he was a consultor of the Holy Office and one of the official theologians at two Roman synods. In 1729 Pope Benedict XIII (1724-30) appointed him bishop of Bovino, a small town south-west of Foggia in southern Italy. He was an exemplary pastoral bishop and a firm defender of the rights of the poor and helpless as well as a reformer of his clergy. He established free elementary schools, provided sets of tools for young men starting work, and built a seminary, a number of churches, and a cathedral. As bishop he continued to lead a life as close to the Franciscan ideal as he could, and he gained a reputation for his evangelical simplicity and poverty, as well as the nickname "the angel of charity." He died in July 1752 after twenty-three years as bishop and was buried in his cathedral, where his tomb soon became a place of pilgrimage because of the miracles reported to have taken place there. He left a number of writings, chief among which was a *Manual of Theology*, which remained the Order's official textbook for many years. He also wrote *Ragioni istoriche*, which argued that all the early Franciscan saints were Conventuals. Antonio was beatified in June 1989.

A.A.S. 81, pt. 2 (1989), pp. 1200-5, gives the papal address on the occasion of the beatification; this stressed the social gospel and its demands, and Bd Antony's apostolate in this respect. See also *Bibl.SS.*, 8, 235-6.

ST ANNE (over page)
The silver border "masoned" in black denotes her care
of the Virgin Mary, while the silver lily on blue field
refers to the girlhood of Mary.

26

SS JOACHIM AND ANNE (First Century)

According to tradition Joachim and Anne were the parents of Our Lady, but neither of them is mentioned in the scriptures. They feature by name for the first time in the so-called *Book of James*, an apocryphal gospel about the infancy of Our Lord also known as the *Protevangelium of James*. This probably dates from the middle of the second century and is of no historical value. With the increasing popularity of the cult of Our Lady in the Middle Ages, however, it became a useful source for stories about her birth and early life and provided inspiration for a number of artists.

Joachim and Anne are portrayed as old and childless. For Joachim in particular the childlessness was a source of public reproach, and he retired to the desert to fast and pray about it. Anne was meanwhile praying at home when an angel appeared to her and told her that she would conceive, the same message that Joachim had received in his desert retreat. This legend is very reminiscent of the birth of Samuel to Anne, as related in 1 Sam. 1:9-20, and the early Eastern Fathers saw this as a deliberate parallel. Apart from this legend, Joachim hardly featured in Christian legend until much later—in the East rarely before the seventh century and in the West rarely before the Middle Ages, when he became a subject in religious art (*O.D.C.C.*). Official attitudes to his cult have been somewhat ambiguous: Julius II (1503-13) authorized his feast-day, but St Pius V (1566-72; 30 Apr.) suppressed it, only for Gregory XV ((1621-3) to allow it again; Leo XIII (1878-1903) raised its rank to that of a double of the second class (*O.D.S.*). From 1913 he had his own feast-day in the West, on 16 August, but from 1969 it has been celebrated along with St Anne today. The supposed site of his tomb is a minor place of pilgrimage in Jerusalem.

Anne was given more prominence as Our Lady's mother. The emperor Justinian built a church in her honour in Constantinople in the sixth century, while relics and pictures in Rome (in Santa Maria Antiqua) date from the eighth century; Pope St Leo III (795-813; 12 June) presented a vestment to Santa Maria Maggiore embroidered with the Annunciation and SS Anne and Joachim. The feast of "the conception of St Anne" was kept in Naples in the tenth century and soon afterwards in Ireland and England, where Canterbury, Reading, and Durham claimed to have relics of her. By 1350 her feast was being generally observed in the West, and Pope Urban VI (1378-89) ordered it to be celebrated throughout England, at the request of "English petitioners," perhaps in order to popularize the marriage of Richard II to Anne of Bohemia in 1382. Her most famous English shrine was at Buxton, and she was patron of various guilds in a number of towns. In the late Middle Ages she was also prayed to by wood-cutters on the grounds that she was the root of the tree whose flower was Our Lady and whose fruit was Jesus. In order to explain the Gospel references to the "brothers of Jesus," she was sometimes credited with having three husbands and a large number of children. For Luther and other early Protestants the cult of St Anne was particularly obnoxious, especially when it involved pictures of her with Mary and Jesus, but in 1584 her feast was extended to the universal Church, and Gregory XV (1621-3) made it a holyday of obligation. The cult of St Anne is especially strong in Canada and Brittany (of which she is the patron saint), and she is the patroness of childless women and expectant mothers and of miners.

O.D.C.C., pp. 71, 877; *O.D.S.*, pp. 22, 253-4. For an interesting interdisciplinary examination of the cult of St Anne see K. Ashley and P. Sheingorn (eds.), *Interpreting Cultural Symbols. St Anne in Late Medieval Society* (1993).

In art, St Anne was often shown teaching Our Lady to read, and this picture may have had an English origin, as it exists in English manuscripts of the thirteenth century and in a number of stained-glass windows, for example in All Saints, York. The earliest cycle of scenes showing the two saints seems to be on the west portal of Chartres, while a series of paintings of both saints by Giotto from the beginning of the fourteenth century is in the Arena Chapel in Padua. In England depictions of the marriage of Anne and Joachim exist in stained glass in Great Malvern, Hereford, Worcester, and elsewhere.

BB John Ingram and George Swallowell, *Martyrs* (1594)

John Ingram was born at Stoke Edith in Herefordshire in 1565. He was brought up a Protestant, and Challoner claims that he was expelled from New College, Oxford, when he became a Catholic and then went to Douai to finish his studies. Anstruther, however, says that he was sent to Douai at an early age to study the humanities and that his mother was a Catholic, at least in later life; his own recollections of his youth and education make no reference to Oxford. From Douai he went to Reims in 1582, but he and his companions were captured by some Calvinist soldiers and held for ransom; he and another boy escaped and made their way to Reims, "two little boys in rags, having escaped by stealth from the hands of their enemies," as the Douai Diary puts it— though at seventeen years old he was hardly a "little boy." In October 1584 he was admitted to the English College in Rome, where he was one of the signatories to the petition of 1585 in favour of the Jesuits continuing to run the college. He was ordained in 1589 and left Rome two years later; the English government knew of his ordination and was hoping to arrest him as soon as he landed, but he sailed to Scotland instead and served for eighteen months as chaplain to Sir Walter Lindsay of Balgavies Castle near Forfar. When persecution broke out in Scotland he crossed the border into England, but was immediately arrested and taken to Berwick for questioning. At first he claimed to be a Scot, using the aliases Ogleby and Bourne, but then he admitted to having been in Rome; he seems to have used other aliases, including Messingham and Lingen. In 1594 he was taken to the Tower of London, where he was tortured, but he refused to give the names of those who had helped him as a priest, saying afterwards, "I take God to witness that I have neither named house, man, woman, or child, in the time of or before my torments." He was sent to Durham for trial at the July assizes in 1594 and was tried along with St John Boste (24 July) and George Swallowell. He was condemned for being a seminary priest working in England and hanged, drawn, and quartered at Gateshead on 26 July. He was beatified in 1929.

John was an expert Latinist and composed a large number of epigrams and verses, some of which he scratched on his cell walls while in the Tower—these have since disappeared. We have a copy in his own hand and two of his letters written from prison. He tells us that the epigrams and verses were written mainly to keep his mind off the "expectation of death," which itself was "another death which grins at me, her grey hairs steeped in gore." They are recollections of his life, of the places where he ministered as a priest, and of his arrest. In one of them he writes:

If thou wouldst with Christ spend eternal days,
Begin to scorn in heart the days of earth.

In one of the prison letters he asked the other Catholics in prison "in the name of my sweet saviour Jesus" to pray that he would have "constancy, courage, and zeal in my holy enterprise, for the spirit is ready, but the flesh is weak." In the other letter he wrote: "And although in my native country I have taken great pains in God's vineyard, yet I doubt not, if God will strengthen me . . . (that) I shall purchase for our Babylonic soil more favour by my death." These writings, and the official letters of the Earl of Huntingdon, make him one of the best documented of all the martyrs (Anstruther).

George Swallowell was a native of County Durham, where he was brought up a Protestant, and taught for a time in Houghton-le-Spring as a minister. He later became a Catholic, and Challoner tells how he announced to his congregation "that he had previously been in error, but was now convinced that they had no true mission in their Church, and therefore he would no longer officiate there." He was arrested and spent a year in prison in Durham before being tried alongside John Ingram and John Boste. At first he wavered under examination and offered to go to church again, but he was convinced by the example and words of John Boste and said that "in that faith wherein those two priests did die, he would also die, and that the same faith which they professed he did also profess." He was condemned to death for having been converted to Catholicism and was hanged, drawn, and quartered at Darlington on 26 July 1594; he was beatified in 1929.

For John Ingram see *M.M.P.*, pp. 204-6; C.R.S., 5, pp. 240-4, for the official letters concerning his arrest, and pp. 165-8, 270-85, for his own writings; Anstruther, 1, pp. 182-

4. For George Swallowell see *M.M.P.*, pp. 206-8; C.R.S., 1, pp. 88-91. See also the general entries on the English and Welsh Martyrs under 4 May and 25 October.

BB Edward Thwing and Robert Nutter, *Martyrs* (1600)

Edward Thwing was born in 1565 in Heworth, now a suburb of York. He went to the English College in Reims in 1582 and on to Rome five years later, where he received minor orders. He had to leave Rome for health reasons and returned to Reims in 1590; he was ordained priest the same year at Laon. After teaching for about four years at the college he was sent to work in England, but there are no details of his whereabouts between then and his arrest early in 1600, when he was imprisoned in Lancaster Castle. He was tried at the July assizes together with Robert Nutter. An official account of the trial said that he used the alias Hilton and was also sometimes known as Nysaunce, and that "it appeared that he had been a scholar of some understanding and much esteemed among the papists." His interrogators made much of the fact that he had lied to hide his identity and that he believed that the law banning Jesuits and seminary priests was "wicked and unjust." Both he and Robert Nutter were condemned for being seminary priests working in England. Before their execution they were asked about their attitude to Queen Elizabeth; Edward Thwing said that he accepted her as his lawful queen and would pray for her, but refused to say whether he thought she should be queen in the light of the pope's excommunication of her in 1570.

Robert Nutter was born in Clitheroe in Lancashire about the year 1556 and was educated at the grammar school run in Blackburn by the Catholic Lawrence Yates. From there he went to Reims in 1579 and was ordained priest at Soissons in 1581. Using the alias Askew he returned to England shortly afterwards and worked around London and in Oxfordshire and Hampshire until his arrest in Oxford in 1584. He spent forty-three days in the Tower and was tortured; during that time his brother, Bd John Nutter (12 Feb.), was executed at Tyburn—their last meeting was in the notorious Pit in the Tower. In early 1585 Robert was banished from the country and went back to Reims for a few months, but he set out for England again before the end of the year, this time using the alias Rowley. The ship he and three other priests were in was intercepted by an English naval ship, and the four priests were landed at Gravesend in November 1585 and imprisoned in the Marshalsea. When challenged with having broken the terms of their banishment, they argued that they had been going to Scotland and had been brought to England by force. Robert Nutter was later identified by a former school-mate from Blackburn but for some reason was not sent for execution, the automatic penalty for exiles who returned without permission. By 1588 he had been transferred as a prisoner to Wisbech, where he remained for twelve years. He and five others escaped in March 1600, but he was captured in Lancashire and tried along with Edward Thwing. Before his execution he said that he had become a Dominican during his years in Wisbech, where he had made his profession with a number of priests as witnesses.

According to a contemporary Catholic account, their joint execution in Lancaster was watched by a large crowd of Catholics who began to seize parts of the martyrs' clothing and hair, and even their fingers, before the executioner had finished his work. This started a minor riot, and while the soldiers were dealing with this some women snatched the martyrs' hearts from the fire and made off with them; some days later the Catholics also obtained their heads and quartered limbs, so that these could not be displayed about the town in the normal way. Both martyrs were beatified in 1987.

M.M.P., pp. 247-9; Anstruther, 1, pp. 259-60, 356-7. See also the general entries on the English and Welsh Martyrs under 4 May and 25 October.

Bd William Ward, *Martyr* (*c.* 1565-1641)

As Anstruther says, there has been considerable confusion over the name and origins of this martyr. According to the Douai records he was William Webster from Westmorland, and no mention is made of an alias, but while he was working in England as a priest he was known as William Ward, and this is the name given him by Challoner and most subsequent writers. His place of birth is given as "Thornby in Westmorland," but Thornby is near Wigton in Cumberland, and he may have come from Thrimby in Westmorland instead. Claims that he was the son of Robert Ward of Cumberland and studied for seven years at Brasenose College, Oxford, before becoming a Catholic in Spain are not supported by the evidence, and the Douai records, usually keen to mention degrees and conversions, make no reference to either, while Challoner says that he was brought up a Catholic.

We do know that he entered Douai as a student in 1604 *aetate provecta* (at an advanced age) and was ordained priest four years later. In October 1608 he set out for the north of England but landed in Scotland instead, was captured almost immediately, and spent the next three years in prison. When he entered England he was again arrested and imprisoned in Newgate, and he was banished from the country in 1613. He seems to have spent about twenty years in various prisons, working between times in London. Being in prison did not prevent him from carrying on his ministry, both to the other Catholic inmates and to visitors, who had fairly easy access to prisoners at the time. In 1641 Parliament ordered persecution of the Catholics to be intensified, and William was arrested for the last time in July 1641 at the house of his nephew in Pye Corner, Smithfield. He was tried, condemned for being a seminary priest working in England and hanged, drawn, and quartered at Tyburn on 26 July 1641. It is reported that on the morning of his execution a friend brought him a new coat, and William replied, "You are right to dress me better than usual, since I am going to a more splendid banquet and a more joyful wedding than any at which I have ever been present." When told on the scaffold that he was being executed for seducing the people, he exclaimed, "Would to God I had converted more! Nay, even all England!" William Ward was beatified in 1929.

M.M.P., pp. 382-92, gives a very full account of the trial and execution by a priest who was one of the martyr's penitents. See also Anstruther, 2, pp. 344-5.

St Bartolomea Capitanio, *Foundress* (1807-33)

Bartolomea Capitanio was born in 1807 in Lovere, Lombardy. Her parents sent her to the convent of the Clarist Sisters for her education, and it was during her time there that she developed the idea of founding an active Congregation to deal especially with the needs of the times, although she also felt strongly attracted to an enclosed life of prayer. Her schooling ended when she was sixteen years old, and she threw herself into a range of church activities, partly to assess the needs of different groups and partly to decide her own vocation. She wrote mini-treatises for herself on devout practices, the rules of various religious associations, and different ways of life, as well as a large number of letters to her friends about all of these matters, but kept returning to her original idea of founding a new Congregation. She had developed a particular devotion to the young St Aloysius Gonzaga (21 June), later to be the patron saint of young people, and established a number of guilds or societies under his patronage for young people in the town. It seemed to her that her future apostolate should lie increasingly with the young of all ages. In 1823 she joined forces with St Vincentia Gerosa (29 June), whose main interest lay in providing nursing for the poor and who had already founded a hospital for that purpose. Under the guidance of Don Angelo, an enthusiastic but level-headed spiritual director, the two women decided to merge their apostolates of teaching and nursing by founding a new sisterhood; they moved into a house opposite the hospital and in November 1832 consecrated themselves totally to a life of charity; this was effectively the foundation of their Congregation, although at the time they were its only members. Don Angelo asked Bartolomea to draw up a provisional Constitution, which she based, as she put it, on "the rules and example left us by our Redeemer," especially his love, gentleness, and humility. The particular apostolate of the Sisters was to lie in the instruction and education of young people, the spiritual and physical care of the sick, and an active participation in the life of their local churches.

Bartolomea died from tuberculosis eight months later, on 26 July 1833, without ever having been clothed as a religious or having taken official vows. She was obviously a forceful character but was noted for her tact, simplicity, and openness. That she could achieve so much at such a young age speaks for her ability to influence both older women and the clergy. She seems to have had inexhaustible energy and great ability as an organizer as well as total dedication to a life lived in imitation of Christ. She was canonized in 1950, along with

Vincentia Gerosa (29 June), who had died in 1847. Bartolomea's principal relics are venerated in Lovere; others are in the generalate in Milan.

Vincentia Gerosa continued the work, and gradually other women joined her. At the time, new Congregations had to adopt the Rule of an already established one, and initially the foundresses chose the Rule that had been drawn up by St Antida Thouret and approved in 1819 for use in Besançon; the Sisters became known simply as the Sisters of Charity (of Lovere). In 1840 the pope gave them permission to be independent of the Thouret Congregation, and in 1841 the bishop of Brescia erected the Congregation canonically and admitted Vincentia and eight companions to their religious professions. The Rule they were to follow was much closer to the Constitution outlined by Bartolomea shortly before her death. From 1884 people began to refer to them as the Sisters of the Infant Mary (*Suore di Maria Bambina*) because of a miracle associated with an image of Our Lady as a child that the Congregation had acquired in 1842. After the canonization in 1950 the Congregation took the official name of the Sisters of Charity of SS Bartlomea Capitanio and Vincentia Gerosa but continued to be known popularly in Italy as the Sisters of the Infant Mary. At the time of Vincentia's death in 1847 it had consisted of 171 Sisters in twenty-eight houses; it reached its peak in the 1970s, with 8,500 members in six hundred houses, including those in India, Latin America, Africa, and the United States. In England the Sisters now call themselves the Capitanio Sisters.

I. Mazza, *Scritti spirituali della B. Capitanio*, 3 vols. (1904-6), and *Della vita e dell'istituto della ven. B. C.* (1905), are fundamental. See also A. Stocchetti, *Le ss. B. C. e Vincenza Gerosa* (1950); E. Belgari, *Il profilo di una maestar santa* (1951); *Diz. Ist. Perf.*, 1, 1063-5, and 2, 386-9.

Bd Titus Brandsma (1881-1942)

Anno Sjoerd Brandsma was born in 1881 in the Friesland province of The Netherlands. His family were farmers and staunchly Catholic in a mainly Calvinist region; three of his four sisters became nuns, and his only brother became a Franciscan priest. Anno received a good education, showing particular ability in philosophy and languages, and went on to gain a doctorate. It is said that when he announced his intention of becoming a Carmelite, the only objection from his parents was that he should become a Franciscan instead, but he stuck to his intention and was ordained as a Carmelite priest in 1905, taking the name Titus in religion. After ordination he went to Rome to study philosophy for three years.

On his return to The Netherlands he was appointed to the staff of the Order's seminary, where he taught for fifteen years. During this time he was extremely active in Catholic affairs, founding a journal of Marian devotion, editing a local newspaper, setting up a Catholic library and a Catholic secondary school that specialized in the sciences, and undertaking the translation of

St Teresa of Avila's (15 Oct.) works into Dutch. In 1923 he became professor of philosophy and of the history of mysticism at the Catholic University of Nijmegen, a post he held for nineteen years. Mysticism became his special area of research, and he established an Institute for the Study of Dutch Mysticism, organized three international congresses on the subject, and lectured on it in the United States and different European countries. He soon became a national figure, contributing to journals and newspapers and becoming the official national spiritual adviser to Dutch Catholic journalists. He served a term as rector of the university from 1932 to 1933.

In addition to his official duties Titus promoted Christian unity and worked to gain official recognition for the Frisian language. He was unpaid chaplain to an old people's home, where he said Mass every Sunday because they could not afford to pay a regular stipend to a diocesan priest. In 1935, when the German government issued new marriage laws against the Jews, he protested in the press and undertook a lecture tour in The Netherlands to explain the iniquity of the legislation. It was about this time that he drew up plans for evacuating Jews to a Carmelite mission in Brazil, but the outbreak of war and the German invasion prevented its implementation.

After the German occupation of The Netherlands early in the Second World War, Titus believed that it was his duty to issue guidelines to the Dutch press on how they should deal with the enemy. He declared that it was not possible for newspapers to carry Nazi propaganda or advertisements and still be regarded as Catholic. He also defended the right of Catholic schools to continue to teach religion. When his friends warned him of the likelihood that he would be arrested he replied, "Well, now I am going to get what has so seldom been my lot, and what I have always wanted—a cell of my own. At last I shall be a real Carmelite." The Nazis were already referring to him as "that dangerous little friar," and he was arrested shortly after his declaration to Catholic journalists. He spent some months in various prisons, using the time to write a biography of St Teresa of Avila and keep a diary. At Amersfoort, where the guards were very strict, he urged the other prisoners to pray for them; when the prisoners replied that they found this very difficult, Titus answered, "You don't need to pray for them all day long; God is quite pleased with a single prayer." On a later occasion he said about the guards, "They too are the children of the good God, and who knows whether something (good) remains in them."

Eventually Titus was sent to the concentration camp at Dachau. Whether he was offered his freedom in return for promising to remain silent is not known, but the guards implied this on a number of occasions when they told other inmates that he could easily have walked out a free man. He was in the camp for only five weeks but made a deep impression on the other prisoners, suffering beatings without complaint and again seeking prayers for their persecutors. German priests in the camp were allowed to say Mass in a separate barrack block, and they passed consecrated hosts to Titus, who ran severe risks in distributing them in his part of the camp. The physical labour proved too much for him, however, and he was sent to the camp hospital. After undergoing a number of inhumane experiments he was finally put to death by lethal injection on 26 July 1942. His body was cremated.

The nurse who administered the injection had herself been a Dutch Catholic. Titus had spoken to her while he was in hospital and had tried to persuade her to start praying again. She had refused and when he gave her his rosary had protested that she no longer knew the prayers, to which Titus replied, "Well, surely you can still say 'Pray for us sinners.'" After the war she returned to the Faith and gave evidence of how he had suffered patiently during the experiments carried out on him and how he had accepted his death with the words, "Not my will, but thy will be done." His cult became very popular in The Netherlands, especially after the publication of his prison writings. His cause was introduced in 1973 and he was beatified in 1985.

There are a large number of biographies and studies. See J. Alzin, *Ce petit mine dangereux* (1954); E. D. Rhodes, *His Memory Shall Not Pass* (1958); M. M. Arribas, *Un periodista martir* (1984); F. Vallainc, *Un giornalista martire: Padre Tito Brandsma* (1985); C. Dolle, *Titus Brandsma—Karmeliet* (1985). See also *Bibl.SS.*, Suppl. 1, 214-6; Ann Ball, *Modern Saints, Their Lives and Faces* (1983), pp. 368-71; *A.A.S.* 78, pt. 1 (1986), pp. 235-9, for his beatification.

27

St Pantaleon, *Martyr* (? Early Fourth Century)

There is no doubt about the existence of a martyr named Pantaleon or Panteleimon ("the all-compassionate"), but the various legends that deal with his life and execution have no credibility. He is said to have been born in Nicomedia of a pagan father and Christian mother and to have studied medicine, becoming famous enough to be appointed physician to the emperor Galerius (305-11). The legends tell of miraculous cures, the raising of a dead child to life, and of trials of strength with the imperial magicians. He was condemned to death as a Christian and, after many tortures, beheaded. His early cult is well attested—sanctuaries in his honour already existed in the reign of Justinian (527-65)—and seems to have centred on Nicomedia in Bithynia. He was venerated as one of the Fourteen Holy Helpers, honoured for the special help that they could provide in human need, and in the Eastern Church as the "Great Martyr and Wonder-worker," and one of the "Holy Moneyless Ones," who were venerated because they treated the sick without payment. Supposed relics of his blood exist in Constantinople, Madrid, and Ravello; those at Ravello are said to liquefy on his feast-day in the same way as does that of St Januarius (19 Sept.) in Naples. Other relics are claimed by Lyons and Venice.

The "wildly fabulous story of St Pantaleon" (*B.T.A.*) exists in a large number of both Latin and Greek versions, and there also Syriac, Armenian, Coptic, and Georgian versions. See Delehaye, *Origines du culte des martyrs* (1911), p. 189; *Bibl.SS.*, 10, 108-17, with a range of illustrations; I. Grant, *The Testimony of Blood* (1929), pp. 17-44, deals with the liquefaction at Ravello.

While many ancient representations of Pantaleon do not link him with the practice of medicine, this was the most usual way of depicting him, as in the eighth-century fresco in Santa Maria Antiqua in Rome, the tenth-century cycle of pictures in the crypt of San Crisogono, Rome, and a window in Chartres Cathedral. A painting by Veronese in the church of St Pantaleon in Venice (1587) shows the saint healing a child, while another painting in the same church, by Fumiani, shows the saint's martyrdom and entrance into glory.

St Celestine I, *Pope* (432)

Celestine was a native of the Campagna who became one of the Roman deacons under St Innocent I (401-17; 12 Mar.). He rose to the position of archdeacon and on the death of St Boniface I (4 Sept.) was unaninmously elected pope, in September 422. He was energetic in defence of orthodoxy and put down the Novationists, a rigorist sect that had survived in Rome in some numbers; he confiscated their public churches, forcing them to worship in private. He was responsible for the building of the basilica of Santa Sabina and for the restoration of Santa Maria in Trastevere, which had been destroyed in the sack of Rome in 410.

Celestine firmly believed that as Bishop of Rome he had authority over both the Western and the Eastern Churches. Part of this authority lay in the hearing of appeals, and this brought him into conflict with the Church in North Africa. He ordered the re-instatement of a disgraced priest, Apiarius, who had previously been restored by Pope St Zosimus (417-8; 26 Dec.) but had been excommunicated by the African bishops when he lapsed again. At a council in Carthage in around 426 Apiarius confessed his guilt, and the bishops wrote to Celestine to remind him of their traditional autonomy and urged him not to deal with people whom they had excommunicated. Other interventions by Celestine were received more favourably: as successor of St Peter, he directed the bishops of Illyria to accept the bishop of Thessalonica as his vicar; he reminded the bishops of southern Gaul of his authority and condemned a number of abuses in their region; the following year, in 429, he sent a mission to Britain under St Germanus of Auxerre (3 Aug.) to root out Pelagianism, and in 431 he sent St Palladius (7 July) as bishop to Ireland. Finally, he wrote again to the bishops of southern Gaul to condemn Semi-Pelagianism (a heresy that allowed the human will some initiative in turning to God independently of divine grace), urging them to follow the doctrines of St Augustine (28 Aug.).

Celestine held a synod in Rome in 430 to consider the rival teachings of Nestorius of Constantinople (428-31) and St Cyril of Alexandria (412-44; 27 June). St Cyril had denounced Nestorius because of his attacks on the title "Mother of God" as applied to Our Lady and his general teaching that there were two persons, one human, one divine, in Our Lord. Celestine regarded this as an appeal from the Eastern Chuch to Rome to settle a crucial point of doctrine. The synod condemned Nestorius and threatened him with excommunication if he did not recant. The pope empowered Cyril to carry out the sentence "in our stead" (*O.D.P.*). The emperor, Theodosius II (408-50), then called a general council at Ephesus in 431 to decide the issues involved; he invited Celestine to attend but the pope was content to send three legates. As it happened, Cyril held the council before they arrived, and all they could do was to approve its findings. The council Fathers did not send its decrees to Celestine for ratification, although it is clear from his letters of 432 that he did agree in the main with what it had decided. His letters and his instructions to his legates make it very clear, "with an unprecedented insistence," that he believed that as the "successor and living representative of St Peter (he had) paternal oversight of the entire church, eastern no less than western" (*O.D.S.*).

Celestine died on 27 July 432 and was buried in the cemetery of Priscilla, near San Silvestro. His feast used to be celebrated on 6 April; it has not been "suppressed" (*O.D.C.C.*) but reduced in status and removed from the universal Calendar.

The so-called Chapters of Celestine, summarizing the Roman position on the question of grace and free will, were attached to the letter to the bishops of southern Gaul. These were most likely written by St Prosper of Aquitaine (*c.* 390-465; 25 June) and not by Celestine.

O.D.P., pp. 41-2, is the best short account. Celestine's letters are in *P.L.*, 50, 417-558; a critical edition by E. Schwartz is in *A.C.O.*, 1 (1925-6 and 1929). See also *O.D.C.C.*, p. 309.

SS Aurelius, Natalia, and Companions, *Martyrs* (852)

During the eighth century the Christians of Spain were treated tolerantly by their Muslim masters, provided that they did not attempt to convert anyone from Islam or openly attack it. When Córdoba became an independent emirate, however, its emirs Abdur Rahman I and Mohammed I initiated a much more positive persecution. One of those who suffered was Aurelius, the son of a Moorish father and a Spanish mother. He had been brought up a Christian and had converted his half-Moorish wife, Sabigotho, who had taken the name Natalia at her Baptism, but outwardly they conformed to Islam while continuing to practise their Christianity in secret. One day he saw a Christian merchant being publicly beaten for stating that Islam was a false religion, and this made him think about his own cowardice in hiding his religious beliefs. It was not easy to know what to do, for he had two young children, and so he and Natalia consulted St Eulogius (11 Mar.), a distinguished priest of the city who had done a great deal to encourage the Christians there not to conform and who was himself to die as a martyr some years later. He advised them to make proper provision for their children, materially and spiritually, and then to admit openly to their Christianity. Aurelius and Natalia gave their children into the care of Isabella, widow of a martyred Christian, and then began to visit Christian prisoners in the city.

They were joined by Felix, a relative of Aurelius, who had accepted Islam but now returned to Christianity, and his wife Liliosa, who had remained faithful. When SS Flora and Mary (24 Nov.) were executed as Christians, Natalia and Liliosa became even more open about their religion, visiting the city's churches with their faces unveiled. The four of them and a number of other Christians, were arrested while attending Mass in Aurelius' house. They were charged with having apostasized from Islam and were condemned to death. A monk named George, who had gone to Córdoba to seek alms for the monastery of Saint Sabas, near Jerusalem, had been arrested with them; when the court was about to release him as a foreigner, he openly attacked Islam and was executed along with the rest of the group. They died in 852.

Information about this group of Spanish martyrs comes from St Eulogius' *The Memorial of the Saints*. See *Bibl.SS.*, 6, 544-5. See also the entry for St Abundius of Córdoba under 11 July, and for St Eulogius and the Martyrs of Córdoba, 11 March.

St Clement of Ohrid and Companions (Ninth to Tenth Century)

Boris I, ruler of the Bulgars, was baptized about the year 865, mainly, it seems, for political reasons, and imposed Christianity on his people. Both German and Greek missionaries were working in the region at the time, and it seems that Boris was at first undecided between giving his allegiance to Rome or to Constantinople; his indecision was deliberate in that what he wanted was a strong native Church independent of both East and West. When Pope Adrian II appointed St Methodius (14 Feb.) to be archbishop in Moravia and Pannonia, his jurisdiction extended to the borders of Bulgaria, and he and St Cyril (14 Feb.) are regarded by the Bulgars as their first apostles, though there is no evidence that either ever preached among them. After the death of Methodius his followers were forced by persecution to leave Moravia, and a number of them were welcomed by Boris, including Clement, Nahum, Sabas, and Angelarius. Less prominent members of the group were sold to Venice as slaves because they were considered to be heretics. Another of them, Gorazd, may have worked in what is now Albania; he had a reputation as a great missionary, and his relics were venerated at Berat in Albania. These five along with Methodius and Cyril became known as the Seven Apostles of Bulgaria.

Clement seems to have been the leader of the group, or at least its most important figure. He came from southern Macedonia (then part of Bulgar territory) and is credited with a great amount of missionary and educational work. Boris chose him to be the chief instrument of his ecclesiastical policy to displace Greek influences and create a Bulgarian clergy, and this became the theme of Clement's subsequent career. He worked mainly in south-west Macedonia, where he was given a number of centres to work from, including Ohrid and Glavenitsa. He was head of a Slavic school at Devol, which educated well over three thousand pupils during his time there, most of whom appear to have gone on to become readers, singers, deacons, or priests. Under Boris' successor, Simeon, he became bishop of the dual see of Debritsa and Belitsa, near Prilep in present-day Macedonia; Nahum took over the running of the school. Clement was later credited with having founded the primatial see of Ohrid, although this only became the leading see in 971. Clement died in 916. He translated a large number of works from Greek, including many sermons; it is not always clear whether these sermons, clearly intended for people newly converted to Christianity, were his original work or translations.

Some accounts say that Nahum succeeded Clement as bishop. He had been a convert of Methodius and Cyril in Moravia and had accompanied them to Rome. He is venerated in Bulgaria and Russia as a great wonder-worker. Their joint feast-day in the West used to be 17 July.

Under Simeon (893-927) the Bulgarian kingdom attained cultural prominence, with a rich Christian literature in Slavonic. The foundations for this were laid by Clement and his co-workers, "organizers of the Slavic Bulgarian church and creators of a great deal of Slavic literature" (Spinka). It was due to them that the Bulgarian Church exerted a profound and creative influence upon other Slavic national Churches, providing them with priests who were able to conduct services in the Slavic tongue, as well as liturgical and devotional books (*ibid.*).

M. Spinka, *A History of Christianity in the Balkans* (1933), pp. 1-72. There is a late eleventh-century Greek version of a Slavonic Life of Clement written shortly after his death by a disciple. See *O.D.C.C.*, pp. 248-9, on Christianity in Bulgaria.

Bd Berthold of Garsten, *Abbot* (*c.* 1075-1142)

Berthold de Rachez was born toward the end of the eleventh century on the shores of Lake Constance (the Bodensee). One account says that he married but that his wife died when he was about thirty years old and he then joined the monastery at Sankt-Blasien in the Black Forest. Other accounts, however, say that he entered the monastery at a very young age and make no mention of his marriage. He rose to be librarian and then prior before moving at some stage to become prior of Göttweig, also in the Black Forest. His time at Sankt-Blasien was very important, since it put him in touch with the Cluniac reform, which had made only sporadic progress in the German Empire, and he became a keen promoter of this when he moved to Garsten. The margrave of Styria, Ottokar, had founded a house of secular canons at Steyer-Garsten some years before this, about the year 1105, but the community had not lived up to his expectations, and so he dismissed it and about 1111 installed Benedictines there instead. He appointed Berthold to be the first abbot, and he soon established a rigorous discipline and reform along Cluniac lines, so much so that the abbey became a place of pilgrimage. His kindness to the local poor and to the pilgrims, for whom he built a hospice and a hospital, strained the resources of the young abbey, leading to stories of how God intervened miraculously to keep it going. Berthold was reputed to have led a secret life of severe penance, never eating meat or fish and spending most of his nights in prayer. His advice was sought by the many visitors who went to the abbey to hear him preach, and he built up a reputation as a wise and effective director, especially in the confessional. He died in 1142, and his cult began immediately; it was approved by the local bishop in 1236, and in the nineteenth century an Office in his honour was approved for local use. In 1951 the Austrian Benedictines took up his cause and had it officially recognized by the Sacred Congregation, where it is still ongoing.

J. Lenzenweger, *Berthold, abt von Garsten* (1958), sorted out and re-examined the two Lives of Berthold, the earliest parts of which date from before 1195 and were written at Garsten. See also *Bibl.SS.*, 3, 109-10.

St Raymund Palmarius (1140-1200)

Raimondo Zanfogni was born in Piacenza in the year 1140. When he was fifteen he and his mother, by then a widow, went on pilgrimage to Jerusalem and stayed in the Holy Land for some time. On their way home his mother died, and Raymund returned alone to Piacenza, carrying a pilgrim's palm branch—hence his nickname, "Palmarius." He married and worked as a cobbler to support his family of five children. His main interests, however, were attending religious talks and receiving instruction, and he soon became quite learned in spiritual matters, although he may well have been unable to read. After a time he developed a special apostolate, gathering groups of workers together on feast-days and giving them simple religious lessons; this was so successful that he was asked to preach publicly, but he refused, saying that that was only for priests and other learned people.

His five children all died in the same year, and when a sixth was born sometime later Raymund consecrated him to God. When his wife died after a long illness Raymund decided to go on pilgrimage to visit as many shrines as he could, starting with that of St James at Compostela. His journey took in Provence to see the relics of St Mary Magdalen (22 July), Pavia to see those of St Augustine (28 Aug.), and Rome. While he was preparing to go to Jerusalem he had a vision of Christ telling him to return to Piacenza to take on an apostolate to the poor. This was probably in 1178, and the rest of his life was spent looking after the needy in Piacenza. He was given a large building and developed it into a hostel for poor and sick people, begging alms for food and medicines; when the project attracted too many for him to cope with he began parading through the streets carrying a cross and crying, "Help us, you hard-hearted and cruel Christians; we're dying of hunger while you're living in plenty!" He became the voice of the poor in the city and their defender before the judges, accompanying them in court and threatening their oppressors with divine punishment if they showed no mercy. He founded other institutions to help those in need, including a hostel for women who had nothing and for repentant prostitutes; he tried to raise money for dowries so that they could either marry or become nuns. He looked after abandoned children, orphans, and pilgrims and did what he could for the care of prisoners.

While he seems to have received considerable support from the authorities for this work, he was less successful when he intervened in politics, trying to stop a war between Piacenza and Cremona and urging the bishop to stop the violent confrontations between the political factions in Piacenza itself. Raymund died on 27 July 1200. He was buried in a chapel close to the church of the Twelve Apostles, and the city fathers paid for a splendid tomb. Miracles were soon being reported, and his cult became very strong locally; lists of the miracles worked through his intercession were kept both in Piacenza and in other neighbouring cities, but moves to introduce his cause were held up by conflicts between Piacenza and the papacy. A Life was written in 1212 by a canon of

Piacenza who had known Raymund personally. It is not clear why later attempts to have him canonized failed, but by the late fourteenth century there was something of a decline in his cult. Some Cistercian nuns took over the care of his shrine and restored it, so that it again became a place of pilgrimage, and in 1576 and 1588 papal indulgences were granted to those visiting it; finally, in 1602, an Office in honour of Raymund was approved. In later centuries Raymund would have founded a religious Order to perpetuate his valuable work; it would be a pity if his apostolate were forgotten and not recognized as an exemplary living-out of the social gospel inspired by a simple devotion to Our Lord.

C. Mollinari, *Compendio della Vita di S. Raimondo* (1899); I. Bianchedi, *Il pellegrino della Croce* (1936); *Bibl.SS.*, 11, 26–9.

Bd Robert Sutton, *Martyr* (1544-88)

Robert Sutton was born in 1544 in Burton-on-Trent in Staffordshire, the son of a carpenter and the eldest of three brothers who became priests. He was educated at Christ College, Oxford, and given the living of Lutterworth in Leicestershire in 1571. He was ordained deacon five years later but resigned from the living the following year and went to the English College in Douai in March 1577; by March the following year he had been ordained and sent back to England. A report to the government of 1584 claimed that he had said Mass at Sir Thomas Gerard's house in Fleet Street on a number of occasions, and in 1585 he was banished. He returned to England, however, later the same year and seems to have worked as a priest in his native Staffordshire for about three years. In July 1588 he was captured in the house of Erasmus Wolsey in Stafford, was sent to London for questioning, and was then returned to Stafford to be tried. He was condemned for being a seminary priest ordained abroad and working in England and was hanged, drawn, and quartered in Stafford on 27 July 1588. Wolsey was granted a special pardon for having knowingly had the priest in his house. Robert Sutton was beatified in 1987.

M.M.P., pp. 122-3, puts the execution in 1586, but Anstruther, 1, p. 343, proves that 1588 is the correct date. A Catholic layman of the same name was executed in London in October 1588.

Bd William Davies, *Martyr* (*c.* 1558-93)

William Davies was born about the year 1558 at Croes-yn-Eirias in North Wales. He entered the English College in Reims in 1582 and was ordained priest there in April 1585. Two months later he left for England, but he was arrested on landing and spent from July 1585 to September 1588 in the Tower. For some reason he was released, despite the severe persecution that followed the defeat of the Armada in July 1588. He went to North Wales and seems to have worked there successfully for a few years until he was captured again, this time in Holyhead, in March 1592; he was about to leave for Ireland with four students who wanted to go to Valladolid in Spain. All five were condemned to death, but the judge took pity on the young students and declared them guilty only of refusing to attend church, which was not a capital crime. Challoner tells us that William was taken from Beaumaris to Ludlow to face the Council of the Marches and a number of Protestant divines, who tried to persuade him to attend the services in the local church. He refused and so was taken back to Beaumaris, where he was imprisoned with the students again but was able to say Mass for them through the kindness of the gaoler. According to Challoner, William two or three times refused the assistance of people who might have helped him to escape, so keen was he to die a martyr's death. On the scaffold he declared that "the cause for which he died was no other than his priestly character, [and he] prayed that his innocent blood, which he joyfully shed for his religion, might not cry to heaven for vengeance, but rather plead for mercy for that island, that it might once more be illustrated with the light of faith which it had lost" (*M.M.P.*). William was hanged, drawn, and quartered at Beaumaris in Anglesey on 27 July 1593. He was beatified in 1987.

M.M.P., pp. 190-6, using an account by one of the students; Anstruther, 1, p. 98. See also the general entries on the English and Welsh Martyrs under 4 May and 25 October.

Bd Mary Magdalen Martinengo, *Abbess* (1687-1737)

Margherita Martinengo da Barca was born into a noble family in Brescia in northern Italy in 1687. As a child she showed precocious signs of piety; she practised physical mortification and experienced psychological disturbances in connection with her spiritual exercises. At some early stage she determined "to imitate *everything* in the lives of the saints," a determination that the previous editors of this work dubbed "heroic . . . but hardly a wise programme at any age." When she was eighteen years old she joined the Capuchin abbey of Our Lady of the Snows in Brescia and was professed in 1706, taking the name Mary Magdalen in religion. She served three terms as novice-mistress and in 1732 and again in 1736 was elected abbess. In these offices she showed considerable ability and a welcome balance of judgment that seems at times to have deserted her in her private life. Her strongest devotion was to Our Lord's passion and especially to his sufferings from the crown of thorns; after her death a circlet of sharp points was discovered around her head. Others of her practices were so extreme that to detail them "would not necessarily tend to edification"; they have, indeed, been dismissed by a Benedictine writer as "the feats of a fakir" (*B.T.A.*). Those who knew her, however, spoke of her humility, her love of silence, her gentleness of speech, and her obvious selfless devotion to the religious life, and she carried on a fruitful apostolate among visitors to the abbey. Her spirituality was essentially christocentric, based as it was on the suffering Saviour, the Incarnation, and the Eucharist. Mary Magdalen Martinengo died in 1737 and was beatified in 1900.

She left a number of writings, some of which have been published: an *Autobiography*, written in 1725 on the orders of her spiritual director and edited by G. M. Pugnetti (1964); *Avvertimenti spirituali ed esortatorii . . . novizie*, a series of notes for her novices on how to acquire a deep humility, published in 1779 along with other documents; reflections on the *Spiritual Maxims composed by Fra Giovanni . . . carmelitano*, published in 1926 as *Lumi per i superiori scritti dalla B. M. M. Martinengo*; *An Explanation of the Capuchin Constitutions;* a *Treatise on Humility*; 170 letters; some poems; and a long *Miscellany*. A number of French and Italian biographies were published around the time of the beatification. See also F. von Scala, *Die selige Maria . . .* (1961); M. da Nembro, *Quattrocento scrittori spirituali* (1972), pp. 447-51; *Dict.Sp.*, 10, 575-6.

28

St Victor I, *Pope* (198)

Victor was born in north Africa. When he was elected pope in 189 he became the first Latin to hold that office and was "certainly the most forceful of the second-century popes" (*O.D.P.*). His first concern was to persuade other Churches to follow the Roman method of calculating the date of Easter, and he was responsible for a number of synods held as far apart as Mesopotamia and Gaul to decide the issue. Most of these agreed to follow the Roman custom; Victor excluded those in Asia Minor that did not form communion with the rest of the Church. This action brought protests even from some of his supporters, such as St Irenaeus of Lyons (28 June), who pointed out that differences over Easter had been tolerated by previous popes and should not lead to exclusion from the Christian community. We do not know what action Victor took in response, but the fact that the excluded Churches remained in communion with Rome indicates that he withdrew the sentence. He also excommunicated Theodotus of Byzantium, who had moved to Rome and was the leader of an Adoptionist sect (Adoptionists believed that Jesus was only human until "adopted" by the Father at his Baptism), and deposed a Gnostic writer, Florinus. All these actions showed that Victor was convinced of his authority over both Eastern and Western Churches.

As far as is known, Victor was the first pope to deal with the imperial court. Marcia, a mistress of the emperor Commodus (180-92), was a Christian, and Victor gave her a list of the Christians currently condemned to work in the Sardinian mines; she was able to have them released, including the future pope, St Callistus I (217-22; 14 Oct.), although Victor had excluded his name from the list. St Jerome (30 Sept.) attributes a number of Latin works to Victor, but these were probably just his encyclical letters, which would have been written in both Greek and Latin. Victor died in 198. He has traditionally been regarded as a martyr and was supposed to have been buried near the tomb of St Peter, but there is no historical evidence to suggest that he was martyred—he died before the next outbreak of persecution under Septimius Severus.

O.D.P., p. 12; *O.D.C.C.*, p. 1693.

St Samson of Dol, *Bishop* (*c.* 565)

While no one doubts that Samson was probably the most important British missionary of the sixth century, there is considerable uncertainty about the authenticity of some of the historical detail surrounding his story. He was probably Welsh by birth, his father being from Dyfed and his mother from Gwent. When he was five years old his parents offered him in thanksgiving to St Illtud (6 Nov.) at Llanilltud Fawr, where he was later ordained priest. The jealousy of Illtud's nephews made Samson retire to an island monastery, possibly on Caldey Island off the coast of Pembrokeshire, where he became cellarer and then abbot. At some stage he went to Ireland and reformed a monastery there (perhaps on Howth, near Dublin), before returning to live as a hermit near the Severn—one account says that he was joined there by his father. He became abbot of a nearby monastery and was consecrated bishop by St Dyfrig (or Dubricius, 14 Nov.)—again the circumstances are not clear. He worked for some time as a missionary in Cornwall, and St Mewan (or Méen, 21 June), St Austell (28 June), and St Winnoc (6 Nov.) were among his disciples and fellow-workers. The early Life is rich in reliable detail about this part of the saint's activities, including the conversion of bands of pagan revellers on Bodmin Moor. There are a number of Cornish places associated with Samson, including Padstow, Saint Kew, Southill, and Golant, and one of the Isles of Scilly is named after him.

From Cornwall he travelled to Brittany, perhaps by way of the Channel Islands, where a town on Guernsey bears his name. He founded monasteries at Pental in Normandy and Dol in Brittany, where he was also recognized as bishop, although there was no regular see there at the time. He visited the royal court in Paris and was given grants of land by the king for his foundations. In 557 the acts of a council in Paris were signed by *"Samson peccator episcopus"* ("Samson the bishop, a sinner"), and it is likely that this was the same person, although Doble says that the signature was *"Samson subscripsi et consensi in nomine Christi"* ("I, Samson, have signed and agreed in the name of Christ"). Samson died in Brittany about the year 565.

His cult was popular in Brittany, where he was the chief of the "Seven Saints of Brittany," the founders of the key sees there. When King Athelstan of Wessex (924-39) acquired some of his relics for the monastery at Milton Abbas in Dorset, the cult gained ground in England—the king gave some of the relics to Canterbury and Salisbury as well. There are six ancient English dedications in his honour. He was normally shown with a cross or staff, and with a dove and a book. A church was dedicated to him in Cricklade in Wiltshire, and this may have been the origin of the medieval legend that associated him with the Greek schools supposed to have been founded there by Brutus and later moved to Oxford by King Alfred; St Samson's Hall in Oxford was said to represent Samson's foundation (Orme). He is "an excellent example of the wandering Celtic monk-bishop" (*O.D.S.*).

The date of an early Life of Samson is disputed; some say it was probably written in the late eighth or early ninth century and have dismissed it as historically worthless; others date it from the early seventh century at the latest and believe that it is fundamentally reliable; see the details in *B.T.A.*, 3, pp. 203-4. The above account is based on *O.D.S.*, pp. 426-7. See also G. H. Doble, *The Saints of Cornwall*, 5 (1970), pp. 80-103, who describes the Life as the earliest and most authentic of any Welsh, Cornish, or Breton Lives. See Nicholas Orme (ed.), *Nicholas Roscarrock's Lives of the Saints; Cornwall and Devon*, (vol. 35 [NS] of Devon and Cornwall Record Society), (1992), pp. 109-12, 169-70. The most up-to-date commentary on the early Life is by B. Lynette Olson, *Early Monasteries in Cornwall* (1989), pp. 9-20.

Bd Benno of Osnabrück, *Bishop* (1088)

Benno as born at Löhningen in Swabia and educated under Bd Herman "Contractus" (25 Sept.) in the monastery of Reichenau. He became a skilled architect and builder and later served the emperor Henry III (1039-56) as his builder-in-chief. In this capacity he worked on the new cathedral in Speyer to save its foundations from being undermined by the Rhine. At some stage he was ordained, and in 1047 he was put in charge of the cathedral school in Hildesheim. He had to leave fairly soon afterwards to accompany his bishop on Henry's campaign against the Hungarians, for which he was in charge of organizing supplies, and he seems to have done this so successfully that he was promoted: he became provost of the cathedral and *vicedominus* of Henry's court at Goslar, where he oversaw the imperial finances, agriculture, and construction. In 1068 the emperor appointed him bishop of Osnabrück.

The German bishops became involved in the serious dispute between Pope St Gregory VII (1073-85; 25 May) and the new emperor, Henry IV (1056-1106), which started over the issue of investiture. In 1075 Henry refused to accept Gregory's decrees forbidding lay investiture of bishops and, in answer to papal threats of excommunication, called the German bishops together at Worms, where they deposed Gregory. Benno was one of those who signed the attempted deposition, but when the pope excommunicated everyone who had taken part in the proceedings, he and the other bishops went to Italy to ask for forgiveness and absolution. Henry also submitted, at Canossa in 1077, but was soon in trouble again and was excommunicated for a second time in 1080. Benno acted as imperial envoy to the pope on a number of occasions, but after 1080 he appears to have gone into hiding to avoid having to take sides against Gregory.

Benno's stance in all this was certainly less than heroic. As pastor of his people, however, he won their esteem for his justice, honesty, and personal integrity. He spent his last years in peace at Iburg, where he had founded a monastery, and died there in the year 1088. Benno's cult was restricted mainly to Osnabrück and Iburg. His first biographer was Norbert, third abbot of Iburg, who was elected while Benno was in retirement there. He described Benno as a distinguished master-builder and an "ingenious layer of stonework." We know that he built a chain of defensive castles against the Saxons, but attempts to link him with other building projects, apart from that on the foundations at Speyer, are open to question.

For a long time no text of Norbert's *vita* was known, and the Bollandists stated that they could find no evidence of a Life or a cult; a text was discovered early in the twentieth century and was published in *M.G.H., Scriptores*, 30, pt. 2 (1926). There is a short entry on Benno as a builder, with a bibliography, in Jane Turner (ed.), *The Dictionary of Art*, 3 (1996), p. 732.

St Botvid (1100)

Botvid of Hammarby was born in the Swedish province of Södermannland and brought up a pagan. At some stage he travelled to England as a merchant, where he became a Christian, and then returned to Sweden to preach the gospel. He worked as a lay missionary in the provinces of Våstmannland and Norrland and is regarded as one of the apostles of Sweden. He is also venerated as a martyr, but there does not appear to be anything in the manner of his death to warrant this. He bought a Finnish slave, instructed and baptized him, and then set him free to go back to Finland to preach the gospel. Botvid and a companion accompanied the new convert across the Baltic by boat, but during the night the Finn murdered the two men and stole the boat. Legend has it that Botvid's brother, Björn, was led to the body by a white bird of a type never seen before and that a spring of fresh water flowed where the blood had stained the ground; a servant had his eyes cured by bathing them in this water. The grave became a place of pilgrimage as stories of miracles spread throughout the country, and Björn built a wooden chapel there that became known as Botkyrka; this was replaced in 1176 by the present stone church. Botvid features in the revelations of St Bridget of Sweden (23 July), who had a strong devotion to him; he is depicted in the nineteenth-century frescoes in her house in Rome.

There is a fourteenth-century Life of Botvid written by a monk of Bodensee. See *Bibl.SS.*, 3, 372-3.

St Melchior García Sampedro, *Bishop and Martyr* (1858)

Melchior García Sampedro was born in Cortes in Asturias, Spain, in 1821. His parents were too poor to pay for his education, but he was able to work his way through college. In 1845 he entered the Dominican novitiate at Ocaña, which specialized in training missionaries for the Far East. His first posting was to Tonkin (Vietnam)—a dangerous assignment because of the anti-Christian policies of the emperor, which meant that the missionaries had to travel in disguise and largely by night. Melchior described their hardships in a letter: "Drenched from head to foot, covered with mud; with neither coat nor clothes for change, we deemed ourselves happy . . . and I forget the pains of my feet to praise the Lord. I have no fear of exaggeration in saying that rarely do we have greater joy than during the strongest tribulations." He was appointed coadjutor to St Joseph Díaz Sanjurjo (20 July), vicar apostolic of the eastern region of Tonkin, and succeeded as bishop after his superior's martyrdom. About a year later, in 1858, he was ambushed and taken prisoner; after considerable sufferings he was eventually hacked to death. Two native lay brothers were tortured and beheaded at the same time. Bishop García was beatified in 1951 and canonized in 1988.

An account of the martyrdom of St Joseph Díaz Sanjurjo was written by Bishop García and published in *Missiones dominicanas* 1 (1917), pp. 39-44. He himself features in an Italian account of the Tonkin martyrs of 1857 to 1862 published in 1951. See the entry for 20 July, and the general entry on the Martyrs of Vietnam under 2 February. The quotation above is taken from Mary Jean Dorcy, O.P., *St Dominic's Family* (n.d.).

BB Peter Poveda, *Founder*, and Victoria Díez, *Martyrs* (1936)

The founder of the Teresian Association, Pedro Poveda Castroverde, was born in Linares in the province of Jaén in south-eastern Spain on 3 December 1874. His family was of modest means and solidly Christian. He felt the call to become a priest at an early age and entered the diocesan seminary of Jaén in 1889. His family was financially unable to maintain him there, as his father had become ill and was unable to work, but the bishop of Guadix in the province of Granada, to the south, offered him a scholarship, and he transferred to the seminary there, being ordained in April 1897. He taught in the seminary for a while, obtained a licentiate in theology in Seville, and then returned to work among the desperately poor cave-dwellers of Guadix, a town whose outskirts consist largely of caves cut out of clay hillocks. In three years of exhausting work he built two schools for the children and workshops for the adults to give them some chance of acquiring skills and so becoming employable, while at the same time concentrating on their Christian formation.

This social and educational apostolate, at which he was evidently successful, earned him great popularity among the cave-dwellers and the approval of the town council, which named a street after him, but the jealousy of more traditional Catholics, including some of his fellow-priests in the diocese who conspired to get rid of him (glossed over as "some misunderstandings" in the *Osservatore Romano* biographical note at the time of his beatification). He voluntarily left Guadix and was for a time unattached to any diocese. He was then "promoted" to a prestigious post as canon of the basilica at the shrine of the Virgin Mary known as *la Santina*, in Covadonga, hidden away on the northern slopes of the Cantabrian Mountains in the north-western province of Asturias, almost as far from his previous social apostolate as is possible to go in Spain. An energetic young man of thirty-two was definitely out of place among the retired canons in the vast buildings attached to the basilica. But Covadonga had long ago been the place where the reconquest of Spain from the Moors began, and Fr Poveda made it his springboard for a new apostolate in the field of education through his writings, publishing articles and pamphlets on the professional formation of teachers. In 1911 he opened a student residence in Oviedo named the St Teresa of Avila Academy, which became the starting point for the Teresian Association, devoted to the spiritual and pastoral formation of teachers. In the early years its members were women involved in all levels of education; they opened secondary schools but also fostered higher education for Catholic women—aims rather different from the standard ideal for Catholic women in Spain at the time, where "piety, duty, and domesticity remained the female cardinal virtues, even when practised 'heroically' or 'virilely'" (Lannon, p. 56). In 1912 he joined the Apostolic Union of Secular Priests, opened new educational centres, and started periodicals in the field of education. The first of these had the significant title *La Enseñanza Moderna* (Modern Teaching), and in the first editorial he wrote: "What moves us, then? Love of culture. Where are we going? To awaken this in the people."

Education had been seen as the way out of the economic and spiritual decline of Spain, which reached its nadir with the loss of the last colonies in 1898. The "Generation of '98" sought the solution in the provision of free, secular education, and many of the best minds in the country gathered around the *Institución Libre de Enseñanza* (Free Institute of Education). Most (private) education was provided by religious Orders, but this was seen by liberal thinkers and governments as both reactionary and ineffective—at the turn of the century 68 per cent of Spanish men and 79 per cent of women were illiterate. Poveda sought a "middle way," with teachers as well formed professionally as those from the Free Institute but committed to Catholic principles and working in the State schools. And for him, formed by the teaching of *Rerum Novarum* and his experience in Guadix, these principles had to include social justice. He proposed an *Institución Católica de Enseñanza* to rival the Free Institute but was never quite able to achieve this.

He was nominated canon of Jaén Cathedral in 1913, and there, in addition to teaching in the seminary, he became the spiritual director of *Los Operarios* (the workmen's) catechetical centre and taught religion at the teacher-training school. His Teresian Association developed and received both ecclesiastical and civil approval in Jaén. In May 1914 he was able to open an *academia* (a hall of residence where the students could also get help with their studies and religious formation) for women university graduates in Madrid—the first institution of its kind in Spain. Similar foundations followed rapidly in many of the major cities of Spain. He moved permanently to Madrid in 1921 with an appointment as chaplain at the royal palace. He was nominated to the central board entrusted to combat illiteracy the following year and was involved in all major educational discussions and initiatives throughout the 1920s, but he was still able to devote much of his time to the Teresian Association, which received papal approval in 1924. He handed over its day-by-day direction but personally oversaw the extension of its work to Chile and then to Italy in 1934.

As a prominent proponent of—even liberal-minded—Catholic education he was a target of revolutionary elements at the outbreak of the civil war (see the general entry on Martyrs of the Spanish Civil War, 22 July, above). Despite warnings from friends, he refused to leave Republican Madrid. On the morning of 27 July 1936, when he had just finished saying Mass in the chapel of the Teresian house in Madrid, militiamen broke in and took him away. He was interrogated by a series of revolutionary tribunals throughout the day and then lost to sight. His body was found near the boundary wall of the East Cemetery on the morning of 28 July 1936. The scapular he was wearing still shows the hole from the bullet through the heart that killed him.

Victoria Díez y Bustos de Molina was born in Seville on 11 November 1903, the only child of a devout couple. There was enough money to educate her, but once she qualified, her salary would be needed to help support the family. Following her parents' wishes, she studied to become a teacher and qualified as an elementary school teacher. Her aim, however, was not to teach but to become a missionary. She also attended art classes at the School of Arts and Crafts in Seville. Her artistic talent was matched by a deep spirituality seeking an outlet in service. There was a house of the Teresian Association in Seville, and she saw this as her way to combine her spirituality with a teaching apostolate. She joined the Association, and in 1926 she wrote to Josefa Segovia, whom Poveda had appointed as director: "Since I came to know the ends it pursues I could only love it and I believe that only by belonging to it can I find happiness. How good God is to give according to our wishes!" She stayed in Seville for two years after joining, teaching while studying for her own final examination. She was then sent to teach in Cheles, a small and inaccesssible town to the north-west near the Portuguese border, which she described as "the end of the world." She worked tirelessly for a year to overcome the general apathy with regard to education among the people, her letters showing her love for her pupils and her enthusiasm, but also some pessimism at the size of the task facing her. She then asked to work nearer Seville in order to be able to help her parents and was assigned to Hornachuelos, close to the north bank of the river Guadalquivir, some twenty miles west of Córdoba. Most of its inhabitants relied on casual agricultural work to earn a living, and the town was rife with economic, ideological, and religious unrest.

She stayed there for the rest of her life, a dedicated teacher involved in many aspects of a Catholic educational apostolate and known for depriving herself in order to help the poorest children in her classes. Here too she struggled against parental apathy to get her pupils to attend school. When in 1933 a law was passed making it illegal for teachers in State schools to teach religion, she organized catechetical classes for her pupils' mothers so that they in turn could teach their children. Like Pedro Poveda, she saw that women were to be the most powerful factor in building the Church of the future.

On the outbreak of the civil war she chose to stay in Hornachuelos, despite the formation of a local committee for the defence of the Republic, which began arresting anyone thought favourable to the military uprising, a category that included Catholic educators. She was seized at nightfall on 11 August 1936 and taken first to the town hall and then to a house converted into a prison, from which she and seventeen others were force-marched overnight to the abandoned lead mine on the Rincón estate, some eight miles from the town. At daybreak the next day they were shot against a wall so that their bodies fell down the shaft. The last in line, she encouraged the others with the prospect of an eternal reward and died, as did so many others at this time, with the *Cristero* slogan *"Viva Cristo Rey!"* on her lips.

Both these martyrs were beatified together by Pope John Paul II on 10 October 1993.

For an introduction to the Teresians and their founder see A. Galino, "Pedro Poveda— una pedagogía para nuestro tiempo," in *Textos pedagógicos hispanoamericanos* (1968), cited in F. Lannon, *Privilege, Persecution and Prophecy: The Catholic Church in Spain 1875-1975* (1987), p. 56. Biographical information in N. San Martín, *Historia de un hombre incómodo: Pedro Poveda* (n.d.); *Osservatore Romano*, weekly edition, 13 Oct. 1993; M.-D. Molleda, *Pedro Poveda: A Biographical Essay* (Eng. trans. of *Pedro Poveda, educador de educadores*, 1993); Ana María López, *Así era . . . Pedro Poveda* (1993). His spiritual writings are published in Spanish: *Escritos espirituales* (1968), and there are recent facsimile editions of several of his early pamphlets. In English see *Staunch Friends of God*, a selection of his writings, ed. and intro. M.-D. Gómez Molleda (1997, trans. by T. Barcelón of *Amigos fuertes de Dios*). The Teresian Association has published a short selection in English: *A Christian Challenge: Extracts from the Writings of Pedro Poveda* (1985), and other pamphlets; it also publishes the occasional review *Down to Earth* (Sp. ed. *Aquí y Ahora*).

A biography of Victoria Díez was written three years after her death: Josefa Grosso, *Veo el cielo abierto* (1939), cited in Carmen Fernández Aguinaco, *Victoria Díez: Memoria de una maestra* (1993), on which the above account relies.

The Teresian Association celebrated the fiftieth anniversary of the arrival of its first members in England in 1998 and has houses in Dublin and the U.S.A. among those in thirty-one countries on four continents, with some six thousand members worldwide. Membership now includes both women and men, married and single.

Bd Alphonsa Muttathupadathu (1910-46)

Anna Muttathupadathu was born in Kudamaloor in Kerala, India, in August 1910 and was baptized according to the Syro-Malabar rite. Her parents died while she was young, and so she was brought up and given an elementary school education by her grandmother and an aunt. When she was thirteen the aunt arranged a marriage for her, but Anna was so opposed to the idea that she deliberately burned her feet to avoid the betrothal, inspired, she claimed to her confessor, by the lives of the early saints who destroyed their beauty to avoid unwelcome suitors. As it happened, the burns were more severe than she intended, and the scars remained on her legs for the rest of her life. Eventually her guardians allowed her to enter the Clarist Sisters at Bharananganam in

1927 as a postulant; this was a convent of Franciscan regular tertiaries who took the usual religious vows. Anna took the name Alphonsa of the Immaculate Conception in religion—the Alphonsa was in honour of St Alphonsus Liguori—and received the religious habit in 1930. The Sisters were mainly engaged in teaching, and Anna gained her teaching certificate while still a postulant and started to teach.

From the time she entered the convent Alphonsa suffered increasingly from bad health, so much so that "an account of her physical sufferings reads like a study in pathology" (Ball). Soon she had to give up her teaching, and for the rest of her life she was an invalid. She accepted these physical sufferings as her main apostolate, declaring: "I believe the Lord has chosen me to be an oblation, a sacrifice of suffering. . . . Any day I don't suffer is a day lost as far as I'm concerned." In addition to her physical ailments she faced opposition from some of the Sisters and others, who did not understand her continued illnesses and spread slanderous rumours about her. While she always welcomed and tried to help visitors who came asking for advice and for her prayers, people commented on a certain reserve that some mistook for coldness. Those who came to know her better found that this reserve covered a deeply spiritual charity that extended to everyone. Reports began to circulate of miracles worked through her intercession; these seem to have been mainly predictions of tragic events. In July 1946 Alphonsa asked her confessor for permission to pray for an early death, as she felt that she had become too heavy a burden on the Sisters. She died on 28 July 1946. A remarkable cult began soon after her death, and large crowds of Christians, Hindus, and Muslims visited her tomb, attracted by the miracles of healing that were widely reported and also by the purity of her life. She was beatified in Kottayam in 1986.

Bibl.SS., Suppl. 1 (1987), 949-50; Ann Ball, *Modern Saints: Their Lives and Faces* (1983), pp. 388-95; T. T. Mundakel, *The Story of Blessed Alphonsa* (1989).

ST MARTHA
Serving Jesus, from the account in St Luke's Gospel.
Dark brown cups, pitcher, and bowl; blue tablecloth with
white stripe, all on silver field

29

SS MARTHA, MARY, AND LAZARUS OF BETHANY
(First Century)

Of these three saints, the new Roman Martyrology retains only the feast of St Martha of Bethany, but as they are so closely related both in the Gospel accounts and in legend, they are being treated together here.

Martha is mentioned on three occasions in the New Testament. The first occasion is the best known and has provided the most common image of her for artists. In Luke's Gospel (10:38-42), when the two sisters, Martha and Mary, welcome Jesus into their house, Martha busies herself getting things ready, but Mary sits at Jesus' feet listening to what he has to say. Martha asks Jesus to tell her sister to help her, but he replies that Mary "has chosen the better part" and tells Martha that she worries and frets about too many things, when only one is necessary.

The second occasion is the raising of Lazarus to life (John 11:1-44). Here we are told that Jesus "loved Martha and her sister and Lazarus," and again it is Martha who has the more active role: while Mary sits at home, Martha goes out to meet Jesus. When Jesus tells her, "Your brother will rise again," Martha replies, "I know that he will rise again at the resurrection on the last day," and Jesus uses this to make his great declaration: "I am the resurrection. . . . If any believe in me, even though they die they will live, and whoever live and believe in me, will never die." Martha then replies to Jesus' question whether she believes this or not by making her own declaration: "I believe that you are the Christ, the Son of God, the one who was to come into this world." When Jesus tells the bystanders to take the stone away from Lazarus' tomb, it is the practical-minded Martha who warns him that the body will smell, as it is the fourth day since its burial.

The third appearance of Martha in the Gospel narrative is just before the passion, when Martha, Mary, and Lazarus entertain Jesus at dinner in Bethany; Martha, we are told, "waited on them," while Mary anoints Jesus' feet with valuable ointment and wipes them with her hair (John 12:1-3). Martha does not feature in the post-resurrection narratives at all. According to relatively late Western legends she accompanied her sister and brother to the south of France (see below), where she was supposed to have saved the people of Tarascon from the attentions of a dragon; the principal church of the town is dedicated to her, and this dedication may date from the first quarter of the ninth century or even earlier. In 1187 her supposed relics were discovered when the church was being rebuilt and were placed in a new shrine.

The Gospel accounts of Martha are straightforward and present an attractive picture of a woman who, despite being busy about many things, did learn the one thing that was necessary and recognized Jesus as the Christ. Her sister, Mary, is more problematical. As we have just seen, according to John's Gospel she anointed the feet of Jesus and dried them with her hair in a house at Bethany. Now Luke also describes an anointing (Luke 7:36-50): he does not name the woman but says that she was a sinner; she uses ointment and wipes her tears from his feet with her hair while Jesus is dining with a man named Simon. Both Mark and Matthew mention it as well, saying that it happened in Bethany, in Simon's house; like Luke, they do not mention the woman's name (Matt. 26:6-13; Mark 14:3-9). These accounts raise two questions: was there more than one anointing with ointment and drying of Jesus' feet with a woman's hair, and who was the unnamed woman in Matthew, Mark, and Luke? Traditionally in the West, the woman who was a sinner in Luke's account has been identified with the Mary Magdalen of Luke 8:1-3, and the anointings have been taken as referring to a single event; this, then, would make Mary of Bethany the same person as Mary Magdalen. This is no longer accepted by most Gospel commentators, who now accept the ancient Eastern tradition of seeing the woman who was a sinner, Mary Magdalen, and Mary of Bethany as three separate people, and the anointing described by Luke as different from that described by John (see the discussion of the issue under St Mary Magdalen; 22 July). We are left with a Mary of Bethany who sat and listened to the Lord, was loved by him, and who showed her love in return by anointing his feet and wiping them with her hair. According to Western legend, she went (in the guise of Mary Magdalen) to Provence with Martha and Lazarus; according to Eastern traditions, she went with them to Cyprus (see below).

As we have seen, in St John's Gospel (11:1-44) there is a full account of the raising of Lazarus from the dead by Jesus. He was the brother of Martha and Mary and a much-loved friend of Jesus, but he does not feature again in the New Testament and we know nothing about his subsequent life. Not surprisingly, various traditions developed about him in the early Church.

The pseudo-Clementine writings say that Lazarus followed St Peter (29 June) into Syria. The Eastern Church had a story that he and his sisters and some other Christians were put into a leaking boat by the Jews at Jaffa but survived and landed in Cyprus. There Lazarus became bishop of Kition (Larnaca) and died peacefully about thirty years later. In 890 Emperor Leo VI built a church and monastery in his honour in Constantinople and moved some of his supposed relics from Cyprus.

According to a Western tradition, dating only from the eleventh century, the boat drifted across the Mediterranean and finally landed on the south-east coast of Gaul. Lazarus then preached in Marseilles, making many converts, and became the first bishop of the city. He was martyred under Domitian (81-96) on the site of the later Saint-Lazare prison, was buried in a cave, over which the abbey of Saint Victor was built, and his relics were later translated to Autun. A letter written by Pope Benedict IX (1032-56) on the occasion of the consecration of the abbey church of Saint Victor referred to the abbey having Lazarus' relics but did not refer to the tradition that he had preached and been bishop there.

The Marseilles tradition seems to have arisen from a number of confusions. In the first place, this Lazarus was confused with the fictitious Lazarus in Christ's parable of Dives and Lazarus (Luke 16:20), who was "full of sores." It was the latter, not Lazarus of Bethany, who gave his name to the *lazarettos* of medieval Europe, and this confusion led to the erroneous association with the Saint-Lazare prison in Marseilles. Secondly, Lazarus of Bethany was confused with a fifth-century bishop of Aix named Lazarus: there is an epitaph in the crypt of Saint Victor's in Marseilles to this bishop, who was buried there. Thirdly, there was confusion between the relics of Lazarus and those of St Nazarius (formerly 28 July), supposedly found by St Ambrose (7 Dec.). Some human remains were enshrined in the cathedral of Autun in 1146 and were thought to be those of Lazarus, but they appear to be relics of Nazarius, taken from Milan to Autun in 542.

The military Order of hospitaller-knights of St Lazarus of Jerusalem took its name from the Lazarus of the parable, not the historical one, while the more recent Order of Lazarus, founded by St Vincent de Paul (27 Sept.), takes its name from the church of Saint-Lazaire in Paris.

Despite these doubtful traditions, the cult of Lazarus was recognized in the early Church in Jerusalem and later throughout the Church. The Spanish pilgrim Etheria, who visited the Holy Land about 390, wrote of a procession on the Saturday of Passion Week to the place where Lazarus was raised from the dead and was much impressed by the great crowds that attended. There were many similar celebrations, almost all of them during Lent, in the Western Church. At Milan, Passion Sunday was called *Domenica di Lazaro*, and in North Africa, according to St Augustine (28 Aug.), the Gospel account of the raising of Lazarus from the dead was read at the night Office of Palm Sunday. The tomb of Lazarus is still shown to pilgrims and tourists at Bethany, though some hold that it was only a grain silo.

St Lazarus' feast used to be celebrated on 17 December.

Bibl.SS., 7, 1135-52, on Lazarus; 8, 1204-18, on Martha. On Mary see the entry for St Mary Magdalen under 22 July, and especially Carla Ricci, *Mary Magdalene and Many Others* (1991; Eng. trans., 1994). On Lazarus, see also H. Thurston in *Studies* 23 (1934), pp. 110-23, and the entry for St Victor under 21 July. For depictions of the three in art see Murray, pp. 270-2 for Lazarus and pp. 307-8 for Martha and Mary. For an imaginative account see Tina Beattie, *The Last Supper according to Martha and Mary* (forthcoming).

The raising of Lazarus provided a favourite theme for Christian artists from the age of the catacombs onwards (see Murray for early examples). There is a fresco by Giotto in the Arena Chapel, Padua, and one by Fra Angelico in San Marco, Florence, while the National Gallery in London has a magnificent *The Raising of Lazarus* by Sebastiano del Piombo

(1517-9), originally painted for Narbonne Cathedral. Two large panels in Chichester Cathedral from the early twelfth century contain carvings of the scene, one showing Christ arriving in Bethany, the other showing Lazarus coming out of the tomb and a disciple unwrapping the bands (Murray). A rarely omitted feature is that of the onlookers guarding themselves against the expected stench from the tomb. On the other hand, depictions of Christ in the house in Bethany only became popular in the sixteenth century, when Dutch artists used it in their still-life and domestic paintings. Tintoretto painted the scene in the 1560s, and one of the finest paintings of the subject was by Vermeer in the following century (National Gallery of Scotland, Edinburgh). Two versions by Velázquez (1618) are in the National Gallery, London, and the National Gallery of Scotland, Edinburgh (Murray).

SS Simplicius and Faustinus, *Martyrs* (? Early Fourth Century)

Legend has it that these two martyrs were Roman brothers who refused to sacrifice to the gods. As a result they were either beheaded or drowned in the Tiber. Their sister, Beatrice, rescued their bodies and buried them in the cemetery of Generosa on the road to Porto. In the seventh century Pope St Leo II (682-3; 3 July) transferred their relics to the church of Santa Bibiana; they were later moved to Santa Maria Maggiore. The fact of their martyrdom and the existence of an early cult seem to be well attested despite the lack of reliable information about their lives and the date when they died. The *Hieronymianum* mentions the veneration on 29 July of Simplicius, Faustinus, and Viatrix; this last name helps to explain the story about Beatrice, who was said to have died a martyr's death herself on 11 or 12 May but whose name should be Viatrix or, possibly, Viatrice. Excavations in the cemetery of Generosa in the mid-nineteenth century unearthed the remains of a small basilica dating from the time of Pope Damasus I (366-84) with frescoes and fragments of inscriptions giving the names Simplicius, Faustinus, Viatrix, and an unknown Rufinianus. Their *passio* has no historical value.

H. Leclercq, *D.A.C.L.*, 6 (1924), 866-900, on the excavations; *Bibl.SS.*, 11, 1204-5.

St Lupus of Troyes, *Bishop* (*c.* 393-479)

Lupus (or Loup) was born in Toul in Gaul, traditionally about the year 383, although 393 now seems more likely. He married a sister of St Hilary of Arles (5 May), but after six or seven years of marriage they parted by mutual consent and Lupus entered the monastery at Lérins, while his wife became a nun. Shortly after this, about the year 426, he was chosen to be bishop of Troyes, a post he held for the next fifty years. He is reputed to have continued to live an austere monastic life, dressing simply, fasting, and spending many hours in prayer. St Sidonius Apollinaris (21 Aug.), a contemporary, described him as "the father of fathers and bishop of bishops, chief of the prelates of Gaul, the rule of morals, the pillar of truth, the friend of God, and the intercessor to God for men."

In 429 he accompanied St Germanus of Auxerre (31 July) to Britain on a mission to prevent the spread of Pelagianism. When the invading Huns under Attila threatened to capture Troyes, Lupus persuaded them to spare the whole province but had to agree to becoming a hostage. When he returned later to Troyes he was accused of helping the enemy and had to go into exile for two years—an early victim of "anti-collaborationist" hysteria, as the previous edition of this work puts it. There is, however, doubt about the story of his resistance to Attila and his subsequent exile. He is said to have spent the two years as a hermit before returning to his see, where he died in the year 479.

An early Life of Lupus probably dates from the beginning of the sixth century and may have been written to defend the rights of the then bishop of Troyes to certain lands and privileges; it is unreliable as a historical account. Lupus is mentioned in a number of Sidonius Apollinaris' letters, and in St Gregory of Tours' *De Gloria Confessorum*. See *M.G.H., Scriptores rerum Merov.*, 7 (1920), pp. 284-302. See also *Bibl.SS.*, 8, 390-1; J. Roserot de Melin, *Le diocèse de Troyes des origines à nos jours* (1957).

St Olaf, *Martyr* (*c.* 990-1030)

Olaf (also Olave or Ola) was the son of a Norwegian lord, Harold Grenske, and was born about the year 990. He spent his youth in fighting and piracy around the Baltic and in Normandy, where he became a Christian, and in 1013 he even fought for Ethelred II in England against the Danes. He inherited his father's estates in 1015 and the following year used his military ability to make himself king of Norway. Given his warlike past, his people were surprised to find that he brought them peace and a certain security, both welcome after years of fighting and occupation of the country by the Swedes and the Danes. He insisted on the rule of law and refused to tolerate bribery or the use of violence by the ruling classes. Above everything else, however, he wanted to make Norway into a Christian country and unfortunately did not always follow his own preaching of non-violence in trying to bring this about—"his zeal was often more than his prudence, and he used force without compunction" (*B.T.A.*). He introduced English missionaries and had an Englishman, Grimkel, as his archbishop, but their efforts to evangelize the people met with only limited success, while Olaf's severity toward his opponents was resented. In the end he was driven from the throne by a rebellion in 1029; King Cnut of England and Denmark helped the rebels and when Olaf tried to regain his position in 1030 with the help of the Swedes, Norway's traditional enemy, he was killed in the battle of Stiklestad on 29 July.

It seems to have been Archbishop Grimkel who started a cult of Olaf by building a chapel over his tomb and declaring him a saint. The dead king gained some posthumous popularity when Cnut's son, who had become king, proved to be very unpopular; when he died in 1035 he was succeeded by Olaf's son Magnus, who did all he could to spread the cult of his father in an attempt to give respectability to the upstart dynasty. Olaf eventually became Norway's principal patron saint, and his shrine in Trondheim Cathedral was an important place of pilgrimage; for medieval Scandinavians he typified both the champion of Christianity and the old Viking military warrior. The cult spread to England and was strong especially in areas that had a Viking connection, with over forty church dedications and mentions in many monastic and cathedral calendars; there are two London churches, St Olave Upwell and St Olave in Hart Street, dedicated to him. Olaf was used as a baptismal name in England and Scotland; in Gaelic it became Aulag, from which the name Macaulay took its origin. In parts of England the name was corrupted to Tooley, and this survives in Southwark, where a street, schools, and the docks were given this form of the saint's name (*O.D.S.*).

O.D.S., pp. 365-6; Gwyn Jones, *A History of the Vikings* (1968), pp. 375-85; *O.D.C.C.*, p. 1179.

Bd Urban II, *Pope* (*c.* 1035-99)

Odo of Lagery was born about the year 1035 in Châtillon-sur-Marne in France and studied at Reims under St Bruno (6 Oct.), the founder of the Carthusians. After being canon and archdeacon there he left to become a monk at the great abbey of Cluny, where he subsequently was elected prior and where, as he later wrote to its abbot St Hugh (28 Apr.), he was re-born "by the life-giving grace of the Holy Spirit." These early monastic influences were important factors in determining his religious and spiritual outlook, and he continued to use Bruno as his adviser when he became pope. Urban was a supporter of Pope St Gregory VII (25 May) in his reforming campaigns, and the pope appointed him cardinal-bishop of Ostia about the year 1080.

In 1088 he was elected pope, taking the name Urban and declaring that he intended to follow the pattern of reform established by his great predecessor, Gregory VII. It was not an easy inheritance, however, since Rome itself was controlled by an antipope, Clement III; it took Urban eight months to enter the city, and there was further fighting before he could take possession of St Peter's. He had also alienated the emperor, Henry IV (1056-1106), through his support for Gregory in the investiture conflict—he had served as papal legate in Germany in 1085 and realized that he would not be able to push ahead with reforms there without making allowances for the emperor's point of view. His tact and diplomacy laid him open to accusations of compromise from the more go-ahead reformers, but on the whole he was successful in strengthening the position of the papacy and, in the end, winning over most of his opponents or at least making their opposition ineffective. The emperor remained unmoved, however, and when he invaded Italy in 1090 Urban was forced to leave Rome and Clement III took over again; by a mixture of persuasion and bribery Urban gradually regained control of the city and made himself secure.

In his dealings with England, Urban made concessions to William II and agreed that future papal legates could only only enter the country with royal permission, but he failed to resolve the quarrel between the king and St Anselm, archbishop of Canterbury (21 Apr.). In France he gained support for his reforming policies, in Spain he extended the feudal rights of the papacy and reorganized the country ecclesiastically, while in southern Italy and Sicily he increased the support he had already received from the Normans by granting the counts considerable rights over the Church.

By holding a number of high-profile and successful synods he advanced the cause of reform and continued the attack on simony, lay investiture, and clerical marriage, which from the start he had condemned as the main evils in the Church. In 1095, at Clermont in France, he proclaimed as law the "Truce of God" (whereby armed hostilities should be suspended on one day each week) and launched his most famous enterprise, the First Crusade. The response to this appeal to the Christian princes to liberate the Holy Land was surprisingly successful and speaks volumes for the prestige enjoyed by the reformed and reforming papacy—"perhaps the most striking proof of the transformation of the papacy into the greatest power in Christendom" (Duffy). From a military point of view the Crusade gained its objectives, and Jerusalem was captured in 1099, but Urban also wanted the Crusade to bring closer links with the Eastern Churches and to heal the schism between them—the first appeal for a Crusade had come from the Eastern emperor. Here Urban failed to achieve any lasting success despite getting partial agreement on some of the disputed theological issues at a joint synod at Bari, and, in the longer term, the activities of the Crusaders only made relations more difficult.

Urban reorganized the central administration of the Church, restructured the papal finances, and established the Roman Curia. There were few areas of church life that did not experience his reforming zeal, and if his interventions did not always produce lasting improvement, they were always motivated on his part by a desire to follow Gregory's example and make the health of Christ's body on earth his only concern. The Church, he had declared at Clermont, "shall be Catholic, chaste and free: Catholic in the faith and fellowship of the saints, chaste from all contagion of evil, and free from secular power" (quoted in Duffy). He died on 29 July 1099, two weeks after the Crusaders captured Jerusalem, unaware of their success. He was beatified in 1881.

Over three hundred of Urban's letters are in *P.L.*, 151, 283-552. See *O.D.P.*, pp. 158-60; *O.D.C.C.*, p. 1668; *D.T.C.*, 15, pt. 2 (1950), 2269-85; *N.C.E.*, 14, pp. 477-8; Eamon Duffy, *Saints and Sinners, A History of the Popes* (1997), pp. 99-105.

St William of Saint-Brieuc, *Bishop* (1234)

There is very little information about the life of Guillaume Pinchon except that he was born in the village of Saint-Alban in the diocese of Saint-Brieuc in Brittany and ordained by Josselin, the local bishop. He served under that bishop's two successors and became a canon in Tours before becoming bishop of Saint-Brieuc about the year 1220. He is said to have been an exemplary pastor of his people, paying special attention to the needs of the poor, particularly in times of food shortages. His early biographer reports that he recited the whole of the Psalter, which he knew by heart, every day. He and the other Breton bishops quarrelled with Peter Mauclerc, duke of Brittany, over the rights of their sees, and William was expelled from it for two years, during which time he took refuge in Poitiers. He was back in Saint-Brieuc by 1230 and died there in 1234. He was buried in the cathedral, and his body was found to be incorrupt when it was exhumed in 1248, the year after his canonization. The speed of his canonizaton argues for a strong cult, at least in his own region; his sufferings in the cause of defending ecclesiastical privilege may also help to explain it. He and St Ivo (19 May) are the only Breton saints to have been formally canonized.

Bibl.SS., 7, 494-5. See also J. Arnault, *Saint Guillaume, évêque de Saint-Brieuc* (1934).

30

ST PETER CHRYSOLOGUS, *Bishop and Doctor* (*c.* 380–*c.* 450)

Peter was a native of Imola in north-eastern Italy. He was a deacon there before being appointed archbishop of the imperial city of Ravenna by the emperor Valentinian III, sometime between 425 and 430. He preached his first sermon as bishop before the empress, Galla Placidia, who became a firm patron and supported him fully in his ambitious building projects and in his plans for church reform. He also won the support of Pope St Leo the Great (440-61; 10 Nov.), stressing the importance and orthodoxy of the pope's teaching on the Incarnation and urging Eutyches of Constantinople, condemned by the Council of Chalcedon in 451, to adhere to Rome in matters of doctrine. He had a great reputation as a preacher. The title "Chrysologus" ("Golden-worded") may have been given him (from the ninth century onward) so that the Western Church would have a preacher of equivalent status to the East's St John "Chrysostom" ("Golden-tongued"). A large number of his sermons remain but almost nothing of his other writings except the letter to Eutyches.

Peter's death took place between 449 and 458, almost certainly at Imola, and there is some evidence that the date was 3 December 450; his feast-day used to be celebrated on 4 December, but the 1969 Calendar reform moved it to today's date. He was declared a Doctor of the Church in 1729. The prayer for his feast-day refers to him as "a most eloquent preacher of Christ, your Word made human," and this may be illustrated briefly by a sermon he preached on the mystery of the Incarnation, in which he stresses the dignity we should feel as human beings because God chose to become human: "The hand that graciously elevated mud into our form, graciously elevated flesh also for our restoration. Therefore the fact that the Creator is found in his creature, and that God is found in flesh, is an honour for the creature and not a humiliation for the Creator. . . . Man, whom he had made an earthly creature, he now has made a heavenly creature; one who was animated by a human spirit he quickens into a divine spirit. Thus he assumes him wholly into God so that he leaves nothing in him of sin, of death, of toil, of sorrow, of earth."

In general, his sermons are marked by "careful preparation, human warmth and the divine fervour of a holy man" (*E.E.C.*). Most of them are homilies on the Gospels and other parts of scripture, or exhortations to penance and conversion. He presents the pastoral attitudes and concerns of the best bishops of his day rather than the polemics against paganism and the Jews that were then commonplace (*Dict.Sp.*). He also provides a wealth of information about the liturgical and cultural life of the Church in fifth-century Ravenna.

The earliest Life dates from 836. There have been various editions of the sermons; see for example A. Olivar, O.S.B., (ed.) in *C.C., Series Latina*, 24 (1975-). See also Eng. ed. of selected sermons and the letter to Eutyches, by G. E. Ganss, S.J., Fathers of the Church, 17 (1953), pp. 3-287. See R. H. McGlynn, *The Incarnation in the Sermons of St Peter Chrysologus* (1956); M. Spinelli, *Pier Crisologo: omelie per la vita quotidiana* (1978); *E.E.C.*, 2, p. 678; *Dict.Sp.*, 12 (1986), 1541-6. The sermon extract above is taken from *The Divine Office*, 3, *Weeks of the Year* (1974), pp. 139-41.

SS Abdon and Sennen, *Martyrs (c. 303)*

According to tradition, Abdon and Sennen were Christians in Persia during the reign of the emperor Decius, when they ministered to those who suffered persecution and buried the bodies of those who were martyred. Their *passio* relates how they were taken to Rome by Decius himself, who had been in Persia, and when they refused to sacrifice to the gods were thrown to the wild beasts and then hacked to pieces when the beasts refused to harm them. The Roman Christians buried their bodies secretly. When Constantine became emperor their relics were moved to the burial place of Pontian, near the Tiber on the road to Porto.

The *passio*, however, is late and unreliable, and it is more likely that they suffered under Diocletian than under Decius. They were certainly venerated in Rome from the fourth century onward, and the date of their feast and place of burial are mentioned in the *Depositio Martyrum* of 354 and in other early sources. A sixth-century fresco on the wall of a catacomb in the cemetery of Pontian represents the two martyrs in Persian dress, with Christ in the act of crowning them, and has their names attached to the figures. The fresco was obviously inspired by the *passio*, but the only reliable elements in the *passio* are their names, the date of their feast, and the place of their burial (*Bibl.SS.*). The remains of the saints were moved to the church of Saint Mark; in 1948 a fifteenth-century casket was discovered there under the high altar, with a parchment of 1474 witnessing to the transfer of the relics of Pope St Mark (7 Oct.) and SS Abdon and Sennen. A new altar was erected to hold the relics of the two martyrs. The list of Roman churches made by order of St Pius V (30 Apr.) in the sixteenth century mentions a church dedicated to SS Abdon and Sennen, which presumably had been built over the site of their martyrdom, between the Flavian amphitheatre and the temple of Venus.

See *Bibl.SS.*, 1, 50-7; *Anal.Boll.* 51 (1933), pp. 33-98, and 56 (1938), pp. 296-300.

St Julitta, *Martyr (c. 303)*

Julitta was a widow living in Caesarea in Cappadocia during the reign of Diocletian. A man who wanted to take over her extensive estates harassed her so much that she went to a local judge for protection, only to find that the man then denounced her as a Christian and her estates were confiscated. When ordered to sacrifice to Zeus she replied: "May my estates be ruined or given to strangers; may I lose my life, and my body be cut in pieces, rather than that by the least impious word I should offend the God who made me. If you take from me a little portion of this earth, I shall gain heaven for it." She was burned and her body decapitated. St Basil (2 Jan.), writing about the year 327, recounts how a spring of fresh water flowed from her burial place and provided water that "preserves health and relieves the sick."

The homily of St Basil is the only source for Julitta's life—it is not a biography but does provide some reliable detail; see *P.G.*, 31, 237-61. See also *Bibl.SS.*, 6, 1239-40.

Julitta features in a fourteenth-century *Annunciation* by Martini in the Uffizi, Florence.

BB Edward Powell, Richard Fetherston, and Thomas Abel, *Martyrs* (1540)

These three martyrs died during the reign of Henry VIII for their refusal to acknowledge the king's ecclesiastical supremacy.

Edward Powell was born in Wales about the year 1478. He became a fellow of Oriel College, Oxford, where he was an outstanding scholar and received a doctorate in theology in 1506. He held the living of Bleadon in Somerset and was a canon of both Lincoln and Salisbury. A book he wrote against Luther in 1523 won high praise, and his reputation was such that he was appointed to be one of the canon lawyers to act as counsel to Catherine of Aragon in the matter of Henry's claim for an annulment. He spoke in favour of the validity of the marriage before Convocation in 1529 and wrote a book on the same subject. By 1534 he was in prison in Dorchester before being removed to the Tower of London; later that year he was sentenced to forfeit his goods and be imprisoned for refusing to take the Oath of Succession, which declared Catherine's marriage to Henry null and void. He remained in strict confinement for the next six years.

Nothing is known about the early life of Richard Fetherston (or Featherstone). He studied in Cambridge, where he became a doctor of divinity, and in 1523 was appointed archdeacon of Brecon in South Wales. He must have been a man of some distinction, for he was Latin tutor to Princess Mary until 1533. Like Edward Powell, in 1529 he spoke in Convocation in favour of the validity of Queen Catherine's marriage, and in 1534 he was named in the bill of attainder that condemned St John Fisher (22 June) and Edward Powell to imprisonment in the Tower.

The early life of Thomas Abel is also unknown. He studied in Oxford and became a doctor of divinity there before being appointed chaplain and tutor in music and languages to Queen Catherine. When Henry was trying to obtain the original papal Bull granting him a dispensation to marry Catherine, Thomas was one of those sent into Spain to get it from the emperor, Charles V. They returned empty-handed, and Thomas seems to have been rewarded by the queen for his part in persuading Charles not to part with the Bull, for he was given the living of Bradwell in Essex by Catherine. About the year 1532 he wrote a book, *Invicta Veritas* ("Truth Unconquered"), supporting the validity of the marriage, and was imprisoned in the Tower. He was released but then re-arrested, allegedly for his part in the so-called "Holy Maid of Kent" affair. He spent about six years in prison and was then allowed out with Edward Powell on parole to beg for alms, an act of kindness that landed the gaoler in prison himself, along with the bishop of Chichester for having given them alms.

The three prisoners were finally attainted of high treason in July 1540 for "adhering to the bishop of Rome" and denying the king's supremacy. They were hanged, drawn, and quartered at Smithfield on 30 July 1540, and beatified in 1886.

L.E.M., 1, pp. 461-501.

St Leopold Mandic (1866-1942)

Bogdan Mandic was born in Castelnuovo near Cattarvo in Dalmatia, the youngest of twelve children of Croatian parents who every year celebrated the conversion to Catholicism of a long-dead ancestor as "the beginning of our faith." At the age of sixteen he went to the Capuchin seminary at Udine in the Veneto region—Venetian Capuchins were working in Dalmatia at that time, and Bogdan was impressed by their humility and how they were highly regarded by the people, Catholic and Orthodox alike. Two years later he entered the novitiate at Bassano, taking the name Leopold in religion. He felt called by God to a special task, to work, as he put it, for the "return of the dissident Orientals to Catholic unity." This vocation lasted as long as he lived, and there are dozens of notes written in his careful Latin detailing his wholehearted commitment to it and the vows he made year by year to pursue what he referred to as the "salvation" or "redemption" of his people. He was ordained priest in 1890 and began his lifelong apostolate as a confessor in the Capuchin monastery in Venice, where he stayed for the next seven years before returning to Dalmatia to be in charge of the monastery at Zara. Eventually, in 1909, he moved to Padua, where he remained for the rest of his life, his "headquarters," as he described it, being a tiny "cell" that was very cold in winter and hot and stuffy in summer—the confessional. He heard Confessions for between ten and fifteen hours a day; from time to time he was given other jobs, such as being chaplain to a convent or being in charge of the Order's students, but these never lasted very long, often because he was thought to be too lenient and easy going, and he returned to his principal work as a confessor.

It is clear that his superiors had a fairly low opinion of his abilities and that he faced a good deal of opposition from them and from some of his colleagues. They accused him of being ignorant of moral theology and too ready to absolve his penitents, nicknaming him "Brother Absolve-all." His usual reply to such accusations was that he had to be kind to sinners, given the example of all the love that Our Lord had shown for them on the cross. He was also, physically, a figure of fun, and was sometimes teased and laughed at in the streets: he was less than four foot six inches (1.35 m) in height, had a bad limp caused by arthritis, and an embarrassing speech impediment that prevented him from preaching. Many thought that his interest in reunion was a stupid obsession, and his superiors refused his requests for an appointment that would allow him to work for its realization, despite his insistence that God was calling him to that particular apostolate. In 1923 he thought his opportunity had come when he was appointed to Fiume, a city on the border with Dalmatia and recently annexed by Italy. Unfortunately, the bishop of Padua objected to losing his services as a confessor, and the appointment was revoked. Leopold accepted this without demur and never again spoke openly of his desire to work for reunion, although it continued to dominate his private writings. Much later he explained his silence by saying that he had had a revelation after Communion one day telling him that "every soul that he helped in the confessional would be his East." He would henceforth fulfill his vow to work for the return of the schismatics among his people by performing to the best of his ability his priestly ministries of saying Mass and hearing Confessions, and in the confessional "he treated every penitent as though the conversion of his people depended on the conversion of that single sinner" (Sicari).

Reports of miraculous cures obtained through his prayers began to circulate, and he was already regarded as a saint when he died on 30 July 1942, after collapsing as he prepared to say Mass. His cult began immediately. The Capuchin church and monastery were destroyed when Padua was bombed in 1944, but Leopold's "cell" remained intact; later a special chapel was built next to it, which holds his body and is a popular place of pilgrimage. He was beatified in 1976 and canonized in 1983.

A. Sicari, *Ritratti di Santi 3* (1993), pp. 115-27; *D.N.H.*, 1, pp. 198-207.

Note: Another entry on him appears in this edition under 14 May, the date on which the Capuchins commemorate him, but today is the date of his death, and future editions will include him here only.

ST IGNATIUS OF LOYOLA (over page)
Gold IHS and rays, for Society of Jesus; silver AMDG for the
Jesuit motto, all on black field

31

ST IGNATIUS OF LOYOLA, *Founder* (1491-1556)

Iñigo López de Loyola was born in the ancestral castle of the Loyola family, about two miles from the small town of Azpeitia in the Basque province of Guipúzcoa. There has been some uncertainty about the date of his birth, but most authorities now agree that it was in 1491. His parents were Beltrán Yañez de Oñaz y Loyola and Marina Sáenz de Licona y Balda, people of substance and reputation in the area. The name Iñigo was a common one among the Basques, and it was only when he moved to Paris and Rome that Iñigo de Loyola began to use Ignacio, or Ignatius, as more recognizable to non-Basques. In 1506 Iñigo left home to become a page in the household of Juan Velázquez de Cuéllar, treasurer to the king of Castile and a leading member of the Castilian nobility, who lived at Arévalo, between Avila and Valladolid. Here Iñigo received the courtly education of the day, accompanied his patron on his travels with the court, and no doubt did all he could to win the notice of the king and his courtiers to assure himself of a financially worthwhile career. A close companion later wrote of him: "Although he was attached to the faith, his life was in no way conformed to it nor did he keep himself free from sin. Rather, he was particularly reckless in gambling, in his dealings with women, in quarrelling, and with the sword" (quoted in Caraman). Iñigo himself later described how it was at this time that he became a keen reader of the books of chivalry and romance that were appearing in Spain: tales of conquest and of glory won by deeds of valour and sacrifice, and of knights who were men of courage and loyalty and who were, above all else, dedicated to the love of their ladies: the ideology of chivalry always had a strongly erotic element (Caraman). An incident that happened in 1515 is often quoted to show his unruly behaviour during these years: on a visit to Loyola, he was involved in a violent brawl when he and his brother Pedro López, himself a priest, attacked some clergy; the case went to court, and it is clear from the records that it was no momentary street clash but a pre-meditated night ambush with Iñigo in armour and carrying sword, dagger, and pistol. Even allowing for some exaggeration in these accounts and in the reminiscences of a saint looking back on his unconverted youth, Iñigo was obviously a fairly typical young blood of the day, enjoying life, proud, and out to make a name for himself in the world.

His plans suddenly seemed to be under threat in 1516 when King Ferdinand died and was succeeded by his grandson, the distant Charles of Burgundy. Velázquez lost his position and influence at court and had to retire, heavily in debt; he died the following year. Iñigo, who seems to have been tiring of court life anyway, took off for Pamplona, the capital of Navarre, and obtained a post in the army of Antonio Manrique de Lara, duke of Nájera and viceroy of Navarre, to whom he was related. His first military action came in 1520, when he was involved in putting down a revolt in Nájera itself, and then in 1521 the French invaded Navarre and he was caught up in the siege of Pamplona, taking charge of the inner fortress of the city. The town council, fearing the damage the superior French troops would do if there was a protracted siege, sued for peace, but Iñigo decided to hold out—an act of great bravery, perhaps, or just rash foolishness. During the siege he was hit by a cannon ball, which broke one leg very badly and injured the other; when he fell, the garrison surrendered, and Iñigo was taken prisoner and cared for by the French. His leg was set and after about two weeks he was well enough to be carried to Loyola. When he arrived his leg had to be re-set and he fell dangerously ill; he made his Confession and prayed to St Peter for help, promising to devote his life as a knight to the apostle if he recovered. He did recover, but the leg had become deformed as a result of the second setting, and Iñigo asked for it to be broken again and re-set, willing to put up with the intense pain mainly out of vanity, it seems. Gradually his health improved, although he needed a convalescence of nine months before he could be active again.

It is important to understand the type of person Iñigo was before this period of inactivity, for it brought about a profound change in him and was the beginning of his conversion. That conversion, of course, did not mean that he became a wholly different person; at the beginning, indeed, it might appear that he had just transferred his knightly qualities to the service of another master and kept his desire for adventure, with his courage and his determination to succeed much as they had been before. It is ironic that for such a man of action conversion should have come from reading: as he lay convalescing, he asked for some of the tales of romance to pass away the time. None were available and he was given instead a copy of Ludolph of Saxony's *Life of Christ* and a selection from the *Golden Legend* collection of saints' Lives. At first he was put off by the tales of bodily penance and self-denial, but slowly he came under the influence of some of the "knights of God," as the Spanish edition called them. St Francis (4 Oct.) had lived a similar dissolute early life, had loved dancing and singing, but then showed courage in going to meet the sultan and in exchanging his fine clothes for the beggar's rags and had become a leader of men and women who were devoted to him. St Dominic had come from near Arévalo and, again, had used his talents to found a great Order—although Iñigo was disgusted at the way he disciplined himself with a chain every night. Another saint who appealed was St Honofrio, a former Persian prince who had spent many years in the desert as a solitary—his total dedication to what he believed to be most important impressed Iñigo. There was, however, no sudden conversion: when he tired of the saints he dreamed, as he said, "of all that he would achieve in the service of a certain lady . . . and the feats of arms he would perform for her." He was so taken by these "conceits" that he did not consider their impossibility, for the lady was of very high standing and not likely to want him as a suitor. Gradually he found that his fancies about following the way of the saints gave more lasting satisfaction than those of his courtly imaginings, and he began to think about his need to do penance for his sins; perhaps a pilgrimage to Jerusalem would be the first step—there were never any half measures with Iñigo, and Jerusalem would provide the thrill of adventure as well as the satisfaction of repentance.

One night when he could not sleep he had a vision of Our Lady, which filled him with an intense joy that lasted several hours. It also gave him a feeling of shame and a total revulsion from his former ways, and he was determined to change. Much later he was to write that after this vision he never again experienced any temptations of the flesh. As soon as he was well enough he set out for Barcelona (by way of the duke of Nájera, who offered him a position of authority) to take ship to Jerusalem as a humble pilgrim. On the way he called at the monastery of Montserrat to make a vigil before the pilgrim shrine of Our Lady and exchange his knightly dress for that of a pilgrim. We do not know what happened at Montserrat, but it is possible that he was convinced from his meetings with the monks there and the general Confession he made that he should defer his pilgrimage until he had made further progress in his new way of life, and so he retired to nearby Manresa to live as a hermit; one of the monks gave him a copy of a work by the monastic reformer, García Jiménez de Cisneros, the *Exercitatorio de la Vida Espiritual*, or "Manual of the Spiritual Life."

He stayed at Manresa for ten months, living at first in a run-down hospice, begging for his food in the streets, occasionally retiring to a quiet place by the river (but never living in a cave, despite later stories that he did), and generally praying and studying how to make progress in the spiritual life he had chosen. While not a solitary existence, in that he made friends and was looked after by a group of mainly well-to-do women, it was an intensely private time for him. He experienced both the joys of conversion and the deep depression of the scrupulous, and the latter was not helped by his severe régime of fasting and bodily penance. He had to be nursed through attacks of fever, and gradually his inner darkness passed: he decided never to confess his past sins again, and his scruples were over; he began to experience the fundamental peace that he enjoyed for the rest of his life, a peace based on knowing that he was doing God's will. The saints were being replaced by the Trinity as the object of his meditations and the impulse for his actions; he would later refer to the beginnings of his mystical life at Manresa as his "primitive church."

Manresa was also fundamentally important in the development of his *Spiritual Exercises*, which were to become his richest single contribution to Western spirituality. Before arriving there he had already started to make notes about what he was reading and about his own experiences as he moved through his conversion process, and he continued the practice during his ten months' "retreat." For the first time he read the *Imitation of Christ*, the outstanding product of the northern *devotio moderna*, which gave him a "model of intensely cultivated inwardness" (Evennett). No matter how much he may have been influenced by what he read, however, Iñigo produced something that was "as original in expression as in general concept and design" (*ibid.*). The *Spiritual Exercises*, the result of his note-taking, prayer, sufferings, and mystical experiences, were intended as a manual for those guiding people toward perfection in the spiritual life, a down-to-earth distillation of his own experiences that was quite different from traditional mystical writings in that it was designed to have a practical use. This marked a stage in Iñigo's own progress toward finding a role. For a time he had thought of entering an enclosed Order to live a life of prayer and penance—he eyed a nearby Cistercian monastery as a possibility—but his make-up included a strong leaning toward activity and being involved with others. After his first conversion, during his convalescence he enjoyed talking to others about his experiences and found that he had an effect on them spiritually; it is clear that at Manresa he began to develop this apostolate, especially to the women who cared for him, and the *Exercises* were also oriented toward helping others to learn from his experiences.

They contain two central elements: a systematized examination of conscience, unrelenting in its concentration on attacking besetting sins, and a planned approach to meditation as a form of prayer that was intended to fix the mind's attention intensely on a particular biblical event or some point of doctrine and, of course, to have practical outcomes in the person's life. A person doing the *Exercises* is forced to make a choice between the "two standards"—to opt for Christ or the world—or to remain a lukewarm "don't know." Not all of this was fully developed by the time Iñigo left Manresa in 1523; some retouching was necessary when he began to take his first followers through the *Exercises* and when the Inquisition examined them for signs of heresy in 1526, and a general revision was made in Paris a few years later. Already, however, he had fixed on personal conversion and individual sanctification as the keys to reform, and they were to remain the aim of his apostolic life: no grand strategy to rebuild the Church meant anything without that double foundation.

Iñigo eventually reached Jerusalem in September 1523. He stayed about three weeks, long enough for the Holy Places to fulfill his devotional needs, and long enough, too, for him to discover that his hidden agenda in going there, to work for the conversion of the Muslims, was impracticable. The Franciscan guardians ordered him to leave to avoid capture and even death at the hands of the Turks. Back in Spain he decided that he needed some formal education if his missionary work was to be fruitful—he did not know any Latin at this stage and had never studied any theology. In his early thirties he started to learn Latin and to study the humanities, and he also developed his vocation by sharing his spiritual insights with others and taking some of them through the early form of the *Exercises*. He began to show the moderation that had been absent from his own spiritual life in Manresa: only moderate penances should be practised, he counselled one correspondent: "The Lord does not bid you do difficult things detrimental to your health, but to live joyfully in Him, giving the body its due" (quoted in Caraman). He was to develop this moderation into a broad principle to be used in guiding souls: later as a confessor he applied it to the interpretation of moral theology, and he urged his followers to make due allowances for local custom and usage. After his death the members of his Society were to face frequent accusations of being "easy confessors."

After two years of studying Latin, Iñigo left Barcelona to begin his university studies at Alcalá. Three young men went with him, and in the university town he gathered a very mixed group of disciples around him—a priest's house-keeper, artisans' wives, a vine-dresser, an apprentice or two, and some prosti-tutes. He had started to wear clerical dress (he had received the tonsure as a youth) and it was not long before the church authorities began to suspect this new group of being another Illuminist sect, or *alumbrados*, claiming special revelations from God and believing themselves to be superior to other Chris-tians. Iñigo was summoned to appear before the Inquisition but was let go on condition that his followers did not dress as though they were members of an Order. Other, more rigorous examinations of his actions and teachings fol-lowed over the next year or so, focussing on the lessons or exercises he was giving to simple people, which included recommendations for fortnightly re-ception of Holy Communion. The inquisitors found nothing unorthodox in either his teaching or his practice, although he was ordered to dress as an ordinary student and not to hold any more meetings until he had done another four years of study. Unwilling to accept this limitation of his ministry, he decided to move to Salamanca to continue his studies, but he was soon in trouble again and spent three weeks in prison while his book of "exercises" was examined. The verdict was the same as before, and Iñigo felt that he had no choice but to leave Spain altogether: he needed to study but would not give up his apostolate while he did so. He decided to move to Paris and arrived there early in 1528.

The impact on his development of the six years that Iñigo spent in Paris can hardly be exaggerated. He entered a wider world of Christian humanism, scrip-ture-based reform, and general intellectual debate, where he studied arts and philosophy and gained a master's degree. He was an archetypal late developer in academic terms, and his Society was to become noted for its learning and its role in developing Catholic higher education, while the higher echelons of that Society were open only to the most gifted intellectually. In Paris he was joined by the followers who were to be the core of that new Society—Francis Xavier (3 Dec.), Alfonso Salmarón, Diego Laínez, Simon Rodrigues, Nicolás Bobadilla del Camino, and Peter Favre (11 Aug.)—and together they bound themselves by a vow to live a life of poverty and to go to Jerusalem to convert the Muslims or, failing that, to put themselves at the service of the pope. He became convinced of the need for organization to make moves toward reform effective, and he refined the *Exercises* by taking his companions through them. A number of successful begging expeditions to Flanders and London gave him some financial security, but his health had been permanently damaged by his early penitential excesses, and when he left Paris in 1535 it was to return to Spain for three months' recuperation, during which he persuaded the authorities to implement a civic scheme for helping the poor such as he had seen in some of the towns in Flanders. The companions promised to meet up again in Venice in two years' time and set out for Jerusalem.

Ignatius, to give him the name that he now used increasingly, went to Venice before the rest and studied theology there privately; while there he met and discussed the state of the Church with leading reformers, two of whom later joined the Society. He continued to use the *Exercises*, and began to develop his skill in giving spiritual direction by letter. When the Paris group (now nine in number and including Claude Le Jay, Paschase Broët, and Jean Codure, two of whom had made the *Exercises* under Favre's direction) joined him, they worked in the city for some months in the hospice for incurables, doing menial work and nursing those dying from typhus and syphilis. Their plans to go to Jerusalem had to be postponed because of Turkish control of the eastern Mediterranean, and they took advantage of the delay to have themselves ordained priests and to make a long retreat together (Ignatius called it his "second Manresa"), and then they split into twos and threes to work in different cities. Before leaving Venice, they decided to call themselves the "Company of Jesus," in line with the brotherhoods and confraternities that had existed for years in parts of northern Europe, and the "Company of Divine Love" that had been founded in Brescia by St Catherine of Genoa (15 Sept.). In no sense did the word "company" have any military overtones in this context, and Ignatius was not calling on his experience as a soldier in organizing his followers in this way—indeed, "organization" is probably too strong a word for the group of companions at this stage, whose strongest link was their common desire for personal conversion and sanctity.

Ignatius, Laínez, and Favre set out for Rome toward the end of 1537. At La Storta, about twelve miles from the city, Ignatius had a momentous spiritual experience. As he prayed to Our Lady to "deign to place him with her Son," he experienced "such a change in his soul and saw so clearly that God the Father had placed him with his Son Christ that his mind could not doubt that God the Father had indeed placed him with his Son" (*Autobiography*). For Ignatius this was the sign that he had been waiting for to show that his work with the companions had divine approval; whether he had thought before this of making them into a formal Order or Congregation is doubtful, and it still may not have been clear even after La Storta, but of one thing he was sure: the name "Company of Jesus" was the right one because it expressed their relationship of service to Christ.

In Rome the three began to teach children the catechism, to hear Confessions, and to preach. There was yet another attack on their orthodoxy, but a judicial inquiry cleared them of all the charges. They were joined by the rest of the group, and the winter of 1538 to 1539 gave them an opportunity to show their practical charity as famine hit the city and they cared for hundreds of the sick and hungry. They had already offered their services to Pope Paul III (1534-49), who had become a keen supporter of their way of life, and he wanted to send them out to different places—the cities where they had already worked were asking for them to return, and the king of Portugal was even asking for them to go to the Indies. Such dispersals would, they were sure, become more frequent and raise the issue of how they could keep their unity in the circumstances; if they took the usual step of forming themselves into an Order, they would owe obedience to two superiors, the pope and their elected head. As their numbers grew, however, the pope could not be expected to deal with them himself in any detail. By June 1539 the companions, after much prayer and open discusion, decided to elect a leader to whom they would take a vow of obedience, and Ignatius was asked to draw up an outline Constitution for them. He produced what he called a "formula," or way of life, rather than a Rule, but already it contained pointers to the later Constitutions: the work of the Company was to teach the catechism, preach, hear Confessions, lecture, and care for the sick and prisoners. An elected superior should exercise authority in council, and each member was subject directly to the pope "without hesitation, irresolution or excuse." There was no mention of saying the office in common, or of prescribed hours of prayer, or of prescribed penances—all features of traditional Rules whose absence, along with the special vow of obedience to the pope, led to objections when the formula was presented for approval. Ignatius would not budge on the issue of the office; the key for him was flexibility, and the ability of the companions to go wherever they were needed at any time—as he said on another occasion, they must always have "one foot on the road, ready to hasten from place to place." It took more than a year for papal approval to be granted in a Bull of September 1540, which called the new foundation the "Society of Jesus." Ignatius was elected superior in 1541, and on April 22 the six companions who were in Rome made their vows. It is interesting to note, in the light of the later work of the Society in the Catholic Reformation, that the "formula" made no reference to Protestantism or to any special role his members might play in counteracting it: Ignatius did not see himself as a champion against heresy and never drew up any strategy for dealing with it; he was himself more concerned with converting the Muslims and taking the gospel to the pagans in foreign countries.

Ignatius spent the rest of his life in Rome, administering the Society and developing his own apostolate to the poor of the city, its prostitutes, its Jews, its sick, and its orphans, for whom he opened a special house and organized a confraternity to run it. He also opened a house for reformed prostitutes, the house of Saint Martha. He kept in touch with members of the Society by correspondence; they had to send him quarterly reports of their activities and he replied with reports of what everyone else was doing. He used their reports as propaganda and to gain more recruits for the Society—particularly useful here were the letters from Francis Xavier, who had gone off to India, the first Jesuit missionary. As well as ordinary administrative letters, Ignatius wrote to kings and queens, to ladies of high repute, to those who asked him for spiritual direction, to those who might support his Roman charities: taken together, these letters "reveal the man only rather less intimately than do the *Spiritual Exercises*; they reflect the whole spectrum of his ideas as they unfolded in the last sixteen years of his life" (Caraman). Nearly seven thousand of these letters have survived, not all, admittedly, written directly by himself. Despite the formality of their language—and Ignatius revised every letter that he wrote at least once and was most careful about how he expressed his thoughts—the letters are strong in human friendship, although there are no intimacies or human touches or chatter; compared with the lively letters of St Teresa of Avila (15 Oct.), these are the prosaic writings of a man totally in control of his emotions who never forgets himself or the importance of what he is writing about (Rahner).

His constant letter writing did not mean that Ignatius interfered in the work of the members; indeed, one of the hallmarks of the Society was the amount of initiative he allowed and encouraged. His loose direction was a long way from any autocratic style of government; he insisted that members should take decisions without referring back to him: "I leave everything to your judgment," he wrote to Rodrigues in Portugal in 1542, "and I shall consider best whatever you decide" (quoted in Caraman). He guided rather than governed, for all the members had done the *Exercises*, and that provided all the assurance he needed: God would be best served in the free and full activity of the committed individual, and few religious superiors can have told members of their Order so firmly to forget the rules and do what they thought best (Bossy).

There was an obvious tension between this flexibility and Ignatius' stress on total obedience as a key virtue for members of his Society, but in most cases it was a creative tension, and he succeeded in allowing the individual the maximum freedom of local action while insisting on total subordination of the individual's will to his superior. Commentators have seen in this an example of a military style of command and delegation; without pushing the analogy too far, it worked because Ignatius' army was composed entirely of officers. There can be no doubting the high value he placed on obedience, and his writings about it are full of traditional language on the subject: the religious should be *quasi cadaver* ("like a corpse"), totally at the disposal of the superior; obedience must be "blind" and the religious like a tool in someone else's hand, while superiors should dismiss those who are disobedient. It was not a theoretical issue for Ignatius, for he was greatly worried by events in Portugal where the lax rule of Bobadilla was causing serious problems, which Ignatius put down to a basic lack of obedience. The long letter that he wrote on the subject in 1553, and the sections that he included in the Constitutions, give a clear picture of his thinking: "The third means to subject the understanding (to accept obedience) . . . is to presuppose and believe, very much as we are accustomed to do in matters of faith, that what the superior enjoins is the command of God our Lord and his holy will. Then to proceed blindly, without enquiry of any kind ... with the prompt impulse of the will to obey" (Letter of 1553, printed in Meissner). Obedience was for Ignatius both the best means of self-denial and the surest sign of its achievement. It should be a willing sacrifice made by the individual to God, and so it should create an atmosphere of love and spiritual joy, not one of fear. The model here, as always for Ignatius, was Jesus, whose "obedience unto death" proved his total acceptance of the Father's will for him. This stress on the importance of obedience had implications for the superior too: his subjects had to be confident that he could lead them closer to Christ, and he had to take into account their talents and their suitability when allotting them particular tasks in the Society, something that Ignatius took considerable trouble over himself.

The position and role of the superior became more clearly defined as Ignatius worked on a formal set of Constitutions between 1544 and 1550, helped by his secretary, Juan de Polanco, who read and commented on all the drafts. They were coloured by the questions that Ignatius was receiving from the members as they interpreted the original "formula," questions that concerned poverty, obedience, their vows, and the authority of local superiors. Jerónimo Nadal went around Europe to gather views on the drafts, and a special meeting of the professed members in Rome approved a version that Ignatius then promulgated, although he continued to work on revisions to it until he died. The radical elements of the "formula" were retained: there would be no office in choir, no set times of prayer or fasting, no special dress, no prescribed penances. The novitiate was extended to two years instead of the usual one and was followed by the scholasticate, or period of study, and then another year of probation, with the taking of solemn vows delayed until after this long course of training. The superior general was to be elected for life—it was to be a monarchical system, highly centralized, with no role for elected bodies and no regular general chapters, though with ample delegation to subordinate superiors. Not all of these elements were novel or unique to the Society, but taken together they produced a new type of Order, suited both to the external needs of the Church and to the internal perfection of the Society's members.

The amount of study imposed on the young member in training was far more extensive than in other Orders, and solemn vows were postponed until his aptitude for such study had been tested. Ignatius was convinced of the need for educated clergy, just as he had been convinced of his own need for study if he were to be successful in taking the gospel to others. The first of the Society's colleges were opened in Padua in 1542, Bologna in 1546, and Messina in 1548. Above all, however, Ignatius wanted colleges in Rome, and the first of these was opened in 1551 to teach grammar, the humanities, and Christian doctrine; courses in philosophy and theology leading to ordination were added in 1553, and thus the famous Gregorian University was born. Ignatius also established a German College in Rome in 1552 to train young Germans as priests who could then work for the reform of the Church in their own country. Within a decade of his death there were colleges in Spain, Portugal, France, Germany, India, Brazil, and Japan. The long-term impact on the education of the clergy and on the general development of secondary education throughout Europe was incalculable.

Apart from what the letters Ignatius wrote in Rome reveal, some insights into his spiritual life can be obtained from two sets of writings, the *Autobiography*, or *Reminiscences,* which he dictated in 1553 and 1555, and the *Spiritual Diary* of 1544-45. The *Autobiography* covers the years 1521, after Pamplona, to his arrival in Rome in 1538, his "years of pilgrimage," as he called them, and give an account of his conversion that is unique, even though the reader must bear in mind that the account was a set of reminiscences and that we do not know how much it was altered by the secretaries who took it down from his dictation. The *Diary*, on the other hand, is a private account of his mystical experiences and spiritual progress, in the form of daily notes. They are difficult to interpret, but they show that he experienced periods of mystical union with God and that his mysticism was wholly Trinitarian in its focus. He described one experience as being "overwhelmed with a great devotion to the Most Holy Trinity, with very increased love and intense tears, without seeing the Persons distinctly . . . but perceiving in one luminous clarity a single essence"(quoted in Caraman). These experiences came to him mainly while preparing for or saying Mass, and their outward sign was nearly always uncontrollable weeping—he seemed to experience very few, if any, of the other physical phenomena of mysticism—but the tears became such a problem that he had to ask the pope to commute saying the office to reciting the rosary. Ignatius was always suspicious of reports of mystical phenomena—the devil, he believed, could too easily deceive people by means of them—and he strongly discouraged members of the Society from aiming at the higher reaches of contemplative prayer, as it so often distracted people from action and laid them open to illusions.

Ignatius died suddenly on 31 July 1556, although he had been ill on several occasions during the previous three years. He was buried by the side of the high altar in Santa Maria della Strada; the church was later pulled down to be replaced by the Gesù, where his remains are now enshrined. A quotation from the last letter that he wrote, shortly before his death, seems to sum up his life: "May it please him through his infinite and supreme goodness to deign to give us his abundant grace, so that we may know his most holy will and perfectly fulfil it." Ignatius was canonized in 1622, along with St Teresa of Avila, St Philip Neri (26 May), St Francis Xavier, and the humble farmer St Isidore (15 May).

By the time of Ignatius' death the Society had already taken on a surprising range of apostolic activities in addition to working among the outcasts of society, preaching, and teaching the catechism at every possible opportunity. In 1542 two members of the Society, Salmarón and Broët, went on a fact-finding mission to Ireland at the request of the pope. The Society was represented among the expert theologians at the Council of Trent, while Francis Xavier had left for India and beyond in 1541 and St Peter Canisius (21 Dec.) and others were busy in Germany, Austria, and Poland; in 1555 a group was sent to work in Ethiopia, with a brief from Ignatius that was "one of the most enlightened missionary documents of any age" (Caraman). In Italy the Society had twenty-two houses or colleges, nineteen in Spain and Portugal, and five centres in Japan. While such rapid expansion brought its own problems, it bears out Evennett's judgment that the Society was to become "the most powerful, active, modernising, humanistic, and flexible force in the Counter-Reformation."

Within the definitive *Monumenta Historica Societatis Jesu* (1894-), there are four series of *Monumenta Ignatiana*, which include the saint's writings, contemporary evidence about him, and documents concerned with the canonization; details may be found in Hugo Rahner, below, and in *O.D.C.C.*, pp. 818-9. For recent English editions of his works see G. E. Ganns *et al.*, *Ignatius of Loyola: The Spiritual Exercises and Selected Works* (1991); W. J. Young, *The Letters of St Ignatius of Loyola* (1959); Hugo Rahner, S.J., *Saint Ignatius Loyola. Letters to Women* (1956; Eng. trans., 1960); J. A. Munitiz, S.J., and P. Endean, S.J., (eds. and trans.), *St Ignatius of Loyola. Personal Writings* (1996), an excellent volume that contains the *Autobiography*, the *Spiritual Diary*, selected letters, and the *Spiritual Exercises*; G. E. Ganns (ed.), *The Constitutions of the Society of Jesus. Translated with an Introduction and Commentary* (1970); J. C. Olin (ed.) and J. F. O'Callaghan (trans.), *The Autobiography of St Ignatius Loyola, with related documents* (1974, 1992). From the very large number of studies, the following more recent works in English may be noted: Hugo Rahner, I*gnatius the Theologian* (Eng. trans., 1968); *Ignatius: the Man and the Priest* (Eng. trans., 2d ed., 1982); *The Vision of St Ignatius in the Chapel of La Storta* (Eng. trans., 2d. ed., 1979); Cándido de Dalmases, *Ignatius of Loyola: Founder of the Jesuits, His Life and Works* (Eng. ed., 1985); André Ravier, *Ignatius Loyola and the Founding of the Society of Jesus* (1974; Eng. trans., 1987); Philip Caraman, *Ignatius Loyola* (1990); W. M. Meissner, S.J., *Ignatius of Loyola, The Psycholgy of a Saint* (1992), which offers a professional psychoanalytical study; John W. O'Malley, *The First Jesuits* (1993); I. Tellechea Idígoras, *Ignatius of Loyola: The Pilgrim Saint* (Eng. trans. by C. M. Buckley, 1994); David Lonsdale, S.J., *Eyes to See, Ears to Hear, An Introduction to Ignatian Spirituality* (1990). See also H. Outram Evennett, *The Spirit of the Counter-Reformation* (ed. John Bossy, 1968), especially ch. 3, still one of the best introductions to the *Spiritual Exercises;* and *Dict.Sp.*, 7.2 (1971), 1266-1318.

No contemporary portraits of the living Ignatius exist, but there is a death-mask and a number of casts. Alonso Coello used one of the masks to make a painting, and this was used as a later model image, as was a painting by Jacopino del Conte made on the day he died. Later pictures are straightforward: Ignatius wears a Jesuit gown and often holds a copy of the *Exercises* or the Constitutions; his motto, AMDG ("to the greater glory of God"), or the monogram IHS, is usually included. There is a statue of him by Legros in the Gesù church in Rome and in the church of Sant'Ignazio a very large painted ceiling by Pozzo (1691-4). Pozzo also painted a fresco portrait a few years earlier to stand over the entrance to Ignatius' rooms; the fresco was discovered during restoration work in 1990. Ignatius' insistence in the *Exercises* that one should visualize as intensely as possible the subject matter of a meditation, whether it be, for example, death, or an event from Our Lord's life, had a very strong influence on the religious art of the late sixteenth and seventeenth centuries (Murray).

St Fabius, *Martyr (c. 303)*

Fabius, "the Standard-bearer," came from Cartenna in North Africa. In the year 303 or 304, at the height of the Diocletian persecution, the Roman governor of Mauretania (present-day northern Morocco and Algeria) called an assembly to meet in Caesarea. There were certain ceremonies attached to the meeting, and Fabius, a standard-bearer, refused to take part in them because they were religious in character. This exposed him as a Christian, and when he refused to change his mind he was sentenced to be beheaded. This is the story as told in the first part of his *passio*, and it appears to be trustworthy; after that, however, it takes off into flights of fancy and tells how his head and his body were thrown separately into the sea, where they miraculously joined themselves together and were carried by the waves to the beach at Cartenna, where the whole body was given a decent burial. This second part of the *passio* appears to be designed to justify his native town's claim to his relics. Fabius features in a number of Latin martyrologies under today's date.

Bibl.SS., 5, 430; *Vies des Saints*, 7, pp. 736-7. An article in *Anal.Boll.* 9 (1890), pp. 123-34, deals with the historicity of the *passio*.

St Germanus of Auxerre, *Bishop (c. 378-448)*

Germanus was born into a Romano-Gallican family in Auxerre (Yonne) in central Gaul about the year 378. He studied law in Rome and was appointed governor, probably of Armorica (present-day Brittany), although some authorities say it was of the province around Lyons. In 418 the bishop of Auxerre, St Amator (1 May), died, and Germanus was chosen by the people and clergy to succeed him. He was a successful pastoral bishop and continued the work of his predecessor in raising the standard of his priests and removing the last elements of paganism from his diocese. He saw in monasticism a way of strengthening the religious life of his diocese and so founded a monastery on the banks of the river Yonne, dedicating its church to SS Cosmas and Damian. Germanus had a number of distinguished disciples, among whom tradition has numbered St Patrick (17 Mar.) and St Illtud (6 Nov.).

In Britain the bishops were worried about the spread of Pelagianism (a heresy that allowed too much initiative to the human will in gaining grace) and sent a request to their fellow-bishops in Gaul for assistance. They chose Germanus and St Lupus of Troyes (29 July) as the most learned advocates of orthodoxy and sent them to Britain in 429. At a conference in Verulamium (St Albans) they countered the arguments of the heretics so successfully that, in Bede's colourful words, "the authors of false doctrines made themselves scarce, grieving like evil spirits over the people who were snatched from their grasp." While he was there, Germanus visited the tomb of St Alban (21 June) and took some earth from it in exchange for relics of the apostles and martyrs. The visit to Britain does appear to have been largely a success, but Germanus had to return sometime after 445 to deal with a group of Pelagians who were still active and who had staged something of a revival; on this second visit he seems to have persuaded the British authorities to exile the dissident leaders. During the first visit he and St Lupus took some part in a battle between the British and an invading army of Picts and Saxons at Easter 430—according to Bede, the bishops led the army into battle and at a strategic moment got all the soldiers to shout "Alleluia" so loudly that it echoed from the surrounding hills and frightened the enemy so much that they fled.

In 448 Germanus went to the imperial court in Ravenna to intercede for the Breton people, who were in revolt against the governor of Gaul. He died there on 31 July 448, much respected by those who had met him, including St Peter Chrysologus (30 July), bishop of the city, and Galla Placidia, mother of the emperor. His body was taken back to Auxerre for burial, which took place with great solemnity on 1 October in a small church that Germanus had built for the purpose. His tomb became an important place of pilgrimage, and his cult was popular throughout France, as well as in Brittany and England. St Clotilda (3 June), who died in 545, built a new basilica dedicated to St Germanus over his tomb. In 841 his body was found to be incorrupt, and in 859 it was moved to a new shrine in the crypt of this basilica and decorated with frescoes that are still there. The Huguenots destroyed the shrine in 1567, but a part of the relics was saved.

A priest of Lyons named Constance wrote a reliable Life in 480; this was edited by W. Levison in *M.G.H., Scriptores rerum merov.*, 7 (1919), pp. 229-83, with Eng. trans. by F. R. Hoare, *The Western Fathers* (1954); it may also be found in S.C., 112 (1965). See also Bede, *H.E.*, Bk. 1, 17-21. A major conference to mark the fifteenth centenary of Germanus' death produced the scholarly *S. Germain d'Auxerre et son temps* (1950). See also *Bibl.SS.*, 6, 232-6; *O.D.S.*, pp. 200-1.

St Helen of Skövde (*c.* 1160)

Helen is said to have come from a noble family and to have been born in Västergötland in Sweden. After the death of her husband she dedicated herself to God's service by giving her property to the poor and to various monastic houses. In circumstances that are not clear, members of her son-in-law's family believed that she had been involved in his murder, and so she went on pilgrimage to Rome to avoid a vendetta breaking out. On her return, however, they murdered her, about the year 1160. Her body was taken from Götene, where she had died, to Skövde, where it was buried in a church that she had built. A spring of water appeared at the place where she had been killed, and a chapel in her honour was built there soon afterwards. On the strength of the miracles reported to have taken place there and at her tomb, Helen's cult was authorized by Pope Alexander IV in 1164. She was sometimes referred to as a martyr. The church in Skövde was repaired after a fire with stones taken from the chapel, which no longer exists.

Her cult was also strong at Tüsvilde, on the Danish island of Zealand, which claimed to have her relics, although there is no record of any translation of these, and the legendary account of their miraculous transportation is incredible. Her cult survived the Reformation at both places, thanks largely, it seems, to its association with holy wells at each site.

A Latin Life was published in *Scriptores rerum Suecicarum*, 3, pt. 2, pp. 135-8. See *Bibl.SS.*, 4, 996-7.

Bd John Colombini, *Founder* (1305-67)

Giovanni Colombini came from Siena, where he was born in 1305. He became a successful merchant, married, and led a rather careless life dedicated to making money and getting on in the world. When he was about fifty years of age he was converted to a more serious way of life, principally, it seems, by reading a book of saints' Lives given to him by his wife—he was moved especially by the account of St Mary of Egypt (2 Apr.). He began to give away large amounts of money in alms and to spend several hours in prayer in the local church. He took poor and sick people into his house, so that it became more like a hospital than a family home, and his wife objected to his new ways even more than she had to his previous neglect and selfishness. Eventually they agreed to part, and, having provided enough money for her maintenance, he devoted himself to full-time work in the city's hospitals and to devotional exercises.

He joined up with another former merchant, Francesco di Mino de' Vincenti, and gradually a group of young men, fired by their enthusiasm and obvious integrity, formed themselves around them. The city authorities became alarmed at what seemed to be an unofficial religious Order, under no one's supervision and similar to the suspect *Fraticelli,* who had been condemned in 1317, and so they banished John. He left Siena with some of his followers and moved around to a number of other cities in the region; at Viterbo they were nicknamed *Gesuati,* or "Jesuats," because of their devotion to the Holy Name and their frequent cry of "Praised be Jesus Christ!" The bishop of Città di Castello, another town that they visited, gave them his blessing, saying that they were "poor, simple, and right-minded men, with no material cares, and so they might well leave all in God's hands." When Pope Urban V passed through Viterbo in 1367 he received John and his companions in audience and eventually recognized them as a new Congregation, with the formal title of Apostolic Clerics of Saint Jerome. They were to be a Congregation of lay brothers, leading a life of great austerity and devoted to the care of the sick and the burial of the dead, and living in small groups in towns and villages. There was also a female branch, consisting of enclosed nuns and named Sisters of the Visitation of Mary, or "Jesuatesses," founded the same year by John's cousin, Bd Catherine Colombini. A few days after receiving papal approval John fell ill; his followers tried to take him back to Siena but he died on the way, on 31 July 1367. He was buried in the convent of Santa Bonda, where his daughter had died. Francis de' Vincenti died a fortnight later. John was never beatified officially, but Pope Gregory XIII (1572-85) inserted his name in the Roman Martyrology. The Congregation flourished in the first half of the sixteenth century but then began to decline; an attempt was made to revive it in 1606 by allowing its members to be priests, but it was finally suppressed in 1688. The nuns continued until 1872 and were known for the extreme rigour of their austere way of life.

John left 114 letters and a large number of hymns, although the attribution of the latter is not certain in many cases; a fifteenth-century Life contains extracts from some of his sermons. All his writings are full of a simple evangelical fervour and show a strong early Franciscan influence. St John of Tossignano (24 July), a member of the Congregation, wrote a short biography.

D. Fantozzi (ed.), *Lettere del beato Giovanni Colombini* (1925). A fifteenth-century Life by the Florentine poet F. Belcari was edited by R. Chiarini (1904), but there does not seem to be a modern edition of John of Tossignano's more historically reliable account. See *Bibl.SS.*, 4, 122-3.

Bd Everard Hanse, *Martyr* (1581)

Everard Hanse was born in Northamptonshire. According to an early manuscript account of his martyrdom he was educated at the university of Cambridge and then held a "fat living" as a Protestant minister. Unfortunately, there is no trace of him at any of the Cambridge colleges, nor has anyone of that name been discovered holding a living. After only two or three years in the ministry he fell seriously ill and began to have doubts about his religion. He consulted a Catholic priest—the manuscript account says that this was his brother, Fr William Hanse, who had arrived from Reims in 1579—was converted, and left England to study in Reims. After being ordained priest in March 1581 he returned to England, but he was arrested very shortly afterwards as he was visiting some Catholic prisoners in the Marshalsea, London. He openly admitted that he was a Catholic priest and was imprisoned in Newgate gaol.

His trial began on 18 July, when he was closely questioned about the authority of the pope and the validity of the excommunication and deposing of the queen by Pope St Pius V (30 Apr.) in 1570. He claimed that the pope had spiritual supremacy in England, but hoped that he had not erred in excommunicating Elizabeth. An official account of the trial circulated by the government made out that Everard had claimed for the pope temporal as well as spiritual authority, but this was a misrepresentation of what he had said. He was also asked if he intended to persuade other people in England to his point of view and replied that he was not sure what was meant here by "persuade," but he "would have all men to believe the Catholic Faith as I do." This was enough to find him guilty under the recent statute of that year, which made it treason to be reconciled or seek to reconcile others to Catholicism. He was condemned on 28 July 1581. While awaiting execution he wrote to his brother, praying him to look after his parents and "to see them instructed in the way of truth . . . my prayers shall not be wanting to aid you by God's grace"; referring to his coming martyrdom, he went on, "The comforts at the present instant are unspeakable; the dignity too high for a sinner; but God is merciful. . . . The day and hour of my birth is at hand, and my master says, 'Take up your cross and follow me.'" He was hanged, drawn, and quartered at Tyburn on 31 July. He was in the first group of martyrs to be beatified in 1886. His feast-day used to kept on 30 July.

M.M.P., pp. 13-8; Anstruther, 1, 145-7, says that the execution aroused great interest in the country as it was the first since the attempted papally backed invasion of Ireland; there are more contemporary accounts of it than of any other martyrdom. See also the general entries on the English and Welsh Martyrs under 4 May and 25 October.

St Justin de Jacobis, *Bishop* (1800-60)

Justin de Jacobis was born in 1800 in San Fele (Basilicata) in southern Italy. The family emigrated to Naples, and when he was eighteen years of age Justin joined the Congregation of the Mission (otherwise known as the Lazarists or Vincentians). After his ordination he was in constant demand as a preacher and confessor and developed a special skill in explaining the faith to the uneducated. At the same time he showed signs of considerable administrative ability and was appointed to help establish a new foundation in Monopoli and then to be superior of the Order's house in Lecce in Apulia. In 1836 and 1837 Naples was hit by a cholera epidemic, and Justin showed outstanding charity in caring for the sick, especially the poor. Then, in 1839, he was appointed to take charge of the recently-founded Vincentian missions at Godar and Adua in Ethiopia. A contemporary newspaper, writing of the appointment, described him as "one of those evangelical workers who knows how to bring the works of nature under the dominion of religion, and to attract to Jesus Christ the wise man and the scholar no less than the ignorant and the simple" (quoted in *B.T.A.*).

Ethiopia was to test both his ability and his determination. The country was politically divided, with constant fighting between local warlords, some of whom supported Justin, but most opposed him as a Westerner. The country was also in a poor state religiously. The Coptic Church, to which about half the population belonged, was theoretically ruled by a non-Ethiopian bishop, or *abuna*, appointed by the patriarch of Alexandria, but for most of the period from 1803 to 1841 there had been no *abuna* in the country at all. There was strong resentment against the small number of Latin Catholics, who were still linked in the popular mind with heavy-handed Western missionary work in the seventeenth century. Western priests had been banned from the country in 1632, and the Vincentian mission was the first to be established since then. Justin was sensitive to this complex situation and studied the country's culture and languages, trying to break down the hostility by kindness and humility. He followed an Ethiopian style of life, wearing local dress and generally doing without furniture, sleeping and sitting on the ground and writing on scraps of paper resting on his knee. He had strong views on the need for an indigenous clergy, arguing that it would be preferable to have poorly instructed Ethiopian priests than large numbers of European missionaries. He insisted on using the Ethiopian rite in his own celebration of Mass, for which he had the backing of Pius IX, and when local priests were later ordained according to the Latin rite he insisted that they should use the local rites in their ministry.

His first official engagement with the Coptic clergy came in 1841, when he was ordered by the local warlord to be part of a delegation to Alexandria to ask for the appointment of an *abuna*. Unfortunately, the patriarch appointed Salama, who was only about twenty years of age, had had no monastic experience, and had, indeed, been educated in an English Protestant school. He was totally unprepared to deal with the problems of the Ethiopian Church.

In 1846 a vicar apostolic, Mgr Massaia, arrived from Rome to open a new mission to the non-Christian people of southern Ethiopia. He ordained some candidates Justin had been preparing for the priesthood and tried to persuade him to become bishop for the northern part of the country. Justin refused, partly out of humility and partly because he was not sure it would help his missionary endeavours: foreign bishops were very unpopular and treated with great suspicion—when Massaia's own presence became known he had to flee to escape an armed band sent to murder him. Eventually Justin agreed to be consecrated, and the ceremony was carried out in secret by Massaia in 1848 after Justin had had to flee to the island of Massawa to avoid an attack by a rebel army. He was able to return to the mainland in 1849, but he kept the fact of his consecration as secret as possible; one of the few ordinations he carried out was of Gabra Michael (28 Aug.) in 1851. Gradually his work made progress, and by 1853 there were twenty Ethiopian Latin priests and about five thousand laypeople, with a sort of peripatetic master-and-disciples seminary.

In 1854 Justin moved south to Gondar, hoping to deal directly with Kassa, now the most powerful of the warlords and soon to be crowned King of Kings by Salama. In July, however, he was imprisoned, along with his followers; instructions to kill the latter originated with Salama—Copts were told that "to kill one who follows their religion [*i.e.,* the Latin] is to earn seven heavenly crowns hereafter" (*O.D.S.*). Justin was sent into exile under armed guard, but the guards allowed him to escape. He returned secretly to Gondar to see if he could help the other prisoners, but when this proved to be impossible he went back north, only to be forced to move to Massawa again in 1855 to avoid Kassa's armies. When one of the warlords applied to the French government for help to regain his territory from Kassa, Justin very reluctantly endorsed the plan and was able to return from Massawa to Halai.

Toward the end of 1859 a French political mission arrived and Justin gave its members hospitality; for this he was arrested by Kassa's troops in 1860 and imprisoned for a few weeks until he was ransomed by his clergy. He went again to Massawa for safety, but, convinced he was dying, set out with most of his followers to return to Halai. He developed a fever and died in the desert on 31 July 1860.

Those who wrote accounts of his work in Ethiopia were unanimous in stressing his humility; as Mgr Massaia wrote, "God raised this great figure of human perfection on a base of humility, to be a lesson to Ethiopia, and to the apostles who should carry on the work he began" (quoted in *B.T.A.*). The Church he founded is "the viable Ethiopian Church of the Ethiopian rite in northern Ethiopia. That it is a church of the Ethiopian rite is not fortuitous but stems from the decisive choice of one man whose heroic dedication to that choice enabled him to establish permanent apostolic roots and leave an indelible mark on Ethiopian history." (O'Mahoney). Justin de Jacobis was buried in the church at Hebo, and his tomb soon became a place of pilgrimage. He was beatified in 1939 and canonized in 1975 for his work as a missionary and ecumenist.

A valuable anonymous account was published in 1866 based on original testimonies and documents, including Justin's letters and journals. See K. O'Mahoney, W.F., *The Ebullient Phoenix—A History of the Vicariate of Abyssinia* (1982); Adrian Hastings, *The Church in Africa* (1994), ch. 6, "Ethiopia in the Nineteenth Century." See also *O.D.S.*, p. 129.

(Names are listed for those saints and blessed who have entries in the main body of the text. Those listed in the RM paragraph at the end of each day are omitted.)

Consultant Editors

DAVID HUGH FARMER. Former Reader in history at the University of Reading. Author of *St Hugh of Lincoln* and other biographical studies of saints. Author of *The Oxford Dictionary of Saints*. General consultant editor.

REV. PHILIP CARAMAN, S.J. Author of numerous biographies of saints and chief promoter of the cause of the Forty English Martyrs (canonized in 1970). Consultant on English Martyrs. Died in 1998.

JOHN HARWOOD. Librarian of the Missionary Institute in London and course lecturer on the Orthodox churches. Consultant on Eastern and Orthodox saints.

DOM ERIC HOLLAS, O.S.B. Monk of St John's Abbey, Collegeville, Minnesota, and director of the Hill Monastic Manuscript Library in Collegeville, where he also teaches theology at St John's University. General consultant, U.S.A.

PROF. KATHLEEN JONES. Emeritus Professor of Social Policy at the University of York. Author of many books and articles on social policy and mental illness. Honorary Fellow of the Royal College of Psychiatrists. Translator of *The Poems of St John of the Cross* (1993). Consultant on social history and abnormal behaviour.

DOM DANIEL REES, O.S.B. Monk of Downside Abbey and librarian of the monastery library. Bibliographical consultant.

DR RICHARD SHARPE. Reader in diplomatic history at the University of Oxford. Author of *Medieval Irish Saints' Lives* (1991), *Adomnán of Iona. Life of St Columba* (1995), and numerous articles on Celtic saints. Consultant on this subject.

REV. AYLWARD SHORTER, W.F. Long experience of African Missions and author of many books on the subject. Former President of Missionary Institute, London, now Principal of Tangaza College, Nairobi. Consultant on missionary saints.

DOM ALBERIC STACPOOLE, O.S.B. Monk of Ampleforth Abbey. Fellow of the Royal Historical Society. Secretary of the Ecumenical Society of Our Lady. Editor of several works, including *Vatican II by Those Who Were There* (1985). Engaged on a study of St Anslem. Consultant on feasts of Our Lady.

DOM HENRY WANSBROUGH, O.S.B. Monk of Ampleforth Abbey, currently Master of St Benet's Hall, Oxford. Member of the Pontifical Biblical Commission. Author of numerous works on scripture and Editor of the *New Jerusalem Bible* (1985). Consultant on New Testament saints.

SR BENEDICTA WARD, S.L.G. Anglican religious. Lecturer at Oxford Institute of Medieval History. Author of numerous works on hagiography, spirituality, and mysticism. Consultant on Middle Ages and age of Bede.